Digital Natives as a Disruptive Force in Asian Businesses and Societies

Omkar Dastane
UCSI Graduate Business School, UCSI University, Malaysia

Aini Aman
Universiti Kebangsaan Malaysia, Malaysia

Nurhizam Safie Bin Mohd Satar
Universiti Kebangsaan Malaysia, Malaysia

A volume in the Advances in Business Strategy
and Competitive Advantage (ABSCA) Book Series

Published in the United States of America by
IGI Global
Business Science Reference (an imprint of IGI Global)
701 E. Chocolate Avenue
Hershey PA, USA 17033
Tel: 717-533-8845
Fax: 717-533-8661
E-mail: cust@igi-global.com
Web site: http://www.igi-global.com

Library of Congress Cataloging-in-Publication Data

Names: Dastane, Omkar, 1983- editor. | Aman, Aini, editor. | Satar,
   Nurhizam Safie, 1972- editor.
Title: Digital natives as a disruptive force in Asian businesses and
   societies / edited by Omkar Dastane, Aini Aman, Nurhizam Safie Satar.
Description: Hershey, PA : Business Science Reference, [2023] | Includes
   bibliographical references and index. | Summary: "The Handbook of
   Research on Digital Natives as a Disruptive Force in Asian Businesses
   and Societies aims to foster multidisciplinary collaboration in order to
   uncover fresh theoretical and empirical views on digital natives as
   disruptive forces, digital technology, and digital revolutions in Asian
   enterprises and society. Quantitative, qualitative, or mixed methods
   research focused on issues surrounding digital natives' interactions and
   behavior throughout digital transformations is invited. Topics"--
   Provided by publisher.
Identifiers: LCCN 2023001142 (print) | LCCN 2023001143 (ebook) | ISBN
   9781668467824 (hardcover) | ISBN 9781668467831 (ebook)
Subjects: LCSH: Mass media and youth--Asia. | Digital media--Social
   aspects--Asia. | Information technology--Social aspects--Asia. |
   Diffusion of technology--Asia. | Disruptive technologies--Asia.
Classification: LCC HQ799.2.M352 A8543 2023 (print) | LCC HQ799.2.M352
   (ebook) | DDC 302.23/10835095--dc23/eng/20230120
LC record available at https://lccn.loc.gov/2023001142
LC ebook record available at https://lccn.loc.gov/2023001143

This book is published in the IGI Global book series Advances in Business Strategy and Competitive Advantage (ABSCA) (ISSN: 2327-3429; eISSN: 2327-3437)

British Cataloguing in Publication Data
A Cataloguing in Publication record for this book is available from the British Library.

For electronic access to this publication, please contact: eresources@igi-global.com.

Advances in Business Strategy and Competitive Advantage (ABSCA) Book Series

Patricia Ordóñez de Pablos
Universidad de Oviedo, Spain

ISSN:2327-3429
EISSN:2327-3437

MISSION

Business entities are constantly seeking new ways through which to gain advantage over their competitors and strengthen their position within the business environment. With competition at an all-time high due to technological advancements allowing for competition on a global scale, firms continue to seek new ways through which to improve and strengthen their business processes, procedures, and profitability.

The **Advances in Business Strategy and Competitive Advantage (ABSCA) Book Series** is a timely series responding to the high demand for state-of-the-art research on how business strategies are created, implemented and re-designed to meet the demands of globalized competitive markets. With a focus on local and global challenges, business opportunities and the needs of society, the **ABSCA** encourages scientific discourse on doing business and managing information technologies for the creation of sustainable competitive advantage.

COVERAGE

- Globalization
- Economies of Scale
- Business Models
- Strategic Alliances
- Innovation Strategy
- Co-operative Strategies
- Outsourcing
- Adaptive Enterprise
- Small and Medium Enterprises
- Tacit Knowledge

IGI Global is currently accepting manuscripts for publication within this series. To submit a proposal for a volume in this series, please contact our Acquisition Editors at Acquisitions@igi-global.com or visit: http://www.igi-global.com/publish/.

Titles in this Series

701 East Chocolate Avenue, Hershey, PA 17033, USA
Tel: 717-533-8845 x100 • Fax: 717-533-8661
E-Mail: cust@igi-global.com • www.igi-global.com

Table of Contents

Detailed Table of Contents

Chapter 1
Fatma Ince, Mersin University, Turkey

Since the conceptualization of entrepreneurship in the digital age is among the current issues, it has not been sufficiently researched yet. Addressing the issue is particularly important for Asian countries that are reorienting competition. This chapter, which deals with the digital ecosystem and entrepreneurship ecosystem in terms of innovation framework, aims to present a comprehensive framework by drawing attention to the sub-dimensions of the subject. In the chapter in which a new research agenda that will fill the gap in the understanding of entrepreneurship in the digital age is outlined, evaluations are made for Asian entrepreneurs after revealing the dynamics of the digital entrepreneurship ecosystem, which is one of the important tools of value creation.

Chapter 2
Ramya Thatikonda, University of the Cumberlands, USA
Bibhu Dash, University of the Cumberlands, USA
Meraj Farheen Ansari, University of the Cumberlands, USA
Srinivas Aditya Vaddadi, University of the Cumberlands, USA

During the last two decades, there have been many shifts in how e-business is conducted. The term "e-business" in this era of industry 5.0 can apply to any commercial or business activity incorporating data exchange over the internet. In industry 5.0, with technological advancements, companies now have access to new clients and markets thanks to the proliferation of the internet. The IBM Internet marketing division coined the phrase "e-business" in 1996, and since then, this word has become more familiar in digitalized enterprises worldwide. Every business performs trade, or the purchasing and selling of products and services among different organizations, as one of its most basic tasks. The adoption and acceptance of digital technology in everyday life affect our societal values, society, and future business prospects, along with its use in industrial production. This chapter will highlight how e-business growth put Asian business as the industrial warehouse of the world and how it impacts social, cultural, and technological sustainability in both the short and long terms.

Chapter 3
Shee Mun Yong, UOW Malaysia University College, Malaysia

Digital natives are Millennials and Gen Zs who grew up under the ubiquitous influence of the internet and digital technologies. As these generations come of age, they represent the largest group of consumers with spending power on the rise, commanding $360 billion in disposable income, and are expected to take the lead in global market growth on online retail sales. As that figure increases, it raises a question in the business community on ways to market to these digital natives as their spending habits differ drastically from the previous generations. The focus of this chapter is to undertake a more in-depth study on the predictors of their buying behaviour and the relationship between the predictors and their determinants.

Chapter 4
Herman Fassou Haba, Université du Québec à Trois-Rivières, Canada

This chapter explores gig workers' opinions in terms of the adoption of online platforms for their work. Based on a qualitative research method, this research study has collected secondary data for the purpose of analyzing them with thematic analysis. A total review of 127 were selected using simple random sampling method. The findings identified four main themes to be considered. The first theme is work, concerning the way gig workers find their job and how interesting it is. The second theme is flexibility, showing how the flexibility the share economy brings to gig workers, the third theme is great, demonstrating how great the online platforms are in terms of earning extra income, and last theme is people, because everything turns around people. The significance of this study is essential in terms of understanding the gig economy and gig workers because it can help in terms of the adoption of share economy platforms around the world.

Chapter 5
Siew Keong Lee, Return Legacy Sdn Bhd, Malaysia
Sam Yee Kho, Return Legacy Sdn Bhd, Malaysia

This chapter provides perspective on the potential for digital natives in the multi-level-marketing (MLM) industry. The chapter commences with an explanation of digital natives and the MLM industry. Thereafter, distinguishing factors for digital natives as customers, as well as opting for a career, are debated. The chapter then discusses digital natives the in MLM industry by considering their unique personality traits prior to providing perspective on recruiting digital natives in MLM, training and engaging digital natives in MLM, and MLM business transformation for Generation Z. Lastly, the chapter proposes attributes for transformed MLM considering above aspects related to digital natives.

Chapter 6
Hafizah Omar Zaki, Universiti Kebangsaan Malaysia, Malaysia
Nurul Atasha Jamaludin, Universiti Kebangsaan Malaysia, Malaysia
Aziatul Waznah Ghazali, Universiti Kebangsaan Malaysia, Malaysia

The main purpose of this chapter is to look at how marketing communications through interactive social media will affect the buying decisions of Gen Alpha. In the end, they want brands and everything they do on social media to give them answers and show that they care more than ever. Young people have been able to meet up with their friends through social media. The fact that young people use technology every day also makes them more likely to use social media to buy things. People who were born in the 21st century and grew up with technology make up Gen Alpha. Young people who know how to use technology well are now called "Gen Alpha." This means that Gen Alpha will be the generation that knows the most about technology. Gen Alpha is the most diverse generation ever, so they care about businesses that are open to everyone. They will keep changing the environment and culture of the whole world. Gen Alphas are likely to keep buying things online or through any other technology-based platform based on how much they are worth.

Chapter 7

    Mahadirin Bin Hj. Ahmad, Universiti Malaysia Sabah, Malaysia
    Kee Y. Sabariah Binti Kee Mohd Yussof, Universiti Malaysia Sabah, Malaysia
    Azizan Bin Morshidi, Universiti Malaysia Sabah, Malaysia
    Badariah Binti Ab Rahman, Independent Researcher, Malaysia

This chapter is about the experience of the authors in nurturing the development of digital natives through the subject during a teaching and learning process. Learning practices are explained based on the subject of Labour History in Malaysia, which becomes a fundamental subject and offered during the second semester from six semesters within three years. Through those courses, authors explain the alignment of the weekly topic of the course, course learning outcome (CLO), and student learning activity (SLT) based on Table 4. After that, authors explain the implication of that learning process by focusing on the element of IR4.0, the adjustment from students during movement control order (MCO) and the implication for the development of digital natives. Based on that experience, finally authors provide the conclusion which emphasizes the adaptation process to achieve the goal of "humans with the ability of technology and at the same time trying to humanize the technology" to enhance the relevance and sustainability of IRP UMS.

Chapter 8

    Mohammad Imtiaz Hossain, Multimedia University, Malaysia
    Md. Kausar Alam, Brac University, Bangladesh
    Zainudin Johari, ALFA University College, Malaysia
    Maherin Tasnim, Brac University, Bangladesh
    Kazi Israk Ferdaous, Brac University, Bangladesh
    Tanima Pal, Brac University, Bangladesh

This empirical paper investigates the role of perceived usefulness (PU), perceived ease of use (PEU), social influence (SI), service trust (ST), user innovativeness (UI), and technological optimism (TO) on intention to adopt Fintech (ITAF) by Malaysian millennials with the moderation of perceived Covid-19 risk (PCR). Theory of planned behaviour, technology adoption model, and social cognitive theory are applied to amalgamate the concept. Data of 313 millennials who are in university were collected using a convenient sampling technique and a structured questionnaire. The data was analysed in partial least squares structural equation modeling (PLS-SEM). The result shows that PU, SI, ST, and TO influence ITAF significantly. Surprisingly, PEU and UI did not evidence significant impact. Moreover, PCR did not show moderating influence. This study can provide important insights for the Fintech users, industry players, policymakers, and government to comprehend the concept so that the adoption of Fintech can be fostered towards achieving a smart and digital Malaysia.

Kasim Khusanov, Turin Polytechnic University in Tashkent, Uzbekistan
Ravshanjon Kakharov, Namangan State University, Uzbekistan
Mushtariybonu Khusanova, Kimyo International University in Tashkent, Uzbekistan
Khamidulla Khabibullaev, Turin Polytechnic University in Tashkent, Uzbekistan
Mukhsina Khusanova, Agency for the Development of Public Service Under the President of
the Republic of Uzbekistan, Uzbekistan

Digital technologies are transforming all aspects of human activity. Uzbekistan also does not stand aside from these transformations—digitalization affects all sectors of the country's economy. The digital transition in education, particularly in higher education, has accelerated during the Covid-19 pandemic. This chapter focuses on studying the digital transformation of higher education in Uzbekistan and the impact of the Covid-19 pandemic on this process. Different aspects of applying online teaching and learning in higher education in that emergency period in Uzbekistan and the perspectives of their development are analyzed here. The chapter's findings highlighted the pandemic's impact on digital higher education and the responses to adapting to the learning environment.

Mustafa Rehman Khan, Shaheed Zulfikar Ali Bhutto Institute of Science and Technology,
Pakistan & UCSI University, Malaysia
Naveed R. Khan, UCSI University, Malaysia
Muhammad Rafique, UCSI University, Malaysia

Market orientation is one of the most widely researched topics in the marketing domain, and has matured over time. The purpose of this chapter is to understand its concept and its gradual growth. The authors put light on the work of four research influencers of this filed, who works in team. First, they proposed a firm base market orientation theory. Second, they view the utile perspective of market orientation. Third, they bring customer perspective of market orientation. And fourth, they introduce the term customer-defined market orientation. Though researchers have conceptualized market orientation differently and bring new contextual factors in the concept, however, all researchers have consensus on the three dimensions of customer-defined market orientation which includes, customer orientation, competitor orientation and inter-functional orientation. Research in this domain reported that a firm who understands and use market orientation makes good profit and remain competitive in the industry in long run.

Subhanil Banerjee, Veni Creator Christian University, USA
Souren Koner, Royal Global University, Guwahati, India

Mother Nature has suffered through many industrial revolutions. Ecology suffered after the first industrial revolution. Industrial revolutions quadrupled CO2. Industrial Revolution 4.0 follows the Stockholm Conference in 1972 and Brundtland's report "Our Common Future" (1983-1987) on sustainable development. The emerging and less developed countries are condemned for their carbon footprint and CO2 emissions from manufacturing and consumption. According to the environmental Kuznets curve hypothesis, developed countries advise developing nations to follow their development path to reduce carbon emissions. Industrial Revolution 4.0 replaced the Fordist style of production with information-based production. In this context, is digitization pro-environment? Regrettably, this has not been empirically studied. This chapter examines the environmental effects of digitalization and Industrial Revolution 4.0. The chapter will examine the link between the environment, digitalization, and Industrial Revolution 4.0 using empirical validation and descriptive analysis.

Chapter 12

Nazhatul Hafizah Kamarudin, Universiti Kebangsaan Malaysia, Malaysia
Mohammad Arif Ilyas, UCSI University, Malaysia

The Internet of Things (IoT) has experienced rapid growth, and as a result, the e-health system has established a robust infrastructure that enables the delivery of viable healthcare services over the network. Healthcare organizations recognize the importance of adopting the latest technologies to improve healthcare services and reduce operational costs. Integrating IoT into the healthcare system offers numerous benefits, including secure patient identification and efficient data collection. However, many existing e-health systems primarily focus on patient data acquisition and medical embedded components, paying little attention to crucial aspects like real-time monitoring and, most importantly, the security of the e-health system. This chapter strives to enable the smooth integration and sustained expansion of digital transformation within the e-health system by addressing the urgent need to strengthen security measures and improve accountability. Securing the extensive advancements in digital transformation within e-health is of utmost importance. To safeguard the security and accountability of digital transformation in the healthcare system, it is essential to develop multilevel authentication protocols alongside the implementation of deep learning techniques.

Chapter 13

Soliha Binti Sanusi, Universiti Kebangsaan Malaysia, Malaysia
Istyakara Muslichah, Universitas Islam Indonesia, Indonesia
Nik Herda Nik Abdullah, Taylor's University, Malaysia
Nabilah Rozzani, Teach for Malaysia, Malaysia

Far from being optional, teaching and learning for education providers at various levels have made online learning the primary medium of delivery, due to Covid 19. As such, this study investigates how students' preparedness, motivation, internet availability, technical support, and psychological support influence students' online learning satisfaction in Malaysian and Indonesian higher learning institutions. An online survey was administered across Malaysia and Indonesia, with three hundred thirty-six (336) responses from Malaysia and two hundred ninety-two (292) from Indonesia. Structural equation model with smart PLS 3.2.4 was used for data analysis, with five hypotheses being tested. The present study found that motivation, psychological support, and technical support significantly affected student satisfaction in Malaysia, whereas an additional factor, students' preparedness, affected Indonesian students. Future research may investigate other aspects that may have contributed to students' satisfaction and which medium is the best for students to satisfy their learning curve.

Marketing automation is becoming an increasingly important topic for marketing managers and practitioners. Despite the well-known use of automation in marketing activities, academic study into marketing automation is minimal compared to, possibly, the recent surge. This chapter addresses this important omission. Findings suggest that to get the most out of automation in digital marketing, organizations need to integrate automation into every part of their operations. Digitalization is an unavoidable prerequisite for the successful adoption of marketing automation. Marketing firms can make better judgments by opting for the excellent use of automation platforms in digital marketing. The creation of effective marketing teams is made more accessible by using marketing automation, although the process is not without its challenges. Automation will allow them to maximize the benefits that marketing automation provides.

Natural language techniques require less personal information to communicate between computers and people. Generative models can create text for machine translation, summarization, and captioning without the need for dataset labelling. Markov chains and hidden Markov models can also be employed. A language model that can produce sentences word by word was created using RNNs (recurrent neural networks), LSTMs (long short-term memory model), and GRUs (gated recurrent unit). The suggested method compares RNN, LSTM, and GRU networks to see which produces the most realistic text and how training loss varies with iterations. Cloze questions feature alternative responses with distractors, whereas open-cloze questions include instructive phrases with one or more gaps. This chapter provides two novel ways to generate distractors for computer-aided exams that are simple and dependable.

Preface

INTRODUCTION

A new generation of Asian entrepreneurs is bringing their creativity, innovation, and digital expertise to market, assisting the region in becoming a disruptive force on the global stage. Live commerce, which combines fast purchases with entertainment, is revolutionizing China's retail industry, and new applications are making users' lives easier and more intertwined. A relatively young and increasingly well-educated population, driven by Millennials and Gen Zs, is driving such high levels of internet and mobile usage. In the following decade, these "digital natives" (born between 1997 to 2012) will account for one-third of Asia's consumption. Despite its relevance, there is a scarcity of research on digital natives and transformation in Asia or reflections of the same in a global context.

The Handbook of Research on Digital Natives as a Disruptive Force in Asian Businesses and Societies fosters multidisciplinary collaboration in order to uncover fresh theoretical and empirical views on digital natives, digital technology, and digital revolutions in Asian enterprises and society. Covering key topics such as the digital divide, internet marketing, and social commerce, this major reference work is ideal for government officials, business owners, managers, policymakers, scholars, researchers, academicians, practitioners, instructors, and students.

CONTENT OF THE BOOK

The handbook is organised into 15 chapters that uncover fresh theoretical and empirical views on digital natives, digital technology, and digital revolutions in Asian enterprises and society.

Chapter 1 titled "The Digital Edge for Entrepreneurship" (author: Fatma Ince) deals with the digital ecosystem and entrepreneurship ecosystem in terms of innovation framework, aims to present a comprehensive framework by drawing attention to the sub-dimensions of the subject. In the chapter in which a new research agenda that will fill the gap in the understanding of entrepreneurship in the digital age is outlined, evaluations are made for Asian entrepreneurs after revealing the dynamics of the digital entrepreneurship ecosystem, which is one of the important tools of value creation. This chapter is contributory because since the conceptualization of entrepreneurship in the digital age is among the current issues, it has not been sufficiently researched yet. Addressing the issue is particularly important for Asian countries that are reorienting competition.

Chapter 2 titled "E-Business Trends and Challenges in the Modern Digital Enterprises in Asia" (authors: Ramya Thatikonda, Bibhu Dash, Meraj Farheen Ansari, Srinivas Vaddadi) highlights how e-business growth put Asian business as the industrial warehouse of the world and how it impacts social, cultural, and technological sustainability in both the short and long terms. During the last two decades, there have been many shifts in how e-business is conducted. The term "e-business" in this era of industry 5.0 can apply to any commercial or business activity incorporating data exchange over the internet. In industry 5.0, with technological advancements, companies now have access to new clients and markets thanks to the proliferation of the internet. The adoption and acceptance of digital technology in everyday life affect our societal values, society, and future business prospects, along with its use in industrial production. Therefore, insights offered by this chapter are valuable.

Chapter 3 titled "Shifting of Paradigm in Buying Behaviour of Digital Natives," (author: Shee Mun Yong) undertake a more in-depth study on the predictors of their buying behaviour and the relationship between the predictors and their determinants. The chapter is vital as digital natives grew up under the ubiquitous influence of the internet and digital technologies. As this generation come of age, they represent the largest group of consumers with spending power on the rise commanding large disposable income and are expected to take the lead in global market growth on online retail sales. As that figure increases, it raises a question in the business community on ways to market to these digital natives as their spending habits differ drastically from the previous generations.

Chapter 4 titled "Gig Economy worker, work and platform perspective from food drivers and freelancers" (author: Harman F. Haba) explores the gig workers opinions in terms of the adoption of online platforms for their work. Knowing that the gig economy has attracted the attention of several scholars. Based on a qualitative research method, this research study has collected secondary data for the purpose of analyzing them with thematic analysis. A total review of 127 were selected using simple random sampling method. The chapter is based on qualitative analysis and explores novel dimensions offering original contribution. The significance of this study is essential in terms of understanding the gig economy and gig workers because it can help in terms of the adoption of share economy platforms around the world.

Chapter 5 titled "Digital Natives and Multi-Level-Marketing (MLM): A Perspective" (authors: Siew Keong Lee, Sam Yee Kho) provides perspective on the potential for digital natives in the multi-level-marketing (MLM) industry. The chapter commences with an explanation of digital natives and the MLM industry. Thereafter, distinguishing factors for digital natives as customers as well as opting for a career, is debated. The chapter then discusses digital natives the in MLM industry by considering their unique personality traits prior to providing perspective on recruiting digital natives in MLM, training and engaging digital natives in MLM, and MLM business transformation for Generation Z. Lastly, the chapter proposes attributes for transformed MLM considering above aspects related to digital natives. This contribution is significant as it has industry insights and data based on real life experiences.

Chapter 6 titled "The Influence of Social Media on Gen Alpha's Purchasing Decisions" (authors: Hafizah Omar Zaki, Nurul Atasha Jamaludin, Aziatul Waznah Ghazali) looks at how marketing communications through interactive social media will affect the buying decisions of Gen Alpha. In the end, they want brands and everything they do on social media to give them answers and show that they care more than ever. Young people have been able to meet up with their friends through social media. The fact that young people use technology every day also makes them more likely to use social media to buy things. People who were born in the 21st century and grew up with technology make up Gen Alpha. The chapter sheds light on digital natives' consumer behaviour and social media as influencing factors. The chapter is of importance when it comes to its practical implications.

Chapter 7 titled "Nurturing Digital Natives UMS Industrial Relations Programme Experience" (authors: Mahadirin Hj.Ahmad, Kee Y Sabariah Kee Mohd Yussof, Azizan Morshidi, Badariah Ab

Rahman). This chapter about experience of the author in nurturing the development of digital natives through the subject during teaching and learning process. Learning practices are explained based on the subject of Labour History in Malaysia which becomes a fundamental subject and offered during the second semester from six semesters within 3 years. Through those courses, authors explain the alignment of the Weekly Topic of the course, Course Learning Outcome (CLO), and Student Learning Activity (SLT) based on Table 4. After that, authors explain the implication of that learning process by focusing on the element of IR4.0, the adjustment from students during Movement Control Order (MCO) and the implication for the development of Digital Natives. Based on that experience, finally authors provide the conclusion which emphasizes the adaptation process to achieve the goal of "humans with the ability of technology and at the same time trying to humanize the technology" to enhance the relevance and sustainability of IRP UMS.

Chapter 8 titled "Structural Modelling on Factors of Adopting Fintech among Malaysian Millennials-Perceived Covid-19 Risk as Moderator" (authors: Mohammad Imtiaz Hossain, Md. Kausar Alam, Zainudin Johari, Maherin Tasnim, Kazi Ferdaous, Tanima Pal) investigates the role of Perceived Usefulness (PU), Perceived Ease of Use (PEU), Social Influence (SI), Service Trust (ST), User Innovativeness (UI), and Technological Optimism (TO) on intention to adopt Fintech (ITAF) by Malaysian millennials with the moderation of Perceived Covid-19 Risk (PCR). Theory of planned behaviour, technology adoption model and social cognitive theory are applied to amalgamate the concept. 313 millennials who are university students' data were collected using a convenient sampling technique and a structured questionnaire. The data was analysed in partial least squares structural equation modeling (PLS-SEM). The result shows that PU, SI, ST, and TO influence ITAF significantly. Surprisingly, PEU and UI did not evidence significant impact. Moreover, PCR did not show moderating influence. This study can provide important insights for the Fintech users, industry players, policymakers and government to comprehend the concept so that the adoption of Fintech can be fostered towards achieving a smart and digital Malaysia.

Chapter 9 titled "Impact of the Covid-19 Pandemic on the Digital Transition in Higher Education in Uzbekistan" (authors: Kasim Khusanov, Ravshanjon Kakharov, Mushtariybonu Khusanova, Khamidulla Khabibullaev, Mukhsina Khusanova) This chapter focuses on studying the digital transformation of higher education in Uzbekistan and the impact of the Covid-19 pandemic on this process. Different aspects of applying online teaching and learning in higher education in that emergency period in Uzbekistan and the perspectives of their development are analyzed here. The chapter's findings highlighted the pandemic's impact on digital higher education and the responses to adapting the learning environment. The study is topical because digital technologies are transforming all aspects of human activity. Uzbekistan also does not stand aside from these transformations - digitalization affects all sectors of the country's economy. The digital transition in education, particularly in higher education, has accelerated during the Covid-19 pandemic.

Chapter 10 titled "Market Orientation: Concept and Progress" (authors: Mustafa Khan, Naveed R. Khan, Muhammad Rafiq). Market orientation is one of the widely research topics in marketing domain and matured over time. The purpose of this chapter is to understand its concept and its gradual growth. We put light on the work of four research influencers of this filed, who works in team. First, Kohli and Jaworski, they proposed a firm base market orientation theory. Second, Narver and Slater who view the utile perspective of market orientation. Third, Deshpandé, Farley, and Webster, they bring customer perspective of market orientation. And fourth, Web, Webster, and Krepapa who introduced the term customer-defined market orientation. Though researchers have conceptualized market orientation differently and bring new contextual factors in the concept however all researchers have consensus on the three dimensions of customer-defined market orientation which includes, customer orientation, competitor orientation and inter-functional orientation. Research in this domain reported that firm who understands and use market orientation makes good profit and remain competitive in the industry in long run.

Chapter 11 titled "Industrial Revolution 4.0 and the Environment - The Asian Perspective" (source: Subhanil Banerjee, Souren Koner) examines the environmental effects of digitalization and Industrial Revolution 4.0. The chapter will examine the link between the environment, digitalization, and Industrial Revolution 4.0 using empirical validation and descriptive analysis. Ecology suffered after the first industrial revolution. Industrial revolutions quadrupled CO2. Industrial Revolution 4.0 follows the Stockholm Conference in 1972 and Brundtland's report "Our Common Future" (1983-1987) on sustainable development. The emerging and less developed countries are condemned for their carbon footprint and CO2 emissions from manufacturing and consumption. According to the Environmental Kuznets Curve hypothesis, developed countries advise developing nations to follow their development path to reduce carbon emissions. Industrial Revolution 4.0 replaced the Fordist style of production with information-based production. In this context, is digitization pro-environment? Regrettably, this has not been empirically studied.

Chapter 12 titled "Securing Digital Transformation in Healthcare System" (authors: Nazhatul Hafizah Kamarudin, Mohammad Arif Ilyas) highlights that to safeguard the security and accountability of digital transformation in the healthcare system, it is essential to develop multilevel authentication protocols alongside the implementation of deep learning techniques. The Internet of Things (IoT) has experienced rapid growth, and as a result, the e-health system has established a robust infrastructure that enables the delivery of viable healthcare services over the network. Healthcare organizations recognize the importance of adopting the latest technologies to improve healthcare services and reduce operational costs. Integrating IoT into the healthcare system offers numerous benefits, including secure patient identification and efficient data collection. However, many existing e-health systems primarily focus on patient data acquisition and medical embedded components, paying little attention to crucial aspects like real-time monitoring and, most importantly, the security of the e-health system.

Chapter 13 titled "Online Learning Satisfaction A Comparative Study on Malaysian and Indonesian Students" (authors: Soliha Sanusi, Istyakara Muslichah, Nik Herda Nik Abdullah, Nabilah Rozzani) investigates how students' preparedness, motivation, internet availability, technical support, and psychological support influence students' online learning satisfaction in Malaysian and Indonesian higher learning institutions. An online survey was administered across Malaysia and Indonesia. The ound that motivation, psychological support, and technical support significantly affected student satisfaction in Malaysia, whereas an additional factor, students' preparedness, affected Indonesian students. Future research may investigate other aspects that may have contributed to students' satisfaction and which medium is the best for students to satisfy their learning curve.

Chapter 14 titled "Automation in Digital Marketing" (authors: Hafizah Omar Zaki, Dahlia Fernandez) suggest that to get the most out of automation in digital marketing, organizations need to integrate automation into every part of their operations. Digitalization is an unavoidable prerequisite for the successful adoption of marketing automation. Marketing firms can make better judgments by opting for the excellent use of automation platforms in digital marketing. The creation of effective marketing teams is made more accessible by using marketing automation, although the process is not without its challenges. Automation will allow them to maximize the benefits that marketing automation provides.

Chapter 15 titled "Study on Sentence and Questions formation using Deep Learning Techniques" (authors: N. Venkateswaran, R Vidhya, Darshana A Naik, Michael Raj TF, Neha Munjal, Sampath

Boopathi) provides two novel ways to generating distractors for computer-aided exams that are simple and dependable. Natural language techniques require less personal information to communicate between computers and people. Generative models can create text for machine translation, summarization, and captioning without the need for dataset labelling. Markov Chains and Hidden Markov Models can also be employed. A language model that can produce sentences word by word was created using RNNs ((Recurrent Neural Networks)), LSTMs (Long Short-Term Memory model), and GRUs (Gated Recurrent Unit). The suggested method compares RNN, LSTM, and GRU networks to see which produces the most realistic text and how training loss varies with iterations. Cloze questions feature alternative responses with distractors, whereas open-cloze questions include instructive phrases with one or more gaps. The findings have several implications for digital learning natives.

Happy Reading!

Omkar Dastane
Graduate Business School, UCSI University, Malaysia

Aini Aman
Faculty of Economics & Management, Universiti Kebangsaan Malaysia

Nurhizam Safie Mohd Satar
Faculty of Information Science and Techology, Universiti Kebangsaan Malaysia

Acknowledgment

We sincerely thank the chapter contributors for their hard work and support which resulted completion of this handbook of research. We also like to thank the members of the editorial advisory board for their assistance, suggestions, and review throughout the book preparation. Last but not the least, we are grateful to IGI Global's editorial and production team for their assistance throughout the editing process.

Omkar Dastane
Graduate Business School, UCSI University, Malaysia

Aini Aman
Faculty of Economics & Management, Universiti Kebangsaan Malaysia

Nurhizam Safie Mohd Satar
Faculty of Information Science and Techology, Universiti Kebangsaan Malaysia

Chapter 1
The Digital Edge for Entrepreneurship

Fatma Ince

ⓘ https://orcid.org/0000-0002-0628-5858

Mersin University, Turkey

ABSTRACT

Since the conceptualization of entrepreneurship in the digital age is among the current issues, it has not been sufficiently researched yet. Addressing the issue is particularly important for Asian countries that are reorienting competition. This chapter, which deals with the digital ecosystem and entrepreneurship ecosystem in terms of innovation framework, aims to present a comprehensive framework by drawing attention to the sub-dimensions of the subject. In the chapter in which a new research agenda that will fill the gap in the understanding of entrepreneurship in the digital age is outlined, evaluations are made for Asian entrepreneurs after revealing the dynamics of the digital entrepreneurship ecosystem, which is one of the important tools of value creation.

INTRODUCTION

There is a significant gap in the conceptualization of entrepreneurship in the digital age. In addressing this gap, it is necessary to consider the digital ecosystem and the entrepreneurship ecosystem together. It cannot be said that the entrepreneurship literature has not adequately addressed the issue yet. Parker (2005) uses the following expressions while explaining this situation; "The reason entrepreneurship literature has not examined the billion-dollar digital startup is because entrepreneurship research has focused on self-employment as both a business owner and self-employed." Entrepreneurship literature focuses on thousands of small startups, which often fail to achieve sufficient success due to a lack of customer base. In other words, entrepreneurship is not focused on finding customers before starting a business. In the digital economy, the opposite is true, each startup can have millions of customers, even though there are far fewer startups. The role of users and customers is therefore worth examining at least as much as the role of entrepreneurship.

DOI: 10.4018/978-1-6684-6782-4.ch001

In a sense, traditional entrepreneurship research has ignored both the role played by digital technologies in entrepreneurship and the role played by users and intermediaries in digital entrepreneurship. In short, there is a major gap in understanding entrepreneurship in the digital age, as a consolidated way of entrepreneurship research has not been sought to examine the impact of digitalization. In other words, entrepreneurship research has not yet been contextualized within the digital economy regarding how it will change due to digitalization. Current knowledge of the impact of digitalization can be obtained from other disciplines related to digitalization and business, such as marketing or management information systems. Therefore, predictions can be made about the impact of digitization and how it might change the way people understand entrepreneurship.

Multidisciplinary studies have great potential to provide a theoretical framework of multilateral platforms to better understand the digital entrepreneurship ecosystem. Because of its broad perspective, this section of the book is important because it outlines a new research agenda that will fill the gap in understanding entrepreneurship in the digital age. In this context, first of all, after the digital entrepreneurship ecosystem, the basic dynamics that make up this system are mentioned and the innovation ecosystem is started. Finally, the study, which preserves its originality with the title of Asian Entrepreneurship, tries to present a different perspective by shifting the reader's direction from the West to the East.

DIGITAL ENTREPRENEURSHIP ECOSYSTEM

When it comes to digital entrepreneurship, it is necessary to talk about digital ecosystems, since there is no single technology. Thus, the subject of the enterprise evolves into entrepreneurs who, in addition to the original discovered in 1911, create digital companies and innovative products and services for many users and agents in the global economy. Stam (2015) takes this assumption further and argues that regional policies toward entrepreneurship will change the focus. According to the author, the main goal of increasing the quantity of entrepreneurship is going through a transition process towards increasing the quality of entrepreneurship today. So, the next step will be the transition from entrepreneurial policy to entrepreneurial economic policy. This perspective highlights the entrepreneurial ecosystem approach as a new framework that accommodates these transitions. Emphasizing the context of productive entrepreneurship, this approach views entrepreneurship not only as the output of the system but also as a critical factor in creating and maintaining a healthy ecosystem. From this point of view, this section, which aims to fill the gap in understanding the role of intermediaries and users in the digital economy, deals with digitalization not from a single aspect, but from an ecosystem that includes different technologies.

Digital ecosystems that mimic biological ecosystems refer to complex and interconnected systems and their underlying infrastructures, in which all components interact and exhibit self-organizing, scalable, and sustainable behaviors as a whole. Starting from a similar point, the concept of the digital ecosystem can also be discussed. The digital ecosystem (DE), a terminology that emerged in the early 2000s, "...to increase system utility, deliver benefits, and promote knowledge sharing, internal and external collaboration, and systems innovation" (Li et al., 2012). DE can be applied in business, knowledge management, service, social networks, and education. Digital ecosystems refer to complex and interconnected systems and their underlying infrastructures in which all components interact and exhibit self-organizing, scalable, and sustainable behaviors as a whole. Digital ecosystems are made up of suppliers, applications, customers, trading partners, third-party data service providers, and all respective technologies (Behera & Dash, 2019).

Despite the different perspectives and the fragmented focus from the various definitions, the convergence or commonality of all the various debates about the concept points to the two pillars of DI; digital technologies and people. Dynamic and continuous changes resulting from the interaction of these two components of digital technologies constitute the behavior of an ecosystem. The assumptions of such an ecosystem inherent in DE are user-centered, bottom-up, and open-source-oriented, emphasizing the important role users or humans play in the ecosystem. The advancement of digital technologies has resulted in a more complex system, digital infrastructure (Tilson et al., 2010). Two key structures, digital infrastructure, and users are the main focus of ecosystem-related digital ecosystem discussions.

An interdisciplinary perspective is required to fill the emerging gap in the conceptualization of entrepreneurship in the digital age. In this section, the digital entrepreneurship ecosystem (DEE) is brought to the forefront by integrating digital ecosystem and entrepreneurship ecosystem issues while presenting a conceptual framework for examining entrepreneurship in the digital age. Thus, the interactions between agents and users are better understood by combining insights into their individual and social behavior. From this point of view, the digital entrepreneurship ecosystem framework consists of four concepts (Sussan & Acs, 2017; Song, 2019; Ince, 2023a; Naudé & Liebregts, 2023):

- Digital infrastructure governance: The term digital infrastructure, which can be used interchangeably with information infrastructure, IT infrastructure, and e-infrastructure, is discussed here from a governance perspective. As digital technologies become increasingly service-oriented, socially embedded, and teeming with intense human interactions, a more open, inclusive, global, dynamic, and resilient view of digital infrastructure (DI) is needed to capture the effects of digitalization. Linked to digital technologies, DI is a socially embedded mechanical system that includes technology and human components, network, systems, and processes that create self-reinforcing feedback loops. Thus, systems and their networks are interconnected at the global, national, regional, industry, or enterprise levels and are constantly changing due to the diverse base of installed digital technologies and users who are the designers or operators of these systems. In this sense, DI has no single defined set of functions or strict boundaries constraining it. Instead, multiple layers of systems and processes operate simultaneously, resulting in a decentralized, shared, and distributed DI that is not subject to the control of a single central stakeholder. The distribution of DI is difficult to manage as control is distributed among multiple actors such as designers, developers, and users. The open access and open standards nature of the Internet allows anyone to develop and share applications on the Internet. DI is constantly evolving and therefore a system that is never fully completed, and members of public and ordinary organizations can be trusted to invent and share good uses. Although there are standards among its members, it is not possible to reach a static set of standards. Also, the bottom-up nature of DI, but still the top-down reality of most organizational structures, makes the governance of DI a particular challenge.
- Digital user citizenship: The second pillar of digital ecosystems is users. Users, were previously viewed as technologists directly interacting with digital technologies, meaning anyone who has access to digital technologies due to the increasing ease of use of ubiquitous computing and devices. It is becoming very common and accessible like smartwatches and mobile phone interaction using IoT infrastructure. As a result, user-centric innovations proliferate as more users develop new products and services for themselves and other users. As an open source-based architecture, the Internet was designed to allow users to participate, and the socio-technological consequence of digitization that allowed anyone to participate in the Web resulted in a culture of volunteerism.

This pro-social behavior is unique in that users provide instant feedback for free labor or time and effort for other users and organizations. Customer-focused researchers have long viewed users as co-creators in product development, service-intensive marketing, service ecosystems, and entrepreneurship. Users are also tagged directly from the situation as citizens or consumers. Users co-create with other consumers and firms and add value to the broader social context. Essentially, the co-creation of ecosystem value is possible due to the generative nature of digital ecosystems and service-heavy factors that explain how users can maximize value from user-producer pairs. Moreover, many of these users have become consumers who participate in the co-creation of new products with organizations and companies, who are also paid nothing, resulting in a procreative class of consumers who are motivated by a combination of utilitarian and emotional reasons. The hedonic goals that result in adding value to the firms that become a part of the intellectual capital of the firms increase the amount of the contribution. In the process of intense interaction with their community, some user entrepreneurs accidentally develop new products or services and become users or entrepreneurs by chance. The entrepreneurial actions of the online community become a productive incubator as the online community is motivated by the attention, they receive from the community to develop new products for other users. In the case of the user-to-entrepreneur transition, they often develop an idea as a user and tap into the knowledge and creativity of the community before commercializing it. From the perspective of users and business models, the philosophical basis of users' willingness to share, contribute, and voluntarily spend time and effort in online communities becomes the most important game-changing element in business models in the digitalization process. New user-intensive business models are emerging that radical change transaction cost-based business models. First, some multilateral platform businesses rely entirely voluntarily on user-generated sharing content from the masses, such as social media. In this model, the core competency of the business depends on the data the business can collect from the users, and thus the revenue of the business comes from advertising without selling anything to a customer. In this model, if all users decide not to voluntarily provide content to the business, there will be no business. Second, businesses like Airbnb rely on users participating in the sharing economy by sharing their unused tangible assets.

- Digital marketplace (DM): This factor is the market, which represents the combination of users and agents in the context of both ecosystems. It considers value creation in the form of a new product, service, or new knowledge that is the result of entrepreneurial activity and user participation, examining intermediaries capable of both opportunistic and conscious foresight. It doesn't matter whether the value created is for profit or not, it may even have a social aspect involving government practices. Electronic applications adopted by users in education, health, or other social services are as interesting and adopted as e-transport, e-social networks, or e-commerce. Social network-based applications make the life of the consumer easier in this area. As can be seen from the descriptions, marketing in this field is the key to a sustainable DEE. Continuous value creation among entrepreneurial agencies and users in DM is one of the main pathways to a sustainable DEE. As users continually produce content and provide free labor, time, and effort to engage and interact with other nonprofit, nonprofit, and government user organizations, their pro-social behavior and efforts will, directly and indirectly, enable entrepreneurial activity. In such a case, the entrepreneurs will optimize the opportunity recognition and take advantage of the opportunities arising from the participation of the users, and at the same time, the users will adopt such use of opportunities that will allow entrepreneurial activities.

This classification makes four important contributions to entrepreneurship literature. First, it contributes to entrepreneurship by bringing the subject to the digital age specifically to digital infrastructure and its implications for entrepreneurship in general. On the other hand, it adds a new dimension to the entrepreneurial economics literature by introducing the role of users in the digital ecosystem. Third, by introducing the interactions of agents and users, it expands entrepreneurial research to include insights into consumers' individual and social behavior across multiple platforms. Finally, digital ecosystem integration provides the opportunity to expand research into entrepreneurial ecosystems.

In addition to the detailed explanations, multilateral platforms should also be mentioned. The platform is being updated due to innovations brought by powerful information and communication technologies that reduce costs and increase access to connecting platform sides. According to Evans and Schmalensee (2016), six new fast and fast technologies have driven matchmaker innovation by reducing cost and expanding the scope of connections between speed users and platform parties. Six technologies help divide the digital infrastructure in our supervisor model: more powerful chips; Internet; World War II Network; broadband communication; programming languages; and pill systems, cloud. Sustaining digital use combined with corporate structure gives us digital infrastructure governance (Evans & Schmalensee, 2016: Matchmaker). A goodwill digital infrastructure makes it possible for digital users to attract users and agents to versatile platforms.

From a platform performance perspective, a matchmaker job is one of the toughest business challenges. In 2007, Apple decided to manage its ecosystem to improve platform performance and announced that it would allow the development of applications for the iPhone by third parties. After the company released the software development kit, it made the App Store available a bit years ago. Developers could only make their apps available to users through Apple's App Store, and Apple was in a position to decide whether to make an app available. therefore, strict standards and processes have been developed to test and review applications. A year after its launch, iPhone has become a bipartisan platform connecting smartphone users and digital entrepreneurs in the digital marketplace. A similar process was followed by Google for Android phones, and it turned out that third-party apps are important to keep users interested in new smartphones. So, the use of the smartphone installed base exploded after 2008, and in 2015 it had over three million users and thousands of apps (Evans & Schmalensee, 2016; CB Insights, 2023).

There is a Peer-to-Peer (P2P) network design that aims to support business activities that create value for participating organizations in a variety of mutually beneficial ways. Temporary virtual networks created by long-term business transactions involving the execution of multiple services from different providers are used as the cornerstone of the scale-independent business network. It is seen how these local interactions, not managed by a single organization, lead to a fully distributed P2P architecture that reflects the dynamics of business operations. Against certain types of failures or attacks, dynamically created resistance systems called Virtual Super Peers (VSPs) are relied upon (Razavi et al., 2009). Adapting to change and restructuring themselves to respond to failures, these designs foster an environment in which business communities can thrive to meet emerging business opportunities and achieve sustainable growth within a digital ecosystem.

It manifests itself at the point of coping with constant change, where improvements are inevitable. For example, Service-oriented architecture (SOA), used as a suite of interoperable services that can be used across multiple separate systems, is not sufficient to face the challenges in the context of the Digital Ecosystem, although it allows for the development of reusable and distributed systems (Monsalve-Pulido et al., 2023). For these reasons, National Innovation Systems (NSI) take steps to ensure the flow of technology and information between people, businesses, and institutions, which are the key to the innovation process at the national level in countries dealing with global competition (Lundvall, 2007). It is possible to multiply these examples further, but it is thought that the broad scope of the digital entrepreneurship ecosystem is discussed in general terms.

In summary, the digital entrepreneurship ecosystem is a wide ecosystem that includes the process of developing innovative business ideas using digital technologies, implementing and growing these ideas. This ecosystem includes entrepreneurs, investors, technologists, academics, government agencies, and other relevant stakeholders. The digital entrepreneurship ecosystem gives entrepreneurs access to the resources they need to test their ideas, develop business models, find financing, market, and grow their businesses. These resources can be cloud-based services, mobile application development tools, data analytics, and technological infrastructures such as artificial intelligence, especially for technology-based entrepreneurs.

The digital entrepreneurship ecosystem also encourages entrepreneurs to communicate and collaborate. This cooperation can take place in many different ways, such as developing joint projects, sharing experience, mentoring, and training programs. The digital entrepreneurship ecosystem is gaining importance in today's rapidly changing and developing world. Investing in this ecosystem provides many opportunities to access innovative business ideas and support the leading entrepreneurs of the future. In the next section, the dynamics of digital entrepreneurship, which is discussed from an innovation perspective, are mentioned.

DYNAMICS OF DIGITAL ENTREPRENEURSHIP AND THE ROLE OF THE INNOVATION ECOSYSTEM

Digital entrepreneurship is an important driving force within the innovation system. It changes the structure, objectives, and networking mechanisms of the overall business system and ultimately affects various levels and dimensions of the innovation system. Bringing inevitable changes to the innovation system, digital technologies not only provide new business opportunities, but they can also be disruptive and cause new vulnerabilities. It is necessary to consider the concept of hybrid digital entrepreneurship and its role in the transformation of the innovation system, taking into account the interaction. Because although digitalization concerns all areas of social life, it primarily determines the transformation of entrepreneurship and business models in different sectors (Satalkina & Steiner, 2020a). This is primarily due to their changing needs for products and services, which determine the adaptations and patterns of communication and collaboration in the value creation process; this process encourages innovative transformations of business models.

The mutual interaction in the factors of change is also in question between innovation and entrepreneurship in the digitalization process. These variables, which are the driving force of each other, are also affected by each other and thus lead the change in an integrated way. Therefore, the innovation system can be considered a meta-system in which entrepreneurial activities become the driving force to take advantage of digital opportunities. Therefore, digital entrepreneurship is a mechanism that takes place in the innovation system both as a result and as a process. In conjunction with the creation of new ventures or the transformation of existing businesses, innovation in new ways of creating value becomes the driving force of development. According to Satalkina and Steiner (2020b), who deal with the issue from this point of view, there are three main determinants of digital entrepreneurship with its sub-dimensions.

- Entrepreneur: Personal characteristics and competencies of entrepreneur, decision-making and bounded rationality, personal outcomes.
- Entrepreneurial process: The prerequisites for digitalization, dynamic shifts in the transformation of business, digital business model innovation, and digital business affordances.
- Ecosystem: Regional digital business environment, digital business infrastructure, collaboration, and social values.

Key performance indicators are handled under different classifications in various studies conducted by OECD, Eurostat, and the World Economic Forum. In the indicators examined, there are the following headings in general terms; Latest trends in e-commerce, digital economy, and society, digital skills, digital economy, digital users, and current situation analysis (OECD, 2023). To see the impact of the innovation ecosystem on entrepreneurship, it may be useful to consider different variables from various perspectives. The innovation variable, which is one of the important ways to benefit from opportunities, is a value-creation tool as well as adapting to the external environment. For this reason, digital entrepreneurship should be evaluated from all aspects due to its potential to adapt and direct external dynamics as well as internal dynamics. From this perspective, different levels of digitization can be examined and various sets of relationships can be modeled (Beliaeva et al., 2020).

To consider the components of the innovation ecosystem in terms of mutual interaction from the systems perspective, first the market, finance, culture and infrastructure support factors should be addressed separately and then holistically, as well as human, cultural and policy factors. Similar to the nature of the ecosystem, the innovation ecosystem includes the interrelationships of factors that are important for the innovative performance of a community of actors. There are substitute and complementary relationships for actors, activities, works and institutions. There is uncertainty as it is difficult to draw clear boundaries of the concept that has the potential to make a beneficial contribution to innovation and innovation management. According to Granstrand & Holgersson (2020), the definitions of innovation ecosystems emphasize cooperation or complementarity as well as competition or substitution for actors. This perspective enables not only cooperating but also competing actors to come to the fore due to information asymmetry. This perspective includes business, product and service, as well as other system inputs and outputs, including tangible and intangible or technological and non-technological resources and innovations. In other words, an innovation ecosystem includes actor systems that contain substitution relationships as well as collaborative, i.e., complementary relationships, with or without a focused firm. Thus, the entrepreneur in the digital world and the innovative change of the external environment meet on a common denominator in an artificial system.

Innovative Business Models in the Digital Ecosystem

With new generation technologies such as Artificial Intelligence (AI), one of the important tools in the world of change, it has the power to change the rules of the game when it comes to customer experience. By making the customer a part of the experience with its interactive participation feature, AI gradually narrows the gap between the product and the customer and blurs the boundaries with chatbots, instant feedback, or participatory applications. What's more, the AI can even recognize and respond to multiple forms of the same question and can be trained and developed to respond instantly using your preferred voice and tone. This type of innovation is an essential part of the process known as the digital business model, which is a form of value creation based on the enhancement of customer benefits using digital technologies. The purpose of these digital solutions is to provide significant advantages that customers are willing to pay for and ultimately improve the features of the business and move it into the future. This can change the entire manufacturing, design, and sales process, from how businesses acquire customers to what products or services you provide. In addition, the foundation of trust is taken into account when using technologies that not only deliver better products and services but also provide personalized and meaningful customer experiences in digital business models. In light of these developments, a digital strategy is seen as a critical factor for the success of brands. In terms of the characteristics of digital business models, for starters, it can be said that digital business models have the following four distinctive features (Ng, 2013; Ranta et al., 2021; Simplilearn, 2023):

- Data-driven system: Ease of collecting information about current and potential customers as well as processes, transactions, and other activities is one of the important advantages of the ecosystem. Data, which is the main driving force of the system, support the consumer-oriented perspective and facilitates the provision of services, tools, or technology suitable for use.
- Customer-oriented value creation process: The system, based on understanding and understanding the consumer and developing new business models, has a collaborative structure to provide the best service with a holistic perspective. This structure, which takes the consumer as the basis of the entrepreneurial journey, also makes it easier to appeal to a wide range.
- Quick feedback and automated processes: Quick turnarounds to increase satisfaction provide strong support for increasing the value stream and easier access to the desired product or service. Data collected from consumers, as well as suppliers and third parties, can be instantly included in decision systems.
- Dynamic and fast decision making: When the speed of the consumer's transition between the pages in the online environment is calculated, it is noticed that there is a risk of losing potential very quickly. For this reason, the existence of skills, processes, and systems such as quick thinking, instant reaction, and instant adaptation to changing market dynamics is inevitable.
- Boundless and global market: The cross-border nature of the digital world necessitates the need for cultural harmony to be achieved already. The assumption that the market is a global village will apply here, as the scaling of such ecosystems cannot be done only with certain countries. Therefore, it is necessary to think visionary for cooperation with subjects such as geography, language, or culture.

The potential roles an initiative can adopt also differ due to the comprehensive context of the ecosystem. First of all, the entrepreneur has to decide, the important thing is to choose the ecosystem. Before the establishment of the business, which ecosystem is important in terms of the business idea should be determined, and then one of the following alternative roles should be preferred. In this context, the 3 roles that can be had in the digital ecosystem are as follows (Kretschmer et al., 2022):

- Modular producer: Companies that can create value in different ecosystems, such as PayPal, are considered in this class. Offering different payment platforms with a unified payment gateway, the business provides an intermediate platform that can enable fast interaction between buyer and seller. It is successful in providing reliable solutions to the basic needs of the business.
- Ecosystem orchestrator: Companies such as Amazon, Alibaba, or Ping, which lead digitalization in the economy, enable others to do business in their newly created ecosystem by illuminating the

dark forest with their pioneering practices. While they get the reward of enduring the difficulties and costs of being the first in the long term, they experience the competitive leadership of being a pioneer.

- Customer: The customer, who is the party that obtains value from the ecosystem, consists of individuals or institutions that become a part of the system while using the digital service. A consumer who makes an online reservation becomes a member of the ecosystem created and managed by that application as soon as he/she enters the system.

In the digital world, it is not always possible to draw boundaries with sharp lines. Applications such as content production, especially from new business areas, enable the participant to be both a creator and a user, so people take on the roles of being both a producer and a consumer at the same time. Similarly, businesses can use multiple platforms and various roles for various activities. It can be said that the borders are fluid in terms of businesses, sometimes with their regulations and sometimes with service activities. On the other hand, it is useful to look at the types of digital ecosystems as well as their roles. The three types of digital ecosystems can be summarized as follows (Ritala & Jovanovic, 2024):

- Platform ecosystem: This classification offers an advanced ecosystem with a large number of digital products and partners. In the system, which is largely data-based, it is possible to quickly present new offers and sell large volumes. The most important reason why it is called a platform is that it has the potential to create value in an order that all business partners can participate in. One of the leading examples of this, Google Home, is developing services such as communicating with home speakers and providing instant responses. Thus, smart home appliances can be developed accordingly. Thus, it provides a wide platform for its business partners to offer new products and services.
- Functional digital ecosystem: This ecosystem, which includes a certain number of partners, offers the opportunity to progress over an existing product or offer. In addition to its easy use, its simple and understandable structure contributes to its global spread. However, the system, which is designed as a relatively closed system, can be drowned in complex activities in data collection and integration processes. For example, digital ecosystems that are limited to one vehicle in the automotive industry can be given.
- Super platform ecosystem: The system, which includes various services and users as well as many different sectors, generally prefers to keep the consumption adventure connected to the ecosystem. These ecosystems, which are as complex as chaos in this aspect, are generally in the hands of companies known as technology giants. Besides known examples such as Amazon, Google and Tencent, the WeChat application can be evaluated in terms of being involved in almost every aspect of users' lives. The system, which constantly focuses on collecting better data, offers different experiences such as social media, banking and shopping on a single platform and becomes an indispensable part of the consumer's life day by day.

In addition to digital ecosystems and various roles in these ecosystems, another issue that the entrepreneur should pay attention to in order to decide on the right step is the digital marketing model. Digitalization, which requires new ways of thinking at every stage of the entrepreneurial process, also requires strategic thinking with different perspectives at the point of marketing. Diversification of business models requires not only reaching the consumer but also keeping the consumer and taking the right action according to the current profile. The mentioned alternative digital business and marketing models are as follows (Ganis & Waszkiewicz, 2018; Talin, 2022; Murali & Krishna-Mohan, 2023):

- On-demand model: This model, which stands for on-demand work, involves improving an existing line of business by adding convenience and speed. This model, which generally reaches the consumer with mobile applications, is generally seen in the transportation, market, and food sectors. Some of the common examples are apps like Fiverr, Apple TV, or Amazon Prime Video.
- Free model (ad-supported): Platforms such as Facebook offer free usage to the user through advertisements. In this business model, while cost and profitability are ensured through advertisements, free service is provided to the consumer. On the other hand, it provides companies with the necessary audience information for advertisements without the knowledge of the user.
- e-Commerce model: While e-commerce applications, which are rapidly spreading, can provide supply and logistics without borders, they are also widely used in the world. In this application, the most known example of which is Amazon, physical products are bought and sold on online platforms.
- Freemium model: Applications that offer free services such as Spotify or YouTube Premium but use ads in this version also offer ad-free content for a certain fee. The consumer who requests additional features agrees to pay a certain fee to have a higher version of the application they are using.
- Marketplace model: A third-party platform is used in this business model, which provides the exchange between the producer and the consumer with examples on a service or product basis. Uber is one of the most well-known examples of double-market practices in the service area, and eBay or Etsy in the products area.
- Model of experience: Aiming to create a new customer-centered ecosystem as well as bring together different experiences, this model focuses on digital experiences. While Tesla focuses on the digital experience in the automotive industry, this model offers a digital ecosystem alongside the digital experience.
- Digital ecosystem model: This ecosystem model, which enables it to be both user and supplier of an ecosystem, is one of the best examples of a comprehensive modular system. The ecosystem, which offers a wide range of services due to its complex but comprehensive structure, has the potential to attract new customers with the database it provides. This structure, which offers suppliers the opportunity to deliver or market more products to existing customers, includes the potential to offer many services such as payment, procurement, and shipping at the same time. The well-known examples of Apple, Google, and Amazon, as well as Alibaba, have great potential to offer ecosystems and other entrepreneurs the opportunity to develop their own businesses.
- Sharing model: Also known as the access through ownership model, this system is based on commercial sharing. In this business model, which provides only the right of use without taking property rights such as renting a vehicle, house or machine, also ensures that property or vehicle, which is seen as a cost element, turns into a source of income.
- Model of subscription: This model, which includes monthly subscription applications such as Office or translation applications as well as paid television platforms, has a structure similar to a subscription to a magazine or newspaper in the classical sense. These services, which are constantly improved with certain updates, are offered for a certain fee in return for monthly or annual contracts. In addition to memberships, services are provided in software or content.
- Model for generating hidden revenue: In this model, which emphasizes that there may be hidden income sources beyond the visible with the help of data provided in the digital environment,

various risks may arise when it comes to interfering with the personal information of consumers. The structure that enables entrepreneurs to earn possible incomes other than the current earning methods requires a good investigation of the potential. The system, which appears in the Mozilla application, when open-source browsers receive copyrights to include other search engines, is one of the models that should be considered well.

- Model of open-source: First of all, this business model, which is offered free of charge, also offers the user the opportunity to contribute. For this reason, applications such as Linux, Red Hat, or Firefox, which are rapidly becoming widespread, are established based on copyright and partnership agreements. While open source itself is presented as a business model, revenue is generated from activities such as additional services or training in addition to the software.

As can be seen from the business models described, choosing the right digital business model is essential. Choosing the most suitable solution is not always easy. There cannot be a single magic formula for the most profitable, successful, or correct solution. First, every entrepreneur needs to be clear about what kind of bids they want to receive and where they want to optimize. Because binary and multi-user markets are highly complex, growth may take time. Because they require large investments, digital ecosystems can contain highly complex and high-risk business models. The key here is to step into the consumer and the unique value proposition they want to have when thinking about new business models. In the beginning, it may be beneficial to turn to clear, simple, and understandable sources rather than hidden or indirect sources of income. For this reason, models such as Freemium or subscription are recommended to make quick money; In long-term options, business models that include binary platforms, as well as digital ecosystems, are recommended. Because while in short-term solutions it is possible to generate income directly by focusing only on demand, in the long-term perspective, problems such as financial burden may arise in addition to the network need. It should not be forgotten that business models are dominated by leading institutions on a global scale.

When it comes to innovative business models in global competition, it will not be enough to think only of new business ideas of profit-oriented giant enterprises. For this reason, developments that support human and technology harmony are also on the agenda in subjects with a social aspect such as education, health, and social services. In addition to hosting different employees in multinational and multicultural structures as one of the requirements of operating on a global scale, employee training is at least as important as compulsory education (Ince, 2022a). While studies on education in the digital world emphasize the distribution of opportunities, they also draw attention to innovation. in their study of the digital education ecosystem. Suleimankadieva et al. (2021), highlight the innovative approach to the features of the modern intellectual economy. According to the authors, it is necessary to pay attention to the following issues in order to effectively manage the inevitably progressing process:

- Development of global education platforms
- Creation of unique or personal training technologies with human-IT compatibility
- Creation of communities of practice that provide support or guidance as well as a collective educational environment
- To create a local education environment that is the social ecosystem of lifelong education
- To create an environment conducive to the self-education of students or participants anytime and anywhere.

Since the perspectives of different sectors on innovative business models may change, the subject of education is considered as an example. Similarly, the health sector, which is very sensitive to technological developments, can be examined. In today's world where developments such as Industry 6.0 are discussed, every sector will be affected by the digitalization process (Ince, 2023b). prefer holistic or holistic methods that involve looking outside the box; ability-based rationality to facilitate working with complex information; Pragmatism that includes all economic, social, and technological possibilities to adequately evaluate results, design, and capabilities.

The Role of ICT in Digital Entrepreneurship

The evolution of ICT, as one of the growing fields, forms the basis of transformation. Companies that are pioneers in this field, taking their place in all definitions of the digital world, develop the sector through their transformational leadership roles and grow with the sector themselves (Ince, 2023c). The ICT sector is taking over huge industries as more and more companies realize its importance in the labor market. Thanks to information technologies, more and more opportunities are created in the field of entrepreneurship, especially for young people. At the same time, more and more businesses are focusing on the development and evolution of ICT-based business applications. ICT has the potential to assist business activities, including design, distribution, manufacturing, sales, R&D, and feedback. For this reason, it may be necessary to direct innovation beyond adapting to change in order to make a business more efficient, effective, and instantly responsive to customer needs. Because the use of ICT is crucial not only for adoption but also for improved corporate performance and competitiveness. ICT and innovation include the opportunity to shape the future beyond increasing the competitive power of the company with the accelerating effect of corporate entrepreneurship. The main reasons for the evolution of innovative solutions in this direction (iED, 2020; Ince, 2023d):

- Changes in the labor market: Entrepreneurship aligning with ICT is one of the results of inevitable change and rapid adaptation. The establishment of modern entrepreneurs in information and communication technologies has taken place rapidly and has become irreversible. It is not possible to stay away from this accelerating change, and the labor market inevitably changes as technology develops. New software and telecommunication systems and applications that increase speed and performance will make their presence even more evident in the future.
- Changing price rates: In addition to compulsory education, events such as in-service and out-of-service training and even global conferences are now held online. This application reduces the cost of service, lowers the prices, and offers equal opportunity. These and similar situations encourage the entrepreneur to create more complex products with multiple functions and take advantage of new opportunities by developing services to meet new applications and needs worldwide.
- New opportunities in entrepreneurship: While the technology change creates new needs, it also eliminates certain needs, especially in applications based on routine activities. This means that some traditional practices will gradually disappear as new businesses emerge in the future. E-commerce, which is one of the clearest examples of this change, accelerates the shopping process by providing convenience in payment and transportation, as well as establishing connections between businesses and consumers on a global scale.
- Sectors changing with informatics: Many sectors, especially marketing, and advertising, are being digitalized by being directly affected by technological developments. Digital advertising activi-

ties, which provide faster and easier access to large audiences, provide many benefits such as saving time and offering opportunities on a global scale. In today's entrepreneurs, where everything can be done online without the need for a physical workplace, product, or warehouse, digital services can be used at every stage of the purchasing and logistics experience.

Advances in digitalization and developments in information and communication technologies are changing the international business environment, transforming business practices, and creating opportunities for new entrepreneurial activities. Due to the mutual interaction, the labor market, the working world, and entrepreneurs are affected by these developments which create constant pressure for innovation (Ince, 2022b). While digital work environments bring new techniques such as hybrid solutions, they also offer opportunities such as independent content production. One of the entrepreneurial activities developing in the new world order is digital entrepreneurship, which is defined as a new job creation opportunity produced by information and communication technologies such as mobile technology, the internet, digital platforms, and social computing (Javalgi et al., 2012: Ngoasong, 2015). Digital entrepreneurs go beyond simply adapting and using ICTs. According to them, ICT is the infrastructure that both triggers entrepreneurial activities and supports stakeholder interactions (Lusch & Nambisan, 2015). From this point of view, how information and processing technologies will affect the nature of entrepreneurship, especially in developing and shared economies, and how these effects will be seen in different dimensions on a local and global scale are the most important issues to be focused on. For this reason, Asian studies on the subject are important.

THE WORLD OF ASIAN ENTREPRENEURSHIP

In order to understand the development of entrepreneurship in Asia in the digitalization process, it can be compared with today's world by first looking at past data. Nam and Lee comprehensively summarize the 2010 data in their study. A trust-based system has been developed since prepaid transactions are made through a common platform. As confidence in the markets increases, the service sector develops and develops. Manufacturing businesses are increasingly dependent on such services. Looking at the figures for 2010, it is seen that the service sector and GDP ratio in developed countries is over 75%. In this period, when the development in information technologies depends on being noticed, the fact that 75% of the employees in developed countries such as England and the USA are in the service sector may have accelerated the adaptation to change. In other developed countries such as Russia, Germany, and Japan, the rates are around 50%. India and China, which draw attention with their rapid growth today, were ready to take their commonplace in the market. For this reason, it is an inevitable fact that service sectors are an important source of opportunity for the global industry.

Looking at the current data in terms of digital entrepreneurship, the identification of m-commerce as well as e-commerce as well as artificial intelligence skills, digital business models, and the appropriate ecosystem that facilitate the emergence of the new economic paradigm, come to the fore. Since each development requires its own infrastructure, m-commerce initiatives have gained technological momentum in the following areas; mobile banking, in-app purchases, virtual marketplace apps like Amazon, and digital wallets like Android Pay, Apple Pay, and Samsung Pay. Purnomo et al, 2021 address and highlight m-commerce in their comprehensive research. Examining academic publications, the study proposes a convergence axis classification that includes publications in the field of m-commerce: Telecommunications, Commerce applications, social networking, Sales, Electronic commerce, Technology, and Smartphones. The digital marketing of m-commerce, digital commerce, and digital entrepreneurship discussed in this section are discussed at least as much as e-commerce. The potential of the so-called new normal to contribute to developments in commerce and mobile technology is a frequently studied theme. It has taken its share from these developments with its large market share and high potential in ventures in Asia.

Shukla et al. (2021), in their research on women's entrepreneurship in India, emphasize that information and communication technology penetrates deeply into our personal and professional lives. The results of the study also show that the entrepreneurial attitude of digital women is enhanced when an individual is knowledgeable about ICT skills. Although there are various schemes to promote female entrepreneurship in India, this segment is still underrated due to the lack of awareness and necessary skills. Proposing that public and private universities in India should include various skill development courses in their curricula in order to increase success in the early stages of their professional life, the authors also emphasize that various entrepreneurial activities should be encouraged on campuses. There are similar studies that show that entrepreneurial training and practices positively affect entrepreneurial intention and entrepreneurial attitude (Ince 2018; Liu et al., 2020; Ince, 2022c; Yahya et al., 2023). In this study, which determines that women show more digital skills, suggestions are made to pave the way for new-generation female entrepreneurship roles. In order to increase entrepreneurship in this way, training on financial skills should also be provided (Ince, 2020a). The empowerment of women, especially in Asian societies, means strengthening the foundations of society. For this reason, besides entrepreneurship, practices on the effectiveness of women's role in business life are very valuable.

When the research is examined in depth, Butler et al., (2004) bring the following criticism; in the last two decades, although a great deal of management-related entrepreneurship research has been published, most of them have been conducted in Europe and North America. During the same period, Asian countries, with their rapid levels of economic growth driven by local entrepreneurs, were not sufficiently covered in these surveys. The significant share of small and medium-sized enterprises in employment is one of the reasons for starting research on Asian enterprises. Research is further supported by the establishment of entrepreneurship journals in Asia. In particular, the growth of countries such as China draws attention to initiatives for the economic development of Asia. As a mixed geographical region that includes both developed and developing countries, Asia does not show a proportional distribution in the number of entrepreneurs. Therefore, in entrepreneurship analysis, it is also necessary to examine in terms of sub-components of economic factors, including purchasing power parity per capita or the absolute size of the economy. For example, when the subject is considered in terms of GDP per capita based on purchasing power parity (PPP), a new perspective is obtained for the comparison of entrepreneurial activities. According to this measurement tool, which has the potential to provide information on the rate of entrepreneurial activity that can be expected in a country, there are 10 countries in Asia with PPPs above $15,000. However, four of them are not represented in the research literature as they are oil countries. While it is seen that countries such as Singapore and Hong Kong take place in the literature, South Korea, Israel, and Japan take place relatively less. When the countries at the bottom of the scale are excluded from the comparison, it is seen that the remaining major economies such as India and China are well represented in these ratios.

According to Wu et al. (2022), the emergence of new initiatives that will have a great impact as competitors to Europe and North America is one of the indicators that existing businesses are put under competitive pressure by Asia. The direction of competition in the market changes as these companies, which until recently focused not on global expansion, but on intensive growth in their own economies, broaden their visions and direct their targets to global markets. However, the onset of the COVID-19 pandemic creates new and attractive opportunities that are hard to ignore (Ince, 2020b). These new opportunities enable Asian entrepreneurs to deliver their products, which include new technologies and create trends in various aspects, to the world through fast logistics channels that emerged during the pandemic. These changes, which are seen in every sector, also show themselves in areas that must be continued, such as education. While all sectors have their share of this rapid adaptation, students and instructors, who have reached large numbers with online education, are also included in this system (Ince 2021a). In other industries, similarly, many of the routines and habits at home and work are forcibly changed, and much of the friction associated with adopting new products or services from less established companies is lessened. Consumers are rapidly becoming more open to new options and are faced with new opportunities globally to meet their needs. This means that businesses that seize the opportunity in chaos or crisis environments take advantage of the opportunities by giving the necessary struggle (Ince, 2021b). So Asian entrepreneurs take advantage of these seismic shifts to learn about new markets and use them as sources of growth. Looking at the beginning of the change, it is seen that start-ups, whose value creation styles are different from the traditional ones, play an important role.

Businesses that took important steps in providing synergetic structuring for sustainability were able to use the change positively in evaluating the current market (Ince, 2021c). There are several studies examining this success. In his study of companies, unicorns, businessmen, governments and leaders in Central and Southeast Asia, Castro (2022) conducts a comparative study of pre-pandemic, during, and post-pandemic. According to the author, rapid acceleration was gained after the Asian "take-off" led by Japan in the last quarter of the 19th century. Progress until the pandemic ensures that around 80% of "Unicorns" in 2012-2017 are start-ups in this region. Other developments can be summarized as follows:

- From Keiretsu to the Entrepreneur's Club Japan
- Taiwan's Guanxi Qiye, even the world's major suppliers of Electronic Basic Basket
- Some results of e-Cells, Women Entrepreneurs, World-class Innovation HUB, "Ministry of Skills Development and Entrepreneurship" and "Ministry of Women in India"
- The factory of the world, the references that the world must comply with in consumption and production
- New companies with existing and potentially guaranteed aggregate demand
- Chinese State Enterprise and Angel Capitals
- Second- and First-Generation Tigers, new approaches and organizational innovations

In light of all these developments, it is no coincidence that digital entrepreneurship research focuses on information and communication technologies. In addition to digital innovation and entrepreneurship, there are also governance and social networking studies in this field (Wu et al., 2022). The researches that have just started to attract attention in the digital social fields provide clues that the subject will be addressed in more depth in the future.

FUTURE RESEARCH DIRECTIONS

Addressing Asian countries in terms of various dimensions of digital entrepreneurship and sub-elements of the ecosystem will make valuable contributions to the literature. The inclusion of SMEs as well as global businesses, especially in countries with different levels of development, allows for a closer understanding of the labor market. The Asian continent, which hosts different cultures apart from the countries not represented in the research literature, has various attractions that will attract the attention of researchers from the West to the East. Therefore, addressing digital entrepreneurship not only with visible numbers but also with sub-details of economic indicators will provide diversity and richness.

If some recommendations for practitioners are needed, it can be said that academics should be supported by various grants or other financial resources to support Asian studies. Since businesses of all sizes can take part in the digital entrepreneurship ecosystem, it may be necessary to measure the effects of medium or small-scale economies on the current situation in research. To predict the future situation, it may be useful to consider the rates of entrepreneurship that are not represented in current research groups.

CONCLUSION

Since there is an important gap in the conceptualization of entrepreneurship in the digital age, this section mainly focuses on the digital ecosystem and entrepreneurship ecosystem. By examining these issues, an innovation and technology-oriented perspective is adopted. In the section, which tries to understand users as well as entrepreneurs, it is desired to present a broad framework including all sub-components of the digital entrepreneurship ecosystem. Therefore, digital infrastructure governance, digital user citizenship, digital entrepreneurship, and digital marketplace dimensions in multilateral platforms are examined from various perspectives.

Today, it is seen that the enterprises known as the world giants give direction to different entrepreneurs in the ecosystems, they have created by directing information and processing technologies. Industry leadership is now in the hands of technology-focused companies. In addition to businesses with transformational business models, it is seen that networks created in the digital environment in examples from leading countries contribute to accessibility as well as providing a high level of cost savings (Ince, 2021d). For this reason, there is overwhelming competition in entrepreneurship activities in the digitalized world. Since the dimensions of the competition are on a global scale, it draws attention to the transitions between the West and the East. Considering the place of Asian countries in the digital entrepreneurship race, it is seen that serious progress has been made (Castro, 2022).

Outlining a new research agenda to fill the gap in the understanding of entrepreneurship in the digital age, the study also includes new business models developed independently of physical spaces and the types of ecosystems in which these models can be applied successfully. Since the opportunities offered by the digital world are limited to the creativity of people, the emergence of a wide variety of new business ideas is one of the indicators that development will increase rapidly in the future. There will inevitably be changes in old business habits as new sectors are born in such initiatives where human and technology harmony will be seen in different areas. For this reason, the synergistic effects should be focused on by contributing to the development of entrepreneurial ecosystems that consider humans and nature beyond adapting to technology.

REFERENCES

Behera, M. P. C., & Dash, M. C. (2019). Digital Ecosystems: Challenges and Prospects. *International Journal of Research and Analytical Reviews*, 176-183. https://www.ijrar.org/papers/IJRAR19VP026.pdf

Beliaeva, T., Ferasso, M., Kraus, S., & Damke, E. J. (2020). Dynamics of Digital Entrepreneurship and the Innovation Ecosystem: A Multilevel Perspective. *International Journal of Entrepreneurial Behaviour & Research*, 26(2), 266–284. doi:10.1108/IJEBR-06-2019-0397

Butler, J. E., Ko, S., & Chamornmarn, W. (2004). Asian Entrepreneurship Research. In K. Leung & S. White (Eds.), *Handbook of Asian Management*. Springer., doi:10.1007/1-4020-7932-X_7

Castro, F. A. O. (2022). The Asian Entrepreneurship Core in COVID-19 Period: Value Chains, Specialized Education, Massive Participation of Women and Strategic Accompaniment. *Socioeconomic Challenges*, 6(3), 132–147. doi:10.21272ec.6(3).132-147.2022

Evans, D. S., & Schmalensee, R. (2016). *Matchmakers: The New Economics of Multisided Platforms*. Harvard Business Review Press.

Ganis, M. R., & Waszkiewicz, M. (2018). Digital Communication Tools as a Success Factor of Inter-disciplinary Projects. *Problemy Zarzadzania*, 16, 4(77), 85-96. doi:10.7172/1644-9584.77.5

Gibson, R. (2023). *International Trade Fairs and Inter-Firm Knowledge Flows: Understanding Patterns of Convergence-Divergence in the Technological Specializations of Firms*. Springer Nature. doi:10.1007/978-3-031-20557-6

Granstrand, O., & Holgersson, M. (2020). Innovation Ecosystems: A Conceptual Review and a New Definition. *Technovation*, 90, 102098. doi:10.1016/j.technovation.2019.102098

iED (2020, April 4). *ICT and Entrepreneurship*. IED. https://ied.eu/blog/ict-and-entrepreneurship/

Ince, F. (2018). Entrepreneurship Tendency of Z Generation: A Study on Undergraduates. *Pamukkale University Journal of Social Sciences Institute*, (32), 105–113. doi:10.30794/pausbed.424969

Ince, F. (2020a). Financial Literacy in Generation Z: Healthcare Management Students. *Smart Journal*, 6(36), 1647–1658. doi:10.31576mryj.616

Ince, F. (2020b). The Effects of COVID-19 Pandemic on the Workforce in Turkey. *Smart Journal*, 6(32), 1125–1134. doi:10.31576mryj.546

Ince, F. (2021a). COVID-19 Pandemic Made Me Use It: Attitude of Generation Z Towards E-Learning. *Smart Journal*, 7(54), 3489–3494. doi:10.31576mryj.1215

Ince, F. (2021b). Opportunities and Challenges of E-Learning in Turkey. In B. Khan, S. Affouneh, S. Hussein Salha, & Z. Najee Khlaif (Eds.), *Challenges and Opportunities for the Global Implementation of E-Learning Frameworks* (pp. 202–226). IGI Global., doi:10.4018/978-1-7998-7607-6.ch013

Ince, F. (2021c). Creating Synergic Entrepreneurship as Support of Sustainability: Opportunities and Challenges. In R. Perez-Uribe, D. Ocampo-Guzman, N. Moreno-Monsalve, & W. Fajardo-Moreno (Eds.), Handbook of Research on Management Techniques and Sustainability Strategies for Handling Disruptive Situations in Corporate Settings (pp. 464-486). IGI Global. doi:10.4018/978-1-7998-8185-8.ch022

Ince, F. (2021d). A Revolutionary Business Model for Global Purpose-Driven Corporations: Mobility as a Service (MaaS). In R. Perez-Uribe, C. Largacha-Martinez, & D. Ocampo-Guzman (Eds.), *Handbook of Research on International Business and Models for Global Purpose-Driven Companies* (pp. 22–42). IGI Global. doi:10.4018/978-1-7998-4909-4.ch002

Ince, F. (2022a). The Human Resources Perspective on the Multigenerational Workforce. In F. Ince (Ed.), *International Perspectives and Strategies for Managing an Aging Workforce* (pp. 274–297). IGI Global. doi:10.4018/978-1-7998-2395-7.ch013

Ince, F. (2022b). Creative Leadership: A Multidisciplinary Approach to Creativity. In Z. Fields (Ed.), *Achieving Sustainability Using Creativity, Innovation, and Education: A Multidisciplinary Approach* (pp. 30–49). IGI Global. doi:10.4018/978-1-7998-7963-3.ch002

Ince, F. (2022c). Digital Literacy Training: Opportunities and Challenges. In M. Taher (Ed.), *Handbook of Research on the Role of Libraries, Archives, and Museums in Achieving Civic Engagement and Social Justice in Smart Cities* (pp. 185–199). IGI Global. doi:10.4018/978-1-7998-8363-0.ch009

Ince, F. (2023a). Digital Transformation and Well-Being. In M. Anshari, A. Razzaq, M. Fithriyah, & A. Kamal (Eds.), *Digital Psychology's Impact on Business and Society* (pp. 1–27). IGI Global. doi:10.4018/978-1-6684-6108-2.ch001

Ince, F. (2023b). Socio-Ecological Sustainability Within the Scope of Industry 5.0. In M. Sajid, S. Khan, & Z. Yu (Eds.), *Implications of Industry 5.0 on Environmental Sustainability* (pp. 25–50). IGI Global. doi:10.4018/978-1-6684-6113-6.ch002

Ince, F. (2023c). Transformational Leadership in a Diverse and Inclusive Organizational Culture. In R. Perez-Uribe, D. Ocampo-Guzman, & N. Moreno-Monsalve (Eds.), *Handbook of Research on Promoting an Inclusive Organizational Culture for Entrepreneurial Sustainability* (pp. 188–201). IGI Global. doi:10.4018/978-1-6684-5216-5.ch010

Ince, F. (2023d). Sustainable Eco-Innovation: Some Points to Ponder. In F. Ince (Ed.), *Leadership Perspectives on Effective Intergenerational Communication and Management* (pp. 16–35). IGI Global. doi:10.4018/978-1-6684-6140-2.ch002

Insights, C. B. (2023, April 3). The Complete List of Unicorn Companies. CB Insights. https://www.cbinsights.com/research-unicorn-companies

Javalgi, R. G., Todd, P. R., Johnston, W. J., & Granot, E. (2012). Entrepreneurship, Muddling Through, and Indian Internet-Enabled SMEs. *Journal of Business Research*, *65*(6), 740744. doi:10.1016/j.jbusres.2010.12.010

Kretschmer, T., Leiponen, A., Schilling, M., & Vasudeva, G. (2022). Platform Ecosystems as Meta-organizations: Implications for Platform Strategies. *Strategic Management Journal*, *43*(3), 405–424. doi:10.1002mj.3250

Li, W., Badr, Y., & Biennier, F. (2012, October). Digital Ecosystems: Challenges and Prospects. In *Proceedings of the International Conference on Management of Emergent Digital EcoSystems* (pp. 117-122). ACM. 10.1145/2457276.2457297

Liu, T., Walley, K., Pugh, G., & Adkins, P. (2020). Entrepreneurship Education in China: Evidence from a Preliminary Scoping Study of Enterprising Tendency in Chinese University Students. *Journal of Entrepreneurship in Emerging Economies*, *12*(2), 305–326. doi:10.1108/JEEE-01-2019-0006

Lundvall, B. Å. (2007). National Innovation Systems—Analytical Concept and Development Tool. *Industry and Innovation*, *14*(1), 95–119. doi:10.1080/13662710601130863

Lusch, R., & Nambisan, S. (2015). Service Innovation: A Service-Dominant Logic Perspective. *Management Information Systems Quarterly*, *39*(1), 155–175. doi:10.25300/MISQ/2015/39.1.07

Monsalve-Pulido, J., Aguilar, J., & Montoya, E. (2023). Framework for the Adaptation of an Autonomous Academic Recommendation System as a Service-oriented Architecture. *Education and Information Technologies*, *28*(1), 321–341. doi:10.100710639-022-11172-8

Nam, K., & Lee, N. H. (2010). Typology of Service Innovation from Service-dominant Logic Perspective. *Journal of Universal Computer Science*, *16*(13), 1761–1775.

Naudé, W., & Liebregts, W. (2023). Digital Entrepreneurship. In W. Liebregts, W. J. Van-den-Heuvel, & A. Van-den-Born (Eds.), *Data Science for Entrepreneurship. Classroom Companion: Business*. Springer. doi:10.1007/978-3-031-19554-9_12

Ng, I. C. L. (2013). *Value and Worth: Creating New Markets in the Digital Economy*. Innovorsa Press.

Ngoasong, M. Z. (2015). Digital Entrepreneurship in Emerging Economies: The role of ICTs and local context. In: *42nd AIB-UKI Conference*. Metropolitan University, UK.

OECD. (2023, April 4). *4th Digital for SMEs Roundtable*. OECD. https://www.oecd.org/digital/sme/

Parker, S. C. (2005). The Economics of Entrepreneurship: What We Know and What We Don't. *Foundations and Trends in Entrepreneurship*, *1*(1), 1–54. doi:10.1561/0300000001

Purnomo, A., Susanti, T., Anisah, H. U., Sari, A. K., & Maulana, F. I. (2021, August). Value of M-commerce Research: A Bibliometric Perspective. In *2021 International Conference on Information Management and Technology (ICIMTech)*, (pp. 813-818). IEEE. 10.1109/ICIMTech53080.2021.9534928

Ranta, V., Aarikka-Stenroos, L., & Väisänen, J. M. (2021). Digital Technologies Catalyzing Business Model Innovation for Circular Economy—Multiple Case Study. *Resources, Conservation and Recycling*, *164*, 105155. doi:10.1016/j.resconrec.2020.105155

Razavi, A., Moschoyiannis, S., & Krause, P. (2009). An Open Digital Environment to Support Business Ecosystems. *Peer-to-Peer Networking and Applications*, *2*(4), 367–397. doi:10.100712083-009-0039-5

Ritala, P., & Jovanovic, M. (2024). Platformizers, Orchestrators, and Guardians: Three Types of B2B Platform Business Models. In A. Aagaard & C. Nielsen (Eds.), *Business Model Innovation: Game Changers and Contemporary Issues*. Palgrave Macmillan.

Satalkina, L., & Steiner, G. (2020a). Digital Entrepreneurship and Its Role in Innovation Systems: A Systematic Literature Review as a Basis for Future Research Avenues for Sustainable Transitions. *Sustainability (Basel)*, *12*(7), 2764. doi:10.3390u12072764

Satalkina, L., & Steiner, G. (2020b). Digital Entrepreneurship: A Theory-Based Systematization of Core Performance Indicators. *Sustainability (Basel)*, *12*(10), 4018. doi:10.3390u12104018

Shukla, A., Kushwah, P., Jain, E., & Sharma, S. K. (2021). Role of ICT in Emancipation of Digital Entrepreneurship Among New Generation Women. *Journal of Enterprising Communities: People and Places in the Global Economy*, 1750-6204. doi:10.1108/JEC-04-2020-0071

Simplilearn. (2023). *11 of the Most Popular Digital Business Models and Strategies in 2023*. Simplilearn. https://www.simplilearn.com/digital-business-model-article

Song, A. K. (2019). The Digital Entrepreneurial Ecosystem—A Critique and Reconfiguration. *Small Business Economics*, *53*(3), 569–590. doi:10.100711187-019-00232-y

Stam, E. (2015). Entrepreneurial Ecosystems and Regional Policy: A Sympathetic Critique. *European Planning Studies*, *23*(9), 1759–1769. doi:10.1080/09654313.2015.1061484

Suleimankadieva, A., Petrov, M., & Kuznetsov, A. (2021). Digital Educational Ecosystem as a Tool for the Intellectual Capital Development. In *SHS Web of Conferences. 116: 00060*. EDP Sciences. 10.1051hsconf/202111600060

Sussan, F., & Acs, Z. J. (2017). The Digital Entrepreneurial Ecosystem. *Small Business Economics*, *49*(1), 55–73. doi:10.100711187-017-9867-5

Talin, B. (2022, Nov 28). 11 Digital Business Models You Should Know. *More than Digital.* https://morethandigital.info/en/11-digital-business-models-you-should-know-incl-examples/

Talin, B. (2023, Jan 20). What is a Digital Ecosystem? Understanding the Most Profitable Business Model. *More Than Digital.* https://morethandigital.info/ru/chto-takoyetzifrovaya-ekosistyema-ponimaniye-naibolyeyeviguodnoy-biznyes-modyeli/

Tilson, D., Lyytinen, K., & Sørensen, C. (2010). Research Commentary-Digital Infrastructures: The Missing IS Research Agenda. *Information Systems Research*, *21*(4), 748–759. doi:10.1287/isre.1100.0318

Wu, J., Si, S., & Liu, Z. (2022). Entrepreneurship in Asia: Entrepreneurship Knowledge When East Meets West. *Asian Business & Management*, *21*(3), 317–342. doi:10.105741291-022-00187-1

Yahya, M., Isma, A., Alisyahbana, A. N. Q. A., & Abu, I. (2023). Contributions of Innovation and Entrepreneurship Education to Entrepreneurial Intention with Entrepreneurial Motivation as an Intervening Variable in Vocational High School Students. *Pinisi Entrepreneurship Review, 1*(1), 42-53. https://journal.unm.ac.id/index.php/PEREV/article/view/49

KEY TERMS AND DEFINITIONS

DE: Digital ecosystem is a term based on increasing system utility, providing benefits, and promoting knowledge sharing, internal and external collaboration, and system innovation.

DEE: The digital entrepreneurial ecosystem is an entrepreneurial ecosystem that focuses on intermediation, infrastructure, users, and the role of institutions while integrating the two existing ecosystem literature.

DI: Digital infrastructure is a socially embedded mechanical system that includes technological and human components, networks, systems, and processes that create self-reinforcing feedback loops. This system is one of the necessary elements to capture the effects of digitalization.

NSI: National systems of innovation is the flow of technology and information between people, businesses, and institutions, seen as the key to the innovative process at the national level.

P2P Architecture: A peer-to-peer architecture consists of a decentralized peer-to-peer network, with nodes that are both clients and servers combined. It distributes the workload among peers, and all peers contribute and consume resources within the network without the need for a central server.

PPP: Purchasing power parity is the currency conversion rate that eliminates price level differentiation between countries. Goods and services in the same basket can be purchased in all countries when converted to a different currency at the bulk parity available.

SOA: Service-oriented architecture is a method that exposes its oriented functionality as a suite of interoperable services that can be used on multiple separate systems, allowing the development of reusable and distributed systems.

USP: The unique selling proposition or the unique value proposition (UVP) is a marketing strategy to inform customers about how their brand or product is superior to their competitors.

Chapter 2
E-Business Trends and Challenges in the Modern Digital Enterprises in Asia

Ramya Thatikonda
University of the Cumberlands, USA

Bibhu Dash
iD https://orcid.org/0000-0002-7509-3462
University of the Cumberlands, USA

Meraj Farheen Ansari
iD https://orcid.org/0000-0002-8707-965X
University of the Cumberlands, USA

Srinivas Aditya Vaddadi
University of the Cumberlands, USA

ABSTRACT

During the last two decades, there have been many shifts in how e-business is conducted. The term "e-business" in this era of industry 5.0 can apply to any commercial or business activity incorporating data exchange over the internet. In industry 5.0, with technological advancements, companies now have access to new clients and markets thanks to the proliferation of the internet. The IBM Internet marketing division coined the phrase "e-business" in 1996, and since then, this word has become more familiar in digitalized enterprises worldwide. Every business performs trade, or the purchasing and selling of products and services among different organizations, as one of its most basic tasks. The adoption and acceptance of digital technology in everyday life affect our societal values, society, and future business prospects, along with its use in industrial production. This chapter will highlight how e-business growth put Asian business as the industrial warehouse of the world and how it impacts social, cultural, and technological sustainability in both the short and long terms.

DOI: 10.4018/978-1-6684-6782-4.ch002

1. INTRODUCTION

Any form of commercial or business transaction that takes place via the internet and includes the transfer of data is referred to as a "e-business," and the term "e-business" is used to refer to these kinds of dealings. Business, which may be defined as the purchasing and selling of products and services between different organisations, is one of the most essential responsibilities that any corporation must do. E-business, which stands for "business conducted over the internet," is a subset of electronic business that places an emphasis on the utilisation of information and communications technology (ICT) to facilitate the company's external operations and contacts with individuals, organisations, and other businesses. In 1996, IBM's Internet marketing group coined the term "e-business" to describe online commercial transactions. IBM and the advertising agency Ogilvy & Mather are credited with coining the term "e-business" in 1994. The word was used to characterise the company's strategy of doing business through the Internet. Louis V. Gerstner Jr., the former CEO of the corporation, said that he was prepared to spend one billion dollars advertising this new product line.

1.1 Background of the Study

While doing business online, two aspects that are deeply influenced are a company's expenses and earnings. Online business has the potential to win over a large audience due to the ease with which it may be used in a variety of contexts. The implications of this finding on financial matters are far-reaching. One other advantage of doing business online is the possibility of buying and selling both physical products and information. The phrase "electronic business," which is also often referred to as "web-based business," is used to represent a broad variety of economic operations that are carried out through the Internet with the purpose of selling products and services. The growth of electronic business is causing a shift in the commercial hub because it is changing corporate strategy, rearranging interactions among market participants, and contributing to structural adjustments. These changes are occurring as a direct consequence of the rise of electronic business. The implications of doing business online have been far-reaching and are difficult to pinpoint. Electronic business has the potential to bring about shifts in firm models, shifts in market structure, and prospects for monetary development brought about by authoritative shifts; nevertheless, only a limited number of enterprises really address these challenges. Soni, V. D., (2020)

By supplying a concealed strategy and therefore - not just replace - in plans of action, electronic business raises the possibility of new models for categorising invention and transacting business. Trade conducted through the internet is an important contributor to the growth and well-being of an economy. It's a strategic action that involves things like planning, controlling, promoting, and appropriately appropriating a variety of commodities and enterprises. The "Business soul" and its contribution to the development of the country is the primary topic that will be discussed in this article. In addition, any sort of economic transaction in which the parties involved interact and work together not in person but rather online is considered to fall under this umbrella as well. Orendorff, A. (2019)

The practise of buying and selling goods and services on the Internet is referred to as "online business," as is the conduct of any other sort of transaction that involves the transfer of ownership or usage rights of items or services through a computer-mediated system. Even though it is widely used, this definition is much too limited to include all of the most recent advancements of this game-changing business innovation. Web-based business refers to the utilisation of electronic communications and computerised data management innovation in commercial exchanges to construct, alter, and reclassify connections for the purpose of value production between or among organisations, as well as between organisations and individuals. Sharma, S., Mahajan, S., & Rana, V. (2019).

Despite the fact that online business and e-business are sometimes used synonymously with one another, the two names really relate to entirely separate ideas. Both business-to-business (transactions between firms) and business-to-consumer (sales to consumers) are two of the most prevalent uses of data and interchanges technology in the commercial sector. Business-to-business refers to transactions between organisations, while business-to-consumer refers to sales to individuals (exchanges between business associations and furthermore people). (Lin, X.; Wang, X.; Hajli, N, 2019)

1.2 Motivation to Study

The phrase "e-business" is used to describe the process of trading information, products, and services across digital mediums such as the internet. Incorporating novel approaches into company communication and workflow. This includes the distribution of resources such as data, software, and hardware through computer networks, wireless technologies, and even spiders. It's a tool that reduces the cost and effort of providing government services to companies, citizens, and the state. E-business, sometimes known as "web-based business," is a relatively new and evolving subfield of business administration and information innovation. The practise of doing business in cyberspace has been the focus of several studies and articles in recent years.

This research differentiates between the two terms business and business by treating them as separate concepts. The ability to grasp the notion of exchange, or "trading of stock on a big scale across multiple nations," is crucial to achieving commercial success. It's logical to conclude that the network that facilitates this transaction also belongs to the realm of online trade. So, it is appropriate to describe electronic business as the buying and selling of stocks on a worldwide scale via the use of an electronic medium, especially the Internet, in a number of different nations. Because of the internet, a new economic model has emerged that connects the global financial system, the media industry, and the innovation economy. In concert, these elements provide the bedrock upon which doing business online may be built. Other definitions utilise phrases like "a business endeavour as an ongoing concern" to describe a company's legal standing. To use the term "e-business" in its widest definition, it may mean any part or process of a company's operations that is conducted electronically or which makes use of highly developed technical systems. Examples of direct business activities include marketing, sales, human resource accounting, and management. In contrast, examples of indirect business activities include business process re-building and change management, both of which can have an effect on the effectiveness and cohesion of company forms and procedures.

2. THEORETICAL FRAMEWORK

2.1 The Spread of Innovations

E-business adoption and performance results may be seen from both the customer's and the company's point of view (the latter perspective is more relevant to this study).

2.2 How It Feels to Be a Customer

Thus far, much of the marketing literature on e-business and the Internet-based business world has concentrated on the effects of these phenomena on customer decision-making and conduct. Information flow in computer-mediated environments (Hoffman and Novak 1996); consumer demographics and Internet usage; customer value delivery using the Internet (Keeney 1999); and customer satisfaction online are just a few of the specific research foci. The larger strategic implications of the Internet for consumer markets have also been the subject of research. Glazer (1991) conducted an early conceptual research that analysed the significance of data and expertise in the formulation of marketing plans. Recently, Alba et al. (1997) compared Interactive home shopping to conventional retail formats to investigate the effects of electronic markets on buyers, sellers, and producers. The Internet's potential influence across various products and services and conducted an analysis of multi-channel situations in which customers may use both traditional and digital means of purchasing goods and services.

2.3 View From the World of Business

A novel gadget, system, policy, programme, method, product, or service is considered an innovation if the adopting organisation decides to implement it (Daft 1982). Researchers have taken many different approaches to studying the adoption of innovations across different functional areas, with many of them focusing on the factors both within and outside of the organisation (Chandy and Tellis 1998). Forces that encourage innovation adoption may be roughly classified into two groups:

(a) Those related to the internal economic incentives and features of the firm, and
(b) Those related to the external environment.

2.4 Factors Relevant to Running a Business

Businesses typically embrace innovations in order to acquire a competitive edge or new capabilities over their competitors, in line with the "often unspoken belief that innovations benefit their adopters" (Abrahamson and Rosenkopf 1993). So, many books and articles on the topic of innovation adoption in organisations have concentrated on detailing the factors that contribute to the successful adoption and implementation of new ideas (Kimberly and Evanisko 1981). Functional distinction, administrative intensity, external and internal communication, and vertical integration are among these characteristics (Hull and Hage 1982).

Information technology (IT) innovation adoption has also been the subject of study. In this article, we examine the role that information and organisational designs play as antecedent factors, along with the importance of top-level management's buy-in and the catalytic effect of operational crises. During his research, Rogers (1995) focused on "authority innovation choices," in which a small group of influential, high-ranking, or technically-savvy insiders decides whether or not to implement a new invention.

2.5 Aspects of the Natural World

As a result of (external) normative pressures, i.e. the worry of being left behind, organisations may also accept innovations for the sake of survival. A company may accept a new idea without first determining whether or not it would be beneficial, but rather because similar companies have done so (DiMaggio and Powell 1983). There has been discussion of this "bandwagon effect" in research that takes an institutional view of how innovations spread. Although early adopters of innovations are often motivated by financial considerations, later adopters may be driven by a desire to seem legitimate (Westphal, Gulati, and Shortell 1997). The adoption of an institution is often prompted by the pressure to "keep up," even if this results in the institution gaining little, if any, advantage over its competitors. The organisation may also accept innovations due to influential groups outside of the organisation. In particular, influential customers and suppliers may pressure the central organisation to adopt new methods that they believe would lower their expenses of working with the organisation or provide other advantages from their connection with the company.

2.6 Studying the Effects of Marketing Strategies on the Spread of E-Business

Both capability-driven and institution-driven aspects in innovation adoption have been studied by marketing scholars. Consider Gatignon and Robertson (1986), who use a set of explanatory variables that include demand-side and supply-side competitive qualities, organisational characteristics, and decision-maker characteristics to explain the (discrete) acceptance or rejection of laptop computers. Two new studies have recently looked at how widespread the use of e-businesses has become. The authors Grewal, Comer, and Mehta (2001) investigate the factors that motivate businesses to take part in B2B online marketplaces. They discover that the degree to which people take part is affected by factors such as the organization's capabilities in regards to learning and information technology, as well as motives for efficiency and legitimacy (an institution-driven factor). Technological opportunism is the capacity of an organisation to recognise and adapt to emerging technologies, and Srinivasan, Lilien, and Rangaswamy (2002) investigate its causes and consequences in the context of e-business adoption.

It is especially important to consider this conflict in the context of e-business, because the organisation faces both economic and normative demands to accept innovations (Dash et al., 2022). In the late 1990s and early 2000s, there was a great deal of optimism about the revolutionary potential of e-business, and this optimism drove the widespread adoption of e-business at the time. Studying whether the components of e-business adoption driven more by normative forces have lesser consequences for company success is intriguing from both a theoretical and practical standpoint. To do so, we take a different tack from the existing literature and examine the issue from the perspective of e-business adoption, starting with the factors that lead up to the decision to adopt, moving on to the characteristics of the adoption itself, and finally to the effects of the adoption on performance. Our antecedents were carefully crafted to include indicators that might be used to disentangle the influence of economic incentives and social pressures.

2.7 Deployment of e-Business Technologies

First, we met with eight managers from different industries, including IT hardware, semiconductors, telecom, and manufacturing equipment, for in-depth, face-to-face interviews. The interviews helped to provide context for the study, verify the most critical components, and provide insight into the realities of e-business implementation. We concentrated on these four areas throughout the interview and data collecting phases largely to improve the comparability of the findings across business units. We stayed away from "dot-coms," which are businesses whose very foundation is the Internet. Instead, we zeroed in on a group of linked sectors that are heavily reliant on physical assets for manufacturing. By focusing on

Figure 1. Components of e-business

the theoretically important antecedents, we can explain the variation in e-business adoption without being too preoccupied with the question of whether or not the nature of the organization's business itself is the main source of this variation. Furthermore, while business units in the studied industries would likely have higher average intensities of e-business adoption compared to those in less technology-intensive industries, our central focus is on the co-variation of e-business adoption with various antecedents and outcomes, rather than adoption levels themselves. Our findings give a foundation for future research in this area, even if it turns out that other sectors do need their own studies.

To understand the extent of e-business adoption, we drew on a mix of theoretical concepts and empirical data. According to Porter's value chain paradigm, there are several phases in the value creation process inside a business unit, starting at the incoming interface (where supplier-related procedures are focused) and ending at the outward interface (where customer-related processes are concentrated). We found that managers logically grouped e-business activities into three distinct categories—those involving external vendors, internal processes, and end users—consistent with this perspective. From this vantage point, I was able to see the benchmarks for e-business implementation. Managers have also made a distinction between the many business processes that electronic technology may facilitate. Manager interviews found that four main functions—communication, internal administration, order taking, and procurement—were the primary drivers of e-business adoption.

Based on our observations in the field, we have developed a conceptual framework for e-business adoption, which is shown in Figure 1. Columns in Figure 1 reflect the areas of a company where the processes described in the preceding row are important, and rows represent the business processes that may be enhanced by implementing e-business initiatives. Within the business unit, with consumers, and with suppliers are all possible locations for communications processes (i.e., the flow or exchange of information). Certain administrative tasks (such as financial and managerial accounting, human resource and employee benefit management, travel reimbursement, and the like) are handled internally, within the scope of the business unit. The customer interface is the place where orders are taken (that is, where business is conducted with customers, whether they end users or other companies). In the end, the supplier interface is where procurement activities take place (i.e., connecting with suppliers to buy raw materials). This process-oriented view is especially pertinent given that firms routinely pursue many e-business projects to accomplish the same goals. Sawhney and Zabin (2001) contend that "enterprise applications targeted at building and managing relationships with key constituencies," such as customers, suppliers, employees, and partners, are made possible by the rise of e-business. This is in line with our business process-focused conceptualization of e-business adoption. Have in mind that in a business network, the boundaries between companies may be blurry. One company's method of receiving orders might be the equivalent of another's method of acquiring goods and services. We address this problem by making sure that all survey metrics pertaining to the SBU of the central manufacturer's adoption of e-business are consistent with one another. These procedures diverge at the SBU level.

It's important to note that Figure 1 only depicts four of the many possible e-business application domains. On the other hand, they form the central set of procedures needed to connect its internal and external stakeholders smoothly. It's important to remember that broader activity sets like CRM and SCM provide opportunities for integrating some of these processes. E-business initiatives, however, may be used for certain subsets of the processes that make up these broader groups of actions. Thus, we aim for a process-level viewpoint in order to have clearer conceptualization and more accurate assessment.

3. STRUCTURE OF IDEAS

The conceptual framework shown in Figure 2 establishes connections between (1) the impetus for adopting e-business, (2) its level of intensity, and (3) the performance results that result from it. Based on our review of the literature, we suggest two main classes of antecedents: internal to the company and external factors. Efficiency, sales, customer pleasure, and connection building are all quantified by measurable performance results. In the literature, several factors have been presented as potential precursors to the acceptance of innovations inside organisations. The antecedents for this research were chosen using a two-stage method. First, we acknowledged that the adoption of e-business was distinct

Figure 2. Businesses using the internet for their transactions

	Within-Firm	**Customer Interface**	**Supplier Interface**
Communication processes	Electronic communication within firm	Electronic communication with customers	Electronic communication with suppliers
Administrative processes	Electronic internal administration	--	--
Order-taking processes	--	Online order-taking	--
Procurement processes	--	--	E-procurement

from the adoption of most other innovations because of the potential effect on various business processes, the complexity and boundary-spanning character of e-business initiatives, the significant environmental factors connected to adoption, and the degree to which interdepartmental cooperation was necessary for successful adoption. Based on this knowledge, we extracted the most relevant background information from the current literature. This preliminary list of antecedents was then put through a second round of testing and refinement based on in-depth interviews with managers in the field. We now have reasons to believe some speculations.

3.1 Factors That Shape Companies' Decisions to Use E-Business

E-business is a priority for upper management. Decisions to adopt are heavily influenced by the mind-set of upper management (Damanpour 1991). Most recently, e-business activities have become an integral aspect of many companies' long-term strategic plans. Given that senior management is crucial in determining the course of a company (Kohli and Jaworski, 1990), it stands to reason that they will play a pivotal part in the e-business sphere as well. For instance, by fostering company-wide strategic agreement about e-business adoption, upper management may lessen departmental tension and speed up the rollout of digital services (Dess and Origer 1987). Moreover, the intense adoption of e-business might call for a lot of money and attention from upper management. Without the support of upper management, investments of this kind are very unlikely to be done.

We anticipate that although the level of intensity with which e-business is adopted will be influenced by the attention given to it by senior management, some business processes will get more attention than others. First, e-business technologies improve communication processes by allowing information and knowledge to flow freely inside and beyond the borders of the business unit, as well as by integrating previously fragmented information flows into a unified knowledge management structure (Sawhney and

Figure 3. Antecedents and performance outcomes of e-business adoption: A conceptual model

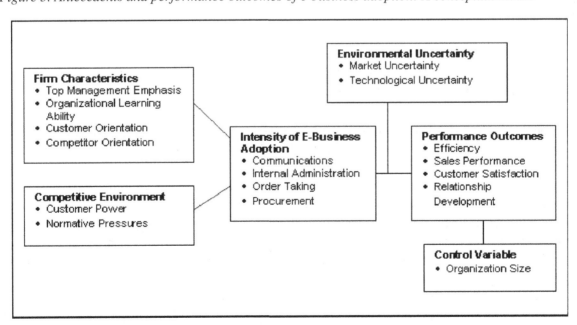

Zabin, 2001). Yet, managers inside and across departments have a tendency to hoard information rather than share it, which impedes the company's ability to regard knowledge as a corporate asset (Brancheau and Wetherbe 1987). In this setting, upper management may ease resistance to and friction between departments exchanging data, which in turn encourages the use of e-business and data sharing inside the organisation. Just as reorganising information sharing networks and other organisational arrangements with customers and suppliers may be necessary when introducing e-business technologies in the order taking and procurement process, so too may internal ones.

4. REVIEW OF LITERATURE

4.1 E-Commerce and Globalization

The Internet removes physical limitations on trade. It is a completely transnational form of trade. E-commerce relies on the broader trend of globalization, to which it has made a significant contribution. That's why e-Commerce is changing the economic structure of countries. The economy is shifting to one based on information and technology (Anil, 2019a). E-commerce has advanced greatly due to globalization. Compared to smaller businesses, multinational corporations make more use of e-Commerce. Companies that operate in a worldwide marketplace are under more pressure to succeed than those that operate locally, therefore they are more likely to swiftly embrace new technologies like e-Commerce to help them stay competitive, grow their market share, and improve their operations. Companies operating on a worldwide scale pay more attention to metrics like operational efficiency and overall cost reduction. With the help of online marketplaces, businesses can streamline their processes and save money by streamlining and speeding up their transactions, as well as by collecting valuable data about their customers and the operations they run. Globalization has different impacts on the adoption of e-Commerce in B2B and B2C commerce, with global companies being more involved in the B2B channel. Therefore, if the vendor has chosen the appropriate platform or e-marketplace to implement an e-Commerce strategy (Semerikov et al., 2019), B2C e-Commerce might be a better possibility for enterprises with regional or local operations.

4.2 The Subject of Discussion Pertains to the Advancement of the Digital Economy and the Transformation of Marketing Strategies

The competitiveness and effectiveness of the business at the present stage of the functioning of the world market is one of the most important areas. The effectiveness and development of an organization's rational strategy can be attributed to its accuracy and formation, which takes into consideration the utilization of innovative techniques and internet technologies, combined with a marketing mix. This approach guarantees the attainment of the desired financial outcomes and customer loyalty. In order to gain an understanding of the fundamental strategies for creating novel marketing techniques and instruments, it is necessary to examine the historical evolution of the utilization of marketing tools and technologies within the realm of commerce. The scientific endeavours of a group of researchers warrant particular attention, as exemplified by the works of Al-Weshah, G. (2020) and Brenstein, R. (2019). These scholars have focused their research on the rapid advancement of internet technologies as the primary driver of modernization in marketing concepts. Their studies are dedicated to exploring the fundamental theoretical aspects of innovative technology development and its application in the field of marketing. This approach is based on the classical method of forming a marketing strategy with more advanced elements of the marketing mix, their planning and promotion, but they do not take into account global transformational features and trends in the organization of electronic marketing, which requires a more detailed study and confirms the relevance of this research topic.

4.3 E-Business

Two English syllables combine to make the term "e-business," which refers to "Electronic business" (B. N. Bhakti, Y. Nurfaizal, and T. Anwar, 2022). This term describes "business activities that are carried out automatically or semi-automatically by utilising computer information systems." IBM, led by CEO Lou Gerstner, was among the first major corporations to adopt internet-based operational systems, and it was Gerstner who coined the term "cloud computing." This kind of electronic commerce provides for more effective and adaptable management of internal and external data processing systems. Communication with suppliers and other business partners, as well as fulfilling and serving customers, are also common uses of e-business. E-commerce is merely one aspect of e-business in the modern world (F. P. Oganda et al., 2020). According to B. D. Wicaksono (2021), "e-commerce is a subset of e-business." E-commerce, on the other hand, is primarily focused on commercial transactions conducted via websites or apps, whereas e-business is everything whose business operations or activities are carried out utilising all electronic data (S. G. Baek and H.-A. Kwon, 2021). By implementing a knowledge management system, this e-commerce has the purpose of boosting firm income.

4.4 E-Commerce-Friendly Online Media Support

In the United States, 42,5 million people regularly use social networking sites like Facebook. It ranks as the fourth tallest in the globe. In Indonesia, around 18% of the population is already active on the four most prominent social networking platforms. The number of Twitter users in Indonesia, at 5.7 million, makes it the third-largest in the world. If the current trend persists, Indonesia will fall further behind in the coming year. It will, without a doubt, be the fourth biggest mobile market in the world. In order to expand their businesses, managers must be able to recognise and respond to changes in the market and other external factors (N. P. Lestari et al., 2021). Behaviour in today's society It's not easy to alter one's ways of behaving. Current cultural norms The finest and fastest approach to see potential in the age of e-business is via the establishment of a consultancy, which is one of the company alternatives available to an entrepreneur. Trend, sustainability, and competitiveness are promoted through virtual consulting, a type of digital business consulting service. The media is the main distinction between conventional and digital enterprises (I. G. Salimyanova et al., 2019), but there are other differences as well. When a new medium appears, it ushers in novel patterns of interaction. "Unique actions suggest an unconventional strategy for doing business." There is a growing body of evidence suggesting that companies that adopt an e-business management approach have a greater probability of success in the long run (Z. Fauziah, et al., 2020). In contrast, businesses that resist going digital have a harder time adjusting to new circumstances. E-commerce, which makes use of digital technology, has been around since December 20 of last year. The military was the first to widely adopt this technology (D. Immaniar et al., 2022). However, both the company and the public participated heavily in building this digital technology facility. All of Tesco Plc's main locations, including those in South Korea, now have an online store where customers can place orders and await delivery. In an effort to streamline the process by which customers purchase food and drink at Hard Rock Cafés across the United States, the chain is implementing a mobile strategy system based on a mobile ordering application model. However, Hertz is an example of a company that provides a self-service kiosk for renting cars (L. Meria, Q. Aini, N. P. Lestari Santoso, 2021). Several other companies do as well. Since we now live in the digital age, it stands to reason that the digital concept would be among the most emblematic channels for launching and promoting increased product sales (H. Nusantoro et al., 2021). As a result, additional managerial skills in application installation in the organization is required, as well as an understanding of market developments such as this.

Inspiration for Online Businesses and Startups Specifically, "Motivation is defined as goal-directed action," as stated by Chung and Meggison. It is the degree to which a person strives to achieve their performance goals. According to the work of J. Gikas and M. M. Grant (2013), motivation may be described as "actions taken with the end in mind." Satisfaction on the work and one's ability to excel at it are both correlated with a person's level of motivation (S. Purnama., 2021). "all the many states of internal conflict that have been labelled as wants, wants, needs, drives, and the like," write Barelson and Steiner to describe motivation. Therefore, we may define motivation as the mental states and mental attitudes that stimulate action, propel goal-directed behaviour, and bring about change in order to meet needs that provide satisfaction or correct inequities (Zaharuddin, U., 2021). Thus, we can ascertain whether or not his sense of purpose in providing and showcasing his work to the community stems from his desire to develop an e-business, thereby aiding the cause of creating a more competitive and competitive business world in today's difficult market.

4.5 Research Gap

While there are several obstacles to e-business adoption, they vary greatly across small and big businesses. According to Arendt (2008), there is still a chasm between the resources available to small businesses and those available to major corporations, despite the fact that both have access to the Internet. Arendt (2008) argues that the obstacles might be classified as either macroeconomic or microeconomic in nature. The absence of an innovation culture is a fundamental impediment to the macro economy. There is not enough of an incentive from the market for businesses to bring new innovations. The climate in which many small businesses function does not foster innovation or the creation of new strategies. Nonetheless, there are times when managers believe that e-marketplace participation is inappropriate because e-business is not relevant to the company.

5. AIM OF THE RESEARCH

Paper aims to highlight current, cutting-edge technologies used in e-business with a focus on how they may be utilised to expand the reach and sales of various goods and services, particularly in the context of building brand awareness.

Objectives of the Study

- The study's primary goal is to examine how e-businesses are putting various theoretical frameworks to work in practise.

- One goal is to investigate the factors that need e-business infrastructure for a corporation to function normally.
- Another goal is to catalogue the many strategic viewpoints that must be taken into account while planning for information exchange.

5.1 Research Question

RQ1. Why does a company choose to do its business online?
RQ2. When it comes to e-business, what are the most pressing concerns right now?

5.2 Hypothesis of the Study

H0: There is a significant impact of e-business factors influencing business Performance
H0: There is relationship towards awareness on e-business strategies among SME practitioners

5.3 Research Methodology

5.3.1 Strategy for Research

Deductive, inductive, and abductive reasoning are the three primary types of research methods that have been identified in the literature. Scanning and analysing previous literature, then drawing inferences from the theory in the form of hypotheses and prepositions, are all hallmarks of the deductive approach. The last part of the process involves presenting conclusions and proofs or refutations after having experimentally verified hypotheses and presuppositions. The steps of a deductive reasoning process look somewhat like this: case | results | rule. The inductive strategy, on the other hand, relies on the inverse methods, with observation leading to a theoretical framework or the pattern-results-case-rule approach (Kovács & Spens, 2005).

A deductive approach was adopted in this study. Being a hybrid of deductive and inductive reasoning, an abductive strategy shifts focus from rules to results to individual cases. As e-business has already been studied extensively, and a theoretical framework has been constructed, an abductive technique is appropriate for this study. By looking at a phenomenon inside a predetermined theoretical framework, Kovács and Spens (2005) argue that an abductive technique may provide a clearer understanding of the phenomenon. Second, we now have a better understanding of the effects of e-business, and we can characterise them. Abduction is a method of reasoning wherein an empirical occurrence is linked to the rule in order to provide light on the situation at hand.

This is why I want to begin my thesis with a review of the relevant literature, before moving on to report the findings of my own experiment. In order to address the initial research questions, the data will next be contextualised and connected with what has already been learned through the aforementioned literature review.

5.3.2 Approach to Research

Several distinct types of research strategies, including qualitative, quantitative, and hybrid, are distinguished in the existing literature. The quantitative approach places an emphasis on the testing of hypotheses and theories, which is a deductive part of the research process. Accumulating and analysing numerical data is a key part of this technique. The qualitative approach, on the other hand, is less concerned with statistics and more concerned with expression, meaning, and description. A wider perspective on the study issue is assumed by qualitative methods (Bryman & Bell 2007).

In order to increase the credibility of their findings, many researchers use a mixed method that employs both qualitative and quantitative approaches. Both primary and secondary sources were employed to compile the results of this qualitative investigation. There is a plethora of justifications for using a qualitative approach. To begin, the human element is crucial in making strategic choices in small businesses. Hence, I can get better answers to the study questions if I interview people with decision-making authority. Second, the qualitative approach is more appropriate since the goal of the thesis is to describe the phenomena of e-business rather than to validate or deny hypothesis. Finally, the approach allows for more wiggle room and revisions, making it more suited to a writer with less expertise. On a fourth point, there have been qualitative studies conducted. At long last, it is possible to do a qualitative study in a manageable amount of time. However it's tough to do comprehensive quantitative research in the time allotted for writing the thesis. Nonetheless, the study does have certain caveats that may be shown.

5.3.3 Research Procedure

This study article seeks to examine the difficulties encountered by organisations in major cities that have integrated e-business into their daily operations. To this end, a questionnaire was developed based on a framework of e-business obstacles, allowing for the gathering of quantitative primary data. The questionnaire employed a 5-point Likert scale, with 5 representing strong agreement, 4 representing agreement, 3 representing neutrality, 2 representing disagreement, and 1 representing significant disagreement. The sample was collected using a stratified sampling strategy. Among the target population of 150 businesses, a sample of 108 was taken to provide a 95% confidence interval. This study employed recently updated publicly accessible data, which covered organisations in the tourism, telecommunications, and banking industries, since there is no definitive list of verified organisations implementing e-business in Metropolitan cities at the time of this research. In a further step, we reached out to organisations within our sample's three target industries that are already making use of e-business to gather our data. The sample was analysed using statistical methods in four different disciplines: technology; economics; law; and culture. These Institutions were sent questionnaires. In order to provide the necessary data, key individuals who are familiar with ICT and the organization's e-business goals took part in the process. The acquired data from the Organizations was finally examined and presented.

5.4 Data Collection

There are two distinct approaches to gathering information, known as secondary and primary data collecting. Although there is a wealth of previously acquired data that may serve as a foundation for analysis, "primary data" is material that has not previously been made public (Bryman & Bell, 2007).

The objective of this study is to boost the validity by using a hybrid approach based on both methods. Yin (2004) claims that using many sources of data improves the reliability of study findings.

5.4.1 Secondary Data Sources

The data utilised in this work is considered secondary since it was obtained for another reason but is relevant to the author's research. The importance of secondary data in management and business is growing (Bryman & Bell 2007). Secondary data analysis has several benefits. Crawford (1997) claims that gathering secondary data is faster than primary data collection, giving the researcher a clearer understanding of the issue than if they had collected it themselves.

A comprehensive understanding of e-business is required for the qualitative approach that has been settled on. By reviewing relevant theory and doing background study, one might gain insight and develop more insightful interview questions. The analysis and result will be more precise as a result. That's the primary justification for relying on secondary sources in my dissertation. In addition, secondary sources, particularly those issued by authorities and commercial groups, may provide more reliable information. Data supplied here is of good quality, and the samples represent a comprehensive range of geographic areas (Bryman & Bell 2007). Official statistics data, supplied by government bodies, may also contribute to a more thorough comprehension of the study issue.

5.4.2 Primary Sources of Data

In-depth interviews with the initially chosen firms were the primary source of information for this thesis. There are several benefits and drawbacks of using interviews to get primary data. Potentially useful information that is necessary for resolving the concerns posed by the article is the key advantage. The interviews, on the other hand, take more time and effort. That's why this thesis makes use of the semi-structured interview method. The expedited timeline and manageability of this method make it ideal for a novice researcher. Although semi-structured interviews need nothing in the way of rearranging the order of questions or rephrasing their language and are thus most appropriate when the author has a solid grasp of the material at hand, they are often used in such cases (Crawford, 1997). In quantitative research, interviews are heavily organised to ensure the reliability and validity of the data, but in qualitative research, the focus is on overarching themes and the respondents' own experiences and perspectives.

The primary benefit of this information is that it facilitates the answering of the first research question and the development of a more complete image of the organisations and their e-business use. The interview's second section consists of nine free-form questions meant to tease out information about the impact, obstacles, and rewards of adopting e-business practises. The interviews lasted between 35 to 45 minutes, and replies were recorded and transcribed so that nothing was forgotten and everything could be scrutinised in detail. With an eye on the potential drawbacks, we sent the questions to the firms so that they could get acquainted with the nature of the study challenge. Such drawbacks include skewed results from responders who were too prepared or persuaded beforehand.

6. RESULTS & DISCUSSION

It's possible to dig into the e-business difficulties to varying degrees that companies in major cities confront while using this strategy. Table 1 displays the results of the study's four surveys, which reveal that the widespread adoption of e-business systems in emerging economies faces a number of obstacles. Low income, low computer and internet penetration, low bank account and credit card penetration, and poor telecommunications infrastructure are all factors cited by Kapurubandara M (2009) as impediments to the growth of e-business.

Efficient and successful operation of an e-business system needs both a dependable network infrastructure and competent staff. Among other issues, lack of ICT infrastructure, hostile environments, lack of macro policies to nurture local e-business structures, and lack of perception of e-business benefits by managers were some of the obstacles to e-business developments in developing countries.

Market size of e-commerce industry across India from 2014 to 2018, with forecasts until 2030:

Figure 4 shows the results regarding Market size of e-commerce with the reference of India. The result values shows drastic increase from 2020 to 2021. The reason behind a drastic enhancement of e-commerce performance is because of Covid-19 pandemic situation, majority has been chosen online purchase of all needy and for the next coming years it is perceived as increase in e-commerce performance in 2025 till 2030.

The statistical results was sourced from Redseer survey (Rana, 2022). The results shows that India have a potential to set a growth in retail sector by 2030.

6.1 CONSTRAINTS POSED by Technology in the Realm of Electronic Business

Seventy-five percent of respondents gave the same response when asked about technical difficulties; another twenty-five percent gave the same response when asked about internet access issues. Bandwidth restrictions on the internet have also been seen as a problem, with 12.5% of users strongly agreeing and 62.5% agreeing. Of the sample, 12.5 percent were unsure whether or not bandwidth posed a problem for their e-business operations, and 12.5 percent flat-out disagreed. However, when asked whether the general public's lack of IT knowledge posed a problem for their e-business operations, 37.5% of respondents strongly agreed, 25% agreed, and 25% disagreed, with 12.5% strongly disagreeing. Firms based in major cities that rely on e-business face additional difficulties because of the scarcity of alternative e-businesses. One-quarter of respondents gave a negative response, while half gave a positive response. The results showed that 12.5% strongly agreed that power interruptions impeded their ability to do every

Table 1. Showing study areas used for questionnaire design.

TECHNOLOGICAL	ECONOMIC
• Connection to the World Wide Web • Inadequate Network Protection • Loss of power • Competent e-business professionals are in short supply.	• Prices associated with new developments and upgrades to existing infrastructure • Internet shopping fees • Expenses associated with acquiring and keeping it talents
LEGAL	**SOCIOCULTURAL**
• Regulatory Acts of Government • Lack of a governing organisation for electronic business	• Users' lack of computer knowledge (Customers) • Educators' Failure to Stress the Importance of Privacy

Figure 4. Market size of e-commerce

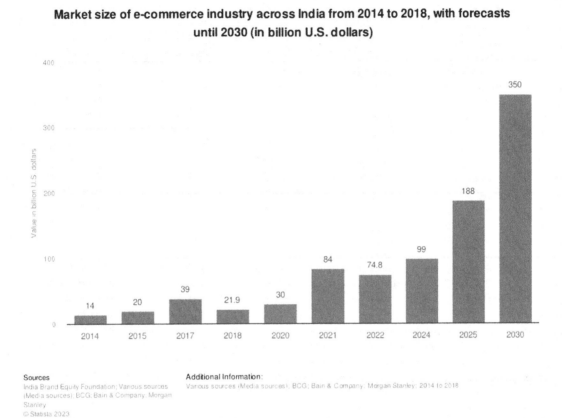

Market size of e-commerce industry across India from 2014 to 2018, with forecasts until 2030 (in billion U.S. dollars)

day e-business, while 25% agreed with the statement. The remaining respondents were split: 25% were in opposition, while 37.5% were on the fence. Organizations in the tourism industry are disproportionately impacted by power outages since they are often situated in outlying, rural locations.

6.2 E-Business and the Economy's Difficulties

Companies doing e-business in major cities have difficulties in terms of both the expenses associated with innovation and the costs associated with adapting to new technologies at a quick pace. 50% of those polled strongly agreed, while another 25% agreed, and 25% opposed, with the remaining 25% unsure. In contrast, fifty percent of respondents strongly agreed that the expense of bringing in e-business professionals was a problem, and twelve percent agreed. Twenty-five percent of respondents disagreed, and twelve percent strongly disagreed. The results showed that 25% of respondents strongly agreed that the expenses associated with e-business administration was a problem, whereas 12.5% agreed that this was a problem. In contrast, 37.5% of people were not in agreement, while 25% were unsure.

Figure 5. Online retail boom

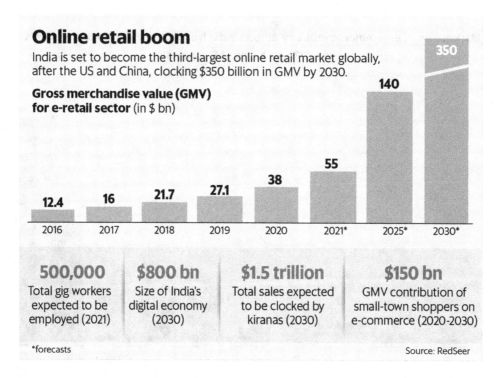

Online retail boom

India is set to become the third-largest online retail market globally, after the US and China, clocking $350 billion in GMV by 2030.

Gross merchandise value (GMV) for e-retail sector (in $ bn)

2016	2017	2018	2019	2020	2021*	2025*	2030*
12.4	16	21.7	27.1	38	55	140	350

500,000
Total gig workers expected to be employed (2021)

$800 bn
Size of India's digital economy (2030)

$1.5 trillion
Total sales expected to be clocked by kiranas (2030)

$150 bn
GMV contribution of small-town shoppers on e-commerce (2020-2030)

*forecasts   Source: RedSeer

6.3 E-Business and the Law's Difficulties

According to the results, it is difficult for metropolitan areas to regulate e-business and keep tabs on digital trades. Respondents were split down the middle on this subject, with 25% disapproving and 12.5% strongly disagreeing while 37.5% were in agreement. Although doing business online presents unique problems, 87.5% of respondents were unsure as to whether or not government regulations and rules were an issue. A further 12.5% expressed extreme agreement.

6.4 E-Business and its Cultural Ramifications

With 25% of respondents strongly agreeing and 37.5% agreeing, the survey indicated that fraud is a barrier to the expansion of e-business in major metropolitan areas. However, 12.5 percent of respondents were unsure and 25% were unconvinced that it posed a threat to e-business processes inside their organisations. Lack of public knowledge has also been identified as a significant barrier. One-quarter of respondents (25%) were very or very agreeable; 37% were agreeable; 25% were not agreeable; 12.5% were severely disagreeable.

7. THE PRACTICAL IMPLICATIONS

Telecommunications businesses need to think about improving internet access by boosting signals in outlying areas, where they have potential specialised industries, like the tourist industry. Companies that have connection issues and power outages can look into implementing failsafe measures. Failsafe is defined as "a system having a backup system that assures ongoing functioning even if the first system fails" in the Random House Kernman Webster's College Dictionary (2010). Solar systems, uninterruptible power supplies (UPS), and generators are just a few examples of automatic backup power sources. Challenged Businesses should use the most dependable ISP available, and ideally have several ISPs as a failsafe. With this, businesses won't have to worry about the income and consumers they would ordinarily lose if their services were temporarily unavailable.

Companies doing business online should use VeriSign on their websites to inspire confidence in their visitors and, perhaps, their customers. With the VeriSign mark, you may reassure your consumers that they are dealing with a reliable company when they do business with you online, as stated by Symantec Corporation (2011). People know they can proceed with confidence in the connection, the site, and the transaction when they see the VeriSign seal.

Companies with comparable economies could benefit from combining forces to implement e-business. By pooling the expense of recruiting and keeping e-business professionals and system maintenance, participating Companies may save money. Another option for cost-cutting is to use reputable public e-business service providers. Furthermore, because India is so close, companies can explore working with Indian e-business Service Providers.

Governments in major urban areas should think about establishing a regulatory and legislative framework to keep tabs on and encourage e-business inside the nation. By ensuring company owners and customers of equal treatment, this would boost confidence and credibility. Similarly, rather of waiting for the government to react to changes, which typically takes longer periods of time when compared to the quick changes in technology, organisations that employ e-business should organise a representative body to express their problems to the government.

E-business operations in megalopolises face obstacles from several cultural factors. According to Mohanna S. et al. (2011), breaking down cultural barriers is necessary to advance the condition of e-business in the nation. Mass education on the benefits of emerging technologies, such as information technology and electronic business, may help accomplish this goal. To do this and lessen the social and cultural effects of e-business myths, mass media may be used to spread the word.

8. LIMITATIONS AND FUTURE DIRECTIONS

This survey may not be representative of all Botswana-based companies because of its small sample size. This is due in large part to the fact that not all organisations that engage in e-business, particularly SMEs, are represented in available information resources. Due to the lack of an e-business regulating organisation, new entrants to the market may not yet be reflected in any of the listings. In addition to the above, only 92 out of 108 Organizations in the sample provided a response. Several organisations, notably banks and other financial institutions, need more time to reply to research requests, and hence the time allotted for data collecting was insufficient. There is a need for further study into how e-business development might be facilitated by influencing public opinion.

9. CONCLUSION

Among the many electronic business sectors, e-business will emerge as a frontrunner in the next years. Because of the ease with which borders may now be crossed and the new possibilities it has presented, the e-business revolution has had a profound impact on the nature of business. It has had a profound effect on the conventional business model and the way of life in major urban centres. Although e-business has many advantages for both buyers and sellers, it also poses serious competitive threats to more conventional industries. Contrasting the situation in industrialised nations, it is clear that developing nations have more hurdles to get over before they can fully embrace e-business. Low internet prices will help e-business grow, which will force many brick-and-mortar stores to close. One of the advantages of doing business online is the convenience it affords customers. One reason for this is that wherever a client has access to the internet, they may make a purchase or place an order. Every consumer is important, thus e-business service providers should make it easy for them to do business with you by providing seamless service, multiple payment methods, and a wide range of online services. The availability of more products and the access into more markets are two more upsides. Yet, there are several obstacles that must be overcome by e-business enterprises before they can succeed.

REFERENCES

Abrahamson, E., & Rosenkopf, L. (1993). Institutional and Competitive Bandwagons: Using Mathematical Modeling as a Tool to Explore Innovation Diffusion. *Academy of Management Review*, *18*(3), 487–517. doi:10.2307/258906

Alba, J., Lynch, J., Weitz, B., Janiszewski, C., Lutz, R., Sawyer, A., & Wood, S. (1997). Interactive Home Shopping: Consumer, Retailer, and Manufacturer Incentives to Participate in Electronic Marketplaces. *Journal of Marketing*, *61*(July), 38–53. doi:10.1177/002224299706100303

Anil, K. (2019a). *Internet and Wold Wide Web (Paper Code: MM-409/IB-419)*. DDEG. https://www.ddegjust.ac.in/studymaterial/mcom/mc-201.pdf

Arendt, L. (2008). Barriers to ICT adoption in SMEs: How to bridge the digital divide? *Journal of Systems and Information Technology*, *10*(2), 93–108. doi:10.1108/13287260810897738

Bhakti, B. N., Nurfaizal, Y., & Anwar, T. (2022). Analisis Komparasi Teknik Rendering Blender Render Dan Cycles Render Pada Video Animasi 3d Tentang Alat Pencernaan Manusia. Technomedia Journal, 6(2), 188–196, 2022

Brancheau, J. C., & Wetherbe, J. C. (1987). Key Issues in Information Systems Management. *Management Information Systems Quarterly*, *11*(1), 23–45. doi:10.2307/248822

Bryman, A., & Bell, E. (2007). *Business research methods. 2*. Oxford University Press.

Crawford, I. (1997). Marketing Research and Information Systems. Food and Agriculture organization of the UN. FAO. https://www.fao.org/docrep/W3241E/W3241E00.htm [2012-04-02]

Daft, R. L. (1982). Bureaucratic Versus Nonbureaucratic Structure and the Process of Innovation and Change. In S. B. Bacharach (Ed.), *Research in the Sociology of Organizations, V.(1)* (pp. 129–166). JAI Press.

Damanpour, F. (1991). Organizational Innovation: A Meta-Analysis of Effects of Determinants and Moderators. *Academy of Management Journal, 34*(3), 555–590. doi:10.2307/256406

Dash, B., Sharma, P., Ansari, M. F., & Swayamsiddha, S. (2022). *A review of ONDC's digital warfare in India taking on the e-commerce giants.* Available at SSRN 4323963.

Dess, G. G., & Origer, N. (1987). Environment, Structure, and Consensus in Strategy Formulation: A Conceptual Integration. *Academy of Management Review, 12*(2), 313–330. doi:10.2307/258538

DiMaggio, P., & Powell, W. W. (1983). The Iron Cage Revisited: Institutional Isomorphism and Collective Rationality in Organizational Fields. *American Sociological Review, 48*(2), 147–160. doi:10.2307/2095101

Fauziah, Z., Latifah, H., Omar, X., Khoirunisa, A., & Millah, S. (2020). Application of Blockchain Technology in Smart Contracts: A Systematic Literature Review [ATT]. *Aptisi Transactions on Technopreneurship, 2*(2), 160–166. doi:10.34306/att.v2i2.97

Gikas, J., & Grant, M. M. (2013). Mobile computing devices in higher education: Student perspectives on learning with cellphones, smartphones & social media. *The Internet and Higher Education, 19*, 18–26. doi:10.1016/j.iheduc.2013.06.002

Glazer, R. (1991). Marketing in an Information-Intensive Environment: Strategic Implications of Knowledge as an Asset. *Journal of Marketing, 55*(October), 1–19. doi:10.1177/002224299105500401

Grewal, R., Corner, J. M., & Mehta, R. (2001). An Investigation Into the Antecedents of Organizational Participation in Business-to-Business Electronic Markets. *Journal of Marketing, 65*(July), 17–33. doi:10.1509/jmkg.65.3.17.18331

Hoffman, D. L., & Novak, T. P. (1996). Marketing in Hypermedia Computer-Mediated Environments: Conceptual Foundations. *Journal of Marketing, 60*(July), 50–68. doi:10.1177/002224299606000304

Hull, F., & Hage, J. (1982). Organizing for Innovation: Beyond Burns and Stalker's Organic Type. *Sociology, 16*(4), 564–577. doi:10.1177/0038038582016004006

Immaniar, D., Cholisoh, N., Putra, F. J. E., Pangestu, P. S., & Sunarya, P. O. A. (2022). Sistem Kartu Ujian Online Menggunakan Framework Yii Pada Universitas Raharja. Technomedia Journal, 6(2), 163–175.

Keeney, R. L. (1999). The Value of Internet Commerce to the Customer. *Management Science, 45*(4), 533–542. doi:10.1287/mnsc.45.4.533

Kimberly, J. R., & Evanisko, M. J. (1981). Organizational Innovation: The Influence of Individual, Organizational, and Contextual Factors on Hospital Adoption of Technological and Administrative Innovation. *Academy of Management Journal, 24*(December), 689–713. doi:10.2307/256170 PMID:10253688

Kohli, A. K., & Jaworski, B. J. (1990). Market Orientation: The Construct, Research Propositions, and Managerial Implications. *Journal of Marketing, 54*(2), 1–18. doi:10.1177/002224299005400201

Kovács, G., & Spens, K. (2005). Abductive reasoning in logistics research. *International Journal of Physical Distribution & Logistics Management*, *35*(2), 132–144. doi:10.1108/09600030510590318

Lestari, N. P., Durachman, Y., Watini, S., & Millah, S. (2021, July). Manajemen Kontrol Akses Berbasis Blockchain untuk Pendidikan Online Terdesentralisasi. *Technomedia Journal*, *6*(1), 111–123. doi:10.33050/tmj.v6i1.1682

Meria, L., Aini, Q., Lestari Santoso, N. P., Raharja, U., & Millah, S. (2021) Management of Access Control for Decentralized Online Educations using Blockchain Technology. *2021 Sixth International Conference on Informatics and Computing (ICIC)*, (pp. 1–6). IEEE. 10.1109/ICIC54025.2021.9632999

Nusantoro, H., Supriati, R., Azizah, N., Santoso, N. P. L., & Maulana, S. (2021). Blockchain Based Authentication for Identity Management. *In 2021 9th International Conference on Cyber and IT Service Management (CITSM)*, (pp. 1–8). IEEE. 10.1109/CITSM52892.2021.9589001

Oganda, F. P., Lutfiani, N., Aini, Q., Rahardja, U., & Faturahman, A. (2020) Blockchain Education Smart Courses of Massive Online Open Course Using Business Model Canvas. *2nd International Conference on Cybernetics and Intelligent System (ICORIS)*, (pp. 1–6). IEEE. 10.1109/ICORIS50180.2020.9320789

Orendorff, A. (2019). *Global ecommerce statistics and trends to launch your business beyond borders.* Global Ecommerce.

Purnama, S., Aini, Q., Rahardja, U., Santoso, N. P. L., & Millah, S. (2021, November). Design of Educational Learning Management Cloud Process with Blockchain 4.0 based EPortfolio. *Journal of Education Technology*, *5*(4), 628. doi:10.23887/jet.v5i4.40557

Rana, M. (2022, December 2). *Digital native brands - transforming retail landscape.* RedSeer Strategy Consultants. https://redseer.com/newsletters/digital-native-brands-transforming-retail-landscape/

Robertson, T., & Gatignon, H. (1986). Competitive Effects on Technology Diffusion. *Journal of Marketing*, *50*(July), 1–12. doi:10.1177/002224298605000301

Rogers, E. M. (1995). *Diffusion of Innovations* (4th ed.). The Free Press.

Salimyanova, G. (2019). Economy digitalization: Information impact on market entities. *Journal of Environmental Treatment Techniques*, *7*(4), 654–658.

Sawhney, M., & Zabin, J. (2001). *The Seven Steps to Nirvana.* McGraw-Hill.

Sawhney, M., & Zabin, J. (2001). *The Seven Steps to Nirvana.* McGraw-Hill.

Semerikov, S., Babenko, V., Kulczyk, Z., Perevosova, I., Syniavska, O., Davydova, O., Soloviev, V., Kibalnyk, L., Chernyak, O., & Danylchuk, H. (2019). Factors of the development of international e-commerce under the conditions of globalization. *SHS Web of Conferences*. SHS. 10.1051hsconf/20196504016

Sharma, S., Mahajan, S., & Rana, V. (2019). A semantic framework for ecommerce search engine optimization. *International Journal of Information Technology : an Official Journal of Bharati Vidyapeeth's Institute of Computer Applications and Management*, *11*(1), 31–36. doi:10.100741870-018-0232-y

Soni, V. D. (2020). Emerging Roles of Artificial Intelligence in ecommerce. *International Journal of trend in scientific research and development, 4*(5), 223-225.

Srinivasan, R., Lilien, G., & Rangaswamy, A. (2002). Technological Opportunism and Radical Technology Adoption: An Application to E-Business. *Journal of Marketing, 66*(July), 47–60. doi:10.1509/jmkg.66.3.47.18508

Westphal, J. D., Gulati, R., & Shortell, S. M. (1997). Customization or Conformity? An Institutional and Network Perspective on the Content and Consequences of TQM Adoption. *Administrative Science Quarterly, 42*(2), 366–394. doi:10.2307/2393924

Yin, R. (2004) *Case study methods.* Cosmo Corp. https://www.cosmoscorp.com/Docs/AERAdraft.pdf

Zaharuddin, U. Rahardja, Q. Aini, F. P. Oganda, & Devana, V. (2021) Secure Framework Based on Blockchain for E-Learning During COVID-19. In *2021 9th International Conference on Cyber and IT Service Management (CITSM),* (pp. 1–7). IEEE. 10.1109/CITSM52892.2021.9588854

Chapter 3
Shifting of Paradigm in Buying Behaviour of Digital Natives

Shee Mun Yong
UOW Malaysia University College, Malaysia

ABSTRACT

Digital natives are Millennials and Gen Zs who grew up under the ubiquitous influence of the internet and digital technologies. As these generations come of age, they represent the largest group of consumers with spending power on the rise, commanding $360 billion in disposable income, and are expected to take the lead in global market growth on online retail sales. As that figure increases, it raises a question in the business community on ways to market to these digital natives as their spending habits differ drastically from the previous generations. The focus of this chapter is to undertake a more in-depth study on the predictors of their buying behaviour and the relationship between the predictors and their determinants.

MAIN FOCUS OF THE CHAPTER

Digital natives are Millennials and Gen Zs who grew up under the ubiquitous influence of the internet and digital technologies. As this generation come of age, they represent the largest group of consumers with spending power on the rise commanding $360 billion in disposable income and are expected to take the lead in global market growth on online retail sales. As that figure increases, it raises a question in the business community on ways to market to these digital natives as their spending habits differ drastically from the previous generations. The focus of this chapter is to undertake a more in-depth study on the predictors of their buying behaviour and the relationship between the predictors and their determinants.

INTRODUCTION

Millennials and Gen Z are digital natives (DN) who grew up surrounded by internet, digital gadgets, and the world of social media. Using digital devices and web apps have become second nature to them. It is not surprising that this generation is synonymous with e-commerce market boom in the early 2000's

DOI: 10.4018/978-1-6684-6782-4.ch003

when consumers were given greater access to an increased variety of e-commerce options available on the internet. Social media accounts for 80% in influencing digital natives' buying decision (Worldline, 2020). They are more creative, curious, and possess agility traits with a higher competence score that set their distinctive consumption characteristics apart from other generations such as Millennials and Gen X (Oxford Economics, 2021).

Different names are used for these new generation of consumers. Tapscott (2008) called them the Internet generation, which is characterized by good know-how and application of information and communication technologies. They are also known as digital natives (DN) because they were born in the computer age (Prensky, 2001). Others called them Millennials and Gen Z due to their high understanding of internet technology and actively using it for entertainment and socialization.

One of the significant contributions of this generation is their active engagement in social media attributed to the revolution of technology and ubiquitous adoption of digital devices. The way digital natives interact and use social media when making online shopping decision has changed consumer behaviour significantly. Mobile channels are now favoured over internet web access. This new norm of integrating shopping apps, location-based services, and mobile wallet is forcing commercial marketing to adopt online platform for brand engagement, online retailing, and market research (The ASEAN Post Team, 2020). Companies are increasingly relying on digital media platforms by incorporating machine learning, real-time data, and smart digital technology into their marketing strategies offering new ways of informing, reaching, engaging, learning, selling, and providing services to these digital natives. Their strong influence of the digital economic culture has resulted in them taking a lead among the 1.6 billion users of eWallet that will surpass 5.2 billion users globally by 2026 (Thistle Initiatives, 2022).

With the entrenchment of 4G telecommunication technology providing seamless connectivity across smart gadgets, digital natives are expected to take the lead in global market growth on online retail sales. The incoming 5G technology once it is broadly available will drive consumer demand even further especially for applications that require high broadband speed such as virtual reality (VR), and augmented reality (AR) shopping and entertainment. Studies such as Ramachandran (2020) have shown that these younger consumers already own the highest number of connected devices. With the advent of 5G technology, it will spur increasing streaming activities among these digital natives.

This phenomenon is exacerbated by lockdown control measures taken by governments during Covid-19 pandemic. The restricted movement in countries worldwide has impacted physical activities. Community events were cancelled, employees were required to work from home, and malls, wet markets, and schools were forced to close to reduce person-to-person contact and human density within confined areas. These actions set off a tsunami wave of social disruption altering market buying behaviour and physical retail business model creating a paradigm shift towards online retail business. Consumers in many instances were forced to purchase products and services online. Over time these consumers adapted to the new way of convenient and time-saving shopping resulting in an influx and growth of online stores. With their familiarity in digital environment, digital natives took the lead and became a big part of the disruptive force. As Gen Z come of age, they represent the largest group of consumers with spending power on the rise commanding $360 billion in disposable income. In Malaysia, Gen Z monthly disposable income is predicted to amount to $327 million (Tjiptono et al., 2020). As that figure increases, it raises a question in the business community on ways to market to these digital natives as their spending habits differ drastically from the previous generations.

BACKGROUND

Consumer Buying Behaviour

The oldest Millennials are now in their mid-40s and Gen Zs in their mid-20s with combined spending of $165 billion (Arifi, 2022). 99% of this segment own a smartphone. With Internet penetration rate as high as 98%, their consumption pattern is different in many ways from previous generations. Most opt to ignore traditional media channels preferring instead news feeds for updates and social media for engagement. As these two generations made up of 55% of the 7.7 billion world population (Miller & Lu (2018) they are becoming the largest consumers in history. Many of these younger adults have the behaviour of buying based on want rather than on need. It is often heard that digital natives keep up with trend regardless of their own financial situation. The ramification is the tendency to overspend resulting in personal and social repercussion such as financial stress and taking on high interest credit card and personal loan that could derail longer term financial goals, getting into debt, and damaging their own credit worthiness.

But despite of it all, spending is an important motivation for their happiness. Their higher spending power allow them to buy items that match their image of success often relying on brands that can help shape their identity with preference given to their trusted brand when comes to making buying decision. This assertion is supported by 45% of Gen Zs that trustworthy and transparent brand is the biggest motivation for engagement (Statistica, 2023).

Therefore, digital natives are considered a disruptive generation which is why studying them becomes important and relevant. According to Shaw (2020), when comes to making buying decision, the level of consideration depends on the value of the products that they need to buy. For instance, fulfilling a physiological need such as buying a beverage at a nearby store can be made instantaneously. In comparison, a higher value product such as buying a car requires more deliberation and longer time for consideration. It is also not uncommon to involve multiple parties before making final decision. The higher level of engagement and interactions give consumer greater confidence in making a perceived correct decision for the product or service that they are paying.

Buying Characteristics

From an age generation demographic perspective, this buying decision process seems to differ between younger and older generation. Whilst digital natives are perceived as more impatience or impulsive when making buying decision attributed mainly to multiple commitments such as work, social, and families, older generations are considered a value hunter. As baby boomers and "silent generations" do not have the time constraints of the younger generations, they are able to devote more of their time and effort in focusing on value for money and product quality that include prioritizing reliable, reasonably priced, and budget-friendly products (see Table 1).

Digital natives on the other hand are characterized by users and consumers of technology. Increasingly, development in information and communication technology serves as a transformational catalyst on these new consumer groups resulting in unique behaviour causing disruptions in market consumption behaviour dissimilar from other generations. This generation of consumers demand quick and easy access to information, prefer using online and mobile apps and are obsessed with technology and social media. They extensively utilize online shopping due to greater transparency of information such as product avail-

Table 1. Buying characteristics differences among Gen Z, Millennials, Gen X, and Boomers

Generation Z	Millennials	Generation X	Baby Boomers
Born between 1997-2015	Born between 1981-1996	Born between 1965-1980	Born between 1946-1964
Prefer online shopping	Shop online and physical stores	Buy in stores	Buy in stores
Have least patience	Switch channels frequently	Like to do research	Do physical shopping

ability, price, and value of products (Santander, 2020.). On the flip side, they are not loyal to a brand, care more about the experiences, and have higher expectations (Schlossberg, 2016). Past study such as Decouz (n.d.) has shown that although attempts were made to capture these digital natives' loyalty via traditional loyalty programs of promotions, and cards, they were not successful. One of the contributing factors is their familiarity with using web and mobile app enabling them to access and share information faster than other generations so much so that traditional marketing communication no longer appeals to them. It becomes a new challenge for companies to stay abreast with the changing trend and respond quickly and adequately to stay relevant in this competitive business world.

Although marketing can greatly affect consumer behaviour in the market, there are other factors such as trust and buyer's own disposable income that have the same influence on an individual's buying decision. These influences are not the same as each customer has a different experience and perception of price, familiarity, and trust.

As the entity of trust is symbolic in nature, consumers' trust can be defined by their willingness to rely on brand that is aligned with their own value when faced with risks (Lau and Lee, 1999). When trust is built over time from consumer's own experience complemented by the influencing power and actions demonstrated by producer, trust is considered an important factor when making purchasing decision.

As opposed to previous generations, digital native shoppers are more likely to choose following influencers on Instagram, and other social media than put their trust into a particular brand. In addition, they like experiencing omnichannel that include both in store and online shopping. In essence, they want more than just browsing physical products and complement this experience through social media interactions and their own inner social circles among friends to add to their overall experience (Morgan, 2019). It raises a question of how important digital natives view trust when making an online buying decision and the contribution of consumer experience towards building this trust? Whilst trust plays an intermediary and influencing role in social media communication and online shopping attitudes (Chetioui, Lebdaoui, and Chetioui, 2021), trust in buying a product is moderated by customer's own disposable income and economic situation.

Brand Loyalty

Brand trust and loyalty are key market elements in determining market price. Brand loyalty refers to the degree of customer attachment to a particular brand is made up of two-dimensional notion of consumer behaviour and attitudes. These two dimensions determine the loyalty of customers for a specific brand (Sarwar, Aftab and Iqbal, 2014). In this sense, brand loyalty is generated when products or services are in line with values, philosophies, and passions of the customer. It refers to a tendency of consumers to purchase a specific brand within a product category because they believe that a certain brand offers the right product in the right features (Inegbedion and Obadiaru, 2019).

Customer who are loyal to a brand often repeatedly purchase the same product or service without looking for alternative brands when needed (Ashraf, Ilyas, Imtiaz, and Ahmad, 2018). However, this holds true only when the firm's internal structures such as price and quality, and market forces such as superior rival products remain within the perceived expectation of customers. Any changes to these factors could trigger a shift in an individual's trust for the brand and hence his brand loyalty (Erdumlu, Saricam, Tufekyapan, Cetinkaya, and Donmez, 2017). Therefore, brand loyalty is a state that correlates with a particular condition at a specific timeframe. This loyalty remains so long as there are no significant changes to the condition.

In the determination of this state, past studies have mainly focussed on attitudinal loyalty (Kressmann, Sirgy, Herrmann, Huber, Huber, and Lee, 2006) and behavioural loyalty (Romaniuk and Nenycz-Thiel, 2013). However, behavioural loyalty is deemed as an unreliable predictor of customer behaviour (Cornell, 2019) as it measures only the continuous tendency to buy a brand but does not account the reasons for not switching to another brand. For example, the reason why customer does not switch to another brand could be attributed to habitual buying behaviour or just plain laziness. Therefore, behavioural loyalty is not a reliable predictor of customer behaviour. Conversely, attitudinal loyalty reflects the overall attitude towards a particular brand loyalty including whether a brand fulfils the key functional or emotional needs of its customers (Ailawadi, Neslin and Gedenk, 2001). In this regard, customer loyalty for a brand is related to their values and lifestyle.

In the context of digital natives, studies such as Brodzik, Young, Cuthill and Drake (2021) has shown 94% of this generation are willing to buy products from companies that stand for important social issues such as Diversity, Equity, and Inclusiveness (DEI) values. 57% are more loyal to brands that clearly demonstrate their commitment in promoting equitable outcomes in their spheres of influence. It testifies that digital natives are more passionate about inclusive branding and brands that fail to represent DEI accurately in adverts and practices would lose a large portion of their existing and future market (James, 2022). Furthermore, as brand ambassador and committed activist loyal customers inspire others of the same value to purchase and think twice before switching to alternative brands (Ilias and Shamsudin, 2020). Although brand loyalty is without a doubt an important outcome variable in the marketing literature, the question is how much influence does brand loyalty has on digital natives and to what extend does DEI influence lead to building brand loyalty? Compared with the previous generations, these generation of consumers is deemed to have shown less brand loyalty and confidence in a brand (Kitchen and Proctor, 2015). Unravelling this question would help companies respond to the challenge leading to higher market share and competitive edge over their market rivals.

Price Perception

Price consciousness and price sensitivity are usually attributed to the impact of price on consumer behaviour. However, they do not present the same pattern. The disposable income of digital natives is the primary factor in actual purchases. Past studies conducted in Malaysia show similar correlations. Price perception is known as predictor of consumer demand (López-Fernández, 2020), purchase intention (Cham, Ng, Lim, and Cheng, 2018) and buying behaviour (Jaafar, Lalp, and Naba, 2012). The insight gained from these experiments is leveraged by product merchants in using digital natives in particularly Gen Z to influence customers' perceived value and purchase intentions for a brand when setting prices and marketing strategies. With the increasing popularity of social media as a means of communication, many companies at home and abroad are using influencer marketing to promote their products and services on social media (Yong and Renganathan, 2019).

Price perception has always been an important research question in understanding consumer buying behaviour. The effect of price perception can be determined by external information from influence of a brand's marketing communication and the consumer's own intrinsic perception of the brand's quality and value from past purchase experience. This concept helps to understand the psychological factors in the minds of customers and the form in which purchasing decisions are made. It allows retailers and producers of goods to increase the chance of sales by making the pricing adjustment according to perceived value of a product. For instance, price-ending numbers in uneven numbers ($9.99) are a better price than even numbers ($10.00). This is because the 00-ending price number is applied for high-priced or high-quality products, whereas the 99-ending price is used for average-price or moderate quality products (Kumar and Pandey, 2017).

Price has two alternate roles in consumers' minds. One is positive, which means it is a cue for high quality; the other is negative which is an unwilling monetary sacrifice in exchange for higher good or service quality. For instance, price-quality schema and prestige sensitivity is the positive role of pricing and believed to influence customers' willingness to buy positively whereas value and price consciousness are negative role of pricing that impact customer's buying intention (Burton, Lichtenstein, and Netemeyer, 1998). Ruff (2019) asserted that digital natives are more susceptible to price fluctuation and have lower brand loyalty than previous generations. This is because digital natives are more informed due to their familiarity with digital channels that enable easy access to information. As a result, they are less loyal to brands when making a purchase decision preferring to weigh various options giving them a reputation as thrifty consumers. On the contrary, there were others such as Voyado (2023) posited that digital natives are willing to pay higher price for sustainable, high-quality products as they value personalised products that are drawn to their own viewpoint. Hence, the question is whether digital natives are price-quality schema and prestige sensitivity, or value and price consciousness and what is the role of quality towards the manifestation of this attitude?

Buying Attitude

Whilst determinants of price perception can be rational, prestige or psychological, attitude towards buying intention is a result from a set of emotions, beliefs and behaviours towards a specific object, person, thing, or event. It is a significant determinant of an individual propensities that decidedly correspond with behaviour and characterized as the level at which people make positive or adverse evaluations of behaviour (Ajzen and Fishbein, 1977). Accordingly, an attitude comprises of three components of emotion of thought, information or cognitive, and behaviour (Kahawandala and Peter, 2020). Furthermore, attitude to purchase can be measured based on four different semantic scales. Two of these scales refer to attitudinal emotions, such as unpleasant or pleasant. The remaining two are consumer attitudes which are composite of a consumer's beliefs, feelings, and behavioural intentions towards some objects (Spence, et. al., 2018).

Attitude is a mental component that is learned and grown in a specific timeframe (Lien and Cao, 2014). When set, it is hard to change. This is because the mind has subconsciously been programmed towards fulfilling certain mental inspiration. However, perspective changes over time as people react and adapt to new developments happening around them. Digital Natives' perspectives towards online shopping have gotten a ton of attention as of late. These perspectives like previous generation trends have shown reliability in shaping mental aspirations and models of future shopping attitude and behaviour. The question is in what way could these perspectives influence digital natives' attitude towards online purchase? Past studies such as Fishbein and Ajzen (1975) have shown that internet shopping readiness is impacted by purchaser attitude and this attitude is found to have strong influence on subsequent commercial trading. Others such as Lavuri, Jindal, & Akram (2022) and Tunsakul (2020) posited the significant impact of hedonic and perceived usefulness values on shopper's online buying attitudes including impulsive online shopping.

Qualitative Research Questions and Objectives

In the quest to understand the paradigm shift, qualitative method was used to explore the raised questions through semi-structured interview providing deeper insights into the phenomena from the standpoint of participants. Using this approach helps to uncover new thoughts that could be used to generate hypotheses for further investigations. In summary, the research questions are:

QLRQ1: How digital natives perceive price when making buying decision?
QLRQ2: How much influence does brand loyalty have on digital natives when making online buying decisions?
QLRQ3: How important do digital natives view trust when making an online buying decision?
QLRQ4: What digital natives' perspective that influences their attitude towards online purchase?

These questions are embedded into a conceptual framework (see Figure 1) that represents the initial two phases of the exploratory sequential mixed method to provide a graphical representation of the theoretical constructs of interest.

Having this conceptual framework enables this study to focus on the construct of Online Buying Behaviour as its core affected by the influencing factors of Price Perception, Brand Loyalty, Trust, and Attitude. Consequently, four qualitative objectives were formulated:

QLRO1: Investigate the effect of price perception on buying behavior of digital natives.
QLRO2: Explore how brand loyalty affects buying behavior of digital natives.
QLRO3: Probe the effect of trust on buying behavior of digital natives.
QLRO4: Examine how attitude of digital natives affects their buying behavior.

METHODOLOGY

In the quest to explore the paradigm shift, this research uses a three-phase exploratory sequential mixed method (see Figure 2). This specific approach is deemed the most appropriate in addressing uncertainties (Creswell, 2003) that are still developing as remaining Gen Zs not in scope of this study are still coming of age of which the end state is not fully known. Understanding of this phenomenon help the study to gain better foothold of the encroaching trend that can be used to generalize current digital native spending pattern and predict behavioural outcome of the remaining Gen Zs and even the next social generation of Alpha. The rationale comes in a threefold purpose. First is its ability to explore the paradigm shift

Figure 1. Qualitative conceptual framework

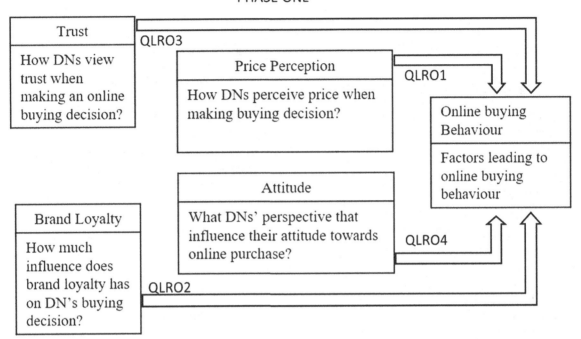

of digital native buying behaviour as depicted in the qualitative conceptual framework and using this framework as a guiding line of thought in transforming reflection from interviews into sets of relationship metaphors. Although qualitative approach provides useful insights, the relatively small sample size impedes generalization statistically required to explain with certainty on how these relationships are formed thus explaining the application of a second, quantitative phase. Behavioural science studies such as buying behaviour are not new. The difference in context is in their application across different social generations. Therefore, by adopting, and reapplying scale items used previously in similar studies, it provides several advantages such as the ability to compare and the parsimonious nature of such study. The final purpose of using this design is its third, integration phase. A top-down deductive approach is good but not enough. Since deductive approach heavily depends on the initial propositions being correct, there is a need to ensure all propositions suggested by the inductive research are true as well. Hence there is a need to verify linkages across both strands of qualitative and quantitative data to increase the credibility and validity of research outcomes. Only through the interpretation of both encompassing data can a study draw conclusion in explaining the cause and effect of digital native buying behaviour.

The first phase is an inductive exploratory primary qualitative phase in which data collected from purposive sampling semi-structured interview was analysed using thematic analysis (Hinkin, 1995). The second phase employs a quantitative deductive approach to explain the first phase outcomes using empirical measurement from a series of mini studies to give deeper meanings on how these factors are manifested. Online survey link was distributed through social media, emails, and other online channels and sample drawn from digital native population was analysed using a combination of descriptive and inferential analytical methods. In the final integration phase, findings from both qualitative and quan-

Figure 2. Exploratory sequential mixed method

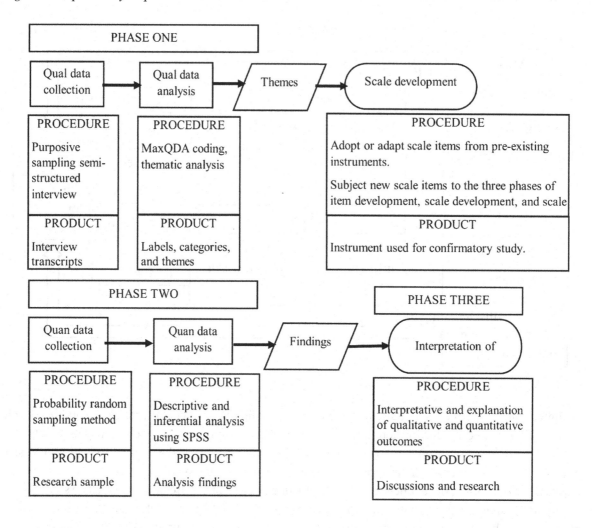

titative study were collated and interpreted to explain the outcomes that connect both strands of data (Fetters, Curry, & Creswell, 2013) efforts.

Mixed Method Phase One: Inductive Exploratory Approach

The first phase involves an inductive exploratory primary qualitative design using purposive non-probability sampling method to provide richer and deeper information for exploring viewpoints, allowing the researchers to reach a better initial understanding of the problem and identify phenomena attitude influences (Healy & Perry, 2000). Seventeen participants (see Table 2) were selected following the definition of digital native age group range of those born between 1981 and 1996 for Millennials and 1997 and 2012 for Gen-Z. Whilst 40 represent the upper age delineation for Millennials at the point when the data was collected, 18 was used to represent the lower age delineation for Gen-Z. The rationale for this selection is based on the participants' experience and maturity in making online purchasing decision.

Table 2. Participant profiles

Actor	Occupation/Industry	Age	Gender
A	Student	22	Female
B	Student	23	Female
C	Student	25	Male
D	Online Grocery	30	Male
E	Online Grocery	28	Male
F	Student	23	Female
G	Logistics	32	Male
H	Technology	30	Female
I	Owned business	36	Female
J	Student	21	Female
K	Financial Institution	28	Female
L	Student	22	Male
M	Student	24	Male
N	Financial Institution	27	Male
O	Technology	33	Female
P	Owned business	31	Male
Q	Food & Beverages	29	Female

The sample size was determined through an attainment of thematic saturation of discursive patterns (Morrow, 2005) and consistency and repetition of findings (Vasileiou, 2018) from encompassing examination of incremental sample data collected during interviews. The thematic saturation of discursive patterns was achieved after having interviewed the seventeenth participant. Prior to the interview an internal pre-test was carried out to verify that the questions used are well understood, comfortable and not confusing with the participants (see Table 3).

Thematic analysis (TA) which uses a flexible process to provide valuable, comprehensive, and complex description of data (Vaismoradi, Jones, Turunen, & Snelgrove, 2016) was used to analyse the sample data. As the central focus of the study is to explore and examine the generalized semantic themes, inductive approach was used to seek and examine if "generalizations" can be drawn by going from the specifics. TA comprises of a six-phase process of 1) data validation, 2) initial codes generation, 3) categories generation, 4) themes patterning, 5) defining, and 6) naming themes and reporting of findings (Maguire, 2017) (see Figure 3).

Table 3. Qualitative questions

Semantic Themes	Question
Buying Behavior	• How do you define your buying behavior?
Price Perception	• How does pricing affect your buying behavior?
Brand Loyalty Trust Attitude	• Do you prefer buying products of your loyal brand? If yes, why? • How would you view the importance of trust in your buying behavior? • How do you think personal attitude affect your buying behavior?

Figure 3.

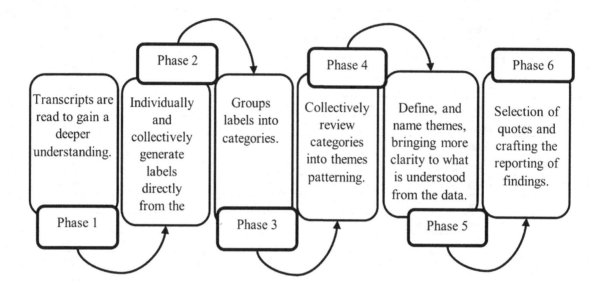

Thematic Analysis: Transcript and Coding

Phase 1 involves interview sessions that were audio recorded after giving participants the assurance of descriptive validity on the data collected and receiving their consent. The data including non-verbatims were transcribed and verified by an independent party before the participants were asked to give their concurrence that the contextualized data was in accordance with the conversation and observations captured during the interview. In phase 2, initial codes were generated based on key words and patterns of the participants' statements. The labels represent the important features of the data and thus, help to summarize and synthesize the responses. Labels congruent in meaning are kept in the same category to help with the provision of details for analytical theme development (Vaismoradi et al., 2016). For example, participant B stipulated "I think my buying behaviour is intellectual because before buying things, I would do research about them first or think about what I want to buy before buying it." Two key words were derived from the expressed sentence. "intellectual" and "research" were annotated as "cognitive experience" in a way information about a product is synthesized, interpreted, and understood to build consumer's belief and buying attitude. In total, forty-one labels were extracted (see Table 4). These labels were further scrutinized on the meaning of their codes and how they relate to one another.

Thematic Analysis: Category Formation

In phase 3, related labels were collapsed to form categories for more efficient analysis. It led to the formation of fifteen categories. From these categories, possible themes were analysed as overarching categories of common information that would be used to assist in explaining the research phenomenon.

Reliability, Consistency, and Experience. Trust refers to a belief or a set of beliefs toward reliability of a brand. There was consensus among the participants that trust plays an important role towards their propensity in buying a product. As they possess better market knowledge, technological know-how

Table 4. Labels and Categories

Category	Primary Label
Affordability	Choice difficulties, disposable income, spending limit
Habitual	Without doing research, familiarity
Psychology	Gut feelings, Impulsive buying
Belief	Cognitive experience, individual belief, sense of encouragement
Emotion	Mood, reaction to situation
Hedonic value	Pleasure shopping, visual impact, influencer impact, user friendly website, mobile apps
Fair price	Budget, price evaluation
Prestige sensitivity	Brand bias, status, prominent feelings
Price to quality	Value purchase
Attachment	Emotion attachment, comfort feelings, brand image, feeling of closeness
Cognitive loyalty	Brand familiarity, reduced risk of relearning, less tension, better brand product knowledge
Customer loyalty	Customer service impact, customer loyalty programs, caring brand, close bond between brand and customers
Reliability	Fulfilled customers' needs, derived satisfaction, product suitability
Consistency	Delivered as expected anytime, keeps to its promise
Experience	Past purchase impact, brand review, learning from past shopping

and are better connected socially than previous generations, such structures are needed to build trust in consumer behaviour. In the response to question, "How would you view the importance of trust in your buying behaviour? Participant Ms. F testified, "If customer trust the brand, we wouldn't hesitate to decide whether we want to buy the brand and will keep repurchasing it. For me the reason why I always trust a brand is because it always keeps our promise and fulfil our need". Participant Ms. A exclaimed, "I would choose a brand because it fulfils my needs. Because I think that if it is suitable for me and keeps to its promise, I won't easily change my choice to try other brands". It can be deduced from here the importance of "Reliability" and "Consistency". Further testimonial of these factors was made by participant Ms. I, "From a customer viewpoint, when we trust a brand, we assume it satisfies us in terms of reliability and quality, and we will have more repeat purchases so long as they continue to deliver to my expectation. Otherwise, we do not feel convinced in buying a product or brand no matter how great it is portrayed or advertised". These responses led to the formation of "Reliability" and "Consistency" as categories representing accuracy, precision, quality and stability of a brand's product or service.

These statements were supported by the viewpoint of business owner participant Mr. P, "We like to carry the brand ourselves, like almost every day. Trust is a very important element in business as gaining customer trust is the forefront of our marketing strategy". Therefore, brand with good track record usually help to reinforce customers' trust for the brand. This is because over time, people who have tried using the brand can testify to its consistency and reliability which support the notion of the contribution effect of shopping experience towards building trust. For instance, participant Ms. A remarked, "We trust a brand because of our past purchase experience. Reviews of the brands' products by others also help reinforce that belief". Participant Ms. K stipulated, "I choose brands that I used before rather than the other." and participant Ms. B said, "I would not touch or try products I never used before". There is clearly enough evidence to suggest the importance of experience in building trust perception. These experiences arise from various sources such as learning from shopping at physical or online stores, acquiring knowledge from social media, or having conversations with friends and relatives about a particular brand. As such "Experience" is created as an additional category to represent familiarity of customers for a brand from past interactions.

Attachment, Cognitive Loyalty, and Customer Loyalty. Brand loyalty is determined by how customers perceive and feel about a brand giving a perception of superiority. Together with trust, these factors can shape customer attitude increasing the likelihood of repeat purchase. As asserted by participant Ms. B, "Because if the things I use is suitable for me and I trust the product I will buy it again.". Past studies such as Markey (2020) reported that brand and customer loyalty can grow a company revenue by 2.5 times faster than its competitors that is translated into two to five times on return of investment to shareholders over a 10-year time frame. Customers who are loyal to brands often purchase 90% more frequently than new customers. In addition, the cost of servicing these customers is far less than cost spent on marketing to entice new customers (Temkin, 2008). This is because brand-loyal customers do not just buy a product and tends to try out other products from the same brand.

To the question, "Do you prefer buying products of your loyal brand? If yes, why?", generally, most agree that trust for a brand can result in emotional attachment or customer's comfort feelings for a brand. This may be built from practices undertaken by the brand. According to participant Ms. F, "Yes, I'll repurchase the brand again that I like. It is because of their great service and the quality of the products that I feel connected with". These feelings of closeness are built over time into a meaningful relationship between customer and brand that help sustain customer interest for the brand. "Attachment" category reflects these feelings of affection.

Besides, some retails provide great customer service in the way they engage and help customer solve problems. Furthermore, having a good customer loyalty programme in place to recognize and reward regular customers would help in establishing brand loyalty. As posited by participant Ms. F, "Some retails put a lot of effort communicating and interacting with customers making them feel that the brand cares about them". It is a testimonial that brand loyalty is more than just emotional attachment. Bonding between brand and consumers is needed to generate this attachment. Constant nurturing of this delicate relationship can be carried out by keeping customer profiles up to date and abreast with the development of the brand. These programmes of relationship nurturing are categorised as "Customer Loyalty" to encapsulate the mutual benefits and lasting relationship from effort expanded by a brand.

Others think that loyalty is derived from familiarity with a brand. Buying from the same brand reduces the risks of relearning the features and operational functions of a product. For instance, participant Mr. O commented, "Okay, yes, of course I do want to buy products from my loyal brand because … I know how it works and the features of it and such will be familiar to me". This statement was supported by participant Ms. A, "Yes. I rarely try new things, mainly because I have some loyal brands that I am familiar with. I do not need to feel the tension of trying other things." and Ms. I asserted "As habitual buyer, we tend to purchase from our loyal brand as there is less risk that the products may not meet my expectations. When we are familiar to one brand, we tend to have the product or brand knowledge … better understanding of the price range which is always within my expected price". From these statements, there are evidence of cognitive loyalty showing that when customers understand and familiar with features, functions, and expectations of products and services of a brand, there is no longer motivation for them to risk trying another brand. As these statements reflect the thinking and belief of a brand that customers are familiar with, "Cognitive Loyalty" would fit well for these labels as its category.

These findings seem to suggest that trust and brand loyalty have an influence on consumer buying attitude. However, buying decision can be influenced by consumers' own economic factors and price perception of the product too. This inference is supported by participants saying that they will continue their loyal so long as the price is within their expectation. However, should the price go up to an unacceptable level it would result in customers seeking alternative brands instead.

Price-to-Quality, Prestige Sensitivity, and Fair Price. Therefore, consumers' perception of product's price has a significant effect on their decision to buy. This is supported by past studies such as Ruff (2019) that claimed digital natives are more susceptible to price fluctuation. However, others such as Voyado (2023) reported that these generations are willing to pay higher price for sustainable, high-quality products. These contradicting outcomes gave an uncertainty to the understanding of price perception which raises the question of "how does pricing affect buying behaviour?"

Participant Ms. F responded, "I think that price could be the one of the factors that influence my buying behaviour, but not entirely as it depends on how much I love the brand. If the price of the brand that I love is very pricey, I would still go ahead regardless of the price. However, if the price did not meet the quality of the product, I won't buy it next time". These statements imply that consumers are conscious of the quality value embedded in their favourite brand when determining price perception. It is encapsulated in Ms. F's expression, "I think pricing will not much affect my buying behaviour because I will still go for my favourite brands regardless". Together these statements portray a favourable perception of the price because of the prominent feelings and status that come with the brand. These favourable perceptions of price cue arising from feelings of prominence and status are best encapsulated under "Prestige Sensitivity" category.

Having said that, quality by itself has an influence on price evaluation. In the case of participant Mr. O, he expressed, "Basically when buying a product, I will choose the cheapest, but it depends. If the cheapest got low quality, then I will move to a bit higher price because basically I also care about the quality". Another participant Mr. M expressed, "The pricing effect have a positive effect on me. Because I think that if I pay a higher price for a product, I will get higher quality". These two statements address the value of price to quality association. It shows that in a consumer's mind, price has a direct correlation with quality. The "Price to quality" category was created to reflect this association.

On the other hand, certain participants evaluate price based on their own disposable income. The price is considered fair when it meets the affordability criteria of customers. Participant Ms. L posited, "If it's too expensive and not within my budget, then I will not buy. However, if the price is within my budget range, then I would consider". These statements imply transaction at fair pricing where the seller represented by the price of a product and buyer represented by their price evaluation and affordability agreed to transact. This price deal between the seller and buyer is classified under "Fair Price" category. Evaluation of what considered as fair depends on the status of their affordability and if their disposable income increases, these customers are willing to pay a higher price for a product. This assertion was aptly supported by participant Ms. A, "The pricing greatly affects my buying behaviour. It depends on whether I have had extra money at the time or not". It goes to show price perception has an influence on the customer buying attitude.

Belief, Emotion, and Hedonic Value. An attitude refers to a set of beliefs an individual accepts. It is formed through the collections of these beliefs about a brand's characteristics moulded into consumers' own cognitive experience or valued principles for the brand. It raises the question of "how digital native attitude affects their buying behaviour?". Participant Ms. F stipulated, "I think is the belief of individual. For example, if the customer has a strong belief for a brand, they will feel happy when using the brand". This expression was supported by participant Ms. I, "So a personal attitude of belief will encourage customers to buy certain brand. For example, I will buy certain brand that portrayed yoghurt to have more protein than milk." These assertions clearly show a strong linkage between an individual's cognitive experience in the way information is interpreted and buying attitude that create a sense of encouragement to buy product of a certain brand. These cognitive experiences were categorised as "Belief".

There are evidence suggesting consumer attitude affected by their own emotion. Participant Ms. K posited, "I feel that my mood is affecting my buying behaviour. For example, if I was scolded by my boss, or that I am in a bad mood all day, I would want to buy a lot of things to express my bad mood". This statement is supported by participant Mr. D, "If I feel not happy, I will just buy something that make me happy" and participant Mr. O said, "Personally, it depends on my mood". These testimonials imply that people can be motivated by their own emotions that could alter their buying behaviour. As this attitude is driven by an individual's mood contrary to his own behavioural norm, we categorised such attribute as "Emotion".

Past studies such as Lavuri, Jindal, & Akram (2022) and Tunsakul (2020) have shown the impact of hedonic and perceived usefulness values. Accordingly, these values must be considered when designing web and mobile apps to attract visitation and usage. As testified by participant Ms. K, "For my case, I love an artist and if the artist appears on my mobile apps or website, I will most likely buy their peripheral supplies for my own satisfaction even though they might not be essential. For example, if BTS (K-pop band) featured on a website, I would buy products from this site and not others". It testifies the importance of creating a pleasurable shopping experience for digital natives through having a user-friendly professional setup websites and mobile apps with great visual impact. Having influencers as part of site content brings high hedonic value that increases user time spent on the sites resulting in a more positive attitude and buying probability. Labels related to such thinking and feeling are categorised under "Hedonic" as an attribute of customer buying attitude.

Affordability, Habitual, and Psychology. Analyses on data collected from question "how do you define your buying behaviour?" reveal that buying behaviours are different even though all the participants are digital natives and young adults. Most of these participants are aware of their own disposable income and try to instil self-discipline of their own consumption by setting limits on their own spending. For instance, participant Mr. G asserted "I think I'm more towards economical because I would set a budget when buying products". Participant Ms. O concurred, "I think I'm more inclined to being an economical buyer because I always buy things that I use". These statements deduce that no matter how attractive the product is to a customer, the final go-ahead decision depends on his or her own financial situation. These labels are placed under "Affordability" category representing spending capacity of customers when making final buying decision.

However, a few participants admitted to being impulsive buying unnecessary products because of their aesthetic appeal or succumb to her own emotions. Participant Ms. A responded, "I would say that I am an impulsive buyer. As you all should know that girls are easily tempted by beautiful and cute things, so I would buy them on impulse without holding back". These participants said that they would buy even if the price were higher than normal not because they reacted impulsively but because buying itself makes them happy. Little consideration was given to the price. These instances show that certain individuals might be enticed to react irrationally without forethought when their visual sensory is stimulated. Purchases based on these impulsive feelings are categorized under "Psychology".

Others are more habitual and do not give much of a thought when buying products from brands that they are familiar with. For instance, participant Mr. N opined "I think I would define my buying behaviour as habitual because I define myself a brand loyalty person. Most times, I would just buy product from the brand that I like without evaluating or researching other brands". Participant Ms. I concurred, "I define my buying behaviour as cautious as I tend to purchase a brand that I'm familiar with". These behavioural disposition from buying certain brand repetitively creates a sense of bias attitude. Unless there is a drastic change in brand offerings, this routine will continue driving buying behaviour of consumers into a category that can be termed as "Habitual".

Thematic Analysis: Themes Patterning and Labelling

In phase 4 and 5 of thematic analysis, these fifteen categories were further reviewed and grouped into semantic themes for better clarity on the meaning of the data. The resultant is five interconnected themes. The first is "Buying Behaviour" representing dimension of psychology, habitual, and affordability in the way digital natives make decision when buying products. While psychology signifies situational impulsive buying, habitual buying behaviour is driven by familiarity or affinity towards a particular brand that requires little consumer involvement. The final "Go" decision hinges on an individual's affordability or the degree in which consumers possess the means to buy the product. This means depends on consumers' own disposable income. Besides its own attributes, digital natives' purchase propensity can be influenced by their trust and by their own predisposition towards a particular brand.

Outcome of qualitative analysis has shown that "Trust" can be dimensioned into three inter-related categories of reliability, consistency, and shopping experience. Having a product that works anytime you use it with the same predicted outcome would result in formidable impression or opinion of the brand. These three dimensions are tightly coupled and when one is missing, it can result in degradation of trust. Participants have indicated their preference in shopping at sites that they are familiar. Pleasant experiences can create perception of trustworthiness in the way website or mobile apps present information that is consistent with actual use of a brand's products. While trust can be nurtured from digital natives' positive feelings toward a brand, having a high level of trust creates a more favourable buying attitude and intention.

"Attitude" is driven by a customer's belief, emotion, and hedonic value of sensory experiences linked to designs of websites and mobile apps. Belief happens when an individual develops valued principles for a brand moulded from one's own cognitive experience with the brand. Sometimes, this belief can be swayed by an individual's mood resulting in making irrational buying decision that goes against buying norm. Whilst impulsive buying is an unplanned buying decision made at the spur of the moment, emotional buying attitude is induced intentionally by digital natives in response to their state of feeling derived from certain circumstances. Although such change in emotional state is triggered mostly by situation, designs of websites and mobile apps that are attractive with high quality content can also induce the same emotional state. It clearly shows that buying behaviour of digital natives can be driven by multifaceted dimensions of buying attitude. However, this attitude is premised on their trust and loyalty for a brand, and perceived price value of the brand's product.

Outcome of the qualitative study suggests that "Brand loyalty" is derived from digital natives' emotional attachment for a brand, cognitive loyalty in the form of brand familiarity and knowledge, and their engagement with a brand via customer loyalty programmes. A deep brand-customer bond can cultivate a positive emotional attachment elevating customer satisfaction. These feelings of closeness can be profitable as it leads to long lasting relationship of repeat sale, cross sale, and up sale of a brand's products. Brand's actions such as customer care programmes, customer reward, keeping customers abreast with latest promotions and establishing two-way communications can instil brand loyalty in customers. However, such business relationship is complex as it requires companies to synthesize customer demographics, behaviour, psychographics, and past transactions using complex analytical tools. One such tools is Customer Relationship Management (CRM) which uses automated customer database to help companies stay connected with customers by managing relationships and streamlining processes with the aim of improving customer relationship and loyalty.

Often, consumers like using brands that are consistent with their own image, and lifestyles. These brands are perceived to possess distinctive features that set them apart from their competitors. For a brand to be seen as unique, it is essential to constantly project this image in their corporate actions, brand communication, and new product launches. For example, digital natives are passionate about inclusive brands and companies should strive to be more diversity, equity, and inclusiveness (DEI) in their approach to addressing community issues and organization objectives. Such actions not only lead to higher customer loyalty, but also result in greater cognitive loyalty for the brand. Furthermore, better familiarity and brand knowledge increases customer satisfaction and reduces cognitive dissonance. In essence, presence of emotional attachment, cognitive and customer loyalty collectively categorised as brand loyalty have an impact on customer's trust, buying attitude, and price perception.

"Price perception" stems from digital natives' interpretation of sensory information on product price to quality, their prestige sensitivity towards certain brand status, and fair price valuation. It is a perceived value that is evaluated based on a product's quality and its corresponding brand's prestige sensitivity determined by the brand's perceived brand image and status. Accordingly, fair price is established when the perceived value of a product matches with customer's own affordability for the product. Although digital natives are willing to pay higher price for sustainable, high-quality products, this happens only when there is favourable brand consciousness. For a sale transaction to take place, a fair price must be established between a brand and its customers. This pricing mechanism has nothing to do with underselling or undercutting competition. It is about giving a brand's target market segment a value that balanced with its own image, matches its perceived product quality, and the amount of money paid by customer is deemed reasonable in getting satisfaction out of the transaction.

Relations of these 6 themes of Buying Behaviour, Trust, Brand Loyalty, Personal Attitude, and Price Perception are illustrated in Figure 4.

Thematic Analysis: Reporting of Findings

The outcome of the qualitative analysis shows that spending habits of digital natives are driven by their own belief for a brand, their state of emotion, and the induced effect of hedonism at shopping sites in which they patronized. Whist belief and emotion are intrinsic motivators, hedonism can shape and amplify the physiological experiences of valence and arousal of an individual towards a certain emotional state. For example, hedonism in an experiential online shopping allows individuals to experience memorable shopping. Having an omnichannel approach that includes experiential physical stores, and mobile apps can exacerbate this experience of hedonism. As this assertion is hypothetical in nature, it raises a question of whether such hedonistic experience would result in a more favourable buying attitude? Or is that not enough, and more should be done. As a saying goes, "Don't deliver a product, deliver an experience" speaks volume for the importance of living up to a brand's own image. Doing this consistently would earn the trust of its customers. It means deliver on your promise every time when a brand engages with its customers providing reliable products that do what they are intended for. However, problem with online

Figure 4. Themes and categories

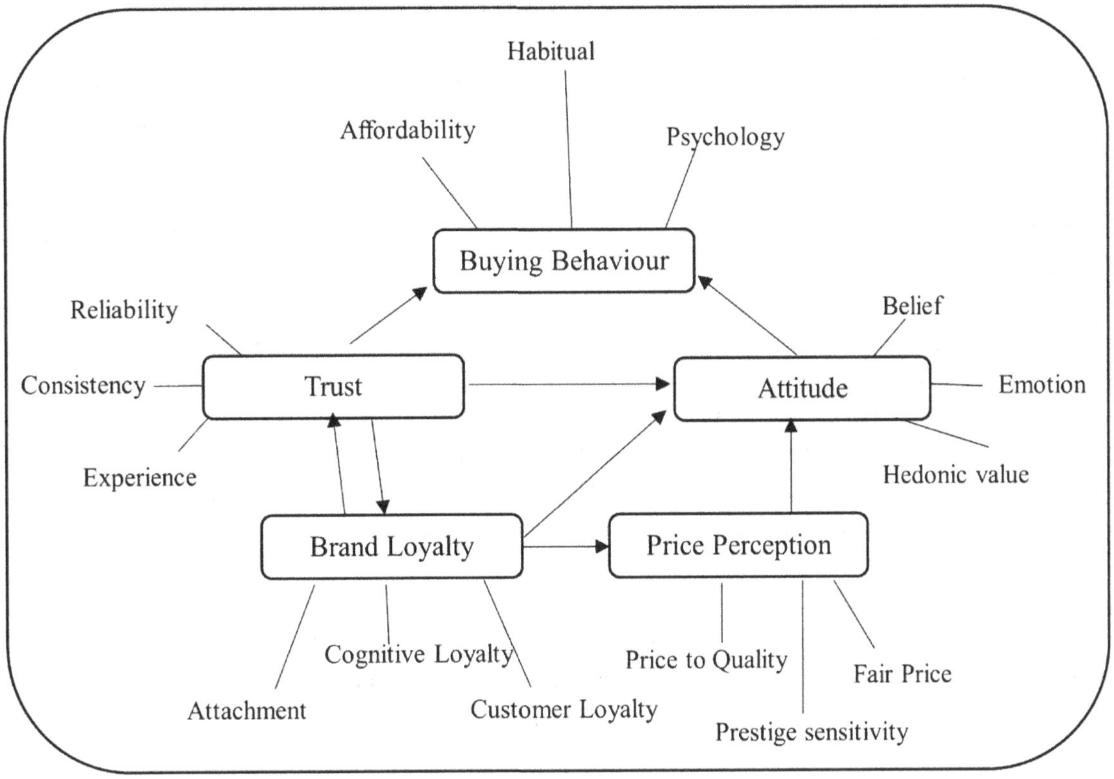

shopping is that a brand is often not in total control when it comes to order fulfilment of its products. This is because customers do not get their products immediately after making an online purchase as fulfilment of an order has to go through various logistic partners. Due to uncertainties during handovers between seller and logistic partners, online shopping is known to carry more risk. It raises a question of whether online shopping experience given the greater exposure and risk would contribute towards building trust?

This trust when built would result in brand loyalty and relationship that is sustainable and profitable. Cost of acquiring a new customer can cost five times more and increasing customer retention by 5% can lead to 25-95% increase in profit. Furthermore, a brand has between 60-70% success in selling to existing customers compare to 5-20% for new customers (Landis, 2022). These statistics imply the importance of "Walk the Talk" or keep to one's promise. The objective is to create an emotional attachment customers have for a brand. This can be done in two ways. The first is to increase cognitive loyalty in customers by designing products and services with look and feel that are consistent with customer experience reducing the need to relearn. The purpose is to inject familiarity into features and functions that serves as motivation for customers to continue using a brand's products instead of taking the risk of trying another brand. The other way is to establish an ongoing emotional engagement by promoting a brand that resonate with consumer lifestyle and image. However, it is not easy for a brand to create such image since digital natives are tech-savvy people who can easily detect a ruse and insincerity from news feeds and other information sources in social media. Therefore, it is important for a brand to really practice what it preaches. Having diversity, equity, and inclusiveness (DEI) would be a great start as digital natives are known to be passionate about inclusive brands. It raises another hypothetical question of whether companies striving to be more DEI in their action would increase digital native's brand loyalty?

Having consistent positive experiences elevate a brand's image and status. They not only create emotional attachment but also lead to a more favourable buying attitude, better trust for a brand and a higher price cue. Furthermore, the prestige sensitivity of a brand would be elevated creating favourable feelings of prominence and status leading to higher price cue of a brand's products. However, a high prestige sensitivity does not automatically translate into buying decision due to its dependence on affordability of customers. Digital natives are young adults with commitments and obligations that often limit their ability to spend beyond their means. To these younger customers, their propensity to buy is based on price cue that is deemed fair and within their means. One contributing factor of fair price is the perceived quality of a product. Although findings indicate that digital natives are willing to pay premium for good quality sustainable products, past studies such as Pitic et al. (2014) asserted that perceived quality is not directly proportional to perceived fair price and that not all increases in quality proportionally contribute to increasing customer value. In contrast to qualitative outcome of high price-to-high quality perception, this study takes a step further to determine the influence of product quality on price perception instead.

These questions were raised with the objective of probing deeper into the phenomenon of understanding of digital natives' buying behaviour. Accordingly, a quantitative study was undertaken as confirmatory approach to help established relationships among the variables under investigation. This is carried out by first defining the quantitative research objectives from the research questions and then developing hypotheses and test them via a collection of data gathered from simple random probability sampling technique. The research questions are summarised as follow:

QTRQ1: How digital natives perceive product quality in relation to price perception?
QTRQ2: Would an inclusive DEI brand increases digital natives' brand loyalty?
QTRQ3: Does online shopping experience contribute towards digital natives' trust for a brand?
QTRQ4: Would hedonic experience from online shopping result in digital natives having more favourable buying attitude?

In the attempt to respond to these four questions, research objectives were developed to describe the intent in which this study desires to accomplish as they would provide better focus in terms of study approach and purpose. As a result, four research objectives were developed:

QTRO1: Establish the relationship between product quality and digital natives' perceived price perception.
QTRO2: Determine the linkage between an inclusive DEI brand and digital natives' brand loyalty.
QTRO3: Understand the contribution of online shopping experience towards digital natives' trust for a brand.
QTRO4: Ascertain the influence of hedonic value from online shopping on digital natives' buying attitude.

Hypothesis Development. Although outcome of this qualitative study testifies the positive effect of perceived price-to-quality, it does not address the quantitative research question of quality-to-price (QTRQ1) in which price value perception for a product is determined by its quality. Whilst there are many proponents of price-to-quality (Voyado, 2023; Ruff, 2019), Chenavaz (2016) suggested the inverse effect of high quality-to-low price due to greater sales generated. Whilst this assertion is possible, having a cheaper price would run the risk of lowering prestige sensitivity of a brand. On a contrary this study hypothesizes that with higher product quality, customers' price perception of the product would increase correspondingly (QTH1).

In the determination of a linkage between an inclusive DEI brand and customer brand loyalty (QTRO2), it is noted that there is consensus among digital natives of a correlation between an inclusive brand and their loyalty for the brand. Companies that consistently commit to their promise over time will establish an emotional bond with their customers. As DEI forms part of an inclusive brand, it is hypothesized that organization which embraces and practices DEI as their human resources management would establish an inclusive image that resonate significantly with digital natives thus contributing to brand loyalty (QTH2).

The third hypothesis (QTH3) is in response to quantitative research object of understanding the contribution of online shopping experience towards building of trust (QTRO3). Online and mobile shopping differs from brick and mortar in terms of its look and feel and distribution method. As it involves third party logistic partners, superior end-to-end experiences are more difficult to achieve. The hypothesis is if it did, it would leave an indelible impression on the mind of consumer building trust and setting expectations for future transactions with the brand.

In response to the quantitative research objective (QTRO4) of hedonic value influence, online store that is user friendly with strong visual impact and high hedonic value is hypothesized to shape and amplify consumer's valence and arousal physiological experiences towards a favourable consumer buying attitude (QTH4).

As these hypotheses are not interdependent and mutually exclusive theories, they were tested separately for parsimonious reason of optimising limited resources. In summary, these hypotheses are:

QTH1: Significant and direct link between product quality and digital natives' perceived price perception.
QTH2: Inclusive DEI brand has significant influence on digital natives' brand loyalty.
QTH3: Online shopping experience has significant contribution towards digital natives' trust for a brand.
QTH4: Digital natives' buying attitude is strongly influenced by hedonic value of online stores.

Although these hypotheses were tested in the second phase of the exploratory sequential mixed method, the quantitative conceptual framework was incorporated into the first phase qualitative research framework to give a broader perspective of how the two phases were linked together (see Figure 5). The quantitative conceptual framework is within the dotted lines. The relationship between the independent variables of Experience, Hedonic, DEI, and Perceived Quality and their corresponding dependent variables are denoted by the thick arrows.

Mixed Method Phase One: Scale Development

Testing of the hypotheses was carried out via four separate confirmatory quantitative studies. Although the studies were independently conducted, the regiment and discipline in undertaking the quantitative studies remain the same. First, scale items for the dimensions of variables under examination were either adopted or adapted from pre-existing instruments. Using instrument of previous studies ensures validity and reliability that can be applied to this study without the need to collect further validity evidence. Furthermore, outcome can be related back to previous research saving time, effort, and cost from developing scale from the scratch in line with the parsimonious nature of the project. Second, a 5-point unidimensional Likert scale is used for collecting respondents' feedback which is then used for measuring the study's key variables. In addition to being an industry measurement standard for quantitative research,

Figure 5. Combined conceptual framework

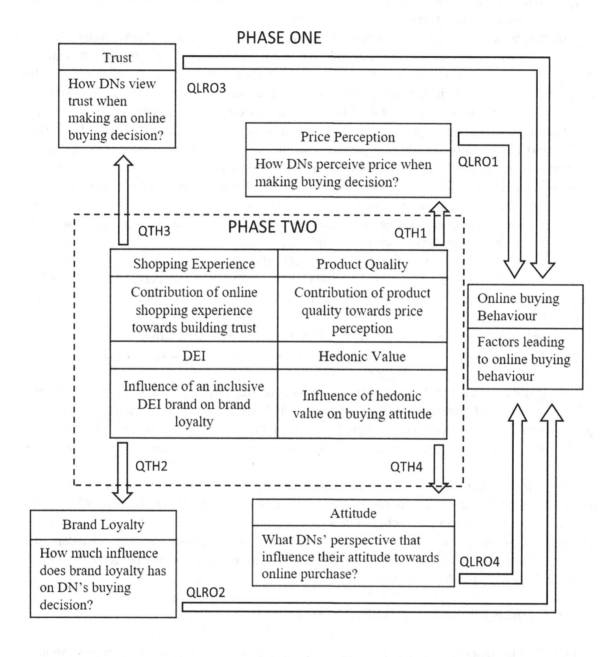

the 5-point scale fits nicely onto mobile device screens allowing for shorter completion time. It includes a choice for neutral option to avoid biases of leading question. As the scale assumes a linear intensity from strongly disagree to strongly agree, it produces data that is reliable in portraying the opinion of the population in study. The scale items used for the measurement of the variables (see Table 5) were tested separately for reliability on samples taken from respective mini studies using Cronbach's alpha.

The results show a Cronbach's alpha range of between 0.797 and 0.922 indicating good to excellent reliability (Sekaran and Bougir, 2016).

Table 5. Scale development

Variable	Scale items	Likert Scale	Source	Cronbach's Reliability
Price Perception (PP)	5	5 points	(Burton et al., 1998)	0.826
Product Quality (PQ)	4	5 points	(Ling and Mansori, 2018)	0.887
Perceived DEI (PD)	7	5 points	(Diversityintech, 2018)	0.917
Brand Loyalty (BL)	5	5 points	(Fan, Ning and Deng, 2020)	0.876
Online Shopping Experience (OSE)	5	5 points	(Roy, Balaji, Sadeque, Nguyen and Melewar, 2017)	0.896
Brand Trust (BT)	5	5 points	(Delgado-Ballester, Munuera-Alemán, and Yagüe-Guillén, 2003)	0.877
Hedonic Value (HV)	5	5 points	(Mohammad, 2016)	0.797
Buying Attitude (BA)	5	5 points	(Park and Kim, 2003)	0.922

Mixed Method Phase Two: Distribution Method and Data Collection

Digital natives of age between 10 – 40 years old form 52.5% or 17.1 million of the total population in Malaysia (DOSM, 2021). According to Krejcie Morgan (1970), the derived sample size for this population based on 95% confidence level with margin error (N) of 5% is 384 responses. To reduce nonresponse bias, the goal was to achieve approximately 60% response rate or a sample size of 230 responses (Fincham, 2008). Probability random sampling method was chosen to select the derived sample size drawn from the defined population size of digital natives. This method allows for lower margin of error due to its randomization principle that would result in better data quality for analysis. The link to the online survey was distributed through social media, emails, and other online channels such as online learning platforms. As a result, the following responses were received (see Table 6).

Majority of the rejected responses were due to non-conformance of 19 to 40 years age bracket criteria used in determining digital natives' spending habits. This is because the minimum age of employment stipulated in Malaysia's Children and Young Persons (Employment) Act is nineteen. Furthermore, those above the age of 40 were not considered as Millennials as at the point of the study.

Mixed Method Phase Two: Analyses

Prior to analysis, the responses were screened for missing data. Normality and parametric statistical homoscedasticity test were carried out to verify normal distribution of sample data drawn and the assumption of similar variances in different groups being compared respectively. Screening and analyses

Table 6. Responses

Survey	Description	Received	Rejected	Accepted
Survey 1	Contribution of product quality on price perception	243	20	223
Survey 2	Influence of an inclusive DEI brand on brand loyalty	236	22	214
Survey 3	Contribution of online shopping experience towards building trust	323	6	317
Survey 4	Influence of hedonic value on buying attitude	270	12	258

of the data including descriptive analysis, and inferential analysis were carried out using Statistical Package for the Social Sciences (SPSS v24). Whilst multiple regression analysis was used in testing hypothesis by measuring relationship model between a single dependent variable and several independent variables, bivariate Pearson correlation statistical testing was chosen to fulfil the objective of measuring the strength and direction of paired linear relationships of different independent and dependent variables tested for this study.

Descriptive Statistics

As shown in Table 7, the profile of respondents participated in the mini surveys carried out sequentially starting from Survey 1 to 4 over a span of two years. The ratio of gender and age group remains similar throughout these four confirmatory studies. As this study is on digital natives, it does not come as a surprise that all respondents indicated that they shop online at least once a year with majority of them shopping online at least once monthly. However, it is fascinating to observe the temporal effect on online buying behaviour pattern over the span of the four surveys. The trend clearly shows that whilst "Once a year" shopping frequency remains constant at around 2%, there is a steady drop of "Once per month" shopping from the initial survey of 48% to 41%. This drop is compensated by an increase in both "Once per week" and "Every few days" online shopping frequency from 30% to 35% and from 18% to 22% respectively.

This phenomenon could be attributed to two reasons. One, the declaration of Movement Control Order (MCO) by the Malaysian government during Covid-19 pandemic compelling closure of education institution campuses, commercial buildings, retail, and public gatherings to prevent the spread of virus have resulted in a change of lifestyle hastening the shift in buying behaviour paradigm towards online shopping. Two, the two-year temporal effect reveals an increasing purchasing power trend of digital natives. As purchasing power increases, consumers tend to purchase more. This behaviour is supported by past studies (Valaskova, Durana, and Adamko, 2021) that consumers' income and age have significant influence in new online shopping patterns. It is not surprising that these two factors when combined results in an accelerated adoption of online shopping.

Inferential Analysis

This research draws conclusion from sample data of digital natives' opinions using inferential statistics as measurements when comparing treatment of related variables and using the outcome to make inference about the larger general population. Due to the parametric distribution of the population from which the sample was taken, Pearson's correlation coefficients were used in measuring statistical strength of the linear bivariate association between the independent and dependent variables. Having these measurements help established the reliability of direction between the variables as indicated by the correlation coefficients and significance of the correlation strength determined by a probability value lower than 5% (p-value < 0.05). The Pearson's statistical correlation (see Table 8) is a collated outcome from the four quantitative studies.

In addition, linear regression was used to examine the relationship between the independent and dependent variables due to the simplicity and independence nature of the relationships. This statistical method allows the study to draw conclusion of causal relationship among the variables in question (see Table 9).

Table 7. Profiles

Profiles		Survey 1	%	Survey 2	%	Survey 3	%	Survey 4	%
Gender	Male	100	45%	121	57%	143	45%	107	41%
	Female	123	55%	93	43%	174	55%	116	45%
Age Group	19 - 26 (Gen-Z)	95	43%	88	41%	174	55%	144	56%
	27 - 40 (Millennials)	128	57%	126	59%	143	45%	114	44%
Employment status	Student	76	34%	52	24%	110	35%	90	35%
	Employed	89	40%	149	70%	139	44%	110	43%
	Others	58	26%	13	6%	68	21%	58	22%
Frequency of shopping online	Every few days	40	18%	42	20%	66	21%	56	22%
	Once per week	67	30%	66	31%	104	33%	90	35%
	Once per month	107	48%	100	47%	142	45%	106	41%
	Once per year	9	4%	6	3%	5	2%	6	2%
	Never	0	0%	0	0%	0	0%	0	0%
Total		223		214		317		258	

Table 8. Collated Pearson statistical correlation

	Price Perception (PP)	Brand Loyalty (BL)	Trust (BT)	Buying Attitude (BA)	Reliability
Product Quality (PQ)	0.853**				Excellent
Perceived DEI (PD)		0.783**			Good
Online Shopping Experience (OSE)			0.708**		Good
Hedonic Value (HV)				0.654**	Fair
**. Correlation is significant at the 0.01 level (2-tailed)					

The outcome of the analysis shows an excellent reliability and significant correlation strength (Pearson coeff. = 0.853, p-value < 0.01) between PQ and PP assuming high correlation between product quality and price perception. The positive coefficients imply a direct relationship inferring a willingness of digital natives to pay a higher price for good quality sustainable product. The correlation is supported by response to the product quality scale item, "The current online seller's product quality is sustainable and meet my quality standard" which carries a mean value of 4.27 and price perception scale item, "I

Table 9. Linear regression

Linear regression model	R-square	Unstd. Coeff. (B)	Sig.
Product Quality (PQ) → Price Perception (PP)	0.746	0.629	0.001
Perceived DEI (PD) → Brand Loyalty (BL)	0.663	0.610	0.021
Online Shopping Experience (OSE) → Brand Trust (BT)	0.605	0.601	0.001
Hedonic Value (HV) → Buying Attitude (BA)	0.437	0.514	0.000

always pay a bit more for quality sustainable product" receiving a mean value of 4.10 from a Likert scale of 1 to 5. From the linear regression perspective, the result (R-square = 0.746, coeff. = 0.629, p-value = 0.001) supports the first hypothesis (QTH1) of a significant and direct link between product quality and price perception. The model accounts for 74% in the variance of PP and every unit increase in PQ causes an increase of 0.629 unit of PP variable.

Testing of the second hypothesis (H2) shows a good and significant direct correlation (Pearson coeff. = 0.783, p-value = 0.01) between PD and BL. The result of correlation is backed by linear regression (R-square = 0.663, coeff. = 0.610, p-value = 0.021) supporting hypothesis (QTH2) of the influencing effect of an inclusive DEI brand on digital natives' brand loyalty. The effect magnitude shows 0.605 unit increase in BL variable for every unit increase in the predictor (PD). This model attributes 66.3% of BL's variation to PD variable inferring digital natives' appreciation of companies committed to being inclusive. However, the relatively weaker strength reflects the sense of perception and interpretation of a brand's actions as reality. This line of thought is portrayed in the DEI scale item, "I believe this organization provides an environment for free and open expression of ideas, opinions and beliefs" which carries a high mean value of 4.09 but not so well in the corresponding Brand Loyalty scale item, "I would choose the brand I currently use because it resonates with my values" which receives a lower mean value of 3.95 inferring a lower albeit significant correlation between the two variables.

Similarly, OSE ® BT variable has a good reliable and significant correlation (Pearson coeff. = 0.708, p-value = 0.01) which correspond with the outcome of linear regression ((R-square = 0.605, coeff. = 0.601, p-value = 0.001) supporting the third hypothesis (QTH3) on the contribution of online shopping experience towards building brand trust. This model accounts for 60.5% variance of BT and an increase of 0.601 BT unit for every unit increase in OSE. The direct relationship between the two variables assumes linearity between digital natives' engagement experience across a brand's omnichannel touchpoints and building trust for the brand. Whilst consistent pleasant online shopping experience can manifest into trust, a single bad experience could quickly derail all previous effort taken towards building of this trust. This assertion is represented in OSE scale item, "My experience will decide whether I continue shopping in an online store" which carries a mean value of 4.16. The challenges faced by today's retail business is in managing an ever-expanding omnichannel that requires integration of internet, mobile, and physical retail channels to work interoperable as one to provide customer a seamless shopping experience. Brand wanting to build trust via provisioning of good shopping experience does not have a choice but pander to the needs of these digital natives who are tech-savvy and use different channels simultaneously in their shopping process.

Finally, although the correlation strength of HV ® BA is rated as fair, it is nonetheless significant (Pearson coeff. = 0.654, p-value < 0.01). The outcome of linear regression (R-square = 0.437, coeff. = 0.514, p-value = 0.000) aligns with Pearson correlation of a strong link between the predictor (HV) and dependent variable (BA) supporting the fourth hypothesis (H4) of hedonic value influence arising from attractive and user-friendly online retail stores on digital natives' buying attitude. The low BA variance percentage of 43.7% attributed to HV ® BA model implies the presence of other latent variables having similar influencing role in moulding the buying attitude. The deduction is that whilst impressive and easy to use online retail stores create pleasure shopping, it is not enough to transform the positive attitude into buying behaviour. This is because other influencing factors such as affordability and trust for the brand must be considered when making the final buying decision.

Mixed Method Phase Three: Interpretation of Results

It can be said that organizations with perceived diversity, inclusiveness, and fair treatment of the organization and environment in which it is operating project a positive image towards increasing digital natives' loyalty for a brand. The results from the inferential analysis of 214 respondents collected using random probability sampling show that digital natives value brands that advocate diversity, equity, and inclusiveness as reflected in their corporate social responsibility programs, social media reviews, and brand communications collectively known as customer loyalty program (QTH2). In addition to not being profiled according to their gender, age, or race, this generation prefers companies that value diverse multicultural environment and are socially responsible that they can relate with a more inclusive feeling. It aligns with qualitative findings that companies striving to be more inclusive in their management and marketing strategies tend to gain higher emotional attachment and cognitive loyalty among their customers. These thoughts and beliefs would manifest into brand loyalty leading to a more positive buying attitude of continuously patronizing a brand.

Hedonic value serves as fundamental online shopping's look and feel reflected in the attractiveness and user-friendly online retail stores can generate excitement and a pleasure shopping experience. In this regard, they are considered as key characteristics to online business success driving consumer attitude towards buying intention. Bivariate correlation and linear regression analyses carried out on a sample size of 258 randomly collected reveals a significant linkage between hedonic value and buying attitude (QTH4) suggesting that positive product reviews, accurate product information, ease of use and impressive online store designs are critical contributors in the formation of digital native attitude towards buying intention. Whilst it generally holds true, qualitative study found that sometimes hedonism can lead to irrational attitude in buying decision when an individual's own emotion goes against his or her better judgement. This type of attitude lends credence to the critical contribution of hedonic value in shaping an emotion of an individual when he or she navigates through the contents of online retail stores. It is therefore a necessity for a brand to inject marketing communication strategies in appropriate areas of its omnichannel retail to incite and transform emotion of digital natives into positive buying attitude.

One of the tenets in building trust is giving customer a great experience at various omnichannel touchpoints to increase their attitudinal and behavioural loyalty towards a brand. This was put to test on responses collected from 317 respondents randomly selected to determine whether digital natives' prior online shopping experience would manifest into trust for a brand. The positive outcome supports the hypothesis (QTH3) of having consistent and reliable online shopping experience as an important influencing factor that accentuates customer's intrinsic motivation leading to the manifestation of trust. The reason is due primarily to the familiarity customers have had with an online retail store that they frequently patronised creating a sense of comfort that reduces their feeling of uncertainty and insecurity. They are accustomed to the navigational process and where to find the items that they are looking for. However, the downside of an online transaction is that the product distribution aspect of an order fulfilment is usually carried out by logistic partners and not under total control of a store owner. This vulnerable part of the supply chain becomes a bane, or an Achilles heel that could derail efforts taken by a company to create a superior customer experience.

As opposed to previous generations that prioritize trust, and price perception over product quality, digital natives are more inclined towards high quality sustainable products and service with the willingness to pay a slight premium on price when making a buying decision. The confirmatory study on 223 randomly selected respondents testifies that although both price and quality are important considerations to digital natives when making buying decision (QTH1), they tend to look for products that give them the best perceived quality value when weighed against the price they pay. When products and services do not live up to its promised quality, these online shoppers would not hesitate to express their disapprovals and opinions in the form of brand reviews and social media.

In conclusion, interpretation of both qualitative and quantitative study indicates that although brand loyalty, trust, price perception and consumer attitude are important factors at various degrees in digital native buying behaviour, the manifestation of these factor values is not the same and different from previous generations. Companies marketing their products and services to digital natives need a change in their strategies to adapt to the paradigm shift. Not only do they need to project good social corporate image that strives on diversity, equity, and inclusiveness, but they also need to translate this image into tangible actions to convince digital natives of their sincerity. Products and services provided by these companies must easily be accessible in omnichannel retail that are user friendly, attractive, and hassle-free. Maintaining two-way brand communication is crucial in generating trust through the provision of factual information and channels for feedbacks and inputs. Finally, value-pricing is a preferred choice of pricing strategy that can be used by companies to match perceived product and service quality to pricing.

DISCUSSION

This study was undertaken to explore the buying behaviour of digital natives from four qualitative objectives of:

QLRO1: Investigate the effect of price perception on buying behaviour of digital natives.
QLRO2: Explore how brand loyalty affects buying behaviour of digital natives.
QLRO3: Probe the effect of trust on buying behaviour of digital natives.
QLRO4: Examine how the attitude of digital natives affects their buying behaviour.

To probe deeper into understanding digital natives' spending pattern around the four qualitative objectives, four corresponding quantitative objectives were developed as confirmatory study to help established relationships and provide focus among the variables under investigation.

QTRO1: Establish the relationship between product quality and digital natives' perceived price perception.
QTRO2: Determine the linkage between an inclusive DEI brand and digital natives' brand loyalty.
QTRO3: Understand the contribution of online shopping experience towards digital natives' trust for a brand.
QTRO4: Ascertain the influence of hedonic value from online shopping on digital natives' buying attitude.

Qualitative analysis shows that trust is an important factor towards a favourable buying behaviour driven by reliability, and consistency of a brand's product or service. When the same experience is felt every time purchase is made, it culminates into an ever-increasing vortex strength of trust. The temporal effect of increasing trust over time accounts for more favourable customer buying behaviour (QLRO3). However, it is easier said than done as experience is not confined to online interactions a customer has had with a brand. It encompasses a holistic supply chain process that includes seamless interface with third parties such as logistic partners in the delivery of goods. However, if it is done well, it would leave an indelible impression in the mind of consumer that goes a long way towards building trust for future transactions with the brand (QTRO3).

The result also signifies the important contribution of hedonic value as part and parcel of an end-to-end customer experience in shaping consumer's valence and arousal physiological experience towards consumer buying attitude. As much as it confirms the contribution of hedonism created from highly engaging website and mobile apps on buying attitude (QTRO4), the linear regression R-square value of 0.437 suggests that hedonic value is not the only contributing factor of consumer buying attitude. The qualitative aspect of this research (QLRO4) reveals other contributing factors such as trust for a brand and customer's affordability. As digital natives are more inclusive in their thinking, companies wanting to create a more favourable buying attitude in digital natives should utilize empathy as part of their emotional appeal to create hedonic value in their marketing communication at various touchpoints in omnichannel retail. Acting on their promise is another important trait companies can employ to earn the belief of consumer on a brand value that aligns with their own.

It resonates with QTRO2 that companies embracing practice of DEI in their action and message tends to manifest into higher customer brand loyalty. Studies have shown that 57% of consumers are more loyal to brands that take action to address social inequities (Deloitte, 2021). Furthermore, companies should be responsive to customer needs, acting fast in solving their problems. Digital natives being digital savvy have many choices. If they are not comfortable with a brand, they will switch from one brand to the next until they find one that meets their expectation. It reflects the importance of designing customer loyalty programmes that speak the language of digital natives. Using these programmes to deepen relationship with consumers at every touchpoint increases brand loyalty and creates a more positive customer buying behaviour (QLRO2).

However, it is not enough without mentioning quality. Although digital natives are known for being price sensitive and often on lookout for value buy, they are willing to pay a slight premium for sustainable, high-quality brands that are deemed prestige sensitive (QTRO1). These contradictory stances imply that digital natives are trying to strike a balance between price sensitivity and having an interest for high quality products. It resonates with QLRO1 that for these digital natives, there is delicate balance between price and quality when making key purchasing decision. Brand should take note of digital natives' impulsive spending habits when they are in spending mood. This is because such spending mood can be induced through engaging marketing communications in omnichannel retail such as online store, mobile apps, social media, influencers, physical stores, and other channels setting up conditions in creating hedonism among digital native shoppers.

Practical and Theoretical Implication

Digital natives are special breed of generation that are grown up in information age and are very accustomed to technology. As their spending power increases, brand wanting to take advantage of the growing demand must re-orient their marketing strategy of using mass and niche marketing to a more personalized and individualized approach. This might be a challenge in the past but with today's technology, companies can leverage on cost-effective connectivity of advanced telecommunication technology such as 5G and fourth industrial revolution (4IR) to deliver superior go-to-market (GTM) strategy using a combination of artificial intelligence, big data analytics, cloud computing, and high-speed broadband to deliver personalized communication geared towards analysing, identifying and offering personalized deals to individual customers. For example, analysing customers' purchase pattern and offering attractive limited time offer deals based on time or event-driven needs such as festivals, or birthdays. It could also be used to encourage non-buying customer to spend at retail outlets by broadcasting attractive promotion on customer mobile device just when he or she is about to exit a store without making a purchase.

With the entrenchment of 4IR, the fusion of cyber-physical systems characterized by a range of new technologies are changing the fundamentals in marketing strategies. Whilst these traditional marketing strategies such as 4Ps of marketing mix or 7Ps of services marketing focus on products or services offered by a company, they are internally driven from a business's point of view with little influence from customers. This is a folly as digital natives are known to be demanding expecting high quality sustainable products that cater to their needs. These inward-looking processes would not solve their needs and manage their expectations resulting in customer dissatisfaction. Therefore, there is a need to rethink marketing strategies.

One way out of this conundrum is using the new 4Cs of Co-creation, Currency, Communal Activation, and Conversation representing a revolutionary model of brand-to customer communication (Pamastillero, 2017). In this model, the one-way communication approach of Marketing Mix is replaced by an interactive multiple-way communication between a brand and customers. Customers such as digital natives are involved at an early ideation stage of Co-creation collaborating with brand designers customizing products desired by their community.

Currency refers to pricing that can be set dynamically according to customer spending pattern, their historical purchase pattern as well as the proximity of the target market's locations. Example such as giving priority purchase to loyal customers and other customer loyalty recognition could help foster great customer experience, and emotional attachment leading to building brand trust and favourable buying behaviour.

Communal Activation is about using 4IR technology such as 3D printing, augmented reality, virtual reality, and online portals to enable peer-to-peer Go-To-Market distribution. Imagine immersing oneself in a metaverse of programmable avatars allows consumer to communicate directly in real time mode with a brand, having instantaneous access to visual image of a product shown in three dimensions, possess the ability to customize product according to individual's needs, and having the product sent directly to the customer's doorstep all done in the confine of one's own location.

Finally, Conversation is all about managing customer experience of digital natives from conversation management, content marketing to brand-to-customer collaboration. Various means can be utilized to achieve this objective such as using in-depth online analytics to understand and address customer interaction pain points, optimizing search engine rankings, and using social media outreach to build one-to-one customer relationship by treating these digital natives as special at a more personal manner.

As these digital natives are digital savvy, they like to be empowered with autonomy of experimenting with new technology. Therefore, companies intending to rollout new products or services should either reduce or eliminate instruction manual and instead embed flexibility in their online store to provide these young adults the freedom of customization by providing different options that they can pick and choose to their satisfaction. Product review and feedback should be part of these options as these customers like to make informed and smart buying decisions.

Finally, companies need to build empathy and diversity in their marketing communication and having representation and inclusiveness in marketing initiative can help to build strong emotional bond with this target market segment. Each interaction with customer across its omnichannel retail must be consistent. Any mistake in communication that provoke strong negative feelings can go viral and derail the pain taken to building customer loyalty and trust for a brand. To prevent such incident from happening, companies should consider incorporating ethical marketing policies as part of their overall business commitment towards having an open, inclusive, transparent, and fair practices to society, and community at large.

Suggestion for Future Research

One suggestion for future research is to explore effectiveness in using 4Cs brand-to-customer revolutionary marketing model of Co-creation, Currency, Communal Activation, and Conversation. With fourth industry revolution still in its infancy stage especially in the aspect of artificial intelligence in driving virtual and augmented reality, companies do not yet fully exploit the enormous power of cyber-physical systems to create a true experiential cradle-to-customer experience.

It presents an opportunity to ride on the exciting wave of technology tsunami for researchers to function as catalysts in exploring creative ways of utilizing realms of technology for the benefit of both consumers and industries. As such it is no longer about doing basic research study but undertaking it as true experimental or quasi-experimental design approach involving researchers in critical areas of 4Cs brand-to-customer revolutionary marketing model process. For example, using neuroscience-based research method such as a neuromarketing to study sensory-motor response, cognitive, and psychological factors of consumers participating in design modelling at the ideation stage of Co-creation would help producers develop products based on genuine consumer concern.

This pragmatic approach can help industry resolve the current conundrum confronting business marketing strategy. This industry-researcher-consumer tripartite partnership can open numerous possibilities driven primarily by future market needs facilitated by technology-induced research and development and fulfilling objective of producing products and services that are customisable, fit for purpose and cater for demands of future generations (Figure 6).

This is worthwhile exploring as future generations are becoming more and more digital driven and personalized marketing is here to stay.

CONCLUSION

Digital natives are considered a disruptive generation due to their active engagement in social media and ubiquitous adoption of digital devices. Their preference for integrating shopping apps, location-based services, and mobile wallet has forced commercial marketing to adopt online platform for brand engagement, online retailing, and market research.

In the quest to look for ways to market to these internet generation, this study has succinctly and empirically determined the need for companies to build brand trust and develop specific customer loyalty programmes gear towards building brand loyalty and drive determinants of price perception to attain favourable buying behaviour. One of the important differences digital natives have compared with the other social generations is their value for inclusiveness. Companies planning to solicit higher customer brand loyalty would do well by embracing DEI practice in their action and message. That means "walk the talk" and delivering quality products and services in a holistic consistent, and reliable manner that resonates with the brand promises. A word of caution, as much as trust can be elevated through pleasurable shopping experience, it could adversely be derailed from a single bad experience. It is for this reason that companies should take the necessary measures when designing and maintaining websites and mobile apps in their omnichannel retail to create quality brand engagement that entices hedonic

Figure 6. Industry-researcher-consumer tripartite partnership

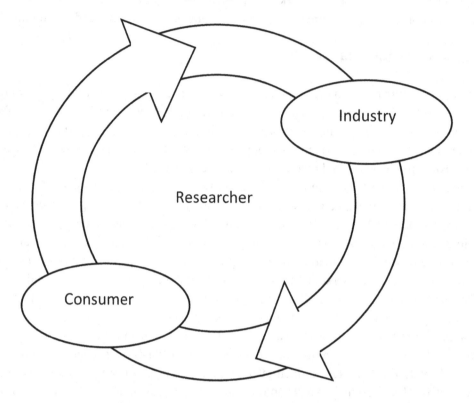

shopping motivation. Doing it correctly might even evoke spontaneous impulsive buying from casual shoppers with no intention of buying.

This study concludes a two-year study that was initially planned to explore the paradigm shift in purchasing pattern caused by the disruptive force of digital natives to eventually involve in excess of a thousand digital native respondents establishing causal relationships between the predictors of buying behaviour and their determinants. As future of marketing becomes more and more digitally driven, companies would do well investing in advanced technology and adopting a more forward-looking marketing approach such as 4Cs in co-creating products which are flexible, and customizable synonymous to open source. The future world is no longer about one party doing what it perceives as best for its customers, rather, collaboration is the key to success. Companies should adopt an open-door policy by involving customers and researchers at an onset of designing new products. From the perspective of a company, this inclusive culture would not only lead to better fit-for-purpose product or service design, but it could also conceivably reduce cost of development and improve profit margin through less wastage and rework. To a researcher, having such an opportunity would increase their contribution to the body of knowledge and add value to industry supply chain. Finally, this process would empower digital natives to add their creativity into developing even better products that are endcaring to future generations.

REFERENCES

Ailawadi, K. L., Neslin, S. A., & Gedenk, K. (2001). Pursuing the value-conscious consumer: store brands versus national brand promotions. *American Marketing Association, 65*(1), 71 – 89. doi:10.1509/jmkg.65.1.71.18132

Ajzen, I., & Fishbein, M. (1977). Attitude-behavior relations: A theoretical analysis and review of empirical research. *Psychological Bulletin, 84*(5), 888–918. doi:10.1037/0033-2909.84.5.888

Arifi, N. E. (2022, July 7). The purchasing power of Millennials and Generation Z. *Insight.* https://www.wundermanthompson.com/insight/the-purchasing-power-of-millennials-and-generation-z#:~:text=According%20to%20two%20US%20studies,on%20their%20Generation%20X%20parents

Ashraf, S., Ilyas, R., Imtiaz, M., & Ahmad, S. (2018). Impact of service quality, corporate image and perceived value on brand loyalty with presence and absence of customer satisfaction: A study of four service sectors of Pakistan. *International Journal of Academic Research in Business & Social Sciences, 8*(2), 452–474. doi:10.6007/IJARBSS/v8-i2/3885

Brodzik, C., Cuthill, S., Young, N., & Drake, N. (2021, October 19). Authentically inclusive marketing - Winning future customers with diversity, equity, and inclusion. *Deloitte.* https://www2.deloitte.com/us/en/insights/topics/marketing-and-sales-operations/global-marketing-trends/2022/diversity-and-inclusion-in-marketing.html

Burton, S., Lichtenstein, D. R., Netemeyer, R. G., & Garretson, J. A. (1998). A scale for measuring attitude toward private label products and an examination of its psychological and behavioral correlates. *Journal of the Academy of Marketing Science, 26*(1), 293–306. doi:10.1177/0092070398264003

Cham, T. H., Ng, C. K. Y., Lim, Y. M., & Cheng, B. L. (2018). Factors influencing clothing interest and purchase intention: A study of generation Y consumers in Malaysia. *International Review of Retail, Distribution and Consumer Research, 28*(1), 174–189. doi:10.1080/09593969.2017.1397045

Chenavaz, R. (2017). Better product quality may lead to lower product price. *The B.E. Journal of Theoretical Economics, 17*(1), 20150062. doi:10.1515/bejte-2015-0062

Chetioui, Y., Lebdaoui, H., & Chetioui, H. (2021). Factors influencing consumer attitudes toward online shopping: The mediating effect of trust. *EuroMed Journal of Business, 16*(4), 544–563. doi:10.1108/EMJB-05-2020-0046

Cornell, J. (2019, January 14). Cultivating behavioral loyalty and attitudinal loyalty among consumers. *Zinrelo.* https://www.zinrelo.com/cultivating-behavioral-loyalty-attitudinal-loyalty.html

Creswell, J. W. (2003). *Research Design: Qualitative, Quantitative, and Mixed Method Approaches.* Sage Publications.

Decouz, H. (n.d). Loyalty programs are failing to engage consumers. *Sogeti.* https://www.sogeti.com/explore/reports/reinventing-loyalty-programs-for-the-digital-age/

Delgado-Ballester, E., Munuera-Alemán, J. L., & Yagüe-Guillén, M. J. (2003). Development and validation of a brand trust scale. *International Journal of Market Research, 45*(1), 35–53. doi:10.1177/147078530304500103

Deloitte. (2021, October 19). *Authentically inclusive marketing.* https://www2.deloitte.com/xe/en/insights/topics/marketing-and-sales-operations/global-marketing-trends/2022/diversity-and-inclusion-in-marketing.html

Diversityintech. (2018, October 1). *Top 20 survey questions for measuring inclusion at work.* https://www.diversityintech.co.uk/top-20-survey-questions-for-measuring-inclusion-at-work

DOSM. (2021). Current population estimates, Malaysia. *Department of Statistics Malaysia.* https://www.dosm.gov.my/v1/index.php?r=column/pdfPrev&id=ZjJOSnpJR21sQWVUcUp6ODRudm5JZz09#:~:text=Malaysia's%20population%20in%202021%20is,to%202.7%20million%20(2021)%20

Erdumlu, N., Saricam, C., Tufekyapan, M., Cetinkaya, M., & Donmez, A. C. (2017). Analysing the consumer behaviour and the influence of brand loyalty in purchasing sportswear products. *Proceedings of IOP Conference Series: Materials Science and Engineering, 254*(17), 172010. 10.1088/1757-899X/254/17/172010

Fan, X., Ning, N., & Deng, N. (2020). The impact of the quality of intelligent experience on smart retail engagement. *Marketing Intelligence & Planning, 38*(7), 877–891. doi:10.1108/MIP-09-2019-0439

Fetters, M. D., Curry, L. A., & Creswell, J. W. (2013). Achieving integration in mixed methods designs – principles and practices. *Health Services Research, 48*(6pt2), 2134–2156. doi:10.1111/1475-6773.12117 PMID:24279835

Fincham, J. E. (2008). Response rates and responsiveness for surveys, standards, and the journal. *American Journal of Pharmaceutical Education, 72*(2), 1–3. doi:10.5688/aj720243 PMID:18483608

Fishbein, M., & Ajzen, I. (1975). *Belief, Attitude, Intention, and Behavior: An Introduction to Theory and Research.* Addison-Wesley.

Healy, M., & Perry, C. (2000). Comprehensive criteria to judge validity and reliability of qualitative research within the realism paradigm. *Qualitative Market Research, 3*(3), 118–126. doi:10.1108/13522750010333861

Hinkin, T. R. (1995). A review of scale development in the study of behavior in organizations. *Journal of Management, 21*(1), 967–988. doi:10.1177/014920639502100509

Ilias, S., & Shamsudin, M. F. (2020). Customer satisfaction and business growth. *Journal of Undergraduate Social Science and Technology, 2*(2). http://abrn.asia/ojs/index.php/JUSST/article/view/60

Inegbedion, H., & Obadiaru, E. (2019). Modelling brand loyalty in the Nigerian telecommunications industry. *Journal of Strategic Marketing, 27*(7), 583–598. doi:10.1080/0965254X.2018.1462842

Jaafar, S. N., Lalp, P. E., & Naba, M. M. (2012). Consumers' perceptions, attitudes and purchase intention towards private label food products in Malaysia. *Asian Journal of Business and Management Sciences, 2*(8), 73–90. https://www.researchgate.net/publication/312762017_Consumers'_perception_attitudes_and_purchase_intention_towards_private_label_food_products_in_Malaysia

James, D. (2022, December 7). Gen Z didn't kill brand loyalty, but it looks different. *Retail Dive*. https://www.retaildive.com/news/gen-z-brand-loyalty-retailers-individuality-pricing/636558/

Kahawandala, N., & Peter, S. (2020). Factors affecting purchasing behaviour of Generation Z. *Proceedings of the international conference on industrial engineering and operations management.* 1153 – 1161. https://www.researchgate.net/publication/349915999_Factors_affecting_Purchasing_Behaviour_of_Generation_Z

Kitchen, P. J., & Proctor, T. (2015). Marketing communications in a post-modern world. *The Journal of Business Strategy, 36*(5), 34–42. doi:10.1108/JBS-06-2014-0070

Krejcie, R. V., & Morgan, D. W. (1970). Determining sample size for research activities. *Educational and Psychological Measurement, 30*(1), 607–610. https://psycnet.apa.org/record/1971-03263-001. doi:10.1177/001316447003000308

Kressmann, F., Sirgy, M. J., Herrmann, A., Huber, F., Huber, S., & Lee, D. J. (2006). Direct and indirect effects of self-image congruence on brand loyalty. *Journal of Business Research, 59*(9), 955–964. doi:10.1016/j.jbusres.2006.06.001

Kumar, S., & Pandey, M. (2017). The impact of psychological pricing strategy on consumers' buying behaviour: A qualitative study. *International Journal of Business and Systems Research, 11*(1/2), 101–117. https://EconPapers.repec.org/RePEc:ids:ijbsre:v:11:y:2017:i:1/2:p:101-117. doi:10.1504/IJBSR.2017.080843

Landis, T. (2022, April 12). Customer retention marketing vs. customer acquisition marketing. *outbound engine*. https://www.outboundengine.com/blog/customer-retention-marketing-vs-customer-acquisition-marketing/#:~:text=Acquiring%20a%20new%20customer%20can,customer%20is%205%2D20%25

Lau, G. T., & Lee, S. H. (1999). Consumers' trust in a brand and the link to brand loyalty. *Journal of Market Focused Management, 4*(1), 341–370. doi:10.1023/A:1009886520142

Lavuri, R., Jindal, A., & Akram, U. (2022). How perceived utilitarian and hedonic value influence online impulse shopping in India? Moderating role of perceived trust and perceived risk. *International Journal of Quality and Service Sciences, 14*(4), 615–634. doi:10.1108/IJQSS-11-2021-0169

Lien, C. H., & Cao, Y. (2014). Examining WeChat users' motivations, trust, attitudes, and positive word-of-mouth: Evidence from China. *Computers in Human Behavior, 41*(1), 104–111. doi:10.1016/j.chb.2014.08.013

Ling, C. H., & Mansori, S. (2018). The effects of product quality on customer satisfaction and loyalty: Evidence from Malaysian engineering industry. *International Journal of Industrial Marketing, 3*(1), 20–35. doi:10.5296/ijim.v3i1.13959

López-Fernández, A. M. (2020). Price sensitivity versus ethical consumption: A study of Millennial utilitarian consumer behavior. *Journal of Marketing Analytics, 8*(2), 57–68. doi:10.105741270-020-00074-8

Maguire, M. (2017). Doing a thematic analysis: A practical, step-by-step guide for learning and teaching scholars. *All Ireland Journal of Higher Education, 8*(3), 33510 - 33514. https://ojs.aishe.org/index.php/aishe-j/article/view/335

Markey, R. (2020, February 1). Are you undervaluing your customers? *Harvard Business Review*. https://hbr.org/2020/01/are-you-undervaluing-your-customers

Miller, L. J., & Lu, W. (2018, August 20). Gen Z is set to outnumber millennials within a year. *Bloomberg*. https://www.bloomberg.com/news/articles/2018-08-20/gen-z-to-outnumber-millennials-within-a-year-demographic-trends?leadSource=uverify%20wall

Mohammad. (2016). *The effects of utilitarian and hedonic online shopping value on consumer perceived value* [Bachelor thesis, Muhammadiyah University Of Surakarta]. https://eprints.ums.ac.id/47992/1/NASKAH%20PUBLIKASI%20PERPUS.pdf

Morgan, B. (2019, December 2). Customer of the future: 5 ways to create a customer experience for Gen-Z. *Forbes*. https://www.forbes.com/sites/blakemorgan/2019/12/02/customer-of-the-future-5-ways-to-create-a-customer-experience-for-gen-z/?sh=73c0c3835a40

Morrow, S. L. (2005). Quality and trustworthiness in qualitative research. *Journal of Counseling Psychology*, *52*(2), 250–260. doi:10.1037/0022-0167.52.2.250

Munuera-Aleman, J. L., Delgado-Ballester, E., & Yague-Guillen, M. J. (2003). Development and validation of a brand trust scale. *International Journal of Market Research*, *45*(1), 1–18. doi:10.1177/147078530304500103

Oxford Economics. (2021, March 10). *Gen Z's role in shaping the digital economy*. Oxford Economics. https://www.oxfordeconomics.com/resource/gen-z-role-in-shaping-the-digital-economy/

Pamastillero. (2017 August 11). Redefining marketing in the digital economy. *Digital Entrepreneur*. http://www.pamastillero.com/2017/08/11/4-redefining-marketing-in-the-digital-economy/

Park, C., & Kim, Y. (2003). Identifying key factors affecting consumer purchase behavior in an online shopping context. *International Journal of Retail & Distribution Management*, *31*(1), 16–29. doi:10.1108/09590550310457818

Pitic, L., Brad, S., & Pitic, D. (2014). Study on perceived quality and perceived fair price. *Procedia Economics and Finance*, *15*(1), 1304–1309. doi:10.1016/S2212-5671(14)00592-9

Prensky, M. (2001). Digital natives, digital immigrants. *On the Horizon*, *9*(5), 1–6. doi:10.1108/10748120110424816

Ramachandran, K. (2020). How will millennials and Gen Z use 5G? *Deloitte*. https://www2.deloitte.com/us/en/insights/industry/technology/5g-impacts-millennials-and-gen-z-technology-usage.html

Romaniuk, J., & Nenycz-Thiel, M. (2013). Behavioral brand loyalty and consumer brand associations. *Journal of Business Research*, *66*(1), 67–72. doi:10.1016/j.jbusres.2011.07.024

Roy, S. K., Balaji, M. S., Sadeque, S., Nguyen, B., & Melewar, T. C. (2017). Constituents and consequences of smart customer experience in retailing. *Technological Forecasting and Social Change*, *124*(C), 257–270. doi:10.1016/j.techfore.2016.09.022

Ruff, C. (2019 February, 26). Price and rewards are crucial to Gen Zers and young millennials. *Retail Dive*. https://www.retaildive.com/news/price-and-rewards-are-crucial-to-gen-zers-and-young-millennials/549166/

Santander. (2020 October, 1). *Malaysia: Reaching the consumer*. Satander. https://santandertrade.com/en/portal/analyse-markets/malaysia/reaching-the-consumers

Sarwar, F., Aftab, M., & Iqbal, M. T. (2014). The impact of branding on consumer buying behavior. *International Journal of New Technology and Research.*, 2(2), 54–64. https://www.researchgate.net/publication/309563927_The_Impact_of_Branding_on_Consumer_Buying_Behavior

Schlossberg, M. (2016, February, 11). Teen Generation Z is being called 'millennials on steroids' and that could be terrifying for retailers. *Business Insider*. http://uk.businessinsider.com/millennials-vs-gen-z-2016-2

Sekaran, U., & Bougie, R. (2016). *Research methods for business: A skill-building approach* (7th ed.). Wiley & Sons.

Shaw, E. H., Pirog, S. F. III, & Hall, J. R. (2020). Household purchasing productivity: Concept and consequences. *Journal of Macromarketing*, 40(2), 156–168. doi:10.1177/0276146720906539

Spence, M., Stancu, V., Elliott, C. T., & Dean, M. (2018). Exploring consumer purchase intentions towards traceable minced beef and beef steak using the theory of planned behavior. *Food Control*, 91(1), 138–147. doi:10.1016/j.foodcont.2018.03.035

Statistica. (2023, January 6). Leading factors motivating Gen Z consumers to engage with a new brand on social media in the United States in May 2022. *Statista Research Department*. https://www.statista.com/statistics/1324765/top-factors-driving-gen-z-engagement-new-brands-social-media-us/

Tapscott, D. (2008). *Grown up digital: How the Net generation is changing the world* (1st ed.). McGraw-Hill.

Temkin, B. (2008, February 19). The state of experience-based differentiation. *Forrester*. https://www.forrester.com/report/The-State-Of-ExperienceBased-Differentiation/RES45114

The ASEAN Post Team. (2020, May 11). Gen Z's use of social media has evolved. *The Asean Post*. https://theaseanpost.com/article/gen-zs-use-social-media-has-evolved

Thistle Initiatives. (2022, December 19). *Digital wallet users expected to exceed 5.2 billion globally by 2026*. Thistle Initiatives. https://www.thistleinitiatives.co.uk/blog/digital-wallet-users-expected-to-exceed-5.2-billion-globally-by-2026#:~:text=A%20new%20study%20has%20found,are%20currently%20considered%20cash%2Dheavy

Tjiptono, F., Khan, G., Yeong, E. S., & Kunchamboo, V. (2020). Generation Z in Malaysia: The Four 'E' Generation. In E. Gentina & E. Parry (Eds.), *The New Generation Z in Asia: Dynamics, Differences, Digitalisation* (pp. 149–163). Emerald Publishing Limited., doi:10.1108/978-1-80043-220-820201015

Tunsakul, K. (2020). Gen Z consumers' online shopping motives, attitude, and shopping intention. *Human Behavior. Development and Society*, 21(2), 7–16. https://so01.tci-thaijo.org/index.php/hbds/article/view/240046

Vaismoradi, M., Jones, J., Turunen, H., & Snelgrove, S. (2016). Theme development in qualitative content analysis and thematic analysis. *Journal of Nursing Education and Practice*, 6(5), 100–110. doi:10.5430/jnep.v6n5p100

Valaskova, K., Durana, P., & Adamko, P. (2021). Changes in consumers' purchase patterns as a consequence of the COVID-19 Pandemic. *Mathematics*, 9(15), 1788. doi:10.3390/math9151788

Vasileiou, K., Barnett, J., Thorpe, S., & Young, T. (2018). Characterising and justifying sample size sufficiency in interview-based studies: Systematic analysis of qualitative health research over a 15-year period. *BMC Medical Research Methodology*, 18(148), 2–18. doi:10.118612874-018-0594-7 PMID:30463515

Voyado. (2023, January 19). *How is Generation Z shopping?* Apptus. https://www.apptus.com/blog/generation-z-online-shopping-habits/#:~:text=Gen%20Z%20consumers%20are%20more,of%20view%20on%20political%20issues

Worldline. (2020, June 15). *How generation affect shopping behavior.* Bambora. https://www.bambora.com/articles/how-do-generation-affect-shopping-behavior/

Yong, S. M., & Renganathan, T. S. (2019). Malaysian Millennial buying behavior and country-of-origin effect. *Jurnal Pengguna Malaysia, 32*(1), 55 - 67. https://macfea.com.my/wp-content/uploads/2020/03/JPM-32-Jun-2019-article-5.pdf

ADDITIONAL READING

Aimé, P., & Grünbeck, J. (2019). *Smart Persuasion: How Elite Marketers Influence Consumers (and Persuade Them to Take Action).* Independently Published.

Pamastillero. (2017, August 11). Redefining marketing in the digital economy. *Digital Entrepreneur.* http://www.pamastillero.com/2017/08/11/4-redefining-marketing-in-the-digital-economy/

KEY TERMS AND DEFINITIONS

Brand Loyalty: A strong feeling of allegiance for a brand perceived as superior resulting in continuous engagement and purchases from the same brand.

Brand Trust: Amount of confidence customers have for a brand to deliver on its promises consistently and reliably.

Buying Attitude: A determinant that decisively affects a purchasing preference or buying decision in a particular situation.

Buying Behaviour: Actions taken by consumer in a commercial transaction to buy a product or service.

Cognitive Experience: Experience on how one sees, understands, and interprets that has implication on his settled way of thinking or feeling for similar future experiences.

Digital Natives: Born in 1981 and onwards who grew up under the ubiquitous influence of internet surrounded by digital technologies.

Diversity, Equity, and Inclusiveness: Policies and practices by an organization designed to promote fair treatment of all people regardless of their race, ethnicity, disability, religion, culture, and sexual orientation.

Habitual buying behaviour: Buying behaviour that is driven by familiarity or affinity towards a particular brand requires little consumer involvement.

Hedonic Value: Pleasant or unpleasant sensation derived from entertaining, emotional, and satisfactory experiences during a shopping process.

Impulsive Buying: An unplanned buying decision taken at the spur of a moment triggered by excitement, and emotions towards buying a product or service.

Price Perception: Customer interprets the worth of a product or service when thinking about a particular brand.

Chapter 4
Gig Economy Worker:
Work and Platform Perspective From Food Drivers and Freelancers

Herman Fassou Haba

Université du Québec à Trois-Rivières, Canada

ABSTRACT

This chapter explores gig workers' opinions in terms of the adoption of online platforms for their work. Based on a qualitative research method, this research study has collected secondary data for the purpose of analyzing them with thematic analysis. A total review of 127 were selected using simple random sampling method. The findings identified four main themes to be considered. The first theme is work, concerning the way gig workers find their job and how interesting it is. The second theme is flexibility, showing how the flexibility the share economy brings to gig workers, the third theme is great, demonstrating how great the online platforms are in terms of earning extra income, and last theme is people, because everything turns around people. The significance of this study is essential in terms of understanding the gig economy and gig workers because it can help in terms of the adoption of share economy platforms around the world.

INTRODUCTION

The gig economy, being a new form of economy relying heavily on contractors or part-time workers within a labour market (Bulian, 2021). People working in this type of economic system are known as the gig workers because of their work flexibility and their independence but little or having no job security (Bulian, 2021). According to Oyer (2020), there has been an increasing holding of this type of jobs by gig workers and it is still growing due to the rise of technology enabling short-term labour contracting. Comprehensively, the growth of gig workers is mostly witnessed in developed economies and some emerging countries due to the use of modern software application such as Uber Technologies apps, DoorDash, Fiverr and others (Oyer, 2020). Thus, the aim of this paper is to understand gig workers opinions and adoption of gig economy from the perspective of Uber Eats, DoorDash, Fiverr and Upwork.

DOI: 10.4018/978-1-6684-6782-4.ch004

Uber Eats and DoorDash are known as disruptive technologies in online food industry resulting to significant changes in terms of how gig workers earn money and consumers get the service in the food industry (Gogul, 2021). There is no doubt that the field has attracted the attention of several scholars such as Ramesh et al, (2021) elaborating a strong empirical study of on online food delivery services from application perspective. However, this type of gig economic system refers to an online channel where consumers use to order food from diverse (Shankar et al, 2022). Online food delivery system uses intermediaries of people guided by a technological app giving them instruction on when they must deliver foods to their clients (Kaur et al, 2020). Moreover, most of the academic literature on the field of OFD system tries to investigate consumers responses to OFD services but does not mostly take into consideration the gig workers (Goods et al, 2019; Behl et al, 2022).

The world of Freelance has changed over the past two decades since the rise of the internet. Online freelancing has been able to provide an opportunity all around to work through internet. They are known as gig workers because they are self-employed persons providing their services to several clients around the world via internet (Masood et al, 2018). Upwork and Fiverr are the two main giants of online freelancing companies around the world, businesses can be able to tap into a global market to gain the professional services they may want beyond their local market (Green et al, 2018). There is no doubt that the gig economy has been the key to the current success of the modern way work, the scope of this study is to understand exactly the views, the opinions, and the perception of gig workers about their jobs and why they fit in terms of doing this type of modern job and why they preferred it. The gig workers are the heart of the gig economy because without them there is no operation of gig economy and that is the crucial reason why the gig workers opinions and views are very important and knowing the scope of it this the objective of this research study.

The aim of this paper is to understand the opinions of gig workers on current online platforms.

Therefore, this research study is going to be significant in the field of gig economy specially with online food delivery industry and online freelancing industry. Trying to comprehend exactly the reason why gig economy workers often adopt this new way of working is crucial for this new economy, it is also crucial for gig platforms for the purpose of improving their systems and adopt their strategy systematically with this new economy of work. Secondly, the work is going to make an academic contribution because of its significance in the field of gig economy, gig workers and platforms specially with the case study of online food delivery and online freelancing sectors.

LITERATURE REVIEW

This literature review is trying to academically elaborate the academic contribution in the field of gig economy associated with gig workers, the theory of social exchange and its contribution in the field of gig economy. Additionally, the exploration of research studies in the field of online food delivery and online freelancing. Thus, the critical analysis of this academic literature is going to be able to help find out the literature gap of the study.

Gig, Gig Economy, Gig Workers

Gig economy known by some other scholars as the sharing economy, it is being characterized by scientists and researchers as a form of short-term contracts based on an exchange between individuals or even firms via digital platforms as moderators facilitating the matching between customers and providers (Mukhopahyay & Mukhopahyay, 2020). The growth of the industry is projected to be $2.7 trillion by 2025, by deriving this type of work which is based on the contingent workforce management which is nothing new but reshaping the introduction of the gig economy. By defining the term gig worker is an independent contractor undertaking short-term jobs for one or more employers via digital platforms (Charlton, 2021). The world has witnessed several models and new companies were born in this era of the gig economy due to the development of the internet and technology (Schmuck, 2015). Internet has made commerce much easier than ever decreasing the transaction costs extremely low for consumers to receive their services (Frenken and Schor, 2017; Mukhopahyay & Mukhopahyay, 2020). From this context, Bocker and Meelen (2016) had given an understandable background concerning the sharing economy based on the environmental, economic, and societal aspects of it. Knowing that the popularity of the gig economy began after the financial crisis of 2008 when technological firms were popular and a lot of people experienced financial difficulties (Kathan et al, 2016; Gorog, 2018).

Understandably, there is a new model of gig work which is well explained in the academic literature of the gig economy, according to De Stefano (2015), the gig work can be divided into two main location-based gig work which is 'work on demand via app' and network-based digital labour sometimes called 'crowdwork'. From the context of understanding crowdwork in the field of gig economy is based on the term conditions of utilisation when the eligible clients agreed that while the providers are agreeing to perform services for you as independent contractors and not as employees (Wood et al, 2019). This is the case for online food delivery companies and gig workers with a repeated and frequent performance of services by the same providers (De Stefano, 2015; Wood et al, 2019). Therefore, a distinct nature of gig work and gig working relations can be demonstrated by contrasting gig work with other forms of work including traditional employment, atypical employment, and independent business (Wang & Wang, 2018). Gig workers often sign up only work or service agreements, not labour contracts, with platform enterprises, their income is based on the piece-rates from which 5% to 30% is deducted in the form of a gig fee (Wei & MacDonald, 2021). Compare to traditional way of working the gig workers do not have permanent jobs, they are independent contractors, the working places are working hours of the gig workers are often directed with technology and the working period is relatively long compared to traditional work (Wei & MacDonald, 2021). In the case of traditional employment, there is a labour contract, the wage is fix with the benefit of social insurance, there is the labour relation and employment relationship with traditional employment, the work time is usually full time and there is also a benefit of retirement (Wei & MacDonald, 2021).

Theory of Social Exchange

Scholars and researchers have associated gig economy with the social exchange theory (SET) for the purpose of understanding why people participate in a sharing economy (Stafford, 2008; Chen, 2013). First, the social exchange theory (SET) is an important theory trying to understand customers' intention to share rather than to own commercial goods and service (Kim et al, 2015). In accordance with the study of Kim et al (2015), the theoretical framework can be able to reflect the characteristics of the sharing economy such as peer-to-peer relationships and how it can be able to address the gig workers sharing behaviour because participants in this type of economy can gain social relationship (Belk, 2010). Therefore, as discuss for the main comprehension of the social exchange theory being a concept based on the notion that the relationship between two individuals is being created throughout cost-benefit analysis process (Davlembayeva & Alamanos, 2022). Comprehensively, it is important to understand the theory tends to take into consideration the sociological and psychological theory that can be able to study the social behaviour of human being based on the interaction of two parties which can be ale to establish the cost-benefit analysis to determine benefits and risks which can be associated with the elements costs and rewards because human often likes the highest reward with the lowest cost leading at having a very important satisfaction in terms of business transaction. The study of Priporas et al (2017) for the purpose of investigating the diverse nature of service quality in the share economy is an important study being associated with the theory of social exchange.

In the case of the gig platforms such as online food delivery (OFD) and online freelancing platforms, scholars in the academic literature had tried to explore exactly how the theory of social exchange can be associated with the gig economy or the economy of platforms which are based on connecting people for the purpose of business transaction (Kumar et al, 2018). It has made the theory more interesting and relevant in today's modern economy where independent workers contribution to customer satisfaction is crucial via online platforms because we currently live in a share economy (Altinay and Taheri, 2019). Additionally, there are several other theories which had been added in the field of share economy or gig economy a part of the social exchange theory, there can be also the discussion of the value co-creation and service dominant theory which is fundamentally associated with the gig workers and the gig world (Camilleri and Neuhofer, 2017; Neuhofer and Johnson, 2017; Zhang et al, 2018). It is also important to mention the social comparison theory of Mauri et al (2018) and the social cognitive theory of Zhu et al (2017).

Gig Workers, Online Food Delivery (OFD), Online Freelancing

However, there are several studies done by researchers and scientists in the field of online food delivery (OFD) system associated with the sharing economy or the gig economy for the purpose of understanding customer satisfaction, experience, and intentions (Raj et al, 2021; Shankar et al, 2022; Behl et al, 2022). There has been strong academic discussion in terms of knowing and importance of OFD in current gig economy context and how several companies such as Uber Eats and DoorDash are changing the face of this modern economy (Wu et al, 2019; Bulian, 2021). Comprehensively, due to the popularity of online food delivery, the customers' expectation for delivery has become very high which is making the cost of delivery very obscured (Bates & Friday, 2018; Dablanc, 2019). Thus, nowadays, a lot of consumers are purchasing online which is making the industry a boom that had never been expected (Lord et al, 2021). Online food delivery (OFD) has transformed exactly the manner the modern world purchase and consume foods lately and there are several varieties of foods which clients can be able to choose from (Lord et al, 2022). By looking at the context of the digitalisation and understanding of online food delivery system, several researchers and scholars have concentrated their area of research on the link that can be able to exist between a huge variety of companies offering on-demand takeaway services and the couriers which had been employed in what is known as the "gig economy" (Song et al, 2018, Galati et al, 2020; Li et al, 2020). Nevertheless, previous research studies had highlighted the augmenting environmental issues and impact which are associated with the same-day delivery activities of gig workers in the field of online food delivery (Allen et al, 2018b; Dablanc et al, 2017). Another consequence of the system is based on the time pressures in the sector prompting gig workers to work longer and faster to meet the clients' expectations (Barratt et al, 2020). Despite the field being explored by a lot of researchers and workers to understand exactly the importance of the gig economy in the field of OFD, most exploration has been directed to the perception of the consumers, regulators trying to understand whether the job being done can be considered as a living job for gig workers or if they can oblige companies to do more about the treatment of their gig workers and environmentalists are concerned about the issue it can be in terms of environmental issues (Christie and Ward, 2019; Lord et al, 2022).

Additionally, in the academic literature, there is no doubt that several contributions have been made in the field of online freelancing, being an important marketplace where individuals can be able to sell their services to potential employers or independent workers around the world (Hannak et al, 2017). Most of the studies had identified that online freelancing provides an opportunity to earn extra money, the freedom to do jobs at their convenience and the benefit to access the global market being a chance to work with clients all over the world (Hannak et al, 2017). From the perspective of some researchers and analyst, the shifting mindset of work is the reason for the rise of the gig economy in the world precisely in the field of online freelancing. It is then important to comprehend in the academic literature there a lot of reason why online freelancing platforms had become popular and why academicians have turned their attentions towards exploring the field and understanding exactly the main reasons for the growth (Sutherland et al, 2019). The contribution of some researchers emphasized on the work precarity and gig literacies for online freelancers in the modern world which tried to understand the temporary employment of workers known to be poorly paid, unprotected with benefits such as health insurance or job security and the inability to be able to support a household in terms of the job being done (Sutherland et al, 2019). Furthermore, some of the researchers shifted their attention on the benefits of the economies of scale which the gig economy can bring in the field of online freelancing explained with clients trying to want their services to be done at the lowest cost possible in developing countries, the economies of scale can also help job creation with a standard of payment in developing countries (Stephany et al, 2021).

Moreover, even though the field of gig economy has been really explored by researchers and scholars, few studies in the academic literature is taking into consideration the views and the perception of gig workers. This research thus is turning its focus on knowing the importance and the explanation of the literature gap the study is trying to cover which is being a new angle of exploration.

Literature Gap

Knowing that there are a lot of research studies done in the field of gig economy based on online food delivery (OFD) industry and online freelancing industry. Moreover, less studies are trying to discuss the opinions of gig workers within these industries for the purpose of knowing their experience and their satisfaction at their jobs. Thus, this study is going to be exploring this new angle of research study leading at making a significant academic contribution in the field. Comprehensively, this research study is going to be looking at the gig economy differently on the basis of knowing the role of the gig workers because it is emphasizing the work of the gig workers in terms of knowing whether the environment of the gig economy is suitable for them and whether or not there is a need to improve the condition of the gig workers by providing them more incentives in terms of regulations because when we cannot talk about the gig economy without the gig workers. This new angle of research is based on fulfilling a research gap which is being rarely explore in the academic literature of the gig economy particularly in the field of online food delivery (OFD) and online freelancing.

RESEARCH METHODOLOGY

This research methodology clearly highlights the research objectives nature with the approach which had been selected to analyse the dataset of the study. Comprehending the key factors and experiences that the gig workers considered in the context of online food delivery (OFD) and online freelancing. Thus, based on inductive approach, this research study adopts the observations of words and moves towards a more abstract generalisation needed and ideas. Knowing that the inductive approach in this research study try to identify factors which can be considered useful for the existing academic literature in the field of gig economy. Furthermore, this research study is based on a qualitative research methodology and the study data collection is going to be a secondary data collection (Creswell, 2013). The research method is based on exploratory research design is known as the methodological approach which can be able to investigate the research questions or problems which had not been explored before and that is why this research study is going to be exploring the literature gap of the study. In brief, the combination of exploratory research design and qualitative research method will be at the heart of this research methodology.

Data collection method: first, the data that is going to be collected in this research study will be on secondary data collection from third party source which is "Glassdoor". Glassdoor is actually an American company where current and former employees of companies anonymously review companies based on ratings and reviews. There are millions and millions of reviews on Glassdoor talking about the gig workers and gig economy in terms of feedbacks on the companies which are going to be using in this research study which are UberEATS, DoorDash, Upwork and Fiverr. Gig workers reviews from Glassdoor for the purpose of knowing their opinions and experience. As the chosen companies are Uber Eats and DoorDash which are two popular American companies operating in North America, Europe, New Zealand, and Australia. Each of the company currently have more than 1 million gig workers as food delivery drivers around the world. The secondary data information is going to be collected from the following websites below:

Regarding online freelancing, the companies which are being chosen are Upwork and Fiverr which are the two major companies operating around the world as a marketplace. Upwork currently have more than 18 million online freelancers and Fiverr currently have more than 19 million online freelancers. Thus, the below is the data source for the two organisations.

In brief, the data which are being collected from Glassdoor will be analysed to be able to find the insight of the question that is research study wants to explore leading at answering the research aim. To doing the analysis, the data which are being collected will be analyse together as the goal is to understand the views and the opinions of gig workers.

Sampling method: this study undertakes a simple random sampling method based on selecting gig workers from two main industries online food delivery (OFD) and online freelancing. However, the selec-

Table 1. Data source for OFD

Data Source for the food delivery companies
https://www.glassdoor.ca/Reviews/Uber-Delivery-Driver-Reviews-EI_IE575263.0,4_KO5,20.htm
https://www.glassdoor.ca/Reviews/DoorDash-Delivery-Driver-Reviews-EI_IE813073.0,8_KO9,24.htm

Table 2. Data source for online freelancing

Data Source for online freelancing companies
https://www.glassdoor.ca/Reviews/Upwork-Reviews-E993959.htm
https://www.glassdoor.ca/Reviews/Fiverr-Inc-Reviews-E750333.htm

tion of each review is done randomly, this means that every review has the same and equal probability to be chosen during the process of the sampling. All the combine reviews are 200 collected during the year 2022 and 74 reviews were eliminated due to inappropriate language and poor English. Then, the total reviews used are 126 reviews which have the following structure below:

Data Analysis Plan: for the purpose of analysing the data, this research study is going to be using Nvivo Enterprise Pro software a fundamental software which is used for thematic analysis. Thematic analysis is going to be used as it entails in terms of searching, identifying, analysing, and reporting repeated patterns (Braun and Clarke, 2006). Thematic analysis is an important qualitative research study which is based on identifying, analysing, and trying to interpret the patterns which of the meaning within the qualitative data collected for the research study (Braun and Clarke, 2006). Thus, the thematic analysis is going to be taking into consideration the word cloud and the word tree which are leading to know exactly the main pattern of the study which patterns are concerning the opinions of gig workers from the context of OFD and online freelancing.

FINDINGS

Thematic analysis is to comprehend and be able to identify the themes, codes, and pattern in a research study dataset for the purpose of getting the insight of respondents or participants opinions (Braun et al, 2016). The finding is based on the data collected in 2022 on the four main platforms of share economy which are Uber Eats, DoorDash, Fiverr and Upwork. The thematic analysis will consist of three main parts consisting of word frequency query, word cloud and word tree.

*Word cloud, the analysis is based on an image made of words that together can resemble a cloudy shape. To interpret the image, the size of the word shows how important the world is by identifying the pattern within the thematic. This analysis is very important to know exactly with the data that has been collected the main importance of words that reviewers had tried to know on the context of online food

Table 3. Review selection and refinement statistics

Criteria	Uber Eats & DoorDash	Fiverr & Upwork
Total Reviews Selected	100	100
Reviews Eliminated (poor English)	20	23
Reviews Eliminated (Inappropriate Language)	26	15
Total Reviews considered	64	62

delivery and online freelancing for their adaptation of the gig work they often do. It is the reason why the word cloud is very important to comprehend views and opinions of the gig workers.

The findings demonstrate words that had been mostly used in the comments based on the opinions of gig workers, it was identified that Work, Great, Good, Flexible, Schedule, Easy, People and Company are the most use words based on their lengths, counts, weighted percentage. However, the word tree is going to show how many comments and patterns are associated to these 8 main words, leading that knowing and findings the opinions of gig workers concerning online platforms. First, it is important to know that

Figure 1. Word Cloud of Gig Workers

Table 4. Word Frequency Results

Word	Length	Count	Weighted Percentage (%)
work	4	57	6.35
Great	5	27	3.01
Flexible	8	18	2.00
People	6	15	1.67

work is the main element which shall be considered for the gig workers because they often use the share economy platforms for the purpose of work, the greatness and the flexibility of the platforms had been also mentioned because it is based on the way gig workers works are being done, it is not fix hours, it depends on them to whether at their own space and hours so that they can be able to earn comparatively to traditional works done by workers and also there is People as a word based on the analysis, the gig economy is all about People, technology is an enabler connecting clients for a service and gig workers providing the services to clients based on their demand. Additionally, there other words which had been counted too such as benefits, culture, hours, schedule, support and others. All these words are being associated to the main 4 words of the analysis such as work, great, flexible and people.

*Word Tree, it is being defined as the depicts multiple parallel sequences of words which can be able to demonstrate and show words which are often follow or precede a target word, the analysis is considered as a very important one for thematic analysis (Nowell et al, 2017). In this section of the research analysis, there is going to be the elaboration of the main 4 words shown in the analysis of the word count which are work, great, flexible and people.

1ˢᵗ word "Work", the analysis is trying to demonstrate the pattern of words associated to the word from the perspective of gig workers, it is trying to know exactly what drive gig workers to work with online platforms and why they have adopted it. Work is actually the first opinions based on the analysis found because it demonstrates what the gig workers thought about work within the context of the share economy, opinions such as good culture that is needed in terms of work, 100% work from home and work life balance, development in terms of skills and careers, being an independent contractor and the ability to do a side hustle for the purpose of earning extra money.

The associated also demonstrate that there is a need of extra income needed for gig workers in function of their goal orientation which is actually satisfactory in terms of making money and doing the job.

Figure 2. Word Tree of Work

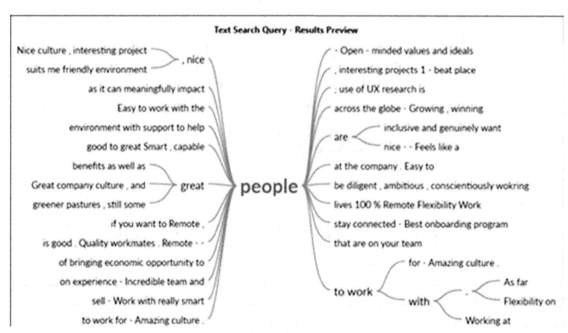

2ⁿᵈ word "Great", discussing about greatness of these platforms is what the gig workers are expressing as the second key word from the analysis of the word cloud. This is due to the benefits that the platforms often brought in terms of pay, onboarding to use the platform, ability to make an extra cash of money with the platform. These are very important aspects which can be leading to the adaptation of the platform. Talking about the greatness of gig economy, it can be a new way forward for a lot of gig workers who do not want the bureaucracy of the traditional employment but work independently even though they are being teleguided by a machine or app but they find it great. Adding more explanation about the word "Great", some gig workers find the share economy platforms easy to use, user friendly and easy to adapt in terms of just registering by putting your information and then be able operate rapidly without a job interview or an exam to get a job.

Gig workers expressed their opinions concerning the greatness of working within an environment of a share-economy such as the benefits it incurred, recognition of achievement via the platform, teamwork, having a very efficient onboarding program for the gig workers, work from home environment with support, and a strong winning culture to help them succeed.

3ʳᵈ word "Flexible", this third word from the analysis very important in terms of expressing the views and opinions of gig workers because it is based on the analysis of word cloud. First, it is known that most gig workers often are looking for flexibility in accordance with several studies done by researchers, when the word cloud identified that flexibility is a key word which shall be analyse of the word tree. Flexibility is associated with so many drivers which are very important and demonstrate the utility of the word, there can be the discussion of time, location, a work which is actually good for students. Gig economy takes into account flexibility because gig workers can work anytime and anywhere in the city where they operating, it is also relaxing as a work, any gig worker can be able to stop working at anytime because they are independent contractors. The freedom of work is the one that had made the gig economy popular among the gig workers because they often think they are they are their own boss even though they are directed by the platform or an artificial intelligence. Additionally, most gig workers think that the work is not so stressful they work with the platforms.

Gig workers have expressed their opinions concerning the flexibility of the work such as having freedom to work, stop working at any time they want. They do express that this type of economic system makes them become their own boss, there is convenience, relaxing time, and be able to work whenever they within the context of making extra money, this means that gig workers can sign in and out at any time.

4ᵗʰ word "People", first and foremost, it is important to know that for any business in the world people are very important specially in the field of technology because if people do not do business transaction, it means that there is no business. This is also the case for the gig economy, even though the platforms are the enablers between the gig workers and the clients, if there is no demand from people the gig workers will not be able to work and earn. Therefore, due to the high demand of clients and gig workers, the popularity of the share economy platforms is undeniable. The word tree demonstrate that there is a great culture, interaction with the platforms in order to connect with people and serve them better. Clients using share economy platforms can create economic opportunity for gig workers, for the gig workers they are also an environment which can be able to support them such as given them tips in terms of food delivery and for online freelancing platform it can be better reviews and recommendations about the work being done. Gig workers do have important opinions about people, the manner they interact with people, the flexibility they do have in their work to serve clients, the benefits they do get while working, all of these are important elements which can be customer experience about their work

Figure 3. Word tree of great

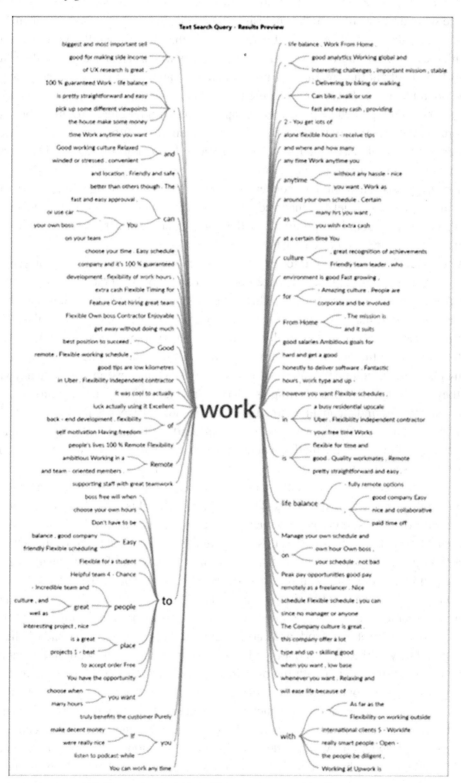

Figure 4. Word tree of flexible

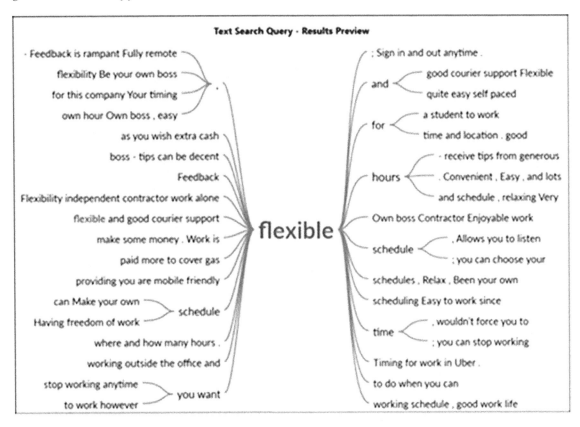

on platforms. From this perspective, it demonstrates that for technology to become an enabler of the gig economy, people are very important in terms of the adoption of it.

*Discussion, from the findings of the thematic analysis based on the analysis of the word cloud and the word tree. It can be said that work is at the heart of the gig economy in terms of connecting the gig workers and the clients. Gig workers often sign up only work or service agreements, not labour contracts, with platform enterprises, their income is based on the piece-rates from which 5% to 30% is deducted in the form of a gig fee (Wei & MacDonald, 2021). The greatness of the application of the app is also an important aspect to consider, first being friendly, easy to use and also easy to subscribe which is the case for online food delivery companies, it is very easy to register as a driver because a gig worker only needs a vehicle or moto bike, a sim card and a smartphone with internet same as the clients in order to be able to connect each other. Nevertheless, for the case of online freelancing it is a bit different because the gig worker needs to have skills and competences that he or she can sell online to potential customers, but it is the same model.

By discussing about flexibility, it is key to the success of gig economy because most gig workers are seeking for flexible hours and be able to stop working at any time and also start working at any time. With the word flexibility, there is no doubt that there are several academic studies which had been associated with the gig economy not only for online food delivery and online freelancing industry but in any kind of industry making it a very promising shift in the way of work and a prospective future which can be considered for the gig economy in the future for all industries (Cheng & Foley, 2018). Lastly,

Figure 5. Word tree of people

there had been the identification of the word "People" from the word cloud trying to understand people is very important, it is key to the social exchange theory which is trying to create the connection between cost-benefit analysis between the gig workers and clients using the share-economy platforms. The study of Priporas et al (2017) for the purpose of investigating the diverse nature of service quality in the share economy is an important study being associated with the theory of social exchange.

In brief, the four main words demonstrate thematically the importance and the reason why the gig economy has been recently adopted in the word and

CONCLUSION

Conclusively, this research study tries to understand the opinions of gig workers from the context of Uber Eats, DoorDash, Upwork and Fiverr leading to comprehend what are the main elements that promote the adoption of online platforms for work among gig workers. Based on a thematic analysis with Nvivo enterprise pro, the findings of the research study identified four main themes this research study can take into consideration. The first theme is work, concerning the way gig workers finds their job and how interesting it is. The second theme is flexible, showing how the flexibility the share economy brings to gig workers, the third theme is great, demonstrating how great the online platforms are in terms of earning extra income and last theme is people because everything turns around people.

Comprehensively, this research study has some limitations which shall be taken into consideration because the study is based on two industries which are online food delivery (OFD) and online freelancing. The data collection of this research study is only for 2022 for the purpose of analysing it as the recent data. Additionally, the focus of the study is only based on the views and perceptions of gig workers in the industries of OFD and online freelancing. Future research studies can be concentrated in this area of gig economy for the purpose of understanding the vies and the opinions of gig workers from other industries because several industries had been disrupted with the share-economy platforms and those platforms now have significant impact on human lives based on the way they interact with their daily services. In brief, the future research scope of this topic is vast because the idea of gig is prosperous and it can be considered as the future of work due to the disruption it is bringing with technology as an enabler and then by seeing the advancement of artificial intelligence and machine learning, there can be a real potential for it in the future.

REFERENCES

Allen, J. (2018). The logistics of parcel delivery: Current operations and challenges facing the UK market. In M. Browne & S. Behrends (Eds.), Urban logistics: Management, policy and innovation in a economy rapidly changing environment (pp. 144–166).

Altinay, L., & Taheri, B. (2019). Emerging themes and theories in the sharing economy: A critical note for hospitality and tourism. *International Journal of Contemporary Hospitality Management*, *31*(2), 180–193. https://doi.org/10.1108/IJCHM-02-2018-0171. doi:10.1108/IJCHM-02-2018-0171

Barratt, T., Goods, C., & Veen, A. (2020) ' I'm my Own Boss…': Active intermediation and 'entrepreneurial' worker agency in the Australian gig-economy. *Environment and Planning A: Economy and Space*, *52*(8), 1643–1661. https://doi.org/10.1177/0308518X20914346

Bates, O., & Friday, A. (2018). Intangible commodities with free delivery [Paper presentation]. Finding the limit in digitally mediated ecommerce and workforce injustice. *Proceedings of the 2018 Workshop on Computing within Limits*. ACM. https://doi.org/10.1145/3232617.3232622

Behl, A., Jayawardena, N., Ishizaka, A., Gupta, M., & Shankar, A. (2022). Gamification and gigification: A multidimensional theoretical approach. *Journal of Business Research*, *139*, 1378–1393. doi:10.1016/j.jbusres.2021.09.023

Belk, R. (2010). Sharing. *The Journal of Consumer Research*, *36*(February), 715–734. doi:10.1086/612649

Böcker, L., & Meelen, T. (2016). 'Sharing for People, Planet or Profit? Analysing Motivations for Intended Sharing Economy Participation.'. *Environmental Innovation and Societal Transitions*, *23*, 28–39. doi:10.1016/j.eist.2016.09.004

Botsman, R. (2015). *Where does loyalty lie in the Collaborative Economy?* Collaborative.

Bulian, L. (2021). THE GIG IS UP: WHO DOES GIG ECONOMY ACTUALLY BENEFIT? *Interdisciplinary Description of Complex Systems*, *19*(1), 106–119. doi:10.7906/indecs.19.1.9

Camilleri, J., & Neuhofer, B. (2017). Value co-creation and co-destruction in the airbnb sharing economy. *International Journal of Contemporary Hospitality Management*, *29*(9), 2322–2340. doi:10.1108/IJCHM-09-2016-0492

Charlton, E. (2021). What is the gig economy and what's the deal for gig workers? World Economic Forum.

Chen, R. (2013). *Member use of social networking sites - An empirical examination*. Decision Consumption. doi:10.1016/j.dss.2012.10.028

Cheng, M., & Foley, C. (2018). The sharing economy and digital discrimination: The case of airbnb. *International Journal of Hospitality Management*, *70*, 95–98. doi:10.1016/j.ijhm.2017.11.002

Christie, N., & Ward, H. (2019). The health and safety risks for people who drive for work in the gig economy. *Journal of Transport & Health*, *13*, 115–127. https://doi.org/10.1016/j.jth.2019.02.007. doi:10.1016/j.jth.2019.02.007

Dablanc, L. (2019). E-commerce trends and implications for urban logistics. In M. Browne, S. Behrends, J. Woxenius, G. Giuliano, & J. Holguin-Veras (Eds.), *Urban logistics. Management, policy, and innovation in a rapidly changing environment* (pp. 167–195).

Dablanc, L. (2017). The rise of on-demand 'instant deliveries' in European cities. *Supply Chain Forum: An International Journal*, *18*(4), 203–217. https://doi.org/10.1080/16258312.2017.1375375

De Stefano, V. (2015). The rise of the 'just-in-time workforce': On-demand work, crowdwork and labour protection in the 'gig economy. *International Labour Office*, *13*(01).

Frenken, K., & Schor, J. (2017). 'Putting the Sharing Economy into Perspective.'. *Environmental Innovation and Societal Transitions*, *23*, 3–10. doi:10.1016/j.eist.2017.01.003

Gogul, K. (2021). A STUDY ON CONSUMER SATISFACTION ON UBER EATS -AN ONLINE FOOD DELIVERY SYSTEM WITH SPECIAL REFERENCE TO KALAPATTI, COIMBATORE. [IJCRT]. *International Journal of Creative Research Thoughts*, *9*(4), 4890–4897.

Goods, C., Veen, A., & Barratt, T. (2019). "Is your gig any good?" Analysing job quality in the Australian platform-based food-delivery sector. *The Journal of Industrial Relations*, *61*(4), 502–527. doi:10.1177/0022185618817069

Green, D., Walker, C., Alabulththim, A., Smith, D., & Phillips, M. (2018). Fueling the Gig Economy: A Case Study Evaluation of Upwork.com. *Management and Economics Research Journal*, *4*, 104–112. doi:10.18639/MERJ.2018.04.523634

Hannák, A. (2017). Bias in online freelance marketplaces: Evidence from taskrabbit and fiverr, *In Proceedings of the 2017 ACM conference on computer supported cooperative work and social computing*, (*vol*. 12, pp. 1914–1933). ACM. 10.1145/2998181.2998327

Hannák, A., Wagner, C., Garcia, D., Mislove, A., Strohmaier, M., & Wilson, C. (2017). Bias in Online Freelance Marketplaces: Evidence from TaskRabbit and Fiverr. *ACM Digital Library*, 1914-1933. doi:10.1145/2998181.2998327

Hassard, J., & Morris, J. (2018). Contrived competition and manufactured uncertainty: Understanding managerial job insecurity narratives in large corporations. *Work, Employment and Society*, *32*(3), 564–580. doi:10.1177/0950017017751806

Kathan, W., Matzler, K., & Veider, V. (2016). 'The Sharing Economy: Your Business Model's Friend or Foe?'. *Business Horizons*, *59*(6), 663–672. doi:10.1016/j.bushor.2016.06.006

Khan, A., & Qureshi, M. (2018). A Systematic Literature Review and Case Study On Influencing Factor And Consequences Of Freelancing In Pakistan. *International Journal of Scientific and Engineering Research*, *9*(12).

Kumar, V., Lahiri, A., & Dogan, O. B. (2018). A strategic framework for a profitable business model in the sharing economy. *Industrial Marketing Management* [Preprint]. doi:10.1016/j.indmarman.2017.08.021

Lord, C. (2022). The sustainability of the gig economy food delivery system (Deliveroo, UberEATS and Just-Eat): Histories and futures of rebound, lock-in and path dependency. *International Journal of Sustainable Transportation*, 15.

Mauri, A. G., Minazzi, R., Nieto-García, M., & Viglia, G. (2018). Humanize your business. the role of personal reputation in the sharing economy. *International Journal of Hospitality Management*, *73*, 36–43. doi:10.1016/j.ijhm.2018.01.017

Neuhofer, B., & Johnson, A.-G. (2017). Airbnb – an exploration of value co-creation experiences in Jamaica. *International Journal of Contemporary Hospitality Management*, *29*(9), 2361–2376. doi:10.1108/IJCHM-08-2016-0482

Nowell, L. S., Norris, J. M., & Moules, N. J. (2017). Thematic Analysis: Striving to Meet the Trustworthiness Criteria. *International Journal of Qualitative Methods*, *2*(1). https://doi.org/10.1177/1609406917733847. doi:10.1177/1609406917733847

Nowell, L. S., Norris, J. M., & Moules, N. J. (2017). Thematic Analysis: Striving to Meet the Trustworthiness Criteria. *International Journal of Qualitative Methods*, *34*(2). https://doi.org/10.1177/1609406917733847. doi:10.1177/1609406917733847

Oyer, P. (2020). Non-traditional employment is a great opportunity for many, but it won't replace traditional employment. Stanford University Graduate School of Business. doi:10.15185/izawol.471

Priporas, C.V. (2017). Unraveling the diverse nature of service quality in a sharing economy: a social exchange theory perspective of airbnb accommodation. *Emerald Insight, 29*(9), 2279–2301.

Raj, M., Sundararajan, A., & You, C. (2021). *COVID-19 and Digital Resilience: Evidence from Uber Eats*. The Social Science Research Network. doi:10.2139/ssrn.3625638

Ramesh, R., Prabhu, S., Sasikumar, B., Devi, B., Prasath, P., & Kamala, S. (2021). An empirical study of online food delivery services from applications perspective. *Materials Today: Proceedings, 12*. doi:10.1016/j.matpr.2021.05.500

Schmuck, R. (2015). *Online üzleti modellek.* [Doctoral Thesis, University of Pécs, Pécs].

Shankar, A., Charles, J., Preeti, N., Haroon Iqbal, M., Aman, K., & Achchuthan, S. (2022). Online food delivery: A systematic synthesis of literature and a framework development. *International Journal of Hospitality Management, 104*(103240), 103240. Advance online publication. doi:10.1016/j.ijhm.2022.103240

Theory Hub. (2022). Social Exchange Theory: A review (2nd ed., Ser. 1). In S. Papagiannidis (Ed), *Theory Hub Book.* TheoryHub. http://open.ncl.ac.uk

Stephany, F. (2019). Online Labour Index 2020: New ways to measure the world's remote freelancing market. *Online labour observatory.* https://doi.org/www.onlinelabourobservatory.org

Sutherland, W. (2019). Work Precarity and Gig Literacies in Online Freelancing. *SAGE Journals, 34*(3). https://doi.org/10.1177/0950017019886511

Wang, Q. X., & Wang, Q. (2018). The labor relationship identification and rights protection of my country's 'online hire workers,'. *Law Science, 4*, 57–72.

Wei, W., & MacDonald, I. T. (2021). Modeling the job quality of 'work relationships' in China's gig economy. *Asia Pacific Journal of Human Resources, 5*. https://doi.org/doi:10.1111/1744-7941.12310

Wood, A. (2019). The Taylor Review: Understanding the gig economy, dependency and the complexities of control. *New Technology, Work and Employment, 34*(2), 111–115. doi:10.1111/ntwe.12131

Zhang, T. C., Jahromi, M. F., & Kizilldag, M. (2018). Value co-creation in a sharing economy: The end of price wars? *International Journal of Hospitality Management, 71*, 51–58. doi:10.1016/j.ijhm.2017.11.010

Zhu, G., So, K. K. F., & Hudson, S. (2017). Inside the sharing economy: Understanding consumer motivations behind the adoption of mobile applications. *International Journal of Contemporary Hospitality Management, 29*(9), 2218–2239. doi:10.1108/IJCHM-09-2016-0496

Chapter 5
Digital Natives and Multi-Level-Marketing (MLM):
A Perspective

Siew Keong Lee
Return Legacy Sdn Bhd, Malaysia

Sam Yee Kho
Return Legacy Sdn Bhd, Malaysia

ABSTRACT

This chapter provides perspective on the potential for digital natives in the multi-level-marketing (MLM) industry. The chapter commences with an explanation of digital natives and the MLM industry. Thereafter, distinguishing factors for digital natives as customers, as well as opting for a career, are debated. The chapter then discusses digital natives the in MLM industry by considering their unique personality traits prior to providing perspective on recruiting digital natives in MLM, training and engaging digital natives in MLM, and MLM business transformation for Generation Z. Lastly, the chapter proposes attributes for transformed MLM considering above aspects related to digital natives.

INTRODUCTION

Each generation is defined by unique, collective experiences. Researchers and marketers' study generational attitudes and behaviors to understand and anticipate each generation's impact. The multi-level marketing (MLM) industry is no different. Through the years, generational perspectives have shaped the evolution of MLM companies and the products and services they deliver. Baby Boomers (born 1946 – 1964) grew up in an era where Tupperware parties and visits from the "Avon lady" were the norm. Gen X (born 1965 – 1980), sometimes called the latchkey generation, was greatly influenced by the increasing number of two-income households with both parents working full-time (Bennett, 2012; Evans & Robertson, 2020). Gen X's "do it yourself" attitude found the entrepreneurial aspects of MLM companies appealing, and party plan-focused direct selling blossomed. The Millennials (born 1981 –

DOI: 10.4018/978-1-6684-6782-4.ch005

1996) came next, and alongside them, the Internet. Millennials are used to adapting to rapidly evolving technology and appreciate the convenience of interacting with MLM companies via E-commerce and mobile communication. Today, Gen Z (born 1997 – 2012) is poised to impact the MLM industry. Even with most of its members still in their teenage years, Gen Z makes up 40 per cent of the global consumer population. As more Gen Z-ers come of age in the years ahead, now is the ideal time to get to know them – and identify ways to shift strategies and marketing messages to align with these already powerful consumers. The cascading social and economic impacts of the COVID-19 pandemic are still evolving, but it's safe to say the working world will be forever changed. When factoring in the generational attitudes of the Millennials and Gen Z-ers who now make up 59 per cent of the global workforce, the change is likely to be transformational. Why is this good news for the Multi-Level Marketing (MLM) industry?

Digital native is a term coined by Prensky (2001) to describe the generation of people who grew up in the era of ubiquitous technology, including computers and the internet. Digital natives are comfortable with technology and computers at an early age and consider technology to be an integral and necessary part of their lives (Bennett & Maton, 2013). Many teenagers and children in developed countries are digital natives, mainly communicating and learning via computers, social networking services, and texting (Wong et al., 2022). Most millennials cannot remember a time before the internet, smartphones, and social media. They are the first digital natives, growing up fluent in technology, constantly connected to an ever-shrinking world, and with instant access to more information than any previous generation (Smith, 2019; Munsch, 2021). Digital natives, born during a time of technological boom and economic doom, Generation Z is fast on technology and hard on savings. They grew up as tech-savvy individuals who used more advanced on-the-go technology in their early life than their predecessors. On the other side, growing up, when the recession hit their families hard, they were more determined to plan their finances. Today, millennials and their younger counterparts, Gen Z, live lifestyles that revolve around their affinity for connectivity, cross-border social circles, and technological skills that have revolutionised how we act, communicate, and work (Lim et al., 2021; Koutropoulos, 2011).

Multi-Level Marketing (MLM) is a marketing strategy where the company's revenue stream is generated by external non-salaried workforces and not by its own internal sales team. Its origin is often disputed; some stated that this marketing idea existed since the 1920s and 1930s (Lee & Dastane, 2019). Instead of retailers purchasing products from manufacturers to mark up and sell to end consumers, MLM representatives, or distributors, sell goods directly to consumers outside traditional stores. MLM distributors allow them to choose their hours of work; they typically choose to exert only part-time effort, tailoring their MLM work hours to dovetail with family and other responsibilities. Many MLM distributors work either part-time or full-time for another employer in addition to their MLM business (Direct Selling Association, 2015). This stands in contrast to traditional salespeople, who generally pursue their job full-time and have less flexibility in structuring their activities.

MLM distributors are often taught the basics of salesmanship, including the importance of reaching out to one's personal network of possible consumers or new downlines. The distributor is thus a conduit to end-users whom the MLM firm would have a much harder time individually targeting. However, there is no requirement that an enrolling distributor agrees to do all of these functions, given the distributors' status as independent contractors. As such, each can choose how hard they work, when they work, what products they personally consume, whether they work on retail selling of products (and which ones in the firm's product line); and whether they work on recruiting and mentoring downlines or not. Some distributors can choose only to personally consume the firm's products at a wholesale price rather than at a marked-up retail price. Some may personally consume and exert sales effort to achieve retail sales to non-distributor consumers. Yet others may try to recruit and mentor downline distributors in addition to retail selling and personal consumption. Regardless of their choices, each distributor pays an annual registration fee to maintain his/her distributorship.

Both retail selling and the development of downline distributors require time, effort, and skill. Just as in any sales force context, here too, a distributor will not be willing to exert this effort without some compensation. Thus, the MLM firm must design and administer a compensation plan that can apply equally to everyone who registers as a distributor – yet can properly reward the different ways in which different distributors take advantage of the MLM business opportunity. Entry into an MLM distributorship and exit from it is very easy, particularly compared to non-MLM sales positions. Any person over 18 years old is typically allowed to pay a typically modest (and generally refundable) registration fee to join as a distributor of an MLM firm. The registration fee entitles the distributor to sell the firm's products, earn money under the firm's compensation plan, use the company's training and educational materials, benefit from the advice and mentorship of his/her upline sponsor, engage in retail selling, and to seek to recruit and mentor downline distributors for a one-year period. Each year the distributor must renew his/her distributorship via the payment of a renewal fee.

DIGITAL NATIVES AS CUSTOMERS

Like the Millennials before them, Gen Z grew up with rapidly developing technologies. But Gen Z-ers are true digital natives who can't remember a world without smartphones, the Internet, and Wi-Fi. The stereotype perception of Gen Z is that kids are glued to their phones and overly dependent on technology. (And yes, Gen Z-ers average five-plus hours per day on their phones, which serve as a primary communication hub.) However, beneath the surface, this generation is a highly connected generation that's plugged into what's happening in their communities and around the world. As a result, their consumer behaviors are unique (Kesharwani, 2020).

Omnichannel All the Time

Gen Z seamlessly blends technology into everything they do, and shopping is no different. Gen Z-ers not only expect to choose from online and in-person shopping options but also expect the different channel experiences to be well-integrated (Wong et al., 2022; San & Dastane, 2021). For MLM companies, this means delivering E-commerce shopping that's focused on ease from browsing through buying. MLM software that facilitates searches with categories and size, style, and colour filters is a must. Beyond optimizing Ecommerce search capabilities, the best MLM software solutions also offer the ability to tag products to highlight bestsellers, low-stock quantities, or sale items. At the same time, Gen Z values connecting with others who share their interests in brands and products, so relationship-building between MLM representatives and their communities – both online and in-person – has never been more important. Look for MLM software and technology tools that make connecting through social media, text, and email easy for reps.

Personalization is a Priority

Because of their comfort levels with technology, Gen Z-ers understand how data can tailor marketing and shopping experiences. As a result, they're more willing than previous generations to share personal data that will drive the customized consumer interactions they expect (Dastane, Goi & Rabbanee, 2023). Forty-four percent of Gen Z say they're willing to share personal information in exchange for a more personalized experience – and 75 percent are more willing to purchase a product if it's personalized for them. MLM companies, with their unique mix of personalized relationships and technology, are a good fit for Gen Z customers. Tap into MLM software functionality that propels personalization, such as real-time alerts sent to reps for new customer purchases, customer anniversaries, or loyalty program achievements. In addition, MLM software can help companies optimize customer data points to design targeted promotional offers and make personalized "you might also like" recommendations as customers engage online.

Purchases Are Driven by More Than Price

Gen Z grew up during the Great Recession, and many saw their parents navigate debt and financial challenges. So, it's not surprising that Gen Z-ers seek out information before making purchase decisions. But the research-based approach to buying isn't solely focused on price. While Gen Z appreciates a good deal, they also focus on quality and getting value for what they decide to spend their money on (Sing, Dastane & Haba, 2021). And, compared to other generational groups, Gen Z-ers place a higher value on service and convenience. In fact, research conducted by IBM found that product choice, availability, convenience, and value are the top drivers behind Gen Z shopping decisions. To win over Gen Z customers, MLM companies can feed their information with detailed product descriptions that emphasize quality and value. Along with written materials, deliver information through videos, both on the web and through social media. Eighty-five per cent of Gen Z search for information and content on YouTube (Lim et al., 2021).

On top of seeking information themselves, Gen Z-ers also appreciate third-party endorsements, such as customer reviews and real-life customer stories. As a first step, make customer reviews easily accessible throughout your E-commerce experience. The best MLM software makes capturing reviews simple and will enable your corporate team to review them before posting. From there, make social sharing easy for customers by inviting them to post about their experiences with your brand and products on social media. Many MLM companies provide customer incentives and rewards to help fuel social posts and post-driven sales.

Digital Natives and Brands

One thing that makes it difficult to cater to this generation is that they are pragmatic and less tolerant toward diverse points of view. They only believe in a practical and holistic approach. A recent study by McKinsey cites that the relationship of Gen Zers with brands is much different from how it was with the earlier generations. It suggests three suggestions for brands to build long-term customer relationships with Gen Z (Bhalla, Tiwari & Chowdhary, 2021). First, "Consumption as access rather than possession" - Members of this generation value products as a service rather than something to own. A brand that delivers a great service is sure to stay in their good books, and they would as well take it to their social circles. They are not interested in exploiting relationships but would rather share the experience to enhance them; they would even consider working for brands they love to extend their relationship. Second, "Consumption as an expression of individual identity" - This case rests both on millennials and Generation Z alike. They like to flaunt the brand as a matter of personal identity i.e., they love brands that complement their individuality. They appreciate brands that give them personalized offerings. Third, "Consumption as a matter of ethical concern" - Generation Z is bound to maintain high ethical standards in everything they do—both in their personal and professional lives. They expect and support brands that also complement their ethical identity.

Health and Well-Being Are Top-of-Mind

Their Gen X parents instilled the importance of eating healthy and exercising regularly. Gen Z-ers take managing their health to the next level through a holistic approach to well-being that encompasses physical, mental, and emotional wellness (Haba, Bredillet, & Dastane, 2023; Dastane & Haba, 2023; Dastane et al., 2023). Gen Z is receptive to all-natural, sustainable, and vitamin-fortified foods. They're also more likely to try natural remedies to supplement traditional healthcare. In addition, they place a premium on mental health, with three in four open to talking about their mental well-being. As a result, Gen Z-ers prioritize self-care by emphasizing work-life balance, actively managing stress and anxiety levels, and tracking steps, heart rates, and sleep. The focus on holistic wellness translates into a desire for products and services that line up with their quest for well-being. MLM companies are not only well-positioned to meet these needs for Gen Z consumers, but they're also able to combine them with Gen Z's desire for convenience and ease. For example, MLM companies are making it easy for customers always to have the products they need on hand with convenient auto-ship functionality that enables buyers to place customized recurring orders. Then, the company's MLM software automates the process by handling the shipping, collecting payments, and communicating with the customer.

Social Responsibility is a Plus

As the most racially and ethnically diverse generation in US history, 56 per cent of Gen Z-ers see themselves as socially conscious, which factors into the brands and products they choose (Buschow, 2020). Most – nearly seven in ten – expect brands to make a positive contribution to society, and six in ten say they're willing to pay more for products produced in ethical and sustainable ways. At the same time, Gen Z is sceptical by nature and has a low tolerance for companies adopting values solely for marketing purposes. To connect with Generation Z, showcase your company's values and how your products and services help to make the world better. When it makes sense, align your MLM brand with relevant social causes and share information and insights about how your company contributes and why the issue is important. Most of all, throughout all of your messaging, strive for a genuine, authentic tone that will resonate with Gen Z.

Just like the generations before them, Gen Z is set to change the consumer landscape. The marketing strategies of the past won't necessarily work with this diverse and plugged-in generation. Instead, stay ahead of the evolving trends by getting to know what's unique about Gen Z customers and optimizing your business strategies to align. Plus, there's another generation on the horizon behind Gen Z – Generation Alpha – who have been immersed in technology since birth and are projected to have the most transformative consumer impact yet. However, the oldest of these potential customers are just turning ten years old, so the next few years will still be all about winning over Gen Z!

DIGITAL NATIVES AND CAREER

For the first digital natives, the way they interact and perceive the world is vastly different compared to previous generations – this is especially so in the workplace, where millennials do not see their jobs as something they do for a pay check. Compared to previous generations, millennials do not expect to hold a stable job over their lifetime: they look for what feels worthwhile and can complement their values and lifestyle choices. This diminishing interest in career stability in favour of personal development and work flexibility has led to the boom of many independent start-ups within the gig economy. Unlike their generational predecessors, Millennials (born 1981 – 1996) and Gen Z (born 1997 – 2009) see their careers as a series of different jobs across a wide range of roles and stages of their lives. They expect to work in some capacity well past retirement age. But they want to do it on their terms (Dingli & Seychell, 2015).

Flexibility and freedom are essential. Their lifelong exposure to technology makes them experts at working wherever and whenever (Prensky, 2010). This doesn't mean that Millennials and Gen Z-ers are lazy. It's the opposite. While they're committed to achieving a healthy work-life balance, they're also highly productive and autonomous. In fact, Gen Z is especially independent. Having grown up with information instantly accessible via Google, they're confident in their abilities to figure things out and get work done. Younger generations sometimes get a bad rap for being job hoppers, but it's why they change jobs that's telling. For Millennials and Gen Z-ers, experience is most important. They want their work to challenge and excite them. They seek a sense of purpose in what they do, and they want to feel like they are making progress toward their goals. When they are not, they don't hesitate to explore other options. Younger generations are also much more likely to have a side hustle or two. Fifty per cent of Millennials have a side gig to supplement their earnings. Beyond earning additional money, gig work is usually tied to a strong sense of passion and purpose. However, Millennials and Gen Z are not the same (Bennett, Maton, & Kervin, 2008). As more Gen Z-ers enter the workforce, research shows that, as a generation, they are more risk-averse regarding their career decisions. Growing up during the Great Recession, many saw their parents struggle financially and professionally. As a result, 69 per cent of Gen Z-ers say having a stable job outranks one they're passionate about. The economic impacts of the COVID-19 pandemic will only reinforce this perspective.

DIGITAL NATIVES IN MLM

The MLM industry, which is perhaps the oldest type of gig business that relies on a distributed workforce, has reinvented itself for the modern world with rapid digitalisation, social media marketing, and interesting products that appeal to the conscious consumer. It is not surprising that the MLM industry has seen a major influx of millennials over the last few years who look to this business as the perfect side hustle that complements their lifestyle. MLM can act as a supplementary source of income for those who are pursuing their passion, or even a full-time career for the entrepreneurial-minded, depending on what the person is looking for.

In MLM, many millennials find this business model appealing because of the easy entry and low start-up cost, they do not have to be tied to a location, they have control over how they want to market the products, especially through social media, and they can work flexible hours. Multi-Level Marketing companies' flexibility, autonomy, and money-making elements align perfectly with what Millennials and Gen Z want from a job. A recent survey by the Direct Selling Association found that 92 per cent of

Gen Z-ers are interested in finding flexible ways to make money, with the low start-up costs and flexibility offered by MLM opportunities particularly appealing. In addition, MLM leverages millennials' social media, technological prowess, strong connection to the community, and powerful sense of social responsibility to generate a sustainable source of income outside of less flexible, traditional career paths. The social networks of previous generations were limited by geography, typically the people they could meet in person, such as family, friends, neighbours, and workplace colleagues.

The first generation of digital natives has built vast online networks that transcend geographic boundaries. According to Goldman Sachs' research, millennials top the chart of highest social media, text messaging, and instant messaging use. Through MLM, millennial entrepreneurs can leverage their natural ability to build and connect with online communities to develop a successful business and earn an income. Studies show that 62% of millennials are likelier to become loyal customers if a business engages them on social media. While millennials grew up in a technological golden age, they have faced more significant financial challenges than previous generations. Stagnant wages, increased debt, higher living expenses, and multiple global financial crises have conspired to cause many millennials to fall short of the economic achievements attained by their parent generation.

Today's job market is also vastly different: intense competition caused by rapid globalisation and the rise of remote work opportunities has led to millennials seeking non-traditional careers to earn a living wage. Though many millennials aspire to become entrepreneurs, the investments and risks associated with starting a business can be daunting for a generation that has struggled financially. However, according to the Direct Selling Association, start-up costs are a few hundred dollars or less for most direct-selling companies. It involves little or no overhead expenses such as retail space, warehousing, or shipping. This gives millennial entrepreneurs an easy, low-cost way to launch their own businesses. Surveys show that millennials view entrepreneurship as a job and a lifestyle that enables them to turn a passion such as art, personal health, or fashion into an income-generating business. They also value a healthy work-life balance and seek flexible schedules that allow time to explore various interests such as travel or volunteering.

Distributors for MLM companies set their own schedules. They are free to devote as much or as little time to their MLM business as they want or need. It can be a full-time job or a part-time that provides supplemental income. Still, the inherent flexibility of direct selling allows the entrepreneur to develop the work-life balance they desire. Millennials are skilled at adapting technology to facilitate their lifestyles. To this end, mobile apps are a powerful tool for millennial entrepreneurs who want the freedom to run their businesses from anywhere at any time, making MLM an even more flexible option. As with any entrepreneurial endeavour, achieving success in direct selling requires commitment and hard work. But many millennials find the reward for their efforts in being their own boss and having the freedom to pursue passions and interests.

In their childhood, technology connected millennials with the world around them and gave them an acute awareness of how their actions impact others. They apply that awareness to their lives as workers and consumers. 80% of millennials are loyal to companies that demonstrate social responsibility. Because entrepreneurs are members of the communities in which they operate, the social structure of MLM naturally fosters a keen sense of social responsibility. Many MLM companies have long histories of giving back to the community, upholding sustainable and responsible business practices and sustainable development goals, and promoting health, hygiene, and gender equality for youth in the community in line with the United Nations Sustainable Development Goals.

Many MLM companies also promote sustainability by banning all single-use plastics in their offices and events and implementing a meat-free policy to reduce greenhouse gases. The millennial generation is looking for businesses to lead the way and create positive change in their communities, who recognise social responsibility, and economic and environmental sustainability. In addition, millennial distributors advocate for projects that positively impact the lives of the communities in which they operate and the environment, especially during the COVID-19 pandemic. Sustainability programmes by MLM companies work to further empower millennial entrepreneurs to collectively mobilise their connections, skills, passions, and businesses to create positive, sustainable change in their communities. MLM companies are well-positioned to feed the entrepreneurial mindsets of Millennials, and Gen Z. MLM distributors control their destinies, with advancement and earnings directly tied to hard work. More importantly, the ability to pursue entrepreneurial goals within the structure of an established company holds appeal. The training, platforms, and tools offered by MLM companies reduce personal risk while still providing ongoing challenges and opportunities for continued growth.

Digital Natives Personality Traits

Acquiring and retaining the digital native's generation as distributors or as customers, for that matter, needs deep research and understanding of the crowd, their ideas, perspectives, and perceptions, and most importantly, how they value brands.

Six core personality traits of digital natives must consider before building digital natives' distributor base:

1. They value individuality and freedom of expression.
2. They do not want to define themselves as a single stereotype.
3. They contribute much toward social causes.
4. Believes in the potential of dialogues to resolve conflicts.
5. Makes decisions based on research, analysis, and understanding of the matter in question.
6. Selfless when compared to the millennial generation.

Each of these together makes up their character whole, and each has an important role to play while recruiting, training, and engaging these astute personalities as MLM distributors.

Recruiting Digital Natives in MLM

Digital natives love flexibility and freedom to work at their own pace and ideas. MLM's potential to deliver this will become an obvious choice, but only if presented in the way they want.

Digital natives, especially Gen Z is the most ethnically and racially diverse generation. They love working with different generations and ethnicities. Hence while considering the work environment, they will consider companies that rank high on diversity and inclusion. Also, they are not the "go for the brand" type; they only recommend brands that deliver quality and value. Fake promises and pompous advertisements will never appeal to them. They consider the quality of the products and value that a brand delivers, an important factor when choosing to enrol with a brand. While recruiting Gen Z, keeping the distributor enrolment process quick and easy is important, including a brand intro and getting them acquainted with the brand values.

Training and Engaging Digital Natives in MLM

These already tech-savvy individuals would not need much technical support to thrive. It would be much easier to launch new tools or technology with Gen Zers. Yet getting them on track would be a topic to look into. Primarily, MLM companies must upgrade their business in all three realms: social, digital, and mobile. Ease of access and staying updated appeal most to Gen Z. Added to this; companies must note that Gen Z is keen on developing their skills, an added advantage to MLM, which gives its workforce overall skill development, both personally and professionally. Revamping the distributor training modules with interactive and gamified training modules will keep the generation with the company for long.

Gen Z is more comfortable working in teams and look forward to mentors for emotional and professional support. So, creating support communities can help engage distributors and improve their confidence. Gen Z will soon overtake millennials as distributors and consumers, achieving dominance in purchasing power. Launching innovative and quality products more often with sustainable business practices can make the brand appeal more to this younger generation.

In its recent survey, Direct Selling Association included one question aimed at analysing the perspectives of its direct-selling member companies on Gen Z as their primary audience. This amassed diverse responses from the participating companies 43% consider digital, mobile, and social channels to attract Gen Zers the most, and 14% believe keeping things simple, easy or quick is the best approach. Another 14% do not consider Gen Z as their primary audience. 10% each had the following reasons that they think appeal to Gen Z: reasonable costs or pricing, personalized service or building trustful relationships, new or quality products, remote or flexible work opportunities and a brand that has a definite purpose or works for a cause.

MLM Business Transformation for Generation Z

Gen Z are a pragmatic group of individuals who are keen on analysing things before making decisions. Convincing them is a herculean task for companies to work on. The MLM companies are needed to establish transparency and flexibility across the business processes, brands to go all mobile, create reliable communication channels and foster the exchange of ideas, showing them outcomes such as progress and promotions. Generation Z is undoubtedly going to be the future of MLM. They are sure to conquer the market with their fresher ideas and diverse expertise. However, creating multi-generational teams is necessary to create a diversified line of thought, and with this diversity comes expertise and the exchange of fresher outlooks. Leveraging the experience of the older generations to the younger one's advantage will be also crucial to their development. Developing these insights will prove the course of success for MLM companies in the future. Despite the quality of products or services, they look out for brands that have a unique value proposition that also impacts the lives of people around them. In short, Gen Zers do not consider the brand as a trend to flaunt but as something that reflects their identity. Brands that capture the Gen Z will surely see a transformation in their businesses in the coming years.

THEORITICAL CONTRIBUTION

As we have presented a perspective based on industry insights and managerial experience, we offer limited but clear and precise academic contribution. This perspective in the form of chapter can guide academicians and researchers to gain insights into various facets of digital natives and their readiness and traits related to MLM marketing. This enhanced understanding can be useful for developing academic programs, training programs as well as setting up specific research objectives in this domain. Although, there is a rising research in the context of digital natives, perspective papers based on industry expertise are sparse and our chapter fill-up this gap. We have clearly specified differentiating factors which makes digital natives stand distinct than millennials in the context of MLM industry. These aspects can be tested empirically by academic researchers and further investigation may result in confirmatory findings which can further enrich the field of digital natives.

REFERENCES

Bennett, S. (2012). Digital natives. In *Encyclopedia of cyber behavior* (pp. 212–219). IGI Global. doi:10.4018/978-1-4666-0315-8.ch018

Bennett, S., & Maton, K. (2010). Beyond the 'digital natives' debate: Towards a more nuanced understanding of students' technology experiences. *Journal of Computer Assisted Learning*, *26*(5), 321–331. doi:10.1111/j.1365-2729.2010.00360.x

Bennett, S., Maton, K., & Kervin, L. (2008). The 'digital natives' debate: A critical review of the evidence. *British Journal of Educational Technology*, *39*(5), 775–786. doi:10.1111/j.1467-8535.2007.00793.x

Bhalla, R., Tiwari, P., & Chowdhary, N. (2021). Digital natives leading the world: paragons and values of Generation Z. In *Generation Z Marketing and Management in Tourism and Hospitality: The Future of the Industry* (pp. 3–23). Springer International Publishing. doi:10.1007/978-3-030-70695-1_1

Buschow, C. (2020). Why do digital native news media fail? An investigation of failure in the early start-up phase. *Media and Communication*, *8*(2), 51–61. doi:10.17645/mac.v8i2.2677

Dastane, O., Fandos-Roig, J. C., & Sánchez-García, J. (2023). It's free! Still, would I learn? Unearthing perceived value of education apps for better entrepreneurial decisions. Management Decision. doi:10.1108/MD-09-2022-1292

Dastane, O., Goi, C. L., & Rabbanee, F. (2023). The development and validation of a scale to measure perceived value of mobile commerce (MVAL-SCALE). *Journal of Retailing and Consumer Services*, *71*, 103222. doi:10.1016/j.jretconser.2022.103222

Dastane, O., & Haba, H. F. (2023). What drives mobile MOOC's continuous intention? A theory of perceived value perspective. *International Journal of Information and Learning Technology*, *40*(2), 148–163. doi:10.1108/IJILT-04-2022-0087

Dingli, A., & Seychell, D. (2015). *The new digital natives*. JB Metzler. doi:10.1007/978-3-662-46590-5

Evans, C., & Robertson, W. (2020). The four phases of the digital natives debate. *Human Behavior and Emerging Technologies*, *2*(3), 269–277. doi:10.1002/hbe2.196

Haba, H. F., Bredillet, C., & Dastane, O. (2023). Green consumer research: Trends and way forward based on bibliometric analysis. *Cleaner and Responsible Consumption*, 100089.

Haba, H. F., & Dastane, D. O. (2019). Massive open online courses (MOOCs)–understanding online learners' preferences and experiences. *International Journal of Learning. Teaching and Educational Research*, *18*(8), 227–242.

Kesharwani, A. (2020). Do (how) digital natives adopt a new technology differently than digital immigrants? A longitudinal study. *Information & Management*, *57*(2), 103170. doi:10.1016/j.im.2019.103170

Koutropoulos, A. (2011). Digital natives: Ten years after. *Journal of Online Learning and Teaching*, *7*(4), 525–538.

Lee, S. K., & Dastane, O. (2019). Building a sustainable competitive advantage for Multi-Level Marketing (MLM) firms: An empirical investigation of contributing factors. *Journal of Distribution Science*, *17*(3), 5–19. doi:10.15722/jds.17.3.201903.5

Lim, W. M., Gupta, S., Aggarwal, A., Paul, J., & Sadhna, P. (2021). How do digital natives perceive and react toward online advertising? Implications for SMEs. *Journal of Strategic Marketing*, 1–35. doi:10.1080/0965254X.2021.1941204

Munsch, A. (2021). Millennial and generation Z digital marketing communication and advertising effectiveness: A qualitative exploration. *Journal of Global Scholars of Marketing Science*, *31*(1), 10–29. doi:10.1080/21639159.2020.1808812

Prensky, M. R. (2010). *Teaching digital natives: Partnering for real learning*. Corwin press.

San, S. S., & Dastane, O. (2021). Key Factors Affecting Intention to Order Online Food Delivery (OFD). *Journal of Industrial Distribution & Business*, *12*(2), 19–27.

Singh, I. J. S. S., Dastane, O., & Haba, H. F. (2022). A Fresh Look on Determinants of Online Repurchase Intention. In *Handbook of Research on Digital Transformation Management and Tools* (pp. 87–116). IGI Global. doi:10.4018/978-1-7998-9764-4.ch005

Smith, K. T. (2019). Mobile advertising to Digital Natives: Preferences on content, style, personalization, and functionality. *Journal of Strategic Marketing*, *27*(1), 67–80. doi:10.1080/0965254X.2017.1384043

Wong, L. W., Tan, G. W. H., Hew, J. J., Ooi, K. B., & Leong, L. Y. (2022). Mobile social media marketing: A new marketing channel among digital natives in higher education? *Journal of Marketing for Higher Education*, *32*(1), 113–137. doi:10.1080/08841241.2020.1834486

ADDITIONAL READING

Dastane, O., & Haba, H. F. (2023). The landscape of digital natives research: a bibliometric and science mapping analysis. *FIIB Business Review*.

Chapter 6
The Influence of Social Media on Gen Alpha's Purchasing Decisions

Hafizah Omar Zaki
Universiti Kebangsaan Malaysia, Malaysia

Nurul Atasha Jamaludin
Universiti Kebangsaan Malaysia, Malaysia

Aziatul Waznah Ghazali
Universiti Kebangsaan Malaysia, Malaysia

ABSTRACT

The main purpose of this chapter is to look at how marketing communications through interactive social media will affect the buying decisions of Gen Alpha. In the end, they want brands and everything they do on social media to give them answers and show that they care more than ever. Young people have been able to meet up with their friends through social media. The fact that young people use technology every day also makes them more likely to use social media to buy things. People who were born in the 21st century and grew up with technology make up Gen Alpha. Young people who know how to use technology well are now called "Gen Alpha." This means that Gen Alpha will be the generation that knows the most about technology. Gen Alpha is the most diverse generation ever, so they care about businesses that are open to everyone. They will keep changing the environment and culture of the whole world. Gen Alphas are likely to keep buying things online or through any other technology-based platform based on how much they are worth.

INTRODUCTION

Social media has been one of the platforms for social events among the younger generation. It has not just encouraged networking but also fortified buying and selling activities. The use of social media to

DOI: 10.4018/978-1-6684-6782-4.ch006

make purchases is also driven by the youngsters' involvement with technology in their daily activities. A new term called the "Gen Alpha" is thus referred to these technology-savvy youngsters. Gen Alpha is made up of people who were born in the 21st century and are surrounded by technology (Razan Saleh, 2022). They are the children of Millennials, and the younger siblings of Generation Z. Gen Alphas will spend more time in front of screens than any other generation, and they will start doing so at very young ages. This means that Gen Alpha will be the most tech-savvy generation ever. With this, they are open to messages about them and making them feel something. Even though they are used to robots and virtual things, they will enjoy a relationship even more if it is personalised and considers what they want and need (Thomas & Shivani, 2020). Eventually, they want brands and every social media pursuit to give them solutions and show they care more than ever.

Gen Alphas will likely continue to buy things online or through any other technology-based platform based on their worth. This means that businesses need to think about both production and marketing to make a supply chain that is honest and fair. Gen Alpha is more diverse than any other generation, so they care about businesses that welcome everyone (The Annie E. Casey Foundation, 2022). If you ignore this generation, you miss the future. They will continue to affect the culture and environment of the whole world. This chapter shows how interactive social media marketing communications affect Gen Alpha's purchasing decisions.

TECHNOLOGY AND THE GEN ALPHA

People who work in an industry that utilises technology need to do everything they can to grow their digital footprint to meet the needs of modern workers and consumers both now and in the future (Chitra, 2020). As the parents of Gen Alpha, Millennials already search, shop, and pay for their travel accommodations and experiences online. This trend will only grow as tech-savvy Alphas become economically active. From online payment engaged by the Millennials, social media platforms have become the primary influence for purchasing activities among Gen Alpha. Generation Alpha has a high level of acceptance of technology because it has been a constant in their lives since they were young children, this has made it easier for them to engage in purchasing activities via a social media platform (Razan Saleh, 2022).

Critical Aspects of Generation Alpha's Adoption of Technology

- Generation Alpha is well-versed in technology, having grown up with gadgets like smartphones and tablets. They feel at ease using technology as a result, and they quickly accept new tools and platforms.
- Generation Alpha uses technology for a range of activities, such as entertainment, communication, and education, and it is fully incorporated into their daily life.
- Generation Alpha is heavily reliant on technology, and many of them see it as a necessary tool for their everyday life. They frequently feel lost without it since they use technology for so many different things.
- Generation Alpha is at ease with cutting-edge technology and is willing to explore and test out new tools, systems, and software. They frequently want to test out the newest technology and software, and they will probably be responsible for future technological improvements.

These youngsters have a high level of technology acceptability and will probably continue to be the engine behind its expansion and advancement in the years to come. Since technology is a big part of their daily life, they are the first generation to have grown up wholly in the digital era.

Generation Alpha Users of Technology

- Mobile devices: Generation Alpha mostly uses smartphones and tablets to access the internet, play games, and interact with others.
- Social media: Generation Alpha connects with friends, shares content, and keeps up with current events through social media sites like Instagram, TikTok, and Snapchat.
- Online learning: As online learning becomes more popular, many Gen Alpha kids are using technology to obtain educational materials, take online classes, and finish their homework.
- Streaming services: Generation Alpha likes to use sites like Netflix, YouTube, and Spotify to stream movies, TV shows, and music.
- Gaming: Generation Alpha enjoys playing video games on their consoles, laptops, and mobile devices.

In general, technology has had a significant impact on how Generation Alpha communicates, learns, and lives. They are quite skilled at using technology, and they will probably continue to drive progress in this area, especially in using the social media in buying and selling activities.

SOCIAL MEDIA AS BUYING AND SELLING PLATFORM

The emergence of social media as a buying platform has significantly disrupted traditional purchasing models and created new business opportunities. Social media can provide companies with a platform to develop relationships with customers, products and services and drive sales (Commission Factory, 2022). Social media is used by millions of people around the world and can reach a larger audience than any other medium.

Companies can now create and manage content shared with people in their networks. This content can be used to promote products and services, build relationships with customers, and increase sales. Companies can use social media to post updates on new product releases, discounts, and special offers. This content can target specific audiences so that companies reach customers most likely to purchase. Another advantage of social media as a buying platform is that it allows companies to interact with customers in real time. Companies can respond to customer inquiries quickly and provide additional information about products and services. Companies can also use social media to engage with customers and build relationships. This engagement can be beneficial for customer loyalty and help build customer trust (Thomas & Shivani, 2020).

Social media can also be used to gather data that can be used to understand customer behaviour and preferences better (Chitra, 2020; Zaki et al. 2021). Companies can track customer interactions with products and services and use this data to develop more effective marketing strategies. Companies can also use data gathered from social media to identify purchasing behaviour trends and create targeted advertisements. The use of social media as a buying platform has revolutionised how companies interact with customers and allow companies to reach a larger audience. Companies can use social media to develop customer relationships, advertise products and services, and drive sales. In addition, companies can use social media to gather data that can be used to understand customer behaviour better and improve marketing strategies.

Furthermore, social media has revolutionised the way businesses operate today. It has become one of the most powerful platforms for marketing, advertising, and selling products and services. Social media platforms such as Facebook, Twitter and Instagram have enabled businesses to reach out to potential customers and effectively and cost-effectively promote their products and services.

Social media is a powerful tool for businesses to engage with customers and build relationships (Chitra, 2020; Zaki et al. 2021). It allows companies to interact with their customers in real-time and gain valuable feedback. Companies use social media to post updates about their products and services, share special offers, and track customer engagement. This helps companies identify customer preferences, target their audience, and create campaigns that increase sales.

Social media can also be used to build personal relationships with customers. Businesses can create customer conversations, respond to queries, and provide customer support. Through social media, companies can create a community of loyal customers who can help spread the word about their products and services.

Finally, social media effectively allows businesses to advertise their products and services. Companies can use paid advertising on social media platforms to reach their target customers. They can also create sponsored content to promote their products and services. Social media is an excellent way for businesses to gain visibility and increase their reach.

In conclusion, social media is invaluable for businesses to promote their products and services and increase sales. Companies can use this powerful platform to interact with their customers, build relationships, and effectively and cost-effectively advertise their products and services effectively and cost-effectively. Social media is an excellent way for businesses to reach out to potential customers and increase their sales.

GEN ALPHA AND THEIR PURCHASING POWER PARITY

Generation Alpha, born between 2010 and 2024, is the most diverse generation in history. Not only are they the most varied in terms of race, ethnicity, and gender, but they are also the first generation to be digital natives. As a result, Generation Alpha has the purchasing power to shape the future of consumer spending.

Generation Alpha's purchasing power is driven by its deep understanding of technology and ability to access information quickly and easily. As a result, they can make informed decisions about what products and services they want to purchase. They are also more likely to use digital payment methods, such as credit cards or mobile wallets, rather than traditional methods, such as cash (Amit Sahni, 2022).

Additionally, Gen Alpha is more likely to use online platforms for shopping. This means they are more likely to purchase from online retailers and services and are willing to pay a premium for convenience and quality (Zaki & Hamid, 2021). As a result, companies must focus on creating an easy-to-use online experience to stay competitive.

Generation Alpha's purchasing power is also driven by its more socially conscious mindset. They are more likely to consider a product's sustainability and ethical standards before purchasing. They are also more likely to seek out transparent brands about their production processes and supply chain practices

(Amit Sahni, 2022). As a result, companies must consider their environmental and social impact when marketing to Gen Alpha to capture their attention.

Finally, Gen Alpha's purchasing power is driven by its desire for personalisation (Chitra, 2020; Zaki et al. 2021). They expect companies to offer products and services that cater to their individual needs and preferences. Companies must make sure that their products are tailored to the needs of Gen Alpha to stand out from the competition and capture their attention.

Overall, Generation Alpha is a powerful consumer group that has the potential to shape the future of consumer spending. Companies must know their purchasing power and understand how to leverage it to stay competitive in the market.

THE RISE OF TECHNOLOGY-SAVVY AMONG GEN ALPHAS

By 2025, gen Alpha will represent more than 2 billion children worldwide (Raja et al. 2022). It is announced as the largest generation in history, in terms of the number of individuals, but also in terms of the level of education according to UNESCO. By 2030, they will represent 34% of the world's working population. These kids will grow up in a world full of new digital devices.

As the world continues to evolve and advance, technology has become increasingly important in people's lives today, particularly the new generation of digital natives, known as Generation Alpha (Dastane & Haba, 2023). Growing up in the digital age, Generation Alpha has been raised on smartphones, tablets, and other digital devices. As a result, they have become adept at using technology to access information, stay connected with friends, and even create content.

Generation Alpha has already demonstrated its technological prowess in a variety of ways. They often quickly pick up new software, apps, and devices and can easily navigate the internet to find what they need. They are also comfortable with coding and robotics, a skill that will become increasingly important. Additionally, members of this generation are tech-savvy enough to create content, such as YouTube videos, podcasts, and websites, that can reach a broad audience (Elad Natanson, 2022; Raja et al. 2022).

Generation Alpha's aptitude for technology will likely benefit them in the future. Technology is becoming an essential part of many jobs, and those who understand how to use it effectively will be at an advantage. Additionally, Generation Alpha's tech-savviness can be used to solve complex problems, innovate, and improve the quality of life in the future.

Generation Alpha is making its mark in the world of technology. They have already demonstrated their aptitude for using technology and will likely continue to be tech-savvy for years. With their growing expertise, Generation Alpha will be able to impact the world in the future positively.

BRANDS AND GEN ALPHA

Generation Alpha is the newest generation to come onto the scene in the digital age. Born after 2010, these young people are the first generation to grow up surrounded by technology. As they grow, they quickly become the most influential generation and change how businesses market their products. Brands must stay in step with Gen Alpha's unique needs and characteristics, appealing to their connected world with personalised and authentic experiences that integrate seamlessly into daily life. Investing early in understanding and building loyalty with Gen Alpha will pay off for brands as this predicted: the "wealthiest generation" grows up.

When we asked kids ages 6 to 16 about their shopping preferences, we changed the dial from purchase inspiration to purchase influence. This is because this generation, also known as Gen Alpha, is not yet a full-fledged buying generation. We found that the matter of power has a significant impact on this generation, as we'll discuss later. When asked what influences them most in terms of things they want to buy, a quarter (25%) said social media - second only to friends (28%) and above family (21%) (What is Generation Alpha, and why is it the most influential, 2022).

Schools, too, staffed by millennials, have shifted learning into more participatory and engaging formats powered by technology. Parents and teachers of this generation also see school as a place to learn life skills and focus on a student's overall well-being. These ways of learning give hints about how Gen Alpha will work, learn, and interact with the world as they get world

YouTube is already filled with homemade videos of children interacting with brands at stores, with their favourite toys, unboxing toys, reviewing toys, and more. Brands should leverage Gen Alpha's favourite influencers on YouTube and other social platforms.

Social media, such as Facebook, Twitter, LinkedIn, YouTube, WhatsApp, Instagram, Tumblr, Pinterest, WeChat, and Google+, permit young users to create personalised online pages, communicate and interact with friends, as well as exchange content that they have made themselves (user-generated content) and information from other brand-related sources (Raja et al. 2022). Television, radio, newspapers, and magazines have conventionally disseminated social behaviour and how consumers think. Still, in the twenty-first century, social media has begun to replace traditional media's enduring and influential role on young consumers. This behaviour change represents both an opportunity and a challenge from an organisation's viewpoint (Chitra, 2020). Marketers progressively depend more on social and mobile ICT channels to market and promote their brands among the youth (Dastane, Goi, Rabbanee, 2023). Additionally, the notion of implementing content that is both entertaining and current would entice young consumers to interact and disseminate the information to their friends. This significant feature, also known as word-of-mouth (WOM), can be considered the future of social media marketing communications (Raja et al. 2022).

Still, brands like Papa John's and Suave are taking advantage of how popular influencer marketing is. By 2022, it is expected that $15 billion will be spent on this channel (Andrea van Wyk, 2022). Wunderman Thompson Commerce found that Gen Alpha likes Amazon, one of the most well-known and liked brands among this group. Earlier this week, Amazon unveiled influencer storefronts that let online celebrities from apps like Instagram and YouTube curate a selection of available products on its e-commerce platform.

Brands have had to adapt to the changing consumer behaviours of Generation Alpha. They must be able to speak to this generation in a way that resonates with them. This means understanding their values, motivations, and how they communicate with each other. Brands must also be able to deliver content that is engaging and entertaining. This can include social media, interactive websites, and different digital experiences.

Generation Alpha is also more likely to trust transparent and authentic brands. Brands must be honest about their products and not make false claims or promises. Furthermore, these young consumers prefer to shop with brands with a positive social and environmental impact. Therefore, brands must ensure that their products and services are ethical, sustainable, and positively impact the world.

Finally, Generation Alpha is more likely to be influenced by its peers. This means that brands must be able to utilise influencers and social media to reach this generation. They must be able to create content that appeals to this generation and create relationships with their influencers. This will help them to create an authentic brand image and build trust with their target audience.

Overall, brands must recognise that Generation Alpha is the future of the consumer market. They must be prepared to meet their needs and create content that resonates with them. By doing this, they can reach this generation and build a lasting relationship with them.

THE FUTURE IS NOW

The future of Generation Alpha (those born between 2010 and 2025) in the use of technology is exciting. As technology rapidly evolves, Generation Alpha will be the first to benefit from the latest and most significant advances in artificial intelligence, virtual reality, and robotics (Raja et al. 2022). Generation Alpha children are growing up in a world where technology is seen as the norm. This generation views technology as an integral part of their lives and is more likely to be tech-savvy than their predecessors. With a new generation of tech-savvy kids, Generation Alpha will develop a deeper understanding of how to use and manipulate technology in innovative ways.

One of the most significant aspects of Generation Alpha's future with technology lies in using artificial intelligence (AI). AI technology is already being used in many aspects of our lives and will only become more and more advanced in the future. AI can automate and improve processes, allowing Generation Alpha to work more efficiently (Elad Natanson, 2022). Furthermore, AI can provide personalised learning experiences to Generation Alpha, providing them with tailored instruction to help them in all areas of their lives.

Virtual reality (VR) is also set to be a significant part of Generation Alpha's future with technology. As VR technology advances, Generation Alpha will be able to experience a more immersive and interactive virtual world. This could be used in education, entertainment, and even the workplace, providing Generation Alpha with a new way to learn and interact with the world.

Finally, robotics will play a significant role in Generation Alpha's use of technology in the future. Robotics technology is becoming increasingly advanced and can be used to do mundane and complex tasks, freeing Generation Alpha to focus on more creative and meaningful activities (Elad Natanson, 2022). Robotics can also be used for medical and engineering applications, allowing Generation Alpha to make significant global contributions.

Finally, robotics will play a significant role in Generation Alpha's use of technology in the future. Robotics technology is becoming increasingly advanced and can be used to do mundane and complex tasks, freeing Generation Alpha to focus on more creative and meaningful activities (Elad Natanson, 2022). Robotics can also be used for medical and engineering applications, allowing Generation Alpha to make significant global contributions.

Robotics will have a big impact on how Generation Alpha uses technology in the future because it will give them fresh, cutting-edge ways to engage with it and their surroundings (Abdelhakim et al. 2023; Shin, 2022). This comprises:

- Education: Robotics can be utilised as a teaching tool to give students practical lessons that will improve their comprehension of science, technology, engineering, and math.

- Automation: Robotics can automate a variety of jobs and procedures, increasing productivity and releasing time for artistic endeavours.
- Personalization: Robotics can be created and programmed to cater to specific requirements and tastes, offering a highly customised experience.
- Healthcare: Robotics can significantly contribute to the delivery of healthcare services, enhancing patient access and care quality.
- Robotics may be utilised to design immersive, interactive experiences, opening new avenues for entertainment.
- Robotics may be utilised to solve difficult issues in a variety of sectors, including environmental protection, space exploration, and disaster relief.

In summary, the future of Generation Alpha in the use of technology is an exciting one. This generation is growing up in a world where technology is the norm, and they will be the first to benefit from advances in AI, VR, and robotics. Generation Alpha will be able to use technology to automate and improve processes, experience an immersive virtual world, and make meaningful contributions to the world through robotics.

CONCLUSION

It has not just encouraged networking but also fortified buying and selling activities. Gen Alpha is made up of people who were born in the 21st century and are surrounded by technology. This means that businesses need to think about both production and marketing to make a supply chain that is honest and fair. Gen Alpha is more diverse than any other generation, so they care about businesses that welcome everyone. Social media can provide companies with a platform to develop customer relationships, advertise products and services, and drive sales. This content can be used to promote products and services, build relationships with customers, and increase sales. The use of social media as a buying platform has revolutionised how companies interact with customers and allow companies to reach a larger audience. It will enable businesses to interact with their customers in real-time and gain valuable feedback. Social media can also be used to build personal relationships with customers.

In conclusion, social media is invaluable for businesses to promote their products and services and increase sales. Brands must stay in step with Gen Alpha's unique needs and characteristics, appealing to worldwide experiences that integrate seamlessly into daily life. We found that the matter of influence significantly impacts this generation, as we'll discuss later. Schools, too, staffed by millennials, have shifted learning into more participatory and engaging formats powered by technology. Brands should leverage Gen Alpha's favourite influencers on YouTube and other social platforms. Social media, such as Facebook, Twitter, LinkedIn, YouTube, WhatsApp, Instagram, Tumblr, Pinterest, WeChat and Google+, permit young users to create personalised online pages, communicate and interact with friends, as well as exchange content that they have developed themselves (user-generated content) and information from other brand-related sources (Elad Natanson, 2022). Wunderman Thompson Commerce found that Gen Alpha likes Amazon, one of the most well-known and liked brands among this group. Brands have had to adapt to the changing consumer behaviours of Generation Alpha. Overall, brands must recognise that Generation Alpha is the future of the consumer market.

REFERENCES

Abdelhakim, A. S., Abou-Shouk, M., Ab Rahman, N. A. F. W., & Farooq, A. (2023). The fast-food employees' usage intention of robots: A cross-cultural study. *Tourism Management Perspectives*, *45*, 101049. doi:10.1016/j.tmp.2022.101049

Annie E. Casey Foundation. (2022). *What Are the Core Characteristics of Generation Z?* AECF. https://www.aecf.org/blog/what-are-the-core-characteristics-of-generation-z

Chitra, A. (2020). Impact of socio-economic status of parents' on the emotional intelligence of generation alpha kids. *International Journal of Latest Technology in Engineering, Management &. Applied Sciences (Basel, Switzerland)*, *9*(5), 46–49.

Commission Factory. (2022). *Marketing to Generation Alpha in Malaysia.* Commission Factory. https://blog.commissionfactory.com/ecommerce-marketing/generation-alpha-malaysia

Dastane, O., Goi, C. L., & Rabbanee, F. (2023). The development and validation of a scale to measure perceived value of mobile commerce (MVAL-SCALE). *Journal of Retailing and Consumer Services*, *71*, 103222. doi:10.1016/j.jretconser.2022.103222

Dastane, O., & Haba, H. F. (2023). The landscape of digital natives research: a bibliometric and science mapping analysis. *FIIB Business Review*, 23197145221137960.

Elad, N. (2022). TikTok, Facebook & Generation Alpha Will Shape The Future Of.... *Forbes*. https://www.forbes.com/sites/eladnatanson/2022/06/28/tiktok-facebook--generation-alpha-will-shape-the-future-of-social-shopping/

Raja, M., Kumar, A. V., Makkar, N., Kumar, S., & Varma, S. B. (2022). The Future of the Gig Professionals: A Study Considering Gen Y, Gen C, and Gen Alpha. In *Sustainability in the Gig Economy* (pp. 305–324). Springer. doi:10.1007/978-981-16-8406-7_23

Razan, S. (2022). Gen Alpha: How to win the customer of 2030. *InfoBip*. https://www.infobip.com/blog/how-to-win-the-customer-of-2030

Sahni, A. (2022). How Each Generation Shops in 2020. *Sales Floor*. https://salesfloor.net/blog/generations-shopping-habits/

Shin, H. (2022). A critical review of robot research and future research opportunities: Adopting a service ecosystem perspective. *International Journal of Contemporary Hospitality Management*, *34*(6), 2337–2358. doi:10.1108/IJCHM-09-2021-1171

Thomas, M. R., & Shivani, M. P. (2020). Customer Profiling of Alpha: The Next Generation Marketing. *Ushus Journal of Business Management*, *19*(1), 75–86. doi:10.12725/ujbm.50.5

van Wyk, A. (2022). *Gen Alpha: The next economic force.* Alberton Record. https://albertonrecord.co.za/322037/gen-alpha-the-next-economic-force/

What is Generation Alpha, and why is it the most influential? (2022). The Drum. https://www.thedrum.com/profile/infobip/news/gen-alpha-the-most-influential-generation-for-cx

Zaki, H. O., & Ab Hamid, S. N. (2021). The Influence of Time Availability, Happiness, and Weariness on Consumers' Impulse Buying Tendency amidst Covid-19 Partial Lockdown in Malaysia. *Jurnal Pengurusan, 62*.

Zaki, H. O., Kamarulzaman, Y., & Mohtar, M. (2021). Cognition and Emotion: Exploration on Consumers Response to Advertisement and Brand. *Jurnal Pengurusan, 63*.

Chapter 7
Nurturing Digital Natives' UMS Industrial Relations Programme Experience

Mahadirin Bin Hj. Ahmad
https://orcid.org/0000-0002-3853-429X
Universiti Malaysia Sabah, Malaysia

Kee Y. Sabariah Binti Kee Mohd Yussof
Universiti Malaysia Sabah, Malaysia

Azizan Bin Morshidi
https://orcid.org/0000-0001-7786-0322
Universiti Malaysia Sabah, Malaysia

Badariah Binti Ab Rahman
Independent Researcher, Malaysia

ABSTRACT

This chapter is about the experience of the authors in nurturing the development of digital natives through the subject during a teaching and learning process. Learning practices are explained based on the subject of Labour History in Malaysia, which becomes a fundamental subject and offered during the second semester from six semesters within three years. Through those courses, authors explain the alignment of the weekly topic of the course, course learning outcome (CLO), and student learning activity (SLT) based on Table 4. After that, authors explain the implication of that learning process by focusing on the element of IR4.0, the adjustment from students during movement control order (MCO) and the implication for the development of digital natives. Based on that experience, finally authors provide the conclusion which emphasizes the adaptation process to achieve the goal of "humans with the ability of technology and at the same time trying to humanize the technology" to enhance the relevance and sustainability of IRP UMS.

DOI: 10.4018/978-1-6684-6782-4.ch007

INTRODUCTION

Notably, when there are changes to the economic climate, the political system and social belief of any nation, education will be the most affected sector. In this context, the higher education system in Malaysia particularly in terms of teaching and learning has become important as the catalyst of change; therefore, these endeavours became diverse and challenging. This paper discusses on the changes and adaptations taken by the Industrial Relations Programme (IRP UMS) to elevate graduates' knowledge and skills in facing the impact of IR 4.0 in the Malaysian context and prepare them to be digital natives for the future. There are three objectives of this paper. The first objective is to explain the teaching and learning development process. Secondly, to address the changes that took place in the curriculum in line with the requirement set-forth by MQA and UMS. Lastly is to record the authors' actual teaching and learning experiences with the new changes to the curriculum that emphasizing on smart learning programmes. Based on that, the explanations in historical development begin with the concept of Industrial Relations and Industrial Revolution, the development of IRP UMS and followed by the practical experience by the program.

Industrial Relations Field Development (Industrial Relations Evolution)

Industrial Relations are an important field of study due to its capability to influence the society and workplaces. It is therefore many scholars, practitioners and management writers in the western countries continue to conduct studies and research that affect the life in every layer of employment and the trends can also be traced in other continents, such as Asia and Africa. According to Kaufman (2004:1):

"The phenomena of industrial relations are found in all countries where people work for others in paid employment. As a generic subject, therefore, industrial relations is ubiquitous. The field of industrial relations, on the other hand, is one approach to studying these phenomena and solving the problems that arise from them. It is only one of a variety of possible ways to produce and organize knowledge, and as such it has a unique frame of reference and its own theories and concepts, techniques and practices, and ideological commitments."

The development of society can be traced back through the historical context of the industrial revolution. During this era, the discussion was centred to people's voice through trade union that possessed the industrial strength to undermine the power of employers. Subsequently, the discussion was focusing on balance power between employer and employee so called by 'win-win' situation. After a few decades the management has regained the power to control over the workers. And now, employer-employee relationship (Employment Relations) tends to vary due to the uncertainties brought by IR 4.0 that warrants organization to think and create new sustainable work relationship; thus the past is what the present is today for a better future as mentioned by Kimura, et. al (2019). This is not to predict what will happen in the future but to create a link or consequence from the past to the present and the future as mentioned by Kimura, et. al (2019:2):

"We cannot predict exactly what will happen by the year 2040: there is much uncertainty about the advancement of new technologies and its consequences. And we must realise that most of the AMS are

not at the very frontier of technological innovation. Thus, the question for us is how to utilize new technologies for our economic development and accelerate our catching-up.

To explain that process, this section will describe the transformation of Industrial Relations into Employment Relations and focus on employee relationships within IR 4.0. The focus is on the Industrial Relations UMS programme development which is relevant to the current practice and needs of new generations, primarily digital natives.

The industrial revolutions that happened in the last 400 years ago can be differentiated by the numbers. IR 1.0 refers to the invention of steam power and later to the invention of more tools and machines. In IR 2.0 with the focus on mass production, the production is mainly concentrated on the factories that supply globally and create globalization, while in IR 3.0, emphasizing more on providing services to people. Finally, after being enhanced by internet and connectivity, IR 4.0 emerged to develop products and services with special requirements with the smart system. Based on that development, IR 4.0 became an important factor to economic growth in ASEAN region. According to Kimura, et.al (2019:19):

"With the help of modern technology, ASEAN has the potential to become a dynamic growth region supplying goods and services globally and generating fulfilling jobs for its workforce. ASEAN in 2040 should aim for a wide adoption of the new technologies to upgrade their economies. It is also possible to modernise traditional industry by use of technology. Any development strategy will require connectivity through improvements in soft and hard infrastructure.

Developing a new type of work and working environment creates a new kind of relationship between actors in the workplace. This relation will enhance flexibility and just in time to meet the consumer's

Figure 1. Differing
Source: Petrillo, et.al (2017)

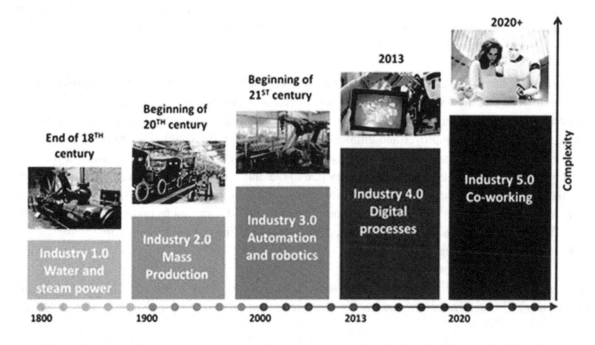

demand. Based on that, the implication of Industrial Relations as an academic and practical activity had shifted to Employment Relations and finally to Employee Relations. This dynamic needs to be enhanced and more attention from the academics and practitioners since the decline of collectivity and increasing individual needs in the workplace. These are crucial followed the flexibility in the workplace and the emergence of new type of employee which known as a Digital Native as by Prensky (2001):

As defined for this study, digital natives today are between the ages of 13 to 29. It is estimated that they have spent over 10,000 hours playing videogames, sent and received over 200,000 emails and instant messages, spent over 10,000 hours talking on cell phones, and over 20,000 hours watching television before they even graduate from college.

That characterization then chosen by Mason, et. al. (2008) for they research as they mentioned:

we will identify this generation as the "digital natives", a term coined by Marc Prensky (Prensky, 2001 Dec) who describes today's youth as "native speakers" of the digital language of computers, video games, and the Internet. This term seems to capture best the idea of one born into an information society where information and communication technologies have become central to the society's economic, social, and cultural identity.

Based on the above, the attribute development of the society can be seen through their special characteristic such as being impatient, socialization, natural multitaskers, intuitive learners, and early adopters (Hoyland, 2022). Therefore, taking into account the said attributes, the dynamic of Industrial Relations undoubtedly turned to Employment Relations and then Employee Relations. In short, the difference according to Jansen (2011:63):

"If industrial relations studies deal with the institutions and actors who define and create the employment relationship, it is obvious when considering the labour market that we must focus on new types of actors who are not the classical collective actors. Companies, managers, professions, and individual employees play a more direct role as actors in IR (ER) regulation. The classical actors (trade unions, employers' associations, and governments) still play an important role in IR regulation, but in some countries and sectors they are supplemented with or replaced by other actors. Simultaneously, the classical players' own roles as actors in IR systems are also changed in some areas."

For that reason, IRP UMS has started the process of adaptation with the concept of Blended Learning (BL) to enhance the student experience and skills. This fact related to the international concern such as practicing in Europe, as explained by Biggs & Tang (2011:3):

"Since 2000 there have been dramatic changes in the nature of higher education. It is not just that participation rates are higher than ever, bringing much greater diversity in the student population, but that these and other factors have altered the main mission of higher education and modes of delivery. One consequence is that the major thrust in teaching is more on professional and vocational programmes and concerns about teaching effectiveness."

Industrial Relations Programme UMS

The industrial relations system and practice in Malaysia have been developed independently by focusing at minor details by the university and corporate managers, particularly relating to human resources management. While, the government more in practically involved in managing the industrial relations matters especially true the Department of Industrial Relations, Labour Department, Industrial Court and Department of Trade Union Affair. Beside that, the contribution of trade union are increasing especially in form of knowledge and mobilization of workers in industrial relations matters. Numerous research and articles on the Industrial Relations field of study have been published mainly to explain the essential elements of Industrial Relations related to Trade Unions, Industrial Conflicts, and many more. Based on that, in 1994, the initiatives to develop IRP in UMS impacted the study of Industrial Relations in Malaysia. Generally, the development of IR programme in Malaysia by UMS mainly to enhance the disciplined of Industrial Relations with a variety of course such as:

"The program introduces students to the relationship between employers, employees, unions and government-based approach to interpersonal relations and interorganizational work. Students will follow courses that emphasize the multi-disciplines such as Labor Legislation, Labor History, Industrial Sociology, Industrial Democracy, The Study Of Industrial Relations, Economic And Political, Safety And Health, Labor Structure, Transnational Corporations, International Human Resource Management And Employment Relations In The Formal and Informal Sectors. The program will also touch on the issue of trade union issues and dispute resolution in the industry."(FSSH UMS Website, https://www.ums.edu.my/fssk/index.php/what-we-offer/undergra duate/uh6347001-industrial-relations)

The multidisciplinary approach has been practiced maintaining and create more opportunities to attract local and international students. For that reason, curriculum development was also reviewed and analysed regularly (3-5 years) by expert to support the changing process to the current needs perform by eight programmed members as shown in picture 1. For the current review, we are starting to focus on "Outcome Based Education" (OBE) which is in line with the national mission of higher education in Malaysia. They are 11 Programme Learning Outcome (PLO) which based on three domains cognitive, affective, and psychomotor as stated below:

i.   Practice knowledge and demonstrate understanding in the field of Industrial Relations. ii. Using cognitive skills in solving problems encountered in the field of Industrial Relations.

iii. Apply practical skills competently in the field of Industrial Relations.
iv.   Exhibit and apply interpersonal skills in the field of Industrial Relations.
v.   Demonstrate effective communication skills in the field of Industrial Relations.
vi.   Use digital technology and applications ethically in solving problems in the field of Industrial Relations.
vii. Demonstrates appropriate quantitative and numeracy skills in the profession. viii. Leading and shouldering responsibilities
ix.   Have personal skills in the field of Industrial Relations.
x.   Apply entrepreneurial knowledge and skills in the work involved.
xi.   Understand and apply professional and ethical practices in the future job.

Picture 1.

Source: FSSH UMS website: https://www.ums.edu.my/fssk/index.php/what-we-offer/undergra duate/uh6347001-industrial-relations

To achieve this outcome, the structure of courses is divided into several phases based on the cohort which contain 3 years of study and divided to 6 semesters. (Picture 2)

Students will start with subjects in categories 1000 which contain 3 main subjects as a foundation to understand the theoretical and the development of IR in Malaysia. This included Basic of Industrial Relations, Malaysian Industrial Relations, and Labour History in Malaysia. After that, in categories 2000, student will be exposed to other subjects as Labour Law, Industrial Safety and Health, Human Resource Management, Organizational Behavior, Industrial Society, Political Economy, Productivity Management, Contemporary Trade Unions Movement, Research Methodology, Collective Bargaining and Arbitration, and Employment Issues. As a final year student, students are exposed to issues and more on practical aspects such as Bargaining strategy, Information Management System, Industrial Relations Law, Wage Compensation, Industrial Democracy, and Employment Law.

Finally, students will be exposed to academic writing skills in which students are required to produce a dissertation systematically. The academic writing begins with proposal defends, data collecting and a dissertation. After completing that, all the students are encouraged to attend an internship training for a minimum period of 2 months within the selected organizations around the world. Students then become alumni of IRP as shown in the graph below:

Programme Learning Outcome and IR 4.0

Most of the PLO required usage of the internet of things. However, the focus of PLO6 displays the importance of using digital technology and applications particularly in solving problems in the field of Industrial Relations. The other PLOs require minimal usage of the internet of things where teaching and learning can be conducted online. These include uploading the written assignments, tutorial presentations, discussions and attending lectures. Besides that, students are required to organize various events such as mini seminars, online discussions and webinars. Such activities can be accessed through the blog

Figure 2. IRP UMS course structured
Source: http://bpa.ums.edu.my/images/dokumen/Prospektus/2019/3YEARS_PROGRAMME_COURSE_STRUCTURE_FKSW_BI.pdf

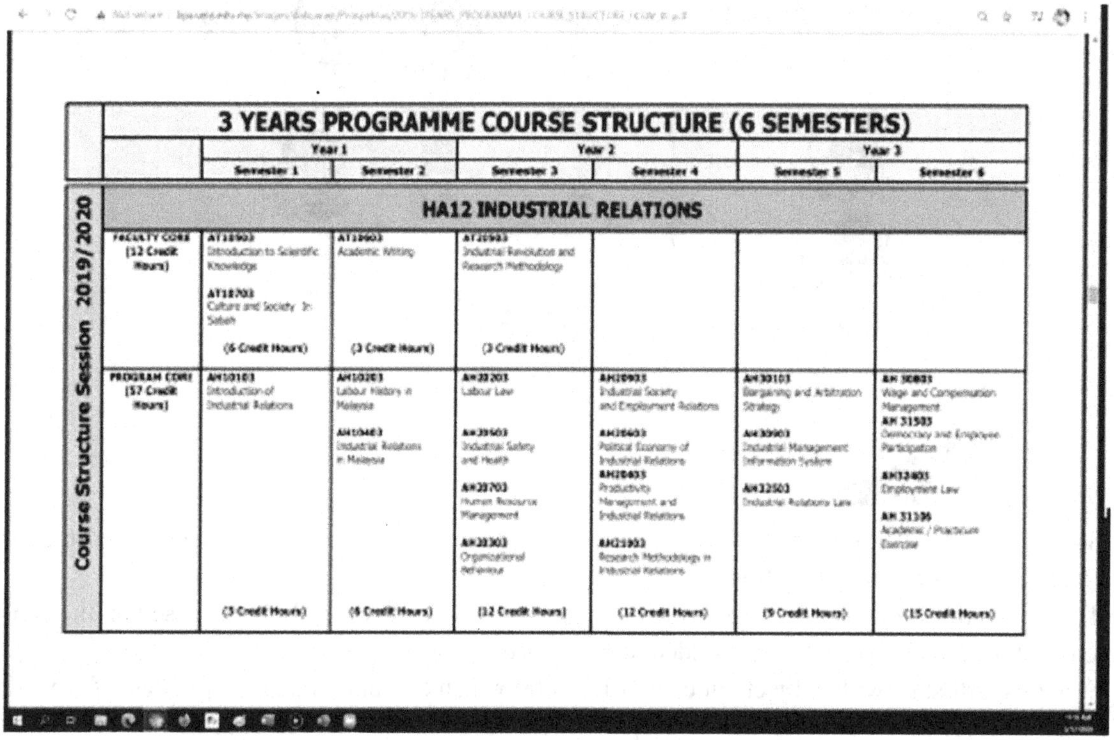

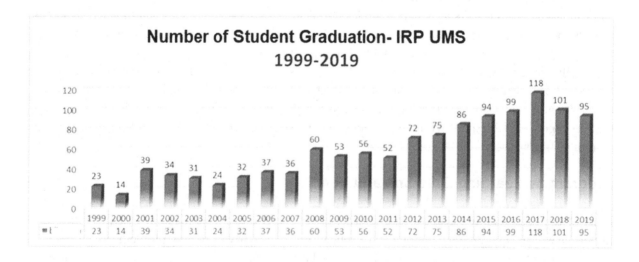

Figure 3. Alumni of IRP UMS
Source: Compile from Convocation Ceremony Book UMS, 2019-2019

Number of Student Graduation- IRP UMS 1999-2019

Year	1999	2000	2001	2002	2003	2004	2005	2006	2007	2008	2009	2010	2011	2012	2013	2014	2015	2016	2017	2018	2019
t	23	14	39	34	31	24	32	37	36	60	53	56	52	72	75	86	94	99	118	101	95

(HA12 Notice Board). At this point of stages, it is utmost important for students to possess the required digital literacy and internet surfing skills which are now becoming a new norm in our life.

Challenges and Changes for Nurturing Digital Native

The significant challenges for a compelling and exciting experience for students during their period of study in UMS, our program had been revised regularly. For the current revision, some changes were proposed to increase the number of courses taken in the program compared to the universities and faculty courses. This percentage is present on Table 1.

The increasing percentage for the courses of the Core Program Module is to 67.5% while decreasing the other module will help to create more content about the program itself. This move is essential for the programme to align and develop a more student-centred learning environment and as a basic for nurturing skills of digital natives. This adaptation will be explained by providing an explanation from various courses which demonstrate the process of Internet of Thing.

Adaptation

Based on the PLO every course offered is aligned to this by providing at least 2 Course Learning Outcomes (CLO) followed by a weekly basis of topics. For example, we provided here a few courses offered to the first, second and third-year students. One of the courses for the first-year students are the understanding

Table 1. The weight of course distribution for IRP UMS

	Component	Requirement Component- MQA	Current Component	New Proposed Component
1.	Compulsory Module (University Courses)	10-17%	18.9%	11.7%
2.	Core Program Module (General & Discipline	63-80%	51.6%	67.5%
3.	Elective Module	5-10%	24.6%	10.8%
4.	Industrial Internship/Academic Exercise	5-10%	4.9%	10.0%

Source: IRP UMS -Program File (2021)

the development of Malaysian Industrial Relations through the course of Labour History in Malaysia that provide knowledge to student on:

"This course provides students with a basic understanding of industrial relations based on the history of workers and labour movement in Malaysia. Students will be exposed to socio-economic development which contributes to the current industrial relations systems. For that purpose, it is vital for students to know and understand the labour history in Malaysia to further learn about Malaysian industrial relations systems and practices.

Therefore, the subject content is divided accordingly based on 3 CLO below and the teaching and learning is spread over 14 weeks:

i.   Explain the process of 'working arrangement' in the colonial era.
ii.   Describe the formation of a labour organization in Malaysia.
iii.   Elaborate the historical contribution on the current industrial relations in Malaysia.

Next is the learning and assessments activity that are created through an online platform by utilizing the Moodle which rebrands as a SmartUMS (Liew, et.al, 2019). There are four major activities which include the i) understanding of syllabus (Table 4-MQA), ii) the access of learning content, iii) participating in online learning activities and iv) submitting an online assessment. These activities enable students to be involved in these activities to get hands-on experience and eventually be assessed based on the assessment and examinations followed by the weekly topics as shown in Table 2.

Elements of information technology have been practiced since 2008 in which students are involved in the making of video. In these activities students are expected to complete their group assignment by creating a documentary on labour history in Sabah. This activity becomes more effective with the introduction of the Blended Learning platform; an online based learning platform provided by JTMK (*Jabatan Teknologi Maklumat dan Komunikasi* - Department of IT and Communication, UMS).

With the implementation of Blended Learning, the subject content was transferred to Smartums (UMS Learning Management System). This platform provides various learning activities such as Forum, Chat, Assignment, Glossary, Workshop, and Wiki. The selection of the activities is subjected to the purpose of the topics and CLO. For example, within six weeks, students will be involved in tutorial classes that need to do a 'video presentation' and 'essay writing,' which fulfils CLO 1. For discussion, students will be divided into small groups containing 13 to 15 students each group. However, for the presentation, it is sufficient for two students to present their topic. The video presentation will be uploaded to each forum during a week, and students are free to watch and raise questions at their times. After the discussion, the final essay needs to be submitted to the assignment for grading marks.

The learning process continue after the midterm semester break, which focused on individual assignments, and students needed to answer quizzes and write an individual essay. Finally, students are exposed to team assignments to enhance interpersonal skills such as communication and teamwork skills. Here, students need to do collaborative work by learning to cooperate in Wiki's by producing the video and essay. All these activities are aligned with CLO and grade according to the number of hours or student learning time (SLT) based on the MQA best guidance practice (MQA, 2011). The example of this learning process can be found in e-book writing by Mahadirin (2022).

Figure 4. Alignment of topics, CLO, and learning activities
Source: Table 4 of AH10203 Labour History in Malaysia

TOPIC/WEEKLY	CLO			Learning Activities	
1. Introduction to Course					
2. Imperialisme and Colonialisme	Explain the process of 'working arrangement' in colonial era (C 1,PLO1)	6 week	Tutorial		
3. Colonial British Labour Policy					Video
4. The development of chinese Labourer					Essay
5. The development of Indian Labourer					
6. The development of Malay and Javanese					
7. Labour in North Borneo					
8. The History of Trade Union	Describe the formation of labour organization in Malaysia (C 3,PLO 9)	3 week	Individual		Kuiz
9. Trade Union and Political Parties					Essay
10. Trade union and industrial conflict					
11. The condition of labour in contemporary	Elaborate the historical contribution on the current industrial relations in Malaysia (A3, PLO 4)	3 week	Group		Essay
11. Labour Issues					wiki
12. The Future of Labour					
13. Revising and Conclusion					

Based on the discussion, the element of IR4.0 can be analysed through the usage of online platform Moodle. First, how does the internet of things produce students with the environment of IR4.0? To answer this question, these online platforms with various activities such as tutorials, examinations, and essay writing have made teaching and learning become visible. Therefore, students are able to perform activities in different locations and at different times as long as internet connection is within their preferences. These innovative systems that emphasize on IR4.0 became an important element in the study of the Industrial Relations field of study. As technology keeps advancing at an accelerated rate, not only students but also workers must prepare to adapt to the emergence of technology under an uncertain economic realm (Salleh and Ab Rahman, 2020) due to widespread global health crises such as Covid-19 pandemic.

Growing evidence shows that IR 4.0 has brought huge opportunities in respective industries, manufacturing, and information technology. Innovation capability has become a distinct possibility, set to serve better product and service reengineering and distinction. Thus, students need to be exposed to the reality of the current workplace phenomenon. The Covid-19 pandemic crisis presents unprecedented challenges and has profound implications for the way people live and work. In IR 4.0 scope, information and communication technologies have played a crucial role in ensuring business continuity as lockdown measures have suddenly forced employees from across the globe to teleworking, often leaving them unprepared and ill-equipped. Further theoretical and empirical studies need to be explored, particularly regarding telework adjustment among employees and managers-union members relations (Azizan, et. al, 2021). Although the IR 4.0 paradigm has emerged worldwide, it is still a challenge for workers to adopt, adapt and adjust, mainly in developing countries such as Malaysia.

This paradigm also impacts the student and various adjustments as mentioned above help the student to adapt with the new environment, especially during MCO. Besides that, ethics and human nature aspects are increased to expose the students to morals and noble values. The feedback from Mr. Aiman as mentioned below:

"In my opinion, assessment experiences such as quizzes, individual/group assignments, tutorials, virtual can be done by daring to try virtual methods that have never been done before such as virtual quizzes, virtual demonstrations, marking through the system, digital storytelling, virtual presentation videos, voice recording, it was a rather interesting experience. In addition, virtual learning as well, I have a feeling of stress with a lot of tasks and less clear task information or miscommunication. In short, virtual learning is a good solution to meet the new norms recommended by the Government of Malaysia. Now is the time to change the pattern of teaching and learning previously practiced to something more flexible by daring to try various current applications/ technologies and subsequently learning outcomes can still be achieved." (Aiman Daniel, Monday, July 13, 2020, 7:27 PM)

Besides that, these courses are delivered by simple methods such as chatting platforms which are advantage for students in terms of data and increasing and improving their reading habit. These are reflections from Miss Era at the end of the semester. According to Miss Era:

"The comment that can be given in this learning course is that the method used for the delivery of this learning is very good especially when students are facing this COVID-19 Pandemic. Lecturers use the hangout app to use during online Lecture. The Hangout app is very easy to use because it does not require strong internet access and is easy to use in my opinion." (Sunday 5 July 2020: 7:31 PM)

Another student responds to the better learning experience during the session which refers to various activities created. Respond from Has:

"Been able to get involved with new learning and teaching methods, namely online learning. It's a lot different from interactive face -to -face learning, yet this method is also effective for me. I was able to re -access notes and discussions with respect to lecture topics already discussed. Although it is not as good as the interactive face -to -face learning session experience where I can meet and interact with friends and lecturers physically. But this learning method is also effective and efficient where there are many new activities that can be done virtually. For example, group activities that form a group collaboration relationship in smartv3 is Wiki." (Thursday, 14 January 2021, 4:13 PM)

Based on that reality, the challenge and adaptation we face here in UMS can be seen as a pilot study of the impact of IR4.0 in teaching and learning process, and more writing is needed in the future. This situation is more visible when the abnormal situation such as MCO due to Covid-19 pandemic (Satar, et.al, 2020) and the affecting factor from the faculty members to elevate their skill and adaptation to the change (Kee Y Sabariah, et.al, 2021).

Future Directions of IR UMS

Moreover, the implications for the future will contribute to the enhancement of digital natives who are prepared and equipped with the necessary abilities. We anticipate that in the future, all of these options will be manageable as more digital workplaces to emerge. This new workplace includes various questions that the individual must answer, including: Are they quick?, personalised?, and flexible? Do they permit multitasking? Do they deliver immediate satisfaction? Utilizes gamification? Do they appeal to innovators and early adopters? Does it comprehend what is essential to digital natives? (Hoyland, 2022).

In addition to posing a threat to public health and safety, the coronavirus pandemic has become a major issue influencing economic activity, employment, and human security. In this case, our graduates are armed and prepared for the worst-case scenario. The hotel and food service, manufacturing, wholesale and retail trade, and commercial real estate industries have all had the greatest impact on working hours and employment. Construction, transportation, and storage; communication; and agriculture, forestry, and fishing all saw reduced work hours and job losses, but on a smaller scale. Uncertainty is a significant issue for businesses, particularly micro, small, and medium-sized enterprises with limited resources to withstand brief periods of inactivity. Priority economic sectors, including their employers and employees, require specialised help to satisfy their skill needs so they may recover and rebuild with a more highly skilled workforce. The crisis has revealed enormous discrepancies in access to high-quality employment and worsened existing imbalances. Those who were already at a disadvantage when it came to seeking a job following the outbreak were hit the hardest and had the greatest need for training and education.

Unemployment and vulnerability have remained beyond pre-crisis levels, contributing to a worsening of inequality and poverty in a number of regions and major demographic categories (women, young people, and informal workers, among others). Millions of low-paid and low-skilled workers face severe reductions in working hours, wage reductions, and layoffs, in part because of limited remote job opportunities or inadequate digital skills and internet access. The provision of opportunities for reskilling and upskilling as part of job retention and employment stimulus packages and long-term comprehensive recovery strategies is one strategy to mitigate their effects. Training and education have been significantly impacted by lockdowns, which have severely disrupted conventional face-to-face skill provision and added to the duties of instructors and trainers. It is anticipated that decreased financing and persistent socioeconomic disparity would have a chilling impact on educational and training programmes. Numerous universities and other institutions of higher education have been forced to close, at least temporarily, as a result of the outbreak. Countries with low learning outcomes, low graduation rates, and inadequate shock resilience are more likely to suffer the impact of university closures. Currently, our graduating students have a challenging transition into the workforce. Threats to our students include an imminent "lockdown generation" and a failure to achieve SDG 4's aim of providing all people with access to high-quality education and fostering lifelong learning.

Academic fields and occupational sectors differ in the extent to which our students adopt digital learning practices. Concerns have been voiced over justice, inclusivity, and the reinforcement of existing disparities, as well as the shutdown of colleges. The "digital divide" threatens to aggravate the achievement gap since low-income households are less likely to have the requisite computer equipment, Internet connection, and other resources for online learning. As a result of its health, humanitarian, and socioeconomic components, the pandemic will have far-reaching effects on the future of employment, education, and skill development. Nevertheless, as a result of the accelerated structural economic and digital transformations, skilling, reskilling, and upskilling will be more vital than ever, particularly in the most impacted industries. To counter the effects of the pandemic on people's ability to earn a living wage, have access to health care, education, and other basic necessities, as well as opportunities for reskilling and upskilling, we will need comprehensive policy responses, including fiscal recovery measures, active and passive labour market policies, and social protection. Despite the significant disruptions in the labour market and the demand for skills, there are still apparent investment targets, such as green, digital, and core skills, occupational safety and health, and skills for the care economy, that may help to re-employ our graduates.

CONCLUSION

The development of the Industrial Revolution and its impact on Industrial Relations, which are explained through teaching and learning by IRP UMS in this paper, can be seen as an adaptation process. This process needs to synchronize and involve all the academics and students, which become more challenging with the fast-changing of digital technology. By aligning the OBE method with the internet of things, the development of students, especially critical thinking and communication skills, are inevitably crucial for the future as digital natives. All this is a continued effort to achieve the situation based on the concept of "human with the ability of technology and at the same time trying to humanize the technology." At the same time, UMS are moving forward in providing more high-speed internet connection structure to ensure the support for sustainable on-line teaching and learning can be upheld for many years to come. The proposition made in this paper is a critical analysis in creating excellent support system to face a new reality in the workplace as digital natives.

ACKNOWLEDGMENT

We thank the Centre of Research and Innovation Management, UMS (PPPI) for the funding and support under SDK (Skim Dana Khas/ Special Grant Scheme) with number SDK0275-2020. This chapter originally based on the paper which present on the 10th ILERA Asian Regional Congress, Quezon City, Philippines, December 3-4, 2020.

REFERENCES

Azizan, M., Kee, Y. S., & Mohammad Idris, B. (2021). Trade Union and Job Changes in Volatile Times: A Systematic Literature Review & Future Research Agenda. *International Journal of Academic Research in Business & Social Sciences, 11*(2), 923–937. doi:10.6007/IJARBSS/v11-i2/9189

Bahagian Perkhidmatan Akademik, U. M. S. (2019) Course Structure Faculty of Social Science and Humanities. *Prospectus 2019*. UMS. http://bpa.ums.edu.my/images/dokumen/Prospektus/2019/3YEARS_PROGRAMME_C OURSE_STRUCTURE_FKSW_BI.pdf

Biggs, J., & Tang, C. (2011). *Teaching for Quality Learning at University What the Student Does* (4th ed) McGraw Hill. https://cetl.ppu.edu/sites/default/files/publications/- John_Biggs_and_Catherine_Tang-_Teaching_for_Quali-BookFiorg-.pd

Hoyland, N. (2022) *What Is A Digital Workplace?* Huler Webpage. https://huler.io/blog/what-is-a-digital-workplace

Hoyland, N. (2022). *Who Are Digital Natives And What Do They Want From The Workplace?* Huler Webpage. https://huler.io/blog/who-are-digital-natives

Jensen, C. S. (2011). Between industrial and employment relations – the practical and academic implications of changing labour markets, *Arbetsmarknad & Arbetsliv, 17*(3), 53-65. https://www.diva-portal.org/smash/get/diva2:513619/FULLTEXT01.pdf

Kaufman, B. E. (2006). *The Global Evolution of Industrial Relations: Events, Ideas and the IIRA*. International Labour Organization and Academic Foundation of India.

Kee, Y., Sabariah, K. M. Y., Mahadirin, A., Jalihah, M. S., Jurry, F. M., Ramlah, D., Hafizi, M., & Liew, T. S. (2021). Penggunaan E-Pembelajaran dan kesannya terhadap kesejahteraan kakitangan akademik di Institusi Pengajian Tinggi di Sabah [MJSSH]. *Malaysian Journal of Social Sciences and Humanities*, 6(4), 108–116. doi:10.47405/mjssh.v6i4.761

Kimura, F., Shrestha, R., & Narjoko, D. (2019). The Digital and Fourth Industrial Revolution and ASEAN Economic Transformation. In F. Kimura, V. Anbumozhi, & H. Nishimura (Eds.), *Transforming and Deepening the ASEAN Community* (pp. 1–23). ERIA. https://www.eria.org/uploads/media/5.AV2040_VOL3_Digital_and _4th_Industrial_Re volution.pdf

Liew, T. S., Haifzi, A., Mahadirin, A., & Dris, M. A. (2019). *Quick Start Guide For UMS Learning Management System*. Institute for Biological Tropical and Conservation, Universiti Malaysia Sabah, OER UMS. https://oer.ums.edu.my/handle/oer_source_files/1099

Mahadirin, A. (2020). HA12 Notice Board – Blog, *Open Electronics Resources (OER)*, Jabatan Teknologi Maklumat dan Komunikasi (JTMK) Universiti Malaysia Sabah. https://oer.ums.edu.my/ handle/oer_source_files/1484

Mahadirin, A. (2022). *Aku Dan Sesuatu Diari*. e-learning Cafe FSSK, UMS. https://indiework.usm.my/ index.php?route=product/product&product_id=458

Malaysian Quality Assurance. (2011). *Guidelines to Good Practices: Curriculum Design and Delivery*. Kuala Lumpur: The Public and International Affairs. https://www2.mqa.gov.my/QAD/garispanduan/2014/ GGP%20REKA%20BENTUK%20N%20KURIKULUM.pdf

Mason, R. M., Barzilai, K., & Lou, N. (2008) The Organizational Impact of Digital Natives: How Organizations are Responding to the Next Generation of Knowledge Workers. *Proceedings of the 17th International Conference on Management of Technology Dubai*. RM Mason. http://faculty.washington. edu/rmmason/Publications/IAMOT_DN_2008.pdf

Satar. M., N.S., H., Azizan, M., & Dastane, O. (2020) Success Factors for e-Learning Satisfaction during COVID-19 Pandemic Lockdown, *International Journal of Advanced Trends in Computer Science and Engineering*, 9(5), 7859-7865. https://www.warse.org/IJATCSE/static/pdf/file/ijatcse136952020.pdf

Petrillo, A., De Felice, F., Cioffi, R., & Federico Zomparelli, F. (2018). Fourth Industrial Revolution: Current Practices, Challenges, and Opportunities. In A. Petrillo, R. Cioffi, & F. De Felice (Eds.), *Digital Transformation in Smart Manufacturing*. IntechOpen. doi:10.5772/intechopen.72304

Salleh, N. M., & Ab Rahman, B. (2020). Part 2 Country Chapter Malaysia. In Nankervis, A.R. Connell, J. and John Burgess,J. (editor) *The Future of Work in Asia and Beyond*. London & New York: Routledge. https://www.taylorfrancis.com/books/edit/10.4324/9780429423567/future-work-asia-beyond-alan-nankervis-julia-connell-john-burgess?refId=b41d9dd3-ffec-414f-be8b-ffa7b1a1a687

Student Feedback. (2020). AH10203 and AH32403. In *SmartUMS. Pusat E-Pembelajaran (PEP) dan Jabatan Teknologi Maklumat dan Komunikasi (JTMK)*. Universiti Malaysia Sabah. https://smartv3. ums.edu.my/

Chapter 8

Structural Modelling on Factors of Adopting FinTech Among Malaysian Millennials:
Perceived COVID–19 Risk as Moderator

Mohammad Imtiaz Hossain
Multimedia University, Malaysia

Md. Kausar Alam
https://orcid.org/0000-0002-9748-5862
Brac University, Bangladesh

Zainudin Johari
https://orcid.org/0000-0001-7571-7020
ALFA University College, Malaysia

Maherin Tasnim
Brac University, Bangladesh

Kazi Israk Ferdaous
Brac University, Bangladesh

Tanima Pal
Brac University, Bangladesh

ABSTRACT

This empirical paper investigates the role of perceived usefulness (PU), perceived ease of use (PEU), social influence (SI), service trust (ST), user innovativeness (UI), and technological optimism (TO) on intention to adopt Fintech (ITAF) by Malaysian millennials with the moderation of perceived Covid-19 risk (PCR). Theory of planned behaviour, technology adoption model, and social cognitive theory are applied to amalgamate the concept. Data of 313 millennials who are in university were collected using

DOI: 10.4018/978-1-6684-6782-4.ch008

a convenient sampling technique and a structured questionnaire. The data was analysed in partial least squares structural equation modeling (PLS-SEM). The result shows that PU, SI, ST, and TO influence ITAF significantly. Surprisingly, PEU and UI did not evidence significant impact. Moreover, PCR did not show moderating influence. This study can provide important insights for the Fintech users, industry players, policymakers, and government to comprehend the concept so that the adoption of Fintech can be fostered towards achieving a smart and digital Malaysia.

1. INTRODUCTION

In the financial services industry, technological developments and digitalisation in every aspect of business process facilitated the increasing converging of the physical and virtual world (Macchiavello & Siri, 2022). Digitised business structures and procedures, new products and services came about as a result of the financial sector's digital transformation. Martinčević et al. (2020) gave several examples, such as digital consulting and trading systems, peer-to-peer (P2P) lending, crowdfunding, artificial intelligence and machine learning, mobile payment systems, and even new monetary capabilities have been cultivating over the past decade, with different types of digital money (such as Bitcoin and other crypto assets). Digital networks have accumulated a solid worldwide retail customer market share and continue to grow consistently. Thus it is not only a cheap way to communicate with clients.

In the financial world, conventional banks have played a key role. The world economy is gradually moving towards digital platforms due to rapid technological evolution. Financial technology (Fintech) firms have quickly changed the disrupted financial markets (Skan et al., 2015). Numerous business models, as well as new consumer requirements, have been developed by advanced financial technology. Payment services, the banking industry and financial regulations, like other aspects of the economy, are being affected (Alsmadi et al., 2022). The gaps in the financial market have been filled increasingly since electronic services were introduced to the market. The new technologies facilitated fast transactions and ease of use to provide a wide variety of service providers. The financial industry has been steadily digitised by the creations like PayPal's online payment portal or the bitcoin currency, followed by the launch of the world wide web (Butt & Khan, 2019; Goel et al., 2022).

"FinTech", a term combined with "finance" and "technology", is known as the advent of emerging information technologies. National Digital Research Centre in Dublin, Ireland, describes it as innovation in financial services. Fintech can be contemplated as any innovative idea that improves the financial service processes by proposing technology solutions in various business situations, according to Leong and Sung (2018, p.75).

Incremental development of innovation for financial service sector processes, applications, products and business models occurred because of FinTech stated by Alt and Puschmann (2012). This study focused on a developing country context, Malaysia. FinTech is challenging the status quo of the financial sector, stated Dato Muhammad bin Ibrahim former governor of the Malaysian central bank, in his speech on Global Islamic Finance Forum 5.0(GIFF 5.0). In the current condition, we will see new business models emerge, which will be challenged by distribution networks and will reduce transaction costs. Instead of referring to FinTech as an aggressive opponent, financial intuition should treat this as an opportunity for them (Vaicondam et al., 2021; Abd Hamid et al., 2023). In terms of attracting consumers and expanding business operations, if Fintech is adopted, it can create an advantage for the companies. Companies adopting FinTech would have an advantage in attracting consumers and expanding their business model. Moreover, Covid-19 fosters the adoption of digital platforms to avoid human interaction (Fu & Mishra, 2020).

According to the Fintech Malaysia Report (2022), Figure 1 shows that FinTech companies and start-ups serve people in many segments and overall fintech sector grew by 27% in 2021 to 294 fintech companies. Payments still dominate the industry, with 60 companies, followed by lending (55), e-wallets (43), and insurtech (31).

All FinTech services are to facilitate the transactions of bank customers across the internet and online facilities to make different financial matters. This is parallel with the medium-term expectation of Bank Negara to make Malaysian society cashless, and Malaysia aims to introduce a virtual bank in the medium term (Saad et al., 2019).

Local businesses, along with international players like Alipay, PayPal, WeChat and Google Pay there, are 39 businesses with e-money licenses competing in the country (BNM, 2019). The top 10 FinTech companies in Malaysia are Neurowave, iMoney, Mpay, Money match, Kapital, MyCash online, Softroom, GHL, Tranglo and Crowdo (Singapore, 2017). Several challenges require the FinTech companies to follow specific laws and regulations and provide products and services according to them; they are required to follow these regulations as the Central Bank of Malaysia imposed financial technology Sandbox (FTSF) for the FinTech companies (Le, 2021).

The Fintech Malaysia report (2018) reported that internet penetration in Malaysia is 85.7 per cent, and online banking penetration has reached 85.1 per cent. However, smartphone penetration for Fintech applications is just 40 per cent. Malaysia is the leading country in Southeast Asia in e-wallet use, numbered 40 per cent and in second place is the Philippines at 36 per cent, Thailand at 27 per cent and Singapore

Figure 1. Segments and Malaysian Fintech companies
Source: *Fintech Malaysia Report (2022)*

at 26 per cent, based on a Mastercard impact study (2020). The adoption of e-Wallet amongst Malaysian show positive growth, and usage almost doubled on 11.11 and 12.12 sales and year-end holidays (Mastor, 2021), but only 22 per cent of millennials uses the e-wallet (Ing et al., 2021). The person who was born between 1981 and is considered a Millennial. While data showed that there is a lower transaction value for mobile Fintech application, it is shown that mobile Fintech application is a favoured alternative for micropayments as the report shows that there is a greater transaction volume (Tun-Pin et al., 2019) which can be inferred those customers still have lousy faith in the security of mobile Fintech application. The cause of lower mobile penetration of Fintech applications may be due to many factors, such as word of mouth, where disgruntled consumers persuade their friends, colleagues and family members to stick to conventional banking and internet banking instead of embracing new alternatives, such as mobile Fintech applications while doing banking activities that offer greater benefits.

However, information violation cases and problems are occurring worldwide, including in Malaysia. Therefore, information security and privacy are crucial areas to look out for in research (Karim et al., 2020). Identity theft, credit card fraud and other cybercrimes occur due to users' lack of information protection, allowing an intruder to take advantage (Barrett-Maitland et al., 2016; Khan et al., 2023). Teoh Teng Tenk et al. (2020) also pointed out low merchant adoption, and poor user interface as crucial reasons for youth's lower e-wallet adaptation rate. Thus, this issue warrants more academic focus. This study identifies important factors such as perceived usefulness, perceived ease of use, social influence, service trust, user innovativeness, technological optimism and perceived Covid-19 risk and their influence on the adoption of Fintech, specially E-wallet by university students. The following section provides the theoretical foundation of the issue; based on that, the association among identified constructs was highlighted. Then, the conceptual framework was proposed, and data analysis results were described. Finally, the contribution and limitations were acknowledged.

2. THEORETICAL BACKGROUND

2.1 Technology Acceptance Model (TAM)

To describe the influence of variables on customer behaviour and intentions, The Technology Acceptance Model (TAM) was proposed by (Davis et al., 1989). TAM has been widely cited in different settings in the field of study since its inception (Martono, 2021). The model describes that the user's intentions to use are influenced by perceived ease of use, perceived utility and attitude.

According to this model, the perceived ease of use explains the degree to which a consumer feels that using a specific device or technology requires much less effort (Wang, 2021). In addition, perceived usefulness describes the extent to which a user feels that specific methods will directly influence his/her output. It has been argued that perceived ease of use and perceived utility directly affect user expectations, which in turn affect the intention of users to use and implement the method (Um et al., 2020). TAM was adopted for this study because it has been used frequently to understand the degree of acceptance of users against a specific method.

2.2 Social Cognitive Theory (SCT)

Social Cognitive Theory (SCT) was developed in the 1960s by Albert Bandura as the Social Learning Theory (SLT). In 1986, it evolved into the SCT and posited that learning occurs with a complex and reciprocal interaction of the individual, environment, and actions in a social context. One of the distinct characteristics of SCT is its focus on social power and its emphasis on external and internal reinforcement. SCT recognises how people assimilate and sustain behaviour while also considering the social contexts in which people carry out those behaviours. To understand whether there will be a behaviour intervention, this theory looks at an individual's past experiences. Whether an individual will engage in a particular behaviour and why they are engaged is influenced by their past experiences, which affect their perceptions, abilities and expectations (Masnita et al., 2021).

Many behaviour models in health promotion concentrate on behaviour initiation rather than behavioural maintenance. The real purpose of public health is not just the initiation of behaviour; instead, it should also be about the continuation of conduct. The goal of SCT is to understand how people manage their actions through control and encouragement to achieve goal-directed behaviour that can be sustained over time (Khan et al., 2021). As part of the SLT, the first five constructs were established; when the theory developed into SCT, the concept of self-efficacy was added.

1. Reciprocal Determinism - The core principle of SCT is this. This applies to the individual's complex and mutual relationship (individual with a collection of experiences learned), environment (external social context), and actions (responses to stimuli to achieve goals).
2. Behavioral Capability – This means the actual capacity of a person to conduct a behaviour who attains it through acquiring necessary information and skill. A person must know what to do and how to do it before carrying out a behaviour effectively. The world where people live is affected by the learning they receive from their behaviours.
3. Observational learning states that individuals can mimic certain behaviours if they have witnessed and observed the same behaviour before. This is also illustrated by the "modelling" of behaviour, and people can effectively complete a behaviour if they see an excellent example of that particular behaviour.
4. Reinforcements – When the probability of continuation or discontinuation of a behaviour depends on the internal or external reactions. Reinforcements can be initiated on their own or in the setting, and reinforcements can be positive or negative. This SCT definition is most closely related to the mutual relationship between actions and the environment.
5. Expectations – Talks about the actions of an individual and their expected effects. Expectations of the result may be related to health or not related to health. Before starting an activity, people anticipate probable consequences, which will impact their performance when he gets into the act. Expectations are usually extracted from past knowledge. Although expectations often derive from previous experience, expectations concentrate on the importance put on the result and are subjective to the person.
6. Self-efficacy – Explains that an individual's ability to perform a behaviour effectively depends on how much trust they put in their ability. This refers to the degree of trust of a person in his or her ability to carry out a behaviour effectively. Self-efficacy is unique to SCT, but other theories, such as the Expected Action Theory, have added this structure at later dates. Individual variables, unique skills and environmental variables (barriers and facilitators) affect Self-efficacy.

2.3 Theory of Planned Behaviour (TPB)

According to Warshaw and Davis (1985), the purpose of the behaviour is defined as the degree to which a person has developed deliberate plans to perform or not perform certain future behaviours. Nevertheless, Ajzen's (1985) planned behaviour theory claimed that behavioural intention is a good predictor of actual behaviour.

The TPB has been used by researchers in social psychology to analyse human behaviour (Chang et al., 2016) and has found support in predicting consumer behaviours in the IS literature (Singh et al., 2020). According to TPB (Ajzen, 1985), individual behavioural intentions can generally be reliably predicted by attitudes towards actions, subjective standards, and expectations of behavioural regulation. Most TPB applications have recently recognised that perceptions, subjective norms, and perceived behavioural regulation are essential for understanding and predicting behavioural intentions in contexts associated with IT acceptance or adoption (Solarz & Swacha-Lech, 2021).

According to TPB, the precedent of any action is the purpose of executing that behaviour (Fishbein & Ajzen, 1975). Intentions measure how challenging individuals are willing to attempt and how much effort they are willing to bring in to carry out a behaviour. If the mindset of individual changes, there is a clear commitment to do something; the actions will change.

3. DISCUSSION ABOUT CONSTRUCTS

3.1 Intention Towards FinTech adoption (ITFA)

The intent to use conduct has become a crucial dimension as the emergence of FinTech occurred, and its confluence with the brick-and-mortar financial industry is a sign that there is a high possibility that consumers will soon embrace FinTech (Hendrikse et al., 2020). The original TAM model (Davis, 1985) argues that the usage pattern is influenced by behavioural intention. Concerning the level of customer awareness, the rate of technological innovation in financial services also significantly impacts an individual's behavioural intent. In addition, FinTech firms may not be able to enjoy the benefits of innovation, or if technological development is faster than customer knowledge and use, the gestation period to earn profits will increase (Haghjooye Javanmardet al., 2022). Therefore, as the use and adoption of the technology hold a lot of several potential researchers are interested in it, and many theories and models are being proposed to study behavioural intent. (Nurlaily et al., 2021).

3.2 Perceived Usefulness (PU) and Intention Towards FinTech Adoption (ITFA)

When one perceives that the use of technology will have a certain degree of boost (Davis et al., 1989), prior studies outlined the influence of perceived utility on behavioural intent (Davis, 1993; Venkatesh et al., 2003). The perceived utility is critical in assessing technology adoption (Sing et al., 2020). The current literature has indicated that perceived utility significantly influences the decision to implement technological technologies, thereby influencing their actual use (Chan et al., 2022), especially Fintech (Shiau et al., 2021).

H1: Perceived usefulness has a significant influence on Intention towards FinTech adoption

3.3 Perceived Ease of Use (PEU) and Intention Towards FinTech Adoption (ITFA)

When someone considers technology use to be effortless to a certain degree (Davis et al., 1989), it is also defined as the degree of effort needed by a technology for its easier use (Venkatesh & Davis, 2000). According to TAM, perceived ease of use is the main factor to explain the difference in perceived usefulness. Regarding reusing technology resources, ease of use has a positive and direct impact (Venkatesh & Davis, 2000; Jünger & Mietzner, 2020). This influences consumers to implement technical services in the long run. The use of technology services, including internet banking, is also influenced by perceived ease of use and increased use by consumers (Utami et al., 2023), as well as other IT-related items. As there are various variants of FinTech services, it is possible to test the impression of ease of use for its impact on the intention to conduct and on the actual use of FinTech services (Nangin et al., 2021).

H2: Perceived Ease of Use has a significant influence on Intention towards FinTech adoption

3.4 Social Influence (SI) and Intention Towards FinTech Adoption (ITFA)

The degree to which others influence the use of a given technology is social influence (Venkatesh et al., 2012). The impact of social knowledge acting similarly to social pressure to adhere to specified actions or opinions has been identified in current literature (Fishbein & Ajzen, 1975). For disruptive innovations, the impact of social norms is far greater as it is presumed that an individual consults his or her social circle about emerging technologies and can be influenced by the knowledge they provide. Individuals rely more on others' views and opinions when they have no experience with a particular technology feature. Also, as the service offered is new, the attitude towards technology is affected by social expectations. Therefore, behaviour, comments and attitudes regarding the use of technology by essential colleagues, friends and family are necessary. Social influence is the most hypothesised and tested construct of UTAUT in the current literature, and there is a substantial relationship between social influence and its impact on the intention to use conduct (Singh et al., 2020; Rahi et al., 2019). Although conflicting findings are documented in some studies (Shin, 2010), they may be partly due to the different methods of applying social control in one's social context. It will therefore be essential to test the relationship between social influence and the purpose and use of behaviour, as users change their actions to achieve social recognition according to the actions of others.

H3: Social Influence has a significant influence on Intention towards FinTech adoption

3.5 Service Trust (ST) and Intention Towards FinTech Adoption (ITFA)

Confidence is focused on the relationships between individuals and individuals, individuals and objects, or people and things. Benevolence, integrity and competence are the three components of faith (Vize et al., 2020). Confidence is considered credible and benevolent, includes fundamental beliefs in capacity, benevolence, and honesty, and is prepared to rely on another group. Trust has been conceptualised as trust (Nangin et al., 2020). A trustor trusts that a trustee will meet the needs of the trustor will trust an individual or a group's intentions or acts (Khatri et al., 2020).

In addition, Lee and Turban (2001) presumed that trust is a belief, expectation, or feeling about certain things; some antecedents will increase or retain the degree of trust that will affect the faith in the transaction of both parties. A person will only take unusual action that would result in the trading partners' negative results or risks (Anderson & Narus, 1990). They are still not popular because of the Fintech service feature;

Fintech Service users sometimes need to browse the website for the services. The brand will help customers decide when the product's consistency and related functions are uncertain (Ratnasingam & Pavlou, 2003). In order to resolve the trust problem of a customer, enterprises should take advantage of the prestige of their brand images, such as its stability, long history, and trustworthiness. The reputation of companies as a brand and service positively influences customer trust (Khatri et al., 2020). Cojoianu et al. (2021) and Heijden, Verhagen, and Creemers (2003) indicated that perception of confidence and interactions would directly influence the buying attitude of a customer when using new technologies. When customer trust in the brand and service increases, the attitude toward buying is more optimistic. Consumers will take a favourable attitude towards this enterprise if consumers feel that the information given by businesses is truthful.

H4: Service Trust has a significant influence on Intention towards FinTech adoption

3.6 User Innovativeness (UI) and Intention Towards FinTech Adoption (ITFA)

User innovativeness is the degree of willingness of individuals to experiment with new technologies (Lu et al., 2005). Optimising external knowledge and information user innovativeness can be accelerated (Setiawan et al., 2021). Meanwhile, Chen et al. (2021) describe the acceptance of new products, technologies and new services can be measured by user innovation. The main driving factor for technology adoption depends on the readiness to accept the presence of new technology. The user innovativeness in this research is defined as an intention to try new technologies, a pioneer in using the latest technology, and be willing to experiment with Fintech services. A prior study showed that user innovativeness positively correlates with technology adoption (Zheng et al., 2018).

H5: User Innovativeness has a significant influence on Intention towards FinTech adoption

3.7 Technological Optimism (TO) and Intention Towards FinTech Adoption (ITFA)

When it is believed positively that technology offers its users increased control, flexibility and efficiency is considered technological optimism. (Parasuraman and Colby, 2015). People perceive Artificial intelligence as hell or heaven. (Kaplan and Haenlein, 2020). Optimists are more willing to use new technologies in certain situations (Ali et al., 2021) compared to pessimistic tech users who put more trust and consider them functional (Walczuch et al., 2007). Thus, optimistic customers are more positively inclined toward new technologies (Godoe & Johansen, 2012). In the financial sector, new technological tools are more desirable to enthusiastic consumers (Clark-Murphy & Soutar, 2004), for example, e-wallets.

H6: Technological optimism has a significant influence on Intention towards FinTech adoption

3.8 Perceived Covid-19 Risk as a Moderator

Bauer (1960) was the first to argue that consumers' buying decisions are influenced by perceived risks (PR). Numerous experts have argued that public relations substantially impact a user's intent to employ technology (Chuang et al., 2016). Regarding digital payments, most research has shown that "privacy and security" are the top risk concerns influencing customers' willingness to use mobile payments (Liébana-Cabanillas et al., 2020; Sinha et al., 2018).

Few research, however, has examined "disease risk" as a factor influencing customers' intent to utilise digital payments. Aji et al. (2020) reported that the outbreak of COVID-19 negatively impacted the intention of Indonesian and Malaysian customers to use cash. However, it expanded its use of electronic wallets for financial transactions. In the same context, mobile payment is viewed as a healthy activity that minimises the likelihood of catching the virus (C.C. & Prathap, 2020; Raj et al., 2023).

Since using cash, banknotes, and contact-based payment systems may contribute to the spread of COVID-19, the WHO recommends that consumers use contactless digital payment methods (Durr, 2020). Based on the present literature and reports from government and healthcare organisations, PC19R will influence Malaysian millennials usage of Fintech for shopping and banking. Consequently, we offer the following hypothesis:

H7: Perceived Covid-19 Risk moderates on Perceived Usefulness and Intention towards FinTech adoption
H8: Perceived Covid-19 Risk moderates on Perceived Ease of Use and Intention towards FinTech adoption
H9: Perceived Covid-19 Risk moderates on Social Influence and Intention towards FinTech adoption
H10: Perceived Covid-19 Risk moderates Service Trust and Intention towards FinTech adoption
H11: Perceived Covid-19 Risk moderates User Innovativeness and Intention towards FinTech adoption
H12: Perceived Covid-19 Risk moderates on Technological optimism and Intention towards FinTech adoption

4. CONCEPTUAL FRAMEWORK

Figure 2. Conceptual framework developed by researchers

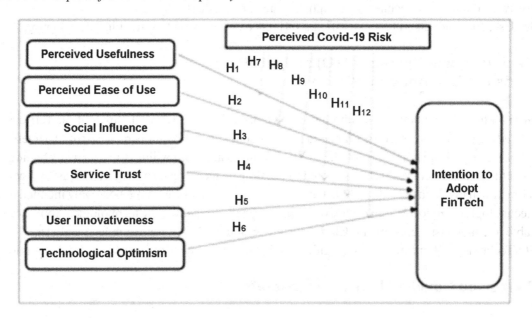

5. METHODOLOGY

The current study followed the positivism paradigm, deductive approach, and quantitative method. A survey was performed on the university students of Malaysian Universities to collect the data through a close-ended structured paper-based questionnaire. The convenience sampling technique was applied for data collection purposes. Data was collected from 15th January 2022 to 30th June 2022, which made the study cross-sectional. The measurement items for each variable were adapted from the prior literature. An industry expert and academia expert conducted a pre-test and pilot study to minimise errors and enhance the quality of the questionnaire. A total of 233 responses were collected, and 213 were taken for the final study after performing proper screening. Among 213 respondents, 78.25% were male, and 21.75% were female. SPSS (v.28) and SmartPLS (v.4) were utilised for analysing the data. SPSS was used for the descriptive analysis and bias test. SmartPLS (v.4) was utilised to assess constructs' reliability, validity, and structural equation modelling (SEM).

6. RESULTS AND DISCUSSION

Construct Reliability and Validity

The reliability and validity of the constructs were determined through the value of Cronbach's Alpha (CA), Composite Reliability (CR), and Average Variance Extracted (AVE). The statistical outcome in Table 1 revealed that CA and CR values for all the constructs were acceptable as the value were above 0.8 and AVE values were above 0.5, which is greater than the recommended threshold of 0.5 (Hair et al., 2017).

Discriminant Validity

The current study assessed discriminant validity through the Fronell-Larcker criterion. The statistical outcome indicated that the value of the Fornell-Larcker criterion is significant and in the acceptable range (Table 3). All the cross-loading and HTMT values (Table 2) were acceptable, as values were above .7 and less than one, respectively (Henseler et al., 2015).

Structural Model Assessment

Coefficient of Determination (R^2)

Statistical data revealed that the coefficient of determination values are 65% and 62%, indicating that the models are substantially acceptable, as coined by Cohen (2013).

Table 1. Construct reliability and validity

Constructs	Cronbach's alpha (CA)	Composite reliability (CR)	The average variance extracted (AVE)
ITFA	0.895	0.898	0.706
PCR	0.856	0.900	0.696
PEU	0.890	0.899	0.696
PU	0.896	0.897	0.763
SI	0.901	0.908	0.669
ST	0.876	0.880	0.670
TO	0.921	0.928	0.717
UI	0.877	0.885	0.670

Table 2. Heterotrait-Monotrait ratio (HTMT) criterion

Constructs	ITFA	PCR	PEU	PU	SI	ST	TO	UI
ITFA								
PCR	0.409							
PEU	0.617	0.338						
PU	0.717	0.410	0.710					
SI	0.647	0.425	0.507	0.644				
ST	0.724	0.325	0.547	0.590	0.536			
TO	0.774	0.447	0.534	0.660	0.567	0.649		
UI	0.601	0.399	0.512	0.459	0.615	0.570	0.613	

Table 3. Fornell-Larcker criterion

Constructs	ITFA	PCR	PEU	PU	SI	ST	TO	UI
ITFA	0.840							
PCR	0.377	0.834						
PEU	0.557	0.316	0.834					
PU	0.644	0.376	0.639	0.873				
SI	0.587	0.390	0.453	0.583	0.818			
ST	0.644	0.280	0.484	0.523	0.478	0.818		
TO	0.708	0.409	0.488	0.603	0.520	0.587	0.847	
UI	0.543	0.365	0.456	0.411	0.551	0.504	0.557	0.818

Figure 3. Measurement model

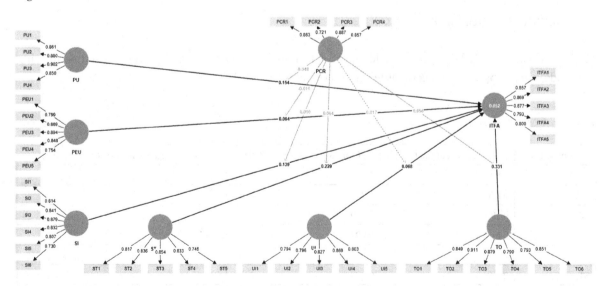

Table 4. Coefficient of determination (R2)

Dependent variable	R-square	R-square adjusted
ITFA	0.652	0.629

Effect Size (f²)

Using Cohen's f2 (Cohen, 2013), the investigator assesses the effect size of the predictor constructs. f2 measures the relative effect on an endogenous construct of a predictor construct (Cohen, 2013). Cohen (2013) considers the f2 values of 0.35, 0.15 and 0.02 as high, medium, and small effect sizes, respectively. In Table 5, the results of the f2 for the current study are presented where the effect size of most of the constructs is small and TO has a medium effect size.

Predictive Relevancy (Q²)

The outcome of Q2 in Table 6 indicates that the Q2 value was found to be 0.53 (higher than zero), indicating predictive relevancy.

Multicollinearity Test (Inner VIF)

Based on the Collinearity result in Table 7, there is no multicollinearity problem in the current study, as the inner VIF values except TO2 is higher than 5.

Table 5. Effect size (f2)

Constructs	ITFA
ITFA	
PCR	0.000
PEU	0.012
PU	0.024
SI	0.027
ST	0.080
TO	0.142
UI	0.007

Table 6. Predictive relevancy (Q2)

Dependent variable	Q²predict	RMSE	MAE
ITFA	0.533	0.693	0.485

Table 7. Multicollinearity test (Inner VIF)

Exogenous Variables	VIF
ITFA1	3.264
ITFA2	3.271
ITFA3	2.837
ITFA4	2.139
ITFA5	2.178
PCR1	1.937
PCR2	1.608
PCR3	2.747
PCR4	2.342
PEU1	2.035
PEU2	2.691
PEU3	3.082
PEU4	2.554
PEU5	1.830
PU1	2.278
PU2	2.714
PU3	3.085
PU4	2.202
SI1	2.547
SI2	3.078
SI3	3.320
SI4	2.495
SI5	2.293
SI6	1.931
ST1	2.292
ST2	2.326
ST3	2.449
ST4	2.390
ST5	1.815
TO1	3.837
TO2	5.344
TO3	3.137
TO4	2.240
TO5	2.449
TO6	2.680
UI1	2.106
UI2	2.316
UI3	2.232
UI4	2.785
UI5	2.101

Figure 4. Structural model

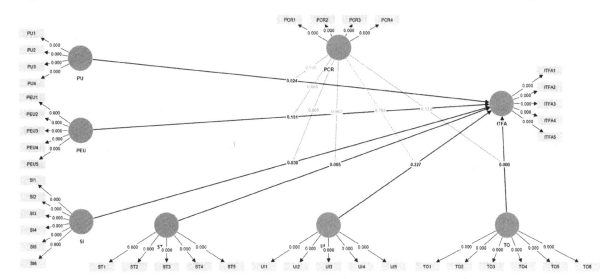

7. HYPOTHESIS TEST RESULT AND DISCUSSION

Table 8 illustrates the results of the hypotheses testing. P values for most the hypotheses except H1, H3, H4, H6 were higher than 0.05, thus H2, H5, H7, H8, H9, H10, H11, H12 were rejected.

Previous research by Aksami dan Jember (2019); Suprapto (2022); Halim et al. (2020) found a positive and significant effect of the usefulness aspect on interest in utilising E-Wallet services, and our findings support this. This suggests that the adoption rate of E-Wallet services, and hence the prevalence of cashless transactions, will rise in proportion to their perceived value.

Table 8. Hypotheses test result

Hypotheses	Original sample (O)	Sample mean (M)	Standard deviation (STDEV)	T statistics (|O/ STDEV|)	P values	Result
H1: PU -> ITFA	0.154	0.153	0.068	2.252	0.024	Accept
H2: PEU -> ITFA	0.094	0.085	0.065	1.435	0.151	Reject
H3: SI -> ITFA	0.139	0.126	0.064	2.177	0.030	Accept
H4: ST -> ITFA	0.229	0.238	0.082	2.797	0.005	Accept
H5: UI -> ITFA	0.068	0.066	0.056	1.209	0.227	Reject
H6: TO -> ITFA	0.331	0.342	0.089	3.703	0.000	Accept
H7: PCR x PU -> ITFA	-0.048	-0.044	0.079	0.614	0.539	Reject
H8: PCR x PEU -> ITFA	-0.010	-0.006	0.069	0.143	0.886	Reject
H9: PCR x SI -> ITFA	0.010	0.008	0.063	0.165	0.869	Reject
H10: PCR x ST -> ITFA	0.004	0.003	0.082	0.046	0.963	Reject
H11: PCR x UI -> ITFA	0.017	0.022	0.064	0.264	0.792	Reject
H12: PCR x TO -> ITFA	0.056	0.029	0.099	0.565	0.572	Reject

Results from H2 align with a study by Setiani (2018), which found that convenience perception did not significantly affect the usage of alternative payment methods. However, some customers who have yet to experience the service's streamlined convenience may be put off by the frequent program changes performed by the E-Wallet provider and may conclude that the E-Wallet app's instructions are too complicated to figure out.

For H3, we find that the hypothesis is supported, with interest in utilising E-Wallet increasing as word of mouth spreads. One of the motivating aspects for E-Wallet adoption is the social influence of those around the user, such as friends and family. Kim et al. (2016) claim that an individual's pattern of behaviour change can be influenced by social influence if we consider compliance as a form of internalised and self-identified belief and social status modification. The study's findings are corroborated by those of (Xu et al., 2017), who explained that consumers benefit from social influence because it helps them obtain more accurate information from social environment factors, such as suggestions and advice from trustworthy information sources when engaging in financial activities.

Service trust affects fintech use (H4). Users must have faith in the services and resources that support Fintech, as this might motivate them to utilise Fintech or remain loyal to it. This study confirms the research of Salam and Abdiyanti (2022) by showing that the frequency of fintech use would increase as consumers' trust in fintech services grows. Users will require Fintech to facilitate their financial transactions if Fintech can give a pleasant experience. This study indicated that the greater users' trust in service, the greater their usage and intention to use Fintech, as well as their loyalty to fintech use.

According to Adeiza et al. (2017), innovation is a fundamental human characteristic that indicates consumer interest in a new subject. As proven by empirical research, Kim et al. (2016) conclude in their study of mobile payment users' adoption behaviour that because most people lack a professional understanding of a wide variety of mobile services, individual inventiveness strongly determines their desire to use (Al Nawayseh, 2020).

The result demonstrated that H6 is acceptable. Technological optimism can be viewed as a mental state caused by the gestalt of mental inhibitors that collectively affect a person's propensity to employ new information. In research on the B2B healthcare sector, Hallikainen and Laukkanen (2016) discovered a correlation between technological optimism and digital service acceptability.

Concerning the moderation of Covid-19, the analyses revealed partially consistent and partially country-specific patterns of results that diverged from the results of the entire sample and, in some instances, indicated paradoxical correlations between variables within our purview. The Malaysian populace adopted digital payment systems before covid-19; hence the covid-19 did not affect their purchasing patterns. Since Bauer's landmark study, the influence of perceived risk on consumer behaviour has garnered the interest of researchers (Bauer, 1960). Bauer identifies two major components: (1) lack of awareness regarding what will occur while using mobile payment systems, often known as client uncertainty, and (2) the likelihood of unfavourable or unanticipated effects from this payment. In addition, Bauer confirms that any client behaviour involving uncertainty carries risk due to unanticipated user repercussions (Bauer, 1960). However, Gerrard and Cunningham (2003) defined perceived risk as the chance that the innovation could be safer to utilise. In diverse models of the adoption of information systems, perceived risk has also been accorded significant weight, as it reflects users' views of uncertainty and the negative repercussions of participation in the activity, hence reducing their intention to use and continue to use the system (Shiauet al., 2020).

8. CONCLUSION AND IMPLICATIONS

This empirical study aimed to examine the factors influencing Malaysian Gen X's intention to make digital payments (Fintech) during the COVID-19 pandemic. The direct and indirect effects of Perceived Usefulness, Perceived Ease of Use, Social Influence, Service Trust, User Innovativeness, and Technological Optimism on intention to adopt Fintech by Malaysian millennials. Moreover, the Perceived Covid-19 Risk acts as a moderator, and the moderator did not show any signs of this context. Including the physical risk of COVID-19 in the technology acceptance model represents a theoretical contribution to the literature. Finally, our study provides practical implications for FinTech payment services during crises such as COVID-19.

Since the financial services sector in Malaysia is primarily controlled by foreigners and faces similar challenges raised by the diffusion of FinTech solutions in the context of the pandemic, our findings may have implications for policymakers in other countries where the financial inclusion of Gen X is a priority. Because of the ongoing pandemic, people's payment practices are shifting. By highlighting the dangers of using traditional payment methods, COVID-19 has raised public support for innovative payment solutions and affected the decisions of millennials.

The adoption of FinTech not only focus on e-wallet and e-payment but also to other FinTech such as digital currency, crowdfunding, and digital insurance. It proves that perceived benefits, in particular, are universal drivers of FinTech adoption. Contrarily, the survey also identified COVID-19 risk as a insignificant moderator on FinTech adoption. Consumers in underdeveloped economies frequently see perceived risk as less serious, which is consistent with prior studies. Although there are some signs that this condition is related to the demographics of the respondents, this study cannot attest to the hypothesis because we did not investigate the impacts of demographics. According to several studies, younger generations with less money are more risk-tolerant and less exposed to risks (Abdul-Rahim et al., 2022). Future research should address this restriction or employ a larger sample size.

The findings endorse Malaysia's strategic initiative to utilize I-4.0 digital technologies in a responsible manner to attain a high-income economy status. It is imperative for governments to enhance their backing and dedication towards the advancement of widespread FinTech adoption in order to achieve financial inclusivity, community resilience, and sustainability both during times of crises and in the long term. The COVID-19 pandemic has significantly facilitated the adoption of FinTech by certain beneficiaries, providing them with advantageous outcomes. It is recommended that stakeholders in the FinTech industry, as well as policymakers, capitalize on the changes in consumer behavior brought about by the pandemic. This can be achieved by encouraging consumers to adopt FinTech as a means of effectively managing financial transactions even after the crisis has subsided. The findings presented in this study can be utilized by policymakers to devise effective interventions and durable policies aimed at leveraging FinTech to address sustainability issues in the actual economy.

Limitations and Future Directions

However, demographic factors unique to the millennials cohort, such as gender, socioeconomic status, and levels of education, were not investigated. In addition to respondents' location (rural vs urban), family composition (single vs married vs no kids), and job status, these variables should be considered in future studies of mobile payment usage. This study does not track participants over time; instead, it is cross-sectional. The sample is tiny, and it only includes people from Malaysia; this could cause problems with generalizability. However, for future studies to have any generalizability, more extensive and representative samples of professional panel providers need to be used.

REFERENCES

Abd Hamid, M. A. A. C., Khairuddin, M. F., Noor, N. A. M., & Mohamad, N. A. (2023). *The study on factors affecting intention to continuously use financial technology (Fintech) among Universiti Malaysia Kelantan (UMK) students post Covid-19* [Doctoral dissertation, Universiti Malaysia Kelantan].

Abdul-Rahim, R., Bohari, S. A., Aman, A., & Awang, Z. (2022). Benefit–Risk Perceptions of FinTech Adoption for Sustainability from Bank Consumers' Perspective: The Moderating Role of Fear of CO-VID-19. *Sustainability (Basel)*, *14*(14), 8357. doi:10.3390u14148357

Adeiza, A., Malek, M. A., & Ismail, N. A. (2017). An Empirical Analysis of the Influence of Entrepreneurial Orientation on Franchisees' Outlet Performance and Intention to Stay. *The Korean Journal of Franchise Management*, *8*(1), 5–18. doi:10.21871/KJFM.2017.03.8.1.5.

Aji, H. M., Berakon, I., & Md Husin, M. (2020). COVID-19 and e-wallet usage intention: A multigroup analysis between Indonesia and Malaysia. *Cogent Business and Management*, *7*(1), 1804181. doi:10.1 080/23311975.2020.1804181

Ajzen, I. (1985). *From intentions to actions: A theory of planned behaviour*. Springer Berlin Heidelberg.

Ajzen, I., & Fishbein, M. (1975). A Bayesian analysis of attribution processes. *Psychological Bulletin*, *82*(2), 261–277. doi:10.1037/h0076477

Aksami, N. M. D., & Jember, I. M. (2019). Analisis minat penggunaan layanan e-money pada masyarakat kota Denpasar. *E-Jurnal EP Unud*, *8*(9), 2439–2470.

Al-Nawayseh, M. K. (2020). Fintech in COVID-19 and beyond: What factors are affecting customers' choice of FinTech applications? *Journal of Open Innovation*, *6*(4), 1–15. doi:10.3390/joitmc6040153

Ali, M., Raza, S. A., Khamis, B., Puah, C. H., & Amin, H. (2021). How perceived risk, benefit and trust determine user Fintech adoption: A new dimension for Islamic finance. *Foresight*, *23*(4), 403–420. doi:10.1108/FS-09-2020-0095

Alsmadi, A., Alfityani, A., & Alhwamdeh, L., Al_hazimeh, A., & Al-Gasawneh, J. (2022). Intentions to use FinTech in the Jordanian banking industry. *International Journal of Data and Network Science*, *6*(4), 1351–1358. doi:10.5267/j.ijdns.2022.5.016

Alt, R., & Puschmann, T. (2012). The rise of customer-oriented banking-electronic markets are paving the way for change in the financial industry. *Electronic Markets*, *22*(4), 203–215. doi:10.100712525-012-0106-2

Anderson, J. C., & Narus, J. A. (1990). A model of distributor firm and manufacturer firm working partnerships. *Journal of Marketing*, *54*(1), 42–58. doi:10.1177/002224299005400103

Barrett-Maitland, N., Barclay, C., & Osei-Bryson, K. M. (2016). Security in social networking services: A value-focused thinking exploration in understanding users' privacy and security concerns. *Information Technology for Development*, *22*(3), 464–486. doi:10.1080/02681102.2016.1173002

Bauer, R. A. (1960). Consumer behavior as risk taking. In *Proceedings of the 43rd National Conference of the American Marketing Association*. American Marketing Association.

BNM. (2019). *List of Regulatees*. BNM.

Butt, S., & Khan, Z. A. (2019). Fintech in Pakistan: A qualitative study of bank's strategic planning for an investment in fintech company and its challenges. *Independent Journal of Management & Production*, *10*(6), 2092–2101. doi:10.14807/ijmp.v10i6.947

C.C., S. & Prathap, S.K. (2020). Continuance adoption of mobile-based payments in Covid-19 context: An integrated framework of health belief model and expectation confirmation model. *International Journal of Pervasive Computing and Communications*, *16*(4), 351–369. doi:10.1108/IJPCC-06-2020-0069

Chan, R., Troshani, I., Hill, S. R., & Hoffmann, A. (2022). Towards an understanding of consumers' FinTech adoption: The case of Open Banking. *International Journal of Bank Marketing*, *40*(4), 886–917. doi:10.1108/IJBM-08-2021-0397

Chang, Y., Wong, S. F., Lee, H., & Jeong, S. P. (2016, August). What motivates chinese consumers to adopt FinTech services: a regulatory focus theory. In *Proceedings of the 18th annual international conference on electronic commerce: e-commerce in smart connected world* (pp. 1-3). ACM. 10.1145/2971603.2971643

Chen, M., Sinha, A., Hu, K., & Shah, M. I. (2021). Impact of technological innovation on energy efficiency in industry 4.0 era: Moderation of shadow economy in sustainable development. *Technological Forecasting and Social Change*, *164*, 120521. doi:10.1016/j.techfore.2020.120521

Chuang, L. M., Liu, C. C., & Kao, H. K. (2016). The adoption of fintech service: TAM perspective. *International Journal of Management and Administrative Sciences*, *3*(7), 1–15.

Clark-Murphy, M., & Soutar, G. N. (2004). What individual investors value: Some Australian evidence. *Journal of Economic Psychology*, *25*(4), 539–555. doi:10.1016/S0167-4870(03)00056-4

Cohen, J. (2013). *Statistical power analysis for the behavioral sciences*. Routledge. doi:10.4324/9780203771587

Cojoianu, T. F., Clark, G. L., Hoepner, A. G., Pažitka, V., & Wójcik, D. (2021). Fin vs. tech: Are trust and knowledge creation key ingredients in fintech start-up emergence and financing? *Small Business Economics*, *57*(4), 1715–1731. doi:10.100711187-020-00367-3

Davis, F. D. (1989). Perceived usefulness, perceived ease of use, and user acceptance of information technology. *Management Information Systems Quarterly*, *13*(3), 319–340. doi:10.2307/249008

Durr, M. (2020). *World Health Organization says cash may contribute to spread of coronavirus, promotes paperless spending* [WWW Document]. M Live. https://www.mlive.com/coronavirus/2020/03/world-health-organizationsays-cash-may-contribute-to-spread-of-coronavirus-promotes-paperlessspending.html (accessed 12.1.22).

Fu, J., & Mishra, M. (2020). The global impact of COVID-19 on FinTech adoption. *Swiss Finance Institute Research Paper*, (20-38).

Gerrard, P., & Cunningham, J. B. (2003). The diffusion of internet banking among Singapore consumers. *International Journal of Bank Marketing*, *21*(1), 16–28. doi:10.1108/02652320310457776

Godoe, P., and Johansen, T. (2012). Understanding adoption of new technologies: Technology readiness and technology acceptance as an integrated concept. *Journal of European psychology students, 3*(1).

Goel, P., Kulsrestha, S., & Maurya, S. K. (2022). Fintech Unfolding: Financial Revolution in India. *Thailand and The World Economy, 40*(2), 41–51.

Haghjooye Javanmard, N., Keymasi, M., & Shah Hosseini, M. (2022). Developing a Model for Measuring the Quality of Fintech Customer Service Using a Systematic Review Approach. *New Marketing Research Journal, 12*(2), 189–216.

Hair, J. F. Jr, Sarstedt, M., Ringle, C. M., & Gudergan, S. P. (2017). *Advanced issues in partial least squares structural equation modeling*. Sage publications.

Halim, F., Efendi, E., Butarbutar, M., Malau, A. R., & Sudirman, A. (2020, October). Constituents driving interest in using e-wallets in generation Z. In *Proceeding on International Conference of Science Management Art Research Technology* (Vol. 1, pp. 101-116). Semantic Scholar.

Hallikainen, H., & Laukkanen, T. (2016). How technology readiness explains acceptance and satisfaction of digital services in B2B healthcare sector? *PACIS 2016 Proceedings*. AIS. https://aisel.aisnet.org/pacis2016/294

Hendrikse, R., Van Meeteren, M., & Bassens, D. (2020). Strategic coupling between finance, technology and the state: Cultivating a Fintech ecosystem for incumbent finance. *Environment and Planning A. Environment & Planning A, 52*(8), 1516–1538. doi:10.1177/0308518X19887967

Henseler, J., Ringle, C. M., & Sarstedt, M. (2015). A new criterion for assessing discriminant validity in variance-based structural equation modeling. *Journal of the Academy of Marketing Science, 43*(1), 115–135. doi:10.100711747-014-0403-8

Ing, A. Y., Wong, T. K., & Lim, P. Y. (2021). Intention To Use E-Wallet Amongst the University Students in Klang Valley. *International Journal of Business and Economy, 3*(1), 75–84.

Jünger, M., & Mietzner, M. (2020). Banking goes digital: The adoption of FinTech services by German households. *Finance Research Letters, 34*, 101260. doi:10.1016/j.frl.2019.08.008

Kaplan, A., & Haenlein, M. (2020). Rulers of the world, unite! The challenges and opportunities of artificial intelligence. *Business Horizons, 63*(1), 37–50. doi:10.1016/j.bushor.2019.09.003

Karim, M. W., Haque, A., Ulfy, M. A., Hossain, M. A., and Anis, M. Z. (2020). Factors influencing the use of E-wallet as a payment method among Malaysian young adults. *Journal of International Business and Management, 3*(2), 01-12.

Khan, M. T. I., Yee, G. H., & Gan, G. G. G. (2021). Antecedents of Intention to Use Online Peer-to-Peer Platform in Malaysia. *Vision (Basel)*, 09722629211039051.

Khan, N. F., Ikram, N., Murtaza, H., & Asadi, M. A. (2023). Social media users and cybersecurity awareness: Predicting self-disclosure using a hybrid artificial intelligence approach. *Kybernetes*, *52*(1), 401–421. doi:10.1108/K-05-2021-0377

Khatri, A., Gupta, N., & Parashar, A. (2020). Application of Technology Acceptance Model (TAM) in Fintech Services. [IJM]. *International Journal of Management*, *11*(12). doi:10.34218/IJM.11.12.2020.328

Kim, Y., Choi, J., Park, Y. J., & Yeon, J. (2016). The adoption of mobile payment services for "Fintech". *International Journal of Applied Engineering Research: IJAER*, *11*(2), 1058–1061.

Le, M. T. (2021). Examining factors that boost intention and loyalty to use Fintech post-COVID-19 lockdown as a new normal behavior. *Heliyon*, *7*(8), e07821. doi:10.1016/j.heliyon.2021.e07821 PMID:34458639

Lee, M. K., & Turban, E. (2001). A trust model for consumer internet shopping. *International Journal of Electronic Commerce*, *6*(1), 75–91. doi:10.1080/10864415.2001.11044227

Leong, K., & Sung, A. (2018). FinTech (Financial Technology): What is it and how to use technologies to create business value in fintech way? *International Journal of Innovation, Management and Technology*, *9*(2), 74–78. doi:10.18178/ijimt.2018.9.2.791

Liébana-Cabanillas, F., García-Maroto, I., Muñoz-Leiva, F., & Ramos-de-Luna, I. (2020). Mobile payment adoption in the age of digital transformation: The case of Apple Pay. *Sustainability (Basel)*, *12*(13), 5443. doi:10.3390u12135443

Lu, J., Yao, J. E., & Yu, C. S. (2005). Personal innovativeness, social influences and adoption of wireless Internet services via mobile technology. *The Journal of Strategic Information Systems*, *14*(3), 245–268. doi:10.1016/j.jsis.2005.07.003

Macchiavello, E., & Siri, M. (2022). Sustainable Finance and Fintech: Can Technology Contribute to Achieving Environmental Goals? A Preliminary Assessment of 'Green Fintech' and 'Sustainable Digital Finance'. *European Company and Financial Law Review*, *19*(1), 128–174. doi:10.1515/ecfr-2022-0005

Martinčević, I., Črnjević, S., & Klopotan, I. (2020). Fintech Revolution in the Financial Industry. In *Proceedings of the ENTRENOVA-ENTerprise REsearch InNOVAtion Conference* (Vol. 6, No. 1, pp. 563-571).

Martono, S. (2021). Analisis Faktor-Faktor Yang Mempengaruhi Minat Menggunakan Fintech Lending. *Jurnal Ekonomi Bisnis Dan Kewirausahaan*, *10*(3), 246. doi:10.26418/jebik.v10i3.45827

Masnita, Y., Rasyawal, M., & Yusran, H. L. (2021). Halal Transaction: Implication For Digital Retail By Using Financial Technology. *Jurnal Ilmiah Ekonomi Islam*, *7*(1), 16–22. doi:10.29040/jiei.v7i1.1492

Mastor, H. (2021). Factors that Affect the Usage Of E-Wallet Among Youth: A Study at a Public Institution of Higher Learning in South Sarawak. Advanced International Journal of Business. *Entrepreneurship and SMEs*, *3*(7), 40–48. doi:10.35631/AIJBES.37004

Nangin, M. A., Barus, I. R. G., & Wahyoedi, S. (2020). The Effects of Perceived Ease of Use, Security, and Promotion on Trust and Its Implications on Fintech Adoption. *Journal of Consumer Sciences*, *5*(2), 124–138. doi:10.29244/jcs.5.2.124-138

Nurlaily, F., Aini, E. K., & Asmoro, P. S. (2021). Understanding the FinTech continuance intention of Indonesian users: The moderating effect of gender. *Business: Theory and Practice*, 22(2), 290–298. doi:10.3846/btp.2021.13880

Parasuraman, A., & Colby, C. L. (2015). An updated and streamlined technology readiness index: TRI 2.0. *Journal of Service Research*, 18(1), 59–74. doi:10.1177/1094670514539730

Rahi, S., Abd Ghani, M., & Ngah, A. (2020). Factors propelling the adoption of internet banking: The role of e-customer service, website design, brand image and customer satisfaction. *International Journal of Business Information Systems*, 33(4), 549–569. doi:10.1504/IJBIS.2020.105870

Raj, L. V., Amilan, S., Aparna, K., & Swaminathan, K. (2023). Factors influencing the adoption of cashless transactions during COVID-19: An extension of enhanced UTAUT with pandemic precautionary measures. *Journal of Financial Services Marketing*, 1–20. doi:10.105741264-023-00218-8

Ratnasingam, P., & Pavlou, P. A. (2003). Technology trust in internet-based interorganizational electronic commerce. [JECO]. *Journal of Electronic Commerce in Organizations*, 1(1), 17–41. doi:10.4018/jeco.2003010102

Saad, M. A., Fisol, W. B. M., & Bin, M. (2019). Financial technology (Fintech) services in Islamic financial institutions. In *International postgraduate conference* (pp. 1-10).

Salam, A., & Abdiyanti, S. (2022). Analisis Pengaruh Celebrity Endorser, Brand Image Dan Brand Trust Terhadap Keputusan Pembelian (Studi Kasus Pada Konsumen Wanita Produk Skin Care Merek Ms Glow Di Kecamatan Sumbawa): Manajemen Pemasaran. *Accounting and Management Journal*, 6(1), 60–68. doi:10.33086/amj.v6i1.2204

Setiani, R. (2018). *Faktor- Faktor Yang Mempengaruhi Penggunaan Alat Pembayaran Non Tunai (Studi di Kota Purbalingga)*. Unviersitas Islam Indonesia. Skripsi.

Setiawan, B., Nugraha, D. P., Irawan, A., Nathan, R. J., & Zoltan, Z. (2021). User innovativeness and fintech adoption in Indonesia. *Journal of Open Innovation*, 7(3), 188. doi:10.3390/joitmc7030188

Shiau, W. L., Yuan, Y., Pu, X., Ray, S., & Chen, C. C. (2020). Understanding fintech continuance: Perspectives from self-efficacy and ECT-IS theories. *Industrial Management & Data Systems*, 120(9), 1659–1689. doi:10.1108/IMDS-02-2020-0069

Shin, D. H. (2010). The effects of trust, security and privacy in social networking: A security-based approach to understand the pattern of adoption. *Interacting with Computers*, 22(5), 428–438. doi:10.1016/j.intcom.2010.05.001

Singh, S., Sahni, M. M., & Kovid, R. K. (2020). What drives FinTech adoption? A multi-method evaluation using an adapted technology acceptance model. *Management Decision*, 58(8), 1675–1697. doi:10.1108/MD-09-2019-1318

Sinha, M., Majra, H., Hutchins, J., & Saxena, R. (2018). Mobile payments in India: The privacy factor. *International Journal of Bank Marketing*, 37(1), 192–209. doi:10.1108/IJBM-05-2017-0099

Skan, J., Dickerson, J., & Masood, S. (2015). *The future of Fintech and banking: digitally disrupted or reimagined?* Accenture.

Solarz, M., & Swacha-Lech, M. (2021). *Determinants of the adoption of innovative fintech services by millennials*. D Space. https://dspace5.zcu.cz/handle/11025/45451

Suprapto, Y. (2022). Analisis pengaruh brand image, trust, security, perceived usefulness, perceived ease of use terhadap adoption intention fintech di Kota Batam. *Journal of Applied Business Administration*, *6*(1), 17–26. doi:10.30871/jaba.v6i1.3396

Teoh Teng Tenk, M., Yew, H. C., & Heang, L. T. (2020). E-wallet Adoption: A case in Malaysia. *International Journal of Research In Commerce and Management Studies (ISSN: 2582-2292)*, *2*(2), 216-233.

Tun-Pin, C., Keng-Soon, W. C., Yen-San, Y., Pui-Yee, C., Hong-Leong, J. T., & Shwu-Shing, N. (2019). An adoption of fintech service in Malaysia. *South East Asia Journal of Contemporary Business*, *18*(5), 134–147.

Um, S. R., Shin, H. R., & Kim, Y. S. (2020). An Analysis of the Factors Affecting Technology Acceptance: Focusing on Fintech in high-end technology. *Journal of Digital Convergence*, *18*(2), 57–71.

Utami, N. (2023). Analysis of the Use of Financial Technology and Financial Literacy Among MSMEs. *MBIA*, *22*(1), 11–21. doi:10.33557/mbia.v22i1.2217

Vaicondam, Y., Jayabalan, N., Tong, C. X., Qureshi, M. I., & Khan, N. (2021). Fintech Adoption Among Millennials in Selangor. *Academy of Entrepreneurship Journal*, *27*, 1–14.

Van der Heijden, H., Verhagen, T., & Creemers, M. (2003). Understanding online purchase intentions: Contributions from technology and trust perspectives. *European Journal of Information Systems*, *12*(1), 41–48. doi:10.1057/palgrave.ejis.3000445

Venkatesh, V., & Davis, F. D. (2000). A theoretical extension of the technology acceptance model: Four longitudinal field studies. *Management Science*, *46*(2), 186–204. doi:10.1287/mnsc.46.2.186.11926

Venkatesh, V., Morris, M. G., Davis, G. B., & Davis, F. D. (2003). User acceptance of information technology: Toward a unified view. *Management Information Systems Quarterly*, *27*(3), 425–478. doi:10.2307/30036540

Venkatesh, V., Thong, J. Y., & Xu, X. (2012). Consumer acceptance and use of information technology: Extending the unified theory of acceptance and use of technology. *Management Information Systems Quarterly*, *36*(1), 157–178. doi:10.2307/41410412

Vize, R., Rooney, T., & Murphy, L. E. (2020). *Digital Technology We Trust: A FinTech B2B Context. In Interdisciplinary Approaches to Digital Transformation and Innovation*. IGI Global. doi:10.4018/978-1-7998-1879-3.ch003

Walczuch, R., Lemmink, J., & Streukens, S. (2007). The effect of service employees' technology readiness on technology acceptance. *Information & Management*, *44*(2), 206–215. doi:10.1016/j.im.2006.12.005

Wang, J. S. (2021). Exploring biometric identification in FinTech applications based on the modified TAM. *Financial Innovation*, *7*(1), 1–24. doi:10.118640854-021-00260-2

Warshaw, P. R., & Davis, F. D. (1985). Disentangling behavioral intention and behavioral expectation. *Journal of Experimental Social Psychology*, *21*(3), 213–228. doi:10.1016/0022-1031(85)90017-4

Xu, X., Li, Q., Peng, L., Hsia, T. L., Huang, C. J., & Wu, J. H. (2017). The impact of informational incentives and social influence on consumer behavior during Alibaba's online shopping carnival. *Computers in Human Behavior, 76*, 245–254. doi:10.1016/j.chb.2017.07.018

Zheng, P., Lin, T. J., Chen, C. H., & Xu, X. (2018). A systematic design approach for service innovation of smart product-service systems. *Journal of Cleaner Production, 201*, 657–667. doi:10.1016/j.jclepro.2018.08.101

Chapter 9
Impact of the COVID-19 Pandemic on the Digital Transition in Higher Education in Uzbekistan

Kasim Khusanov
https://orcid.org/0000-0002-5491-7071
Turin Polytechnic University in Tashkent, Uzbekistan

Ravshanjon Kakharov
Namangan State University, Uzbekistan

Mushtariybonu Khusanova
Kimyo International University in Tashkent, Uzbekistan

Khamidulla Khabibullaev
Turin Polytechnic University in Tashkent, Uzbekistan

Mukhsina Khusanova
Agency for the Development of Public Service Under the President of the Republic of Uzbekistan, Uzbekistan

ABSTRACT

Digital technologies are transforming all aspects of human activity. Uzbekistan also does not stand aside from these transformations—digitalization affects all sectors of the country's economy. The digital transition in education, particularly in higher education, has accelerated during the Covid-19 pandemic. This chapter focuses on studying the digital transformation of higher education in Uzbekistan and the impact of the Covid-19 pandemic on this process. Different aspects of applying online teaching and learning in higher education in that emergency period in Uzbekistan and the perspectives of their development are analyzed here. The chapter's findings highlighted the pandemic's impact on digital higher education and the responses to adapting to the learning environment.

DOI: 10.4018/978-1-6684-6782-4.ch009

INTRODUCTION

Digital transformation has significantly impacted higher education, transforming how institutions deliver education to students. The widespread use of digital technologies has made online learning platforms, virtual classrooms, and digital assessments more accessible to students and faculty, offering a flexible and convenient way to learn (Sharma, 2020). Moreover, the COVID-19 pandemic has accelerated the adoption of digital technologies in education, with institutions forced to shift to remote learning to ensure the safety of students and faculty (Khusanov et al., 2022; UNESCO, 2020).

Despite its benefits, implementing digital transformation has been challenging for many institutions. The digital divide remains a significant issue, with not all students having equal access to digital resources and technology (Johnson et al., 2015). Institutions also face cybersecurity concerns, as the increased use of digital technologies means more opportunities for cyber threats and data breaches (Balanskat & Engelhardt, 2015). Furthermore, adopting digital technologies requires significant faculty and staff training investment, which can be a significant financial and logistical burden (Jukes et al., 2010).

Uzbekistan is one of the countries that has embraced the digital transformation trend and has been actively implementing it in all areas of its economy, including education. The Uzbekistan government recognizes the importance of digital transformation in education and has been working to create a more digitally integrated learning environment. In 2020, the "Digital Development Strategy of Uzbekistan until 2030" was adopted, outlining the strategic goals and directions for digital transformation in education and other sectors (DP, 2020a).

The education sector has been a crucial focus of the digital transformation strategy. The improvement in the material and technical base of higher educational institutions in Uzbekistan has facilitated the introduction of digital technologies, including creating electronic resource centers and adopting cloud technologies (DP, 2019; DP, 2020b). These technological advancements have allowed the use of modern teaching methods based on high-performance information technologies, such as distance and evening forms of education, mobile and online learning technologies, and the recognition of distance education as one of the primary forms of education.

Given the significance of the digital transformation strategy in Uzbekistan's education sector, studying the problems and experiences of developing digital teaching methods and digitalizing other aspects of the higher education system in Uzbekistan is essential.

MAIN FOCUS OF THE CHAPTER

This chapter focuses on the digital transformation of higher education in Uzbekistan and the impact of the Covid-19 pandemic on this process. Different aspects of applying distance teaching and learning in higher education, the challenges faced in implementing digital teaching methods, the best practices for ensuring successful digitalization, and their development prospects are analyzed here.

BACKGROUND OF THE STUDY

Compulsory Digitalization in Education

The COVID-19 pandemic and subsequent lockdowns have disrupted all aspects of human activity, including traditional economic practices and social development. The pandemic has highlighted the need for countries to develop emergency measures to mitigate the consequences of future crises. Bihu (2022) has studied such efforts, including the contingency plan in Tanzania, which includes preserving the educational process during possible lockdowns. One such opportunity is the digitalization of education, which involves transitioning to online teaching and learning.

In this regard, governments and educational institutions play a significant role in overcoming the consequences of the pandemic. Governments and institutions worldwide have launched initiatives to provide students with digital tools and internet access to bridge the digital divide and support students in need. For instance, the Indian government launched the Digital India program to provide affordable internet access to students and promote digital literacy (Ministry of Electronics & Information Technology, n.d.). Similarly, the Brazilian government launched the Connected Education program, which provides internet connectivity to students and teachers in public schools nationwide (Government of Brazil, 2022).

Amaghouss and Zouine (2022) discussed another example of state measures taken to respond to the pandemic crisis. Their study focused on the measures adopted by Morocco to stabilize the education system during the pandemic, which exacerbated pre-existing educational inequalities in developing countries. In response, Morocco introduced digital learning technologies and promoted education development during the pandemic. As part of this initiative, the government introduced the LMS MASSAR platform to facilitate communication between teachers and students, organize online courses, and evaluate student progress. To improve accessibility, universities also introduced a mobile version of the online platform. Additionally, the previously existing TelmidTICE educational platform, which contained over 6,000 titles, was supplemented with new materials. The Ministry of Education has developed and adopted this platform for use in all levels of education in Morocco, from preschool to higher education.

However, challenges remain, particularly in developing countries where adopting digital learning platforms has helped mitigate the harmful effects of the pandemic on education. These challenges include limited access to technology and the Internet, particularly in remote areas, inadequate teacher training, and insufficient funding (World Bank, 2020). Developing countries must address these challenges to ensure equitable access to quality education for all students. Despite these challenges, the countries have used various applications and platforms for organizing online learning, such as the Zoom platform for meetings, Google Meet virtual class platforms, Microsoft Teams, Cisco WebEx, and others (Al-Maroof et al., 2021). Therefore, overcoming the challenges and ensuring adequate access to quality education for all students is essential.

Although distance education has been used for decades and is officially accredited in some countries, such as India (M. S. & Siddiqui, 2022), the Covid-19 pandemic, nonetheless, has highlighted the socioeconomic challenges associated with online learning. The pandemic has compelled educational institutions to adopt online learning as the primary mode of instruction, making issues of accessibility and inclusiveness more prominent. The inclusiveness of online learning is affected by various factors, such as access to electronic devices, internet connectivity, and infrastructure (M. S. & Siddiqui, 2022). While online learning can democratize education and offer equal learning opportunities, it cannot address educational disparities resulting from these inclusion factors and pedagogical aspects (Christensen &

Alcorn, 2014; Ruipérez-Valiente, 2022). Most online courses, including MOOCs, are designed for pre-trained learners and may not cater to the needs of all students. Therefore, to ensure that online learning is inclusive and accessible to all, attention must be paid to addressing socioeconomic challenges and designing courses that cater to diverse learners.

The Covid-19 pandemic has also presented significant challenges for teachers, as highlighted by Lin and Yeh (2022) in their review of research on this topic. The authors identified various challenges teachers face, including primary and additional workloads, inadequate digital literacy, difficulties integrating technology and learning, limited availability of online learning, insufficient institutional support, and communication difficulties between teachers and students. Additionally, the pandemic has made teaching soft skills such as teamwork, communication, time management, creativity, leadership, emotional intelligence, and stress management challenging. The authors recommend various measures to overcome these challenges, including contingency planning, advanced professional learning for teachers, and blended online teaching. UNESCO (2020) also emphasizes the importance of supporting teachers to ensure the effective implementation of digital education. The study suggests that teachers need training and professional development opportunities to use technology for teaching and learning effectively.

Specialists and technicians involved in e-learning must also receive training to ensure the effective implementation of e-learning systems. Holmes et al. (2023) studied the implementation of E-Learning Management Systems in Saudi Arabia, using the Blackboard system as an example. The authors identified financial, administrative, and technical barriers to implementing the system among Saudi university students. To overcome these barriers, the authors recommend addressing the technical aspects of using the system, providing appropriate training to specialists and technicians on the use of this system, as well as teaching students the basics of e-learning. By addressing these challenges, teachers and e-learning specialists can help ensure the effective implementation of digital education, even during challenging times such as the Covid-19 pandemic.

The Environment in Online Learning

During the pandemic, inclusive access to education is essential to the continuity of learning. Building a good learning environment can ensure access, quality, and continuity of education. The most promising approach to developing an online learning environment includes structured online discussions with clear instructions and goals, well-designed courses with interactive content and flexible deadlines, and ongoing instructor involvement, including personalized, timely, and meaningful feedback (Siemens et al., 2015).

Distance education has achieved individualization of learning, including a competency-based, flexible choice of an individual learning path (Iyer et al., 2022; Holms et al., 2018; Magoulas & Chen, 2006; Meeuwse & Mason, 2018; Krishnaswami et al., 2022). However, these opportunities were largely unavailable during the unexpected pandemic. Methodologies for building individual distance learning include creating digital infrastructure, training programs for teachers, defining courses and modules, increasing teachers' digital competence, identifying students, introducing a digital learning environment, adapting the curriculum, assessing, and identifying appropriate technologies, monitoring performance, and organizing feedback. These methods are essential to ensure the effectiveness of online learning and the achievement of learning objectives.

An integral aspect of higher education is developing adequate student assessment systems. Such systems are critical when using online learning technologies. Fung et al. (2022a) considered the socio-economic aspects of building an assessment environment that ensures the continuity and inclusiveness of education and equal opportunities for students to access education. The assessment system for online learning is an integral part of the instructions. Constructing such a system requires special consideration of the inclusive features of online learning. The authors studied the factors influencing the development of an inclusive assessment environment.

In turn, access to implemented learning systems can be limited by the language of instruction if the language of instruction in the offered online courses differs from the native language of the student, for example, English. Then the knowledge or ignorance of a foreign language significantly affects the effectiveness of digital learning platforms. The socioeconomic status of students in the country also affects the digital transformation process of the education system and the effectiveness of the introduction of online learning (Ruipérez-Valiente, 2022). The large-scale study results reveal a strong dependence on access to open online MOOC courses on the HDI Human Development Index of the user's country of residence. Moreover, access, course completion, and certification also depend on the content of the course and the language used: courses in English have stricter content and certification conditions, while courses in national languages are usually easier to understand.

Likewise, the need for digital literacy among the population is also a barrier to successfully implementing online learning. However, as noted by Ansu-Kyeremeh and Goosen (2022), using the example of the education system in Ghana, integrating technology in education, such as online learning methods, contributes to increasing digital literacy in the country.

The Lockdown Effect on Higher Education

The pandemic significantly impacted higher education. Many university campuses were shut down or needed more student access, including classrooms, libraries, hostels, wellness centers, and services requiring in-person interaction. In 2021, the Organization for Economic Co-operation and Development (OECD) conducted a study to assess the pandemic's impact on university education in 27 countries. The report revealed that universities in five countries, including Ireland, Austria, Israel, Canada, and Germany, closed all open-access services from March to December 2020. On the other hand, student campuses in the Baltic countries, New Zealand, Belgium, Finland, Spain, Greece, Denmark, and Slovenia were closed for only two months, from March to May 2020. In other countries, restrictions continued for three to eight months, and 13 countries closed campuses again in 2021 due to the ongoing pandemic (OECD, 2021).

To minimize the impact of campus closures on learning outcomes, universities worldwide widely adopted online distance learning. Before the pandemic, more than half of the countries had limited use of distance learning (OECD, 2021). However, during the quarantine period, universities in many countries had to resort to online teaching methods to prevent gaps in the learning process. Only Spain, Germany, Colombia, and Sweden had 15% to 25% of students using distance technologies before the pandemic (OECD, 2021). Some countries like Italy, New Zealand, Poland, Japan, Turkey, Lithuania, and Hungary legally restricted distance education. Additionally, many universities and teachers needed more time to adapt to digital teaching methods.

The research of OECD (2021) indicates that during the pandemic, digital technologies were used by more than 90% of teachers and students primarily for searching the literature, working on projects, and communicating. As the pandemic continues, higher education institutions actively seek innovative approaches to enhance online learning and ensure students' academic progress. However, it is essential to note that countries differ in their levels of digital development and access to the Internet, which affects the effective use of online learning. Some students could not continue their education during quarantine due to the lack of digital infrastructure. Nevertheless, most European universities implemented online learning within two to three months of the pandemic's onset (Fung et al., 2022b)

There are many issues concerning digital transformation in education. So, Lamsal (2022) discusses issues inherent in digital technologies that have become especially relevant and serious during the pandemic. Providing a supportive and safe digital space for learning is a challenge. One such problem could be cyberbullying. This problem in connection with education has yet to be studied, but it undoubtedly requires research. Another problem of the parent-student relationships during the pandemic and the transition to online learning also requires attention and related research (Treceñe, 2022). Given that the pandemic poses employment and earnings challenges for adults, parents have trouble helping their children learn.

For a compelling study of the issues concerning digitalization in universities, Tomte et. al. (2019) suggested an approach that considers these processes in two aspects: *external*, under the influence of the state and international trends, and *internal*, on the part of institutions. Due to the pandemic, the development of digital technologies in the organization of the educational process and learning has been given priority by states (Bihu, 2022; Amaghouss & Zouine, 2022; DP-5953, 2020). This measure of states is an *external* influence. On the other hand, one of the significant problems for educational institutions, even before the pandemic, is the tremendous ethno-social diversity of the student body. This problem calls for more attention to teaching methods that provide student support, greater individualization, and flexibility in learning (Bates, 2015). One of the solutions to the problem is the introduction of distance education or online teaching methods. The crisis has led educational institutions of all categories, from preschool to higher education, to switch to online forms of education to continue the educational process (Krishnaswami et al., 2022). This institutional measure is an *internal* influence. Considering the digitalization problems in universities by their external and internal influences allows for more constructive systemization and analysis of measures to mitigate them.

METHODS

The research used a qualitative analysis of data gathered from online surveys and literature reviews. The researchers distributed online surveys to students and teachers in higher education institutions in Uzbekistan and analyzed the responses to identify the challenges and opportunities of digital learning. The chapter contains the literature review conducted to gather relevant data on the impact of the pandemic on the education sector globally and in Uzbekistan. The authors applied the quantitative ANOVA statistical data analysis to study the impact of the Covid-19 pandemic on the introduction of online learning methods in universities in Uzbekistan. While investigating the effectiveness of the development of Learning Management Systems, the authors used descriptive data analysis.

Digital Transformation in Higher Education in Uzbekistan

The unexpected outbreak of the Covid-19 pandemic affected the entire education system of Uzbekistan and disrupted the traditional order of education. One hundred fourteen higher education institutions with 423,000 students and about 27,000 teachers have risen to the challenges of the pandemic in the country's higher education in 2020 (The State Committee). Over the next three years of Covid 2019, these figures rose to 127 universities, 461,000 students, and 37.4 thousand teachers (The State Committee).

These figures give an idea of the abnormal proportions of the pandemic problem in higher education in Uzbekistan.

In the context of introducing strict quarantine restricting movement during the pandemic, universities forcibly transfer traditional face-to-face education to online distance learning. This measure, at that time, was the only one to preserve the continuity of the learning process. The beginning of the Covid-19 pandemic has made adjustments to the plans for reforming higher education in Uzbekistan. Distance learning methods and related technical and software tools have emerged, and online learning has become the most popular. In contrast to the school system (Khusanov et al., 2022), there were significant prerequisites for introducing e-learning in higher education in Uzbekistan. Digital technologies, including online distance learning methods, were already being introduced in some universities on an experimental basis before the pandemic. Thus, according to the State Program for the implementation of the action strategy (DP-5953, 2020), as an experiment, in stages from the 2020/2021 academic year, distance learning was introduced at the Tashkent University of Information Technologies named after Muhammad al - Khorezmiy, Tashkent State University of Law and Tashkent State Pedagogical University. The Concept for the Development of the Higher Education System of the Republic of Uzbekistan until 2030 (DP-5847, 2019) approved. According to the Concept, one of the strategic development directions is "the introduction of digital technologies and modern methods in the educational process." The Parliament of Uzbekistan adopted the "Law on Education" (LRU, 2020), which officially defines the distance form of education. Thus, the quarantine conditions of the pandemic only accelerated the introduction of distance learning methods in the country's higher education (Khusanov et al., 2022).

In addition to a large target group of students, a severe problem with the forced widespread transition to online learning was the provision of education participants with access to the Internet. According to the Speedtest Global Index, in April 2020, Uzbekistan had Mobile Internet with a speed of 9.68 Mbps and Fixed Internet with a speed of 25.88 Mbps (Speedtest, 2020). These indicators were significantly inferior to similar indicators in neighboring countries and were a significant barrier to the effective implementation of digital technologies in education. Further, a strategic program for developing Digital Uzbekistan was developed and adopted to accelerate the country's digital transformation and overcome the pandemic's consequences (DP, 2020a). According to this strategy program, one of the indicators of digitalization in Uzbekistan is the speed of the Internet. As a result of implementing the measures provided for by the program, at the beginning of 2023, the speed of the Mobile Internet in the country increased by more than 40%. It reached 13.61 Mbps, and the speed of Fixed Broadband Internet increased by 70% and is equal to 43.94 Mbps (Speedtest, 2023). However, today these figures are significantly lower by 1.7-2.8 times the similar average figures in the world.

Another factor influencing the use of digital technologies in education is the availability of computers and communication. During the pandemic, smartphones and related applications' role in establishing communication between teachers and students and between students has grown significantly. Fortunately, the situation is better here - 96% of the country's adult population owned smartphones (The State Committee). The ubiquity of the Telegram application for smartphones and the creation of discussion groups on subjects made it possible to organize alternative forms of feedback in online learning.

The HDI Human Development Index also determines Uzbekistan's digital transformation prospects. HDI is one of the alternative indicators of a country's development, which allows for assessing economic growth and general socioeconomic development. This index is published annually by the UN. According to the UNDP report for 2021-2022 (Conceição, 2022), Uzbekistan entered the category of High human development countries and ranked 101 out of 195 countries with an HDI index of 0.727. This result is higher than the world average (0.732) and has a positive growth trend (+11 points for 2015-2021 in the ranking of countries in the report table). The index indicators indicate good prospects for introducing digital technologies in Uzbekistan, in particular in the higher education of the country.

RESULTS

The Impact of COVID-19 on the Implementation of Online Learning in Universities in Uzbekistan

To study the influence of the pandemic and related quarantine on higher education in Uzbekistan, the authors select two universities as targets: the Turin Polytechnic University in Tashkent (TTPU) and the Namangan Engineering-Construction Institute (NamECI). The selection of these universities allows for studying digital transformations in the universities from the different regional locations with related challenges. TTPU locates in the capital of Uzbekistan, and NamECI is in the Ferghana Valley - the most densely populated region of Uzbekistan. On the other hand, these universities differ in organizational structure as well. So, TTPU is a joint university with the educational curriculum of the heading university Polito – Turin Polytechnic university in Italy. While NamECI is the state institute with the standard study program approved by the Ministry of Higher Education of Uzbekistan. This difference also influenced their digital transition during the pandemic and the research outcomes. The authors already conducted similar investigations earlier (Khusanov & Kakharov, 2020), but they extended studies and presented additional and new results here.

Learning Management Systems in TTPU

Before the pandemic, the situation with e-learning at TTPU was similar to many other universities in Uzbekistan. The online platform moodle.polito.uz was developed and successfully used in TTPU. Learning materials, exam results, and others were uploaded there. Also, there was the remote access to Polito's didattica.it platform (Didattica) with similar functions. With the help of Didattica, since 2018, TTPU began to conduct remote exams in some disciplines.

With the onset of pandemic-based quarantine, access to BigBlueButton (n.d.) virtual classes integrated into the Didattica platform to organize online training has opened for students and teachers at TPUT. All online video lessons were recorded and stored on a platform, and students can download them for offline study. The Lockdown system restricts students from using third-party applications during the online exam. At the same time, the system provides visual control using a webcam on the student's computer. The exam may conduct in the form of quizzes through the virtual classroom, and the examiner had the opportunity to conduct an additional oral exam for individual students.

In TTPU, to support the continuity of education during the quarantine period during the Corvid-19 pandemic, the LMS TTPU (n.d.) was developed and implemented. The authors participated in testing the system and currently use it in teaching. This platform aims to create an online system for organizing training at the university, covering the main aspects of the educational process: preparation of electronic educational materials, online training of students, monitoring of the educational process, and conducting an adequate assessment of student performance.

The platform's database currently contains 4316 students, 62% of the total student population. This system is used by students, mainly in the 1st year, and students studying according to the national educational program. Senior students have access to the LMS platform Didattica of, the Italian partner of Polito University. Also, users of LMS TTPU are 105 teachers, or 66% of the total composition of teachers. Thus, more than two-thirds of all participants in the educational process at TTPU used LMS TTPU.

The My courses platform option in Figure 1 provides information about the user's courses: for the student, this is the program and content of the mandatory and elective courses for which he enrolled, and for the teacher, these are the courses in which he conducts classes.

In the 2022-2023 academic year, 102 training courses with a total volume of 780 credits are placed on the platform, which is 60% of the entire teaching load of the university. While in the 2021-2022 academic year, there were only 29 courses on the platform with a volume of 198 credits (27%), and in the 2020-2021 academic year, 28 courses and 156 credits, respectively (22%). The chart in Figure 2 shows that over the past three years, the number of courses hosted on the platform has increased from 28 to 102 (an increase of 3.6 times), or credit growth was +38% in percentage terms.

The teacher leading the course can form the course content online. In addition to the program, he can add topics of classes, and various assessment tasks, conduct online surveys of students, regularly monitor learning, conduct online exams, create discussion groups, and much more.

One of the essential features of the platform is the organization of a virtual classroom for online learning. Along with the Didattica platform, which also has this capability, the TTPU LMS has ensured the continuity of education during the period that accompanied the lockdown pandemic.

The platform usage statistics above show that developed during the pandemic as an emergency measure, the TTPU LMS is now actively used in training organizations. It significantly contributes to the university's digital transformation and the introduction of digital technologies in education.

Another online platform developed at TTPU during the pandemic is the Educational Management System TTPU platform (EMS, n.d.). This system's purpose is to support the digital transformation of the management of the activities of the university departments. Such transformation concerns all types of

Figure 1. My courses

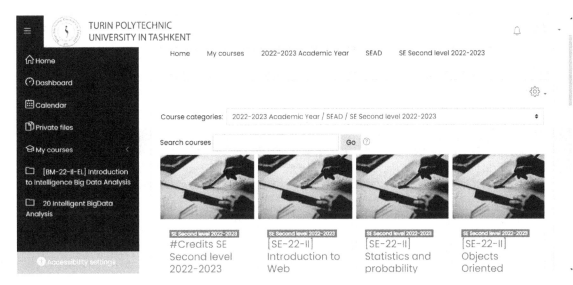

Figure 2. The efficiency of using LMS TTPU

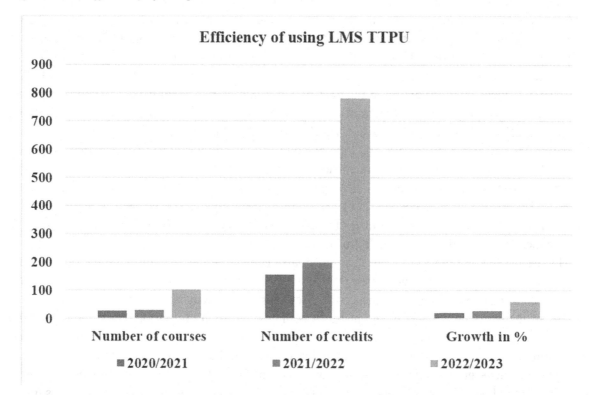

activities of teachers of departments. The platform includes online accounting of teachers' educational, methodological, scientific, and educational work. The authors have also participated in testing EMS and are currently using it. The authors used the platform data during the study. Figure 3 represents the working page of the platform website.

To study the influence of the pandemic on education in TTPU, the authors used LMS TTPU and EMS TTPU systems. The chapter analyzed the training on the subject "Linear Algebra and Geometry" (LAG) taught by one of the authors and an Italian partner professor on the 1st level of the bachelor program. The study covers the period from 2019 to 2023 academic years. The subject consists of LAG1 and LAG2, differentiated by computational technologies applied in LAG2. Before the pandemic, teachers

Figure 3. Educational management system EMS TTPU

☰ TTPU	Profile	**Individual plan**	Publications	Syllabuses	Account	Settings		⤷
Workload and Raise Table			2022-2023 academic years				Document	Comments
Mandatory total workload		350 academic hour		Maximum raise (monthly additional payment)				100%
Planned total workload		350 academic hour		Planned raise				160%
Total workload completed		260 academic hour		Raise completed				90%
Total workload validated		156 academic hour		Raise validated				38%

‹   Calendar plan   Educational work   Educational work (additional)   Educational and methodical works   Scientific and research activity   Administrational and ›

Select subject   ▾ +

taught the subject in a traditional face-to-face format and held academic performance exams in writing mode. Beginning from March 2020 till Dec 2021, during the pandemic, Linear Algebra and Geometry subject taught through online learning. The teachers performed evaluation exams during that period and in current years online.

For the study, the authors chose the aspects of the training which can quantitatively evaluate the effect of online learning. They consider the students' attendance and academic performance before and during the pandemic. To study, the authors selected 299 students on LAG1 and 548 on LAG2 - 847 students who learned the LAG. Tables 1 and 2 present the learning outcomes. Table 1 shows the attendance of 409 students from all selected ones who participated in training on LAG.

The table shows, in general, the low average attendance by studied students both before quarantine and during online lessons caused by the pandemic (20% -40% and 3% -10%, respectively). At the same time, one can see an even more decrease in attendance during the quarantine period (-17% -30%) due to additional problems associated with the pandemic. TTPU students from the regions, which comprise more than 80% of the total number of students, were returned to the residence place during quarantine, so they faced low Internet infrastructure in the regions. This problem negatively influenced their learning ability. It was especially critical during online exams: students often could not connect to the exam server.

To smooth out such limitations and for a more successful process of online learning, TTPU teachers, through the Telegram application, created chat groups for academic disciplines. These virtual groups discussed online issues and problems that students had with studying the subject. The number of participants in such chats also illustrates the effectiveness of this discussion method and additional support for students. So, on the subject of LAG, the number of chat subscribers was 342 people (83.6%), and most of the participating students were active there during the entire training and exams.

Studying the quality of online training results of exams on LAG for the 2019 - 2023 academic years were analyzed separately in LAG1 and LAG2. Table 2 presents exam results. The table presents the results of academic performance evaluations before the Covid-19 pandemic on LAG1 in 2019 and LAG2 in 2020. In other years all exams in TTPU were held in an online format.

According to regulation, students' progress used to assess on a scale of 0-30+ points. To pass the exam, students should take at least 18 scores. Exam results in a range of 18-20 means "satisfactory" level of the study subject. Range 21-25 corresponds to "good" academic level, and range 26-30 evaluates "excellent" academic performance. 30+ points from an exam students can obtain in case of getting extra points, which means an "extraordinary" score. The table includes results of only passed students from 18 to 30 points. The table in the second row shows evaluation scores in the 18 – 30+. The rows below indicate the frequency number of students getting correspondent scores.

According to LAG2, this part of the general LAG course students used to learn in the spring semester and take the evaluation exam in the summer control session. The last pre-pandemic time LAG2 was in the spring of 2019, with the exam in the summer, and the first pandemic teaching was during March-June

Table 1. Attendance in the distance learning at TTPU

Subject	Level	Nº of Students on the List	Before Quarantine		During Quarantine			
			Nº Attended (average)	*% Attended*	*Nº Attended Online*	*% Attended Online*	*Nº Attended Telegram*	*% Attended Telegram*
LAG	1	409	80-150	20-40	10-40	2.5-9.8	342	83.6

Table 2. Academic performance in TTPU during the pandemic; Freq – frequency related to scoring, Av - average

Year/ Subject	N⁰ of students	Freq/Av per year	Scores													
			18	19	20	21	22	23	24	25	26	27	28	29	30	30+
2019/ LAG2	51	Freq	15	4	4	11	1	1	6	1	2	0	6	0	0	0
		Av	21.4 - Average score before Covid-19													
2020/ LAG2	103	Freq	36	0	31	1	0	0	23	0	1	0	5	0	0	6
		Av	21.2 - Average score in year													
2021/ LAF2	343	Freq	88	38	5	0	0	93	10	0	0	64	11	0	0	34
		Av	22.9 - Average score in year													
2022/ LAG2	102	Freq	20	6	0	11	2	10	0	10	0	6	7	0	0	30
		Av	24.4 - Average score in year 22.8 – Average score during the pandemic													
2020/ LAG1	41	Freq	9	4	7	2	2	3	2	4	2	1	3	1	0	1
		Av	22.0 - Average score before Covid-19													
2021/ LAG1	83	Freq	45	4	0	0	21	1	1	7	2	0	0	1	0	1
		Av	20.3 - Average score in year													
2022/ LAG1	188	Freq	24	17	1	0	35	9	0	28	21	0	0	17	17	19
		Freq	24.3 - Average score in year													
2023/ LAG1	28	Freq	12	4	2	0	0	6	0	0	0	0	4	0	0	0
		Av	20.8 - Average score in year 22.9 – Average score during the pandemic													

of 2020 with the summer exam. In the 2019th year, 51 students passed the exam successfully, while in the summer session of the 2020th year, with online learning, 103 students passed the exam. Next 2020, 2021, and 2022 pandemic academic years number of passed students was 103, 343, and 102, respectively. Variation in numbers here is due to TTPU regulation where students can choose subjects to take exams.

The table shows students' performance who passed the distance learning exam before and just at the beginning of the pandemic lockdown (21.4 and 21.2 average scores in 2019 and 2020, respectively). Besides the challenges of the pandemic, it was almost the same.

Thus, the exam results show that online learning maintained the continuity of the learning process and its quality indicators. The measures of the state and the university to organize online learning played an important role. Another reason for such results can be reformatting the content of the exam questions. LAG2 exams, both before the pandemic and during the Covid-19 period, were conducted online in multiple-choice answers questions mode both before and during the pandemic years. Moreover, before the pandemic, the exam involved using the MATLAB program to select the correct answer. However, from 2020 until the last exam in 2023, using any third-party programs, including MATLAB, was prohibited. The content of the examination questions has changed so that the examinee does not need to use technical computing tools. As a result, it became easier for students to prepare for the exam. The ease of the exam offset the adverse effects of the pandemic.

Table 2 also shows the increase in average LAG2 academic scores in subsequent years (22.9 points in 2021 and 24.4 points in 2022). According to the table, the average academic performance during the 20020-2022 pandemic period is 22.8 points. Growth in this way is 1.4 points or 6.5%. Although a statistical study of confidence intervals with an indicator of 95% gives results on the border of critical ones, this increase can be considered statistically significant. The exams' results testify to students' adaptation to this online assessment form.

As for LAG1, the last time before the pandemic was in the fall of 2019, and the final exam was in February 2020. For the first time during the pandemic, this course was in the fall semester of 2020, with the corresponding exam in the winter of 2021. Table 2 shows the average results of these two exams - 22.0 points in 2020 before the pandemic and 20.3 points in 2021 following the results of online learning during the lockdown. The decline in results in the first year of the pandemic was 1.7 points or 7.7%.

All the negative consequences of quarantine have already manifested here, including one of the main ones: insufficient access to the Internet for participants in the educational process. At the same time, many students experienced difficulties even when passing the online exam. In addition, the online exam material corresponds in complexity to the pre-pandemic written exam.

In the following years, the results of the exams differed in variability. So, if in 2022, the average result was 24.3 points - 4 points or 19.7% higher than the previous year - then in 2023, the result was 20.8 points. The indicators worsened and returned to the first year of the pandemic (20.3 points). The average exam score during the pandemic was 22.9 points, corresponding to a slight average increase in marks (+0.9 points). The calculation of the statistical significance of the difference with a 95% confidence criterion shows that these average estimates before and during the pandemic are close to the statistical error.

Learning Management System HEMIS in Uzbekistan

Over the past three years, many higher educational institutions in Uzbekistan, including NamECI, used the HEMIS OTM platform (HEMIS, n.d.) developed as an information management system for educational processes. The authors used this platform to get and analyze data concerning the research. The HEMIS information system provides electronic education services to administrative staff, professors, and students due to the automation of the main activities of higher education institutions. The information system bridges higher education institutions and the Ministry of Higher Education, Science, and Innovation. It drastically reduces the information received from higher education institutions, abandons their paper form, and digitizes the management system. The Ministry of Higher Education, Science, and Innovation of the Republic of Uzbekistan recommended this system platform for use at higher education institutes in Uzbekistan. Currently, 154 universities and over 700 thousand students and teachers use this platform.

This management system includes administrative management, educational process, scientific activity, and financial management modules. The chapter presented a general module description that clarifies the system's objectives.

The administrative management module focuses on managing information about the structure of universities, faculties, and departments, staff and teaching staff, student contingent and their movement, and financing issues.

The Education module manages students' educational programs, subjects, and educational activities, registering and control of university graduates. Figure 4 illustrates the corresponding part of the web platform HEMIS OTM.

The figure shows subdivisions of the Education part: staff, students, students activities, learning process, educational program, semesters, subject syllabuses, enrolled students, timetable, monitoring, exams list, attendance, academic performance, and control evaluations.

Figure 4. Education

The Science module aims to provide informational and organizational support for research and scientific planning processes, publications, intellectual property and methodical educational work processes, and evaluation of teachers' scientific activities.

System HEMIS OTM covers the activities of higher educational institutions. Each staff registered in this system: system administrator, head of department, dean, lecturer, student - all have the opportunity to work within their functional duties. Users can work in the system mainly in the status of an administrator, an employee of the personnel department, an employee of the dean of a faculty, a head of a department, a teacher, and a student. In the system, in addition to the above statuses, an employee can work as an employee of the administration, financial, accounting, engineering and construction, and other departments based on their functional duties.

The system administrator launches the system first, creating general university information and a critical account (HR employee). An HR employee generates a database of employees according to instructions. An employee of the dean's office forms the current curriculum and schedule of classes for this faculty. The head of the department forms a database of subjects and topics related to this department according to the teaching load. The teacher prepares materials on the subjects according to the department's curriculum, determines the topics and hours of the current classes that he conducts, keeps records of student attendance, and posts assignments and tests in the lesson. In turn, the student's status shows the current, intermediate, and final grades on the subject materials of the relevant subjects.

Distance Learning at NamECI

For the study of online learning at NamECI, three groups of 4th-year students (13MT16, 14MT16, 15aMT16, a total of 54 students) were selected, who studied the subjects "Engineering Technologies" (S1) and "Language Practice" (S2) during the 1st semester before the pandemic and in the 2nd semester, where the training took place partially (March-June) during the quarantine period in the 2019-2020 academic year. Based on the current platform, the institute transited learning to online mode during the pandemic. This platform was introduced earlier and used for the electronic organization of the educational process. During the quarantine, the platform was a resource base for educational materials, interactive remote communication with students, and conducting online exams. Later the institute switched to the

HEMIS system. Additionally, the Telegram application supported feedback. Table 3 shows the results of comparing distance learning assessment with traditional learning before the pandemic.

The range of a student's learning performance in NamECI is on a scale of 0%-100%. Analysis of the table data shows an average increase in academic performance during the pandemic by 8%. Students' academic achievement increased in technical subjects (S1, +6 points) and humanities (S2, +5.2 points). Statistical analysis also confirmed a statistically 95% significant increase in academic performance in subjects S1 and S2 during the quarantine. However, according to a discussion with the teachers, this "growth" was achieved in many respects due to a decrease in the general requirements for assessing academic performance under quarantine conditions.

Thus, the study shows an increase in academic performance by 4% - 8%. in both universities. It means that distance learning, forcibly used in universities in Uzbekistan, provides continuity of education. Significantly, it was achieved not only in the capital of Tashkent but also in the regions. The reasons for this situation lie in the fact that despite problems with the Internet, especially in the regions, universities managed to use alternative forms of organizing the educational process (for example, the Telegram application) and establish friendly and almost round-the-clock support for students.

Qualitative Assessment of Online Learning Experience

For a qualitative assessment, interpretation, and confirm obtained results, the authors prepared a questionnaire for a survey of teachers and students participating in the study. The authors mainly kept the Concept of the survey used before (Khusanov et al., 2022). The authors surveyed teachers of different regions of Uzbekistan: 4 teachers on LAG and six teachers on other subjects from TTPU, four teachers from other universities in Tashkent, six teachers on information technologies from Namangan State University, four teachers of engineering subjects and four teachers of English from NamECI. The survey also involved 12 students from Tashkent and 27 students from the regions. Totally 28 teachers and 39 students participated in the review study. Restrictions during the quarantine caused a fewer number of interviewed people. Two logical parts of the questionnaire concern estimated indicators of attendance and students' academic performance in online learning. Questions 1-7 refer to the estimation of students' attendance, and questions 8-11 concern evaluating their academic performance. The questionnaire presents the options explaining the reason for the low or high assessment score of the studied indicators related to online learning during the Covid-19 quarantine period. It includes Questions:

1. Attendance fell due to the communication infrastructure.
2. Attendance fell due to low Internet infrastructure.

Table 3. Academic performance on distance education at NamECI

Period		S1			Average S1	S2			Average S2	Total Average
Period	**Groups**	**13**	**14**	**15**		**13**	**14**	**15**		
	N° of the Students in the List	**20**	**19**	**15**		**20**	**19**	**15**		
Before Pandemic	Performance%	69	69	72	69.8	71	72	76	72.7	71.3
During Pandemic	Performance%	80	72	75	75.8	74	81	79	77.9	76.9
Full	Affect %	+11	+3	+3	+6	+2	+9	+3	+5.2	+5.6

3. Attendance fell due to control decreasing by the teachers.
4. Attendance fell due to control decreasing by the educational institution.
5. Attendance fell due to the poor quality of the proposed educational content.
6. Attendance rose due to the flexibility of the learning environment.
7. Attendance rose due to underestimated requirements.
8. Academic performance dropped due to the poor quality of the proposed educational content.
9. Academic performance dropped due to restrictions on online learning.
10. Academic performance dropped due to the stress situation caused by the pandemic.
11. Academic performance rose due to the flexibility of the learning environment.
12. Academic performance rose due to underestimated requirements.
13. Academic performance rose due to the possibility of cheating.

Figure 5 shows the questionnaire results in the diagram.

The chart in Figure 5 shows that insufficient Internet access (Question 2) is the most significant cause of poor online class attendance. Moreover, this indicator is more critical in the regions than in the capital: 21% and 41% of respondents noted this factor, respectively. Two negative factors, rated approximately equal, are the weakening of control by teachers and universities. Here the estimates are 7% and 14% for Question 3 and 14% and 9% for Question 4. The respondents in the capital and regions (7%) noted the quality of educational materials as a factor in reducing attendance. Although attendance for online learning has declined, most teachers noted the tacit loosening of quarantine requirements for students (Question 7) as a potential factor in a possible increase in attendance.

As the biggest reasons for the decline in academic performance, teachers consider limitations associated with the peculiarities of distance learning (Question 9): 25% and 37%, respectively, in Tashkent and the regions. Although the stress caused by quarantine undoubtedly affected student performance, only

Figure 5. Results of the questionnaire of the teachers

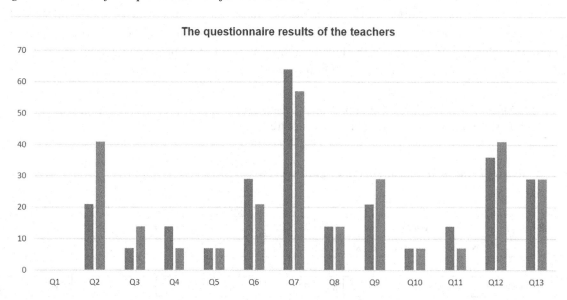

7% of the respondents noted this factor (Question 10) of reducing academic performance. Teachers again noted the main reasons for the possible increase in academic performance as the weakening of student requirements (Question 12) and the possibility of cheating in exams in online learning (Question 13). 36% and 41% of reviewed teachers mentioned these factors for Question 12 and 29% for Question 13.

The results, presented in the chart in Figure 6, show that 50% and 66% of the surveyed students from Tashkent and regions, respectively, like the teachers before, deemed that insufficient Internet access to the Internet (Question 2) is the biggest reason for poor online class attendance. Moreover, this indicator is also more critical in the regions than in the capital. Two negative factors assessed by students and teachers are the weakening of control by teachers and universities (Questions 3 and 4). Here, for the students, the estimates are 33% and 40% for Question 3 and 25% and 32% for Question 4. 17% and 19% of respondents, both in the capital and regions, respectively, noted the quality of educational materials as a factor in reducing attendance. As the teachers, students marked the weakening of quarantine require-ments for students (Question 7) as a possible factor in the increase in attendance (42% and 59% of the students, respectively, in Tashkent and the regions).

Students recognized the most significant cause for the decline in academic performance as the limi-tations associated with the peculiarities of distance learning (Question 9): 21% and 29%, respectively, in Tashkent and the regions. 7% and 5% of students from Tashkent and regions flagged stress caused by quarantine (Question 10) as a negative factor affecting academic performance. The main factors for potential growth in students' academic performance were the loosening of requirements for students (Question 12) - 58% and 33% of the students surveyed chose this factor. 33% and 48% of respondents cited the possibility of cheating on exams in online learning (Question 13) as a reason for improving academic performance.

Thus, summing up the results of the survey, the authors conclude:

Figure 6. Results of the questionnaire of the students

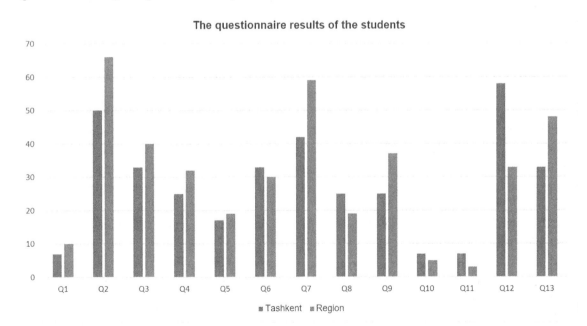

- Student enrollment in online classes has dropped significantly during the pandemic. The main reason for this fall was the lack of availability of the Internet, especially in the regions.
- Academic performance could formally improve. Surveys show that these results were achieved mainly due to the relaxation of general requirements during quarantine.
- The results obtained are consistent with those expected in the study. At the same time, the survey revealed challenges facing teachers and online learning providers.

SOLUTIONS AND RECOMMENDATIONS

The challenges faced in the digital transition of higher education in Uzbekistan due to the COVID-19 pandemic the authors classified into three categories: infrastructure and technology, teacher and student training, and student engagement.

Infrastructure and technology: The lack of infrastructure and technology has been a significant challenge in the digital transition of higher education in Uzbekistan. Many students and teachers need access to the necessary devices, such as computers and reliable Internet, to participate in digital learning. This lack of access has resulted in unequal access to education and limited the effectiveness of digital learning. To address this issue, educational institutions have taken measures by providing devices and internet access to students and teachers.

The government has also launched initiatives to provide internet access to schools and universities in remote areas. In this regard, Uzbekistan adopted the Concept of development of the system of higher education of the Republic of Uzbekistan till 2030 (DP, 2019), Digital Development Strategy of Uzbekistan until 2030 (2020a). These documents focused on further developing digital technologies, particularly in higher education in Uzbekistan.

Teacher and student training: Another challenge of the digital transition is the need for more training of teachers and students in digital learning. Many teachers need more skills and knowledge to teach effectively in the digital environment, resulting in reduced learning outcomes. Similarly, many students need more experience with digital learning and may need help adapting to the new format. Educational institutions have provided teacher training programs to improve digital teaching skills to mitigate this issue. Institutions provided students with support services to assist with the transition to digital learning. The adopted documents above contain measures to adapt to digital education as well.

Student engagement: One of the most significant challenges of digital learning is maintaining student engagement. The lack of face-to-face interaction can reduce students' motivation and engagement. The shift to digital learning has also created a need for new teaching methods to maintain student engagement. Educational institutions have implemented measures to promote student engagement, such as virtual classrooms, online discussions, and interactive learning materials. They developed LMS to provide online learning and manage educational processes. Examples are LMS and EMS developed in TTPU and HEMIS used in NamECI.

Based on the findings of this study, the authors can make several general recommendations to adapt to digital learning in Uzbekistan:

- Increase investment in infrastructure: The government should increase investment in digital infrastructure and technology to improve access to digital learning.

- Provide teacher training programs: educational institutions should provide teacher training programs to improve the skills and knowledge necessary to teach in the digital environment.
- Student support services: educational institutions should provide support services to assist students with transitioning to digital learning.
- Promote student engagement: educational institutions should implement measures to promote student engagement, such as virtual classrooms, online discussions, and interactive learning materials.

FUTURE RESEARCH DIRECTIONS

This article presents some problems concerning the digital transformation of higher education in Uzbekistan linked with the challenges of the COVID-19 pandemic. In their previous article, the authors studied such problems related to secondary schools and vocational education (Khusanov et al., 2022). However, problems of the influence of the pandemic on introducing digital learning in preschool, postgraduate education, and specialists' advanced professional training wait for further investigations. The limitations caused by the lockdown restricted the number of regions, higher education institutes, and participants covered by the study. The measures considered to mitigate the challenges of the pandemic and further development of the country's digital infrastructure will undoubtedly affect the coming years. The comparison study of these digital transformation problems would be perspective and actual in further research.

CONCLUSION

The research shows that online distance learning implemented during the lockdown caused by the pandemic of Covid-19 allowed for a continuation and inclusivity of higher education in Uzbekistan during that period. The study revealed the problems of using online learning for higher education students during the pandemic. The main of these highlighted problems was the need for more high-quality digital infrastructure, especially in the regions.

Universities have gained invaluable experience in using distance learning methods. It includes developing training materials, providing adequate feedback, and receipt of appropriate evaluation of training. Despite problems with the Internet, universities managed to use alternative forms of the educational process (for example, the Telegram application) and establish friendly and almost round-the-clock academic support for students.

The measures of the state and universities to address pandemic problems by targeted support to vulnerable students and their families, reducing Internet costs for education, and extending access to the electronic library funds allowed to mitigate the harmful effects of the pandemic.

The quarantine has accelerated the planned process of introducing distance learning in Uzbekistan. Currently, digital technologies are being implemented widely in the education system of Uzbekistan. These technologies, including distance education, are developed and used not only in teaching but also for reforming the entire system of higher education in Uzbekistan to further its digitization.

REFERENCES

Al-Maroof, R. S., Alnazzawi, N., Akour, I. A., Ayoubi, K., Alhumaid, K., AlAhbabi, N. M., Alnnaimi, M., Thabit, S., Alfaisal, R., Aburayya, A., & Salloum, S. (2021). The Effectiveness of Online Platforms after the Pandemic: Will Face-to-Face Classes Affect Students' Perception of Their Behavioural Intention (BIU) to Use Online Platforms? *Informatics (MDPI)*, *8*(4), 83–103. doi:10.3390/informatics8040083

Amaghouss, J., & Zouine, M. (2022). A Critical Analysis of the Moroccan Education System's Governance in the Online Education Era. In M. Garcia (Ed.), *Socioeconomic Inclusion During an Era of Online Education* (pp. 156–176). IGI Global. doi:10.4018/978-1-6684-4364-4.ch008

Ansu-Kyeremeh, E. K., & Goosen, L. (2022). Exploring the Socioeconomic Facet of Online Inclusive Education in Ghana: The Effects of Technological Advancements in Academia. In M. Garcia (Ed.), *Socioeconomic Inclusion During an Era of Online Education* (pp. 47–66). IGI Global. doi:10.4018/978-1-6684-4364-4.ch003

Balanskat, A., & Engelhardt, K. (2015). *Computing our future: Computer programming and coding.* European Schoolnet.

Bates, T. (2015). *Teaching in a Digital Age (Open Textbook).* Open Textbook. https://opentextbc.ca/teachinginadigitalage/

BigBlueButton virtual classroom. (n.d.). https://bigbluebutton.org/

Bihu, R. (2022). Implications of the COVID-19 Pandemic on Higher Education in Tanzania: A Roadmap for Developing an EPRRM Contingency Plan. In M. Garcia (Ed.), *Socioeconomic Inclusion During an Era of Online Education* (pp. 68–91). IGI Global. doi:10.4018/978-1-6684-4364-4.ch004

Christensen, G., & Alcorn, B. (2014). Are Free Online University Courses an Educational Panacea? *New Scientist*, *221*(2959), 24–25. doi:10.1016/S0262-4079(14)60484-X

Conceição, P. (Director and lead author) (2022). *Human development report 2021/2022. Uncertain times, unsettled lives. Shaping our future in a transforming world.* UNDP. https://hdr.undp.org/system/files/documents/global-report-document/hdr2021-22pdf_1.pdf

Decree of the President of the Republic of Uzbekistan (2019). *Concept of development of the system of higher education of the Republic of Uzbekistan till 2030.* DP-5847 08.10.2019.

Decree of the President of the Republic of Uzbekistan (2020a). *Digital Development Strategy of Uzbekistan until 2030.* DP-6079, 05. doi:10.2020.https://lex.uz/en/docs/5031048

Decree of the President of the Republic of Uzbekistan. (2020b). *On the State Program for the Implementation of the Strategy of Actions in five priority areas for the development of the Republic of Uzbekistan in 2017 - 2021 in the "Year of the Development of Science, Education, and the Digital Economy."* DP-5953 02.03.2020. https://lex.uz/ru/docs/-4751561

Fung, A., Meadows, M., & Xu, Z. (2022a). Online Learning in Higher Education during COVID-19: A Review of Evidence. *International Journal of Educational Research*, *109*, 101865. doi:10.1016/j.ijer.2021.101865

Fung, C. Y., Su, S. I., Perry, E. J., & Garcia, M. B. (2022b). Development of a Socioeconomic Inclusive Assessment Framework for Online Learning in Higher Education. In M. Garcia (Ed.), *Socioeconomic Inclusion During an Era of Online Education* (pp. 23–46). IGI Global. doi:10.4018/978-1-6684-4364-4.ch002

Government of Brazil. (2022). *The Wi-Fi Brazil program: high-speed internet to places with little or no connection.* Government of Brazil. https://www.gov.br/en/government-of-brazil/latest-news/2022/the-wi-fi-brasil-program

HEMIS OTM. (n.d.). *The information management system for educational processes.* HEMIS. https://hemis.uz/

Holmes, W. S. A., Schaumburg, H., & Mavrikis, M. (2018). *Technology-Enhanced Personalized Learning: Untangling the Evidence.* http://www.studie-personalisiertes-lernen.de/en

Iyer, L. S., Bharadwaj, S., Shetty, S. H., Verma, V., & Devanathan, M. (2022). Advancing Equity in Digital Classrooms: A Personalized Learning Framework for Higher Education Institutions. In M. Garcia (Ed.), *Socioeconomic Inclusion During an Era of Online Education* (pp. 225–245). IGI Global. doi:10.4018/978-1-6684-4364-4.ch011

Johnson, L., Adams Becker, S., Estrada, V., & Freeman, A. (2015). *NMC horizon report: 2015 higher education edition.* The New Media Consortium.

Jukes, I., McCain, T., & Crockett, L. (2010). *Understanding the digital generation: Teaching and learning in the new digital landscape.* Corwin Press.

Khusanov, K., & Kakharov, R. (2020). Impact of the Covid-19 pandemic on the development of digital training in higher education in Uzbekistan (Rus). In *Collection "Interconf" (36): with the Proceedings of the 7th International Scientific and Practical Conference "Challenges in Science of Nowadays" (November 26-28, 2020) in Washington, USA,* (pp. 513-522). Endeavors Publisher, 10.4018/978-1-6684-4364-4.ch010

Krishnaswami, M., Iyer, L. S., John, C., & Devanathan, M. (2022). Countering Educational Disruptions Through an Inclusive Approach: Bridging the Digital Divide in Distance Education. In M. Garcia (Ed.), *Socioeconomic Inclusion During an Era of Online Education* (pp. 204–224). IGI Global., . doi:10.4018/978-1-6684-4364-4.ch010

Khusanov, K., Khusanova, G., & Khusanova, M. (2022). Compulsory Distance Learning in Uzbekistan During the COVID-19 Era: The Case of Public and Senior Secondary Vocational Education Systems. In M. Garcia (Ed.), *Socioeconomic Inclusion During an Era of Online Education* (pp. 111–133). IGI Global. doi:10.4018/978-1-6684-4364-4.ch006

Lamsal, B. (2022). Exploring Issues Surrounding a Safe and Conducive Digital Learning Space in Nepal: A Preparation for Online Education in the Post-Pandemic Era. In M. Garcia (Ed.), *Socioeconomic Inclusion During an Era of Online Education* (pp. 246–263). IGI Global. doi:10.4018/978-1-6684-4364-4.ch012

Lin, E. C., & Yeh, A. J. (2022). Fighting Through COVID-19 for Educational Continuity: Challenges to Teachers. In M. Garcia (Ed.), *Socioeconomic Inclusion an Era of Online Education* (pp. 177–203). IGI Global. doi:10.4018/978-1-6684-4364-4.ch009

LRU. (2020). *Law of the Republic of Uzbekistan on Education, 23.09.2020, LRU-637*. LRU. https://lex.uz/ru/docs/5700831

M. S., N. & Siddiqui, I. (2022). How Inclusive Is Online Education in India: Lessons from the pandemic. In M. Garcia (Ed.), *Socioeconomic Inclusion During an Era of Online Education*, 135-155. IGI Global. doi:10.4018/978-1-6684-4364-4.ch007

Magoulas, G. D., & Chen, S. Y. (Eds.). (2006). *Advances in Web-Based Education: Personalized Learning Environments*. IGI Global. doi:10.4018/978-1-59140-690-7

Meeuwse, K., & Mason, D. (2018). *Personalized Professional Learning for Educators: Emerging Research and Opportunities*. IGI Global. doi:10.4018/978-1-5225-2685-8

Ministry of Electronics & Information Technology. (n.d.). *Digital India*. MEIT. https://www.digitalindia.gov.in/

OECD. (2021). The State of Higher Education: One Year into the COVID-19 Pandemic. OECD Publishing. doi:10.1787/83c41957-

Ruipérez-Valiente, J. A. (2022). A Macro-Scale MOOC Analysis of the Socioeconomic Status of Learners and Their Learning Outcomes. In M. Garcia (Ed.), *Socioeconomic Inclusion During an Era of Online Education* (pp. 1–22). IGI Global., doi:10.4018/978-1-6684-4364-4.ch001

Sharma, M. (2020). A study on digital transformation and its impact on education sector. *PJAEE, 17*(7), 16105–16108.

Siemens, G., Gašević, D., & Dawson, S. (2015). *Preparing for the Digital University: A review of the history and current state of distance, blended, and online learning*. Link Research Lab.

The State Committee of the Republic of Uzbekistan on Statistics. (n.d.). *Social Protection*. SCRUS. https://stat. uz/en/official-statistics/social-protection

Tomte, C. E., Fossland, T., Aamodt, P. O., & Degn, L. (2019). Digitalization in higher education: Mapping institutional approaches for teaching and learning. *Quality in Higher Education, 25*(1), 98–114. doi:10.1080/13538322.2019.1603611

Treceñe, J. K. (2022). COVID-19 and Remote Learning in the Philippine Basic Education System: Experiences of Teachers, Parents, and Students. In M. Garcia (Ed.), *Socioeconomic Inclusion During an Era of Online Education* (pp. 92–110). IGI Global., doi:10.4018/978-1-6684-4364-4.ch005

UNESCO. (2020). *Education: from school closure to recovery*. UNESCO. https://www.unesco.org/en/covid-19/education-response

World Bank. (2020). *Remote Learning During the Global School Lockdown: Multi-Country Lessons*. World Bank. https://www.worldbank.org/en/topic/edutech/brief/how-countries-are-using-edtech-to-support-remote-learning-during-the-covid-19-pandemic

ADDITIONAL READING

Alexander, S., & McKenzie, J. (2021). Pedagogical approaches to teaching online: A review of the literature and collaborative exploration of its impact on practice. *Journal of Further and Higher Education*, *45*(4), 479–498. doi:10.1080/0309877X.2020.1796816

Cavanagh, M., & Prescott, J. (2020). Evolving higher education landscapes: The COVID-19 pandemic and implications for the future. *Journal of Higher Education Policy and Management*, *42*(3), 245–252. doi:10.1080/1360080X.2020.1777141

Cheng, G., Chau, J., Chang, H., Liang, J., & Chou, T. (2020). Factors affecting university students' online learning performance during the COVID-19 pandemic. *Journal of Educational Technology & Society*, *23*(1), 32–42.

Dalkir, J. (2020). Lessons learned from the COVID-19 crisis: A content analysis of higher education institutions' communication. *Journal of Education & Social Policy*, *7*(3), 87–99.

Valtonen, T., Nissinen, K., & Rikala, J. (2020). Disruption as an opportunity for innovation: Finnish higher education teachers during the COVID-19 pandemic. *Journal of Vocational Education and Training*, *72*(4), 437–455.

Zawacki-Richter, O., & Qayyum, A. (Eds.). (2019). *Open and Distance Education in Asia, Africa, and the Middle East National Perspectives in a Digital Age*. Springer. doi:10.1007/978-981-13-5787-9

KEY TERMS AND DEFINITIONS

Digital Education: It refers to using innovative information technologies to teach students of all ages.

Digital Transition: It is the transformation of human activities using digital technologies.

Inclusive Education: Providing quality education to all students, regardless of their physical abilities, socioeconomic status, and remoteness or isolation from their residence. It became especially relevant during COVID-19.

Learning Management System (LMS): Universities' software application to deliver educational content and instructions online.

Lockdown: A restriction on people's movement and physical contact. In the context of the COVID-19 pandemic, universities were closed to the public, and the officials transferred the educational process to online distance learning.

Online Distance Education: A form of education where students receive online instructions rather than in physical classrooms.

Chapter 10
Market Orientation:
Concept and Progress

Mustafa Rehman Khan
ⓘ https://orcid.org/0000-0002-0250-9092
Shaheed Zulfikar Ali Bhutto Institute of Science and Technology, Pakistan & UCSI University, Malaysia

Naveed R. Khan
UCSI University, Malaysia

Muhammad Rafique
UCSI University, Malaysia

ABSTRACT

Market orientation is one of the most widely researched topics in the marketing domain, and has matured over time. The purpose of this chapter is to understand its concept and its gradual growth. The authors put light on the work of four research influencers of this filed, who works in team. First, they proposed a firm base market orientation theory. Second, they view the utile perspective of market orientation. Third, they bring customer perspective of market orientation. And fourth, they introduce the term customer-defined market orientation. Though researchers have conceptualized market orientation differently and bring new contextual factors in the concept, however, all researchers have consensus on the three dimensions of customer-defined market orientation which includes, customer orientation, competitor orientation and inter-functional orientation. Research in this domain reported that a firm who understands and use market orientation makes good profit and remain competitive in the industry in long run.

INTRODUCTION

The ultimate objective of any organization operating in the market is to maximize its revenue at its optimum level. The companies ought to acquire a sustainable competitive advantage over their competitor to achieve that goal (Gudlaugsson & Schalk, 2009). Hence, it is essential to realize the orientation

DOI: 10.4018/978-1-6684-6782-4.ch010

that allows companies to gain sustainable competitive advantage (Khan et al., 2022a). Over time, the concept of sustainable competitive advantage has been evolving through various structures. Previously, the sustainable competitive advantage is generally accentuated on economies of scale, standardization (production orientation) or product line expansion (product orientation), that enables organizations to provide their customer an extensive variety of products/services at a reasonable cost. Recently, market orientation has taken the position of strategic orientation, which emphasizes on the capability building of organization to continuously creating superior values to the customers (Kotler et al., 2010). Firstly, market orientation is specified as a strategic framework which assists organizations to execute the marketing ideas. It prompts organizations to continuously observe and respond to market fluctuation by focusing the customer as the core of their strategy (Jaworski & Kholi, 1993). Since the 1990s, a number of published research identify the substantial effect of market orientation on organizational performance (Borazon et al., 2022). The majority of the research findings affirm that the market orientation significantly links with abilities of the organization to create superior values. According to Day (1994) when the organizations do more exertion to contemplate the market, the more probabilities that organizations will successfully identify and react to unpredictable events in the unsteady market.

The idea of market orientation is established on the same principles as the concept of marketing. The literature of marketing provides solid evidence for this statement. According to Lavidge (1966), marketing is a set of actions that focus three aspects of the business; the customer, the marketing operation, and the profit of the company. Alderson and Green (1964) claim that the idea of marketing consists of activities related to finance, production and research and development. Kotler et al. (2010) proposed that the concept of marketing is based on three pillars which include: customer focused, coordinated marketing and profitability. The market orientation has defined by Kohli and Jaworski (1990) as on the basis of literature it would justifiable to conclude that those organizations are market-oriented who operationally manifest three pillars of marketing concept: "customer focus", "coordinated marketing" and "profitability", thus it can be understood that market orientation is the execution of marketing concept into organizational practices.

In successive part, the three pillars of marketing concept: customer focus, coordinated marketing, and profitability are enlightened to define the main concept. Kotler and Armstrong (2010) proposed that customer focus encourage organizations to invest in the research activities that assist organizations to gain information over the customer's ever-changing needs, wants, demands and expectations. When organizations know the demand and expectations of customers, they need to provide products/services that satisfy those needs of customers. The organization should accomplish this process through marketing planning, survey, market intelligence generation and dissemination (Gudlaugsson & Schalk, 2009). The integrated marketing refers that marketing practices of an organization should be well coordinated and align to look after each other. The third aspect profitability focus refers that profit is a substantial gauge for any venture, strategic decision, and management function as the ultimate objective for the operation of any organization is to earn a profit. Based on Kotler and Keller (2012), the three pillars of marketing concept are demonstrated in Figure 1.

According to Osuagwu (2006), the marketing concept has been extensively approved to divide into two categories: the concept of old-marketing and the concept of new marketing. The old marketing concept is considered as a philosophy which mainly concerns for customer-orientation, innovation, and profit. These concern of old marketing assist in creating satisfied customers. The concept of old marketing is seen as more philosophy whereas the concept of new marketing is considered explicit. The new marketing concept consists customer orientation, customer-oriented culture, continuous learning and

Figure 1. The three pillars of marketing concept

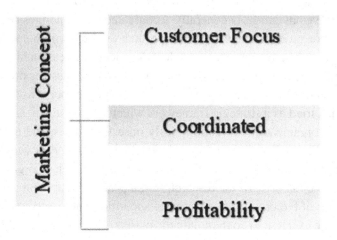

improvement in products/services, value delivery, total quality management, target marketing, market intelligence, coordinated, value creation, and integrated organizational activities. This highlighted an aspect of new marketing are coordinated toward getting proficiency and viability, which assist to accomplish superior competitive advantages. According to Matsuno et al., (2005), "the new-marketing concept implies business culture and an integral part of market economies". Hence it is an effective way to effectively operate an organization.

The market orientation has been introduced through several terms by different researchers (Shapiro, 1988; Kohli & Jaworski, 1990; Narver & Slater, 1990; Harris & Ogbonna, 2001). The recognized terms of market orientation includes: "integrated marketing" (Felton, 1959); "market-oriented" (Gummesson, 1991); "customer-oriented" (Kelley, 1992); "market-led" (Piercy, 1991); "market-oriented culture" (Harris, 1998). Indeed, the concept of marketing orientation has been present by different names, though the most popular term for the concept is "Market Orientation" (Narver & Slater, 1990; Kohli & Jaworski, 1990). Next section will provide the concept of market orientation construct.

Researchers claim that the market orientation implies a design of organizational cultures which systematically arrange human resource of an organization to the process of creating superior customer value (Narver & Slater, 1990; Deshpandé et al., 1993; Day, 1994; Kohli & Jaworski, 1990). The market orientation practices were embodied inside organizations since the start. Though the market orientation is a kind of degree, therefore the execution level of market orientation creates a difference between organizations (Kohli & Jaworski, 1990). The concept proposed by Kohli and Jaworski was asserted by Narver and Slater (1990), and researchers further state that an organization cannot just simply turn on and off the market orientation. A customer-driven organization cannot be categorized as a market-oriented organization. The long-term effort of the whole organization is required to label an organization as market-oriented. Additionally, this long-term effort usually brings significant changes in organizational culture.

The concept of market orientation based on three sub-dimensions which includes: "customer orientation", "competitor orientation" and "inter-functional coordination", and these factors are long term in vision and profit directed (Narver & Slater, 1990). They also claim that market orientation brings improvement and lead to better functioning. Several types of research and empirical studies have found that market orientation positive influence different aspects of business performance such as customer value creation, profitability, growth in sale volume et cetera. The next paragraphs will highlight a few remarks of different researchers on market orientation.

The market orientation is a systematic practice of organizations to obtain, explicate and exert the information about customer and competitors to acquire competitive advantage (Bisp, 1999). Narver et al. (1998) express that the market orientation is a culture of an organization with the interconnection between main factors market orientation, culture, and management. These researchers also believe that to implement market orientation successfully, the top management needs to clearly identify the vision and circulate established vision effectively from top to lower management.

Kotler and Armstrong (2010) claim that the successful implementation of market orientation required equalization of customer and competitor orientation within an organization. The organization will perform poorly who implement market orientation without balancing customer orientation and competitor orientation. Gudlaugsson and Schalk (2009), depict market orientation as the practices that have features of acquiring market data, evaluate and spread the analyzed information throughout the organization. Though, Market orientation is impacted by various factors, such as changes in technology, customer behavior, and the business environment (Zhao et al., 2023). Recently, companies are focusing more on data and analytics to understand customer preferences and make informed market orientation strategies (Zhao et al., 2023). There is also an increased emphasis on delivering exceptional customer experiences and incorporating technology into market orientation. Additionally, sustainability is becoming more important in market orientation strategies. Companies that are able to effectively adapt to these trends will be better positioned for success.

DIFFERENT VIEWS OF MARKET ORIENTATION

Market orientation has received attention from several researchers. Therefore, several researchers have proposed theories in different perspective regarding the concept of market orientation. In the following section, the most widely accepted theories of market orientation are discussed briefly to provide a concrete understanding of the concept.

Market Orientation in Context of Kohli and Jaworski

In July 1990, the research article "Market Orientation; the construct, research propositions, and managerial implications" was published by Kohli and Jaworski. In this article, researchers proposed a firm base market orientation theory. They state that market orientation depicts the practical implication of marketing concept into practices of organizations. Later, Kohli et al., (1993) proposed a measure model (MARKOR) of market orientation. The MARKOR model based on three main elements: market data collection, dissemination of market data and the action plan based on intelligence gathered. Kohli and Jaworski (1990) define market orientation as: "Market orientation is the organization-wide generations of market intelligence pertaining to current and future customer needs, dissemination of the intelligence across departments, and organization-wide responsiveness to it."

According to researchers' market orientation is the implementation of the marketing concept. The organizations who adopt the marketing concept in their practices are considered as market-oriented organizations. In MARKOR model of Kohli and Jaworski, market intelligence plays a basic role to initiate the practice of market orientation. The market intelligence pertains to the collection of data, analyzing customer preferences, government regulations and competitors' strategies that effect the needs, wants, and preferences of their customers. Market orientation implies the development of organizational market intelligence. Hence, researchers considered learning of organization as the key outcome of market orientation. The organizational learning focus on the development of every individual in the organization through involving them in a continuous process of collecting, disseminating, and communicating data to all functional departments of an organization. One of the main considerations of this model is that the organizational learning required the involvement and cooperation from all departments of an organization and it is not only task of sales and marketing department. This school of thought also acknowledge by Slater and Narver (1994), Narver and Slater (1990), and Shapiro (1988). These researchers also emphasized the significance of inter-functional departmental coordination.

Market Orientation in Context of Narver and Slater

In 1990, after three months of Kohli and Jaworski publication, Narver and Slater presented their paper "The Effect of a Market Orientation on Business Profitability", which contributes another significant perspective of market orientation. In this study, Narver and Slater proposed a utile perspective of market orientation and construct a model of market orientation. Narver and Slater conduct extensive research by inviting managers of 140 strategic business unit from both commodity and non-commodity business. The perspective proposed by Narver and Slater is different from previous authors, he considered market orientation to be an organizational culture (Ortega & Criado, 2012). Narver and Slater highlighted another perspective of market orientation by emphasizing that market-oriented organizations adopt a balanced approach to focus on customers as well as competitors equally. This perspective is later embraced in Kotler and Keller's theory (Kotler & Keller, 2012). Furthermore, inter-functional coordination was given eminence as it makes the department's coordinated efforts within the firm and creates it a part of the culture. Narver and slater proposed a definition of market orientation can be separated into two key aspect's behavioral part which consists of three component customer orientation, competitor orientation, inter-functional coordination and the decision principle which direct company behavior includes; long term focus and profitability.

Market Orientation in Context of Deshpandé, Farley, and Webster

Deshpandé et al. (1993) proposed another perspective of market orientation. They proposed a customer perspective of market orientation which is different from previous scholars. Deshpandé et al. (1993) asserts that the assessment of the intensity of how much an organization is customer-oriented should base on customers perception rather than completely reflect the company itself perception. In this study, researchers aim to answer four questions related to organizational culture and business performance: the relationship between customer orientation (customers' and marketers' perspective) and business performance, the differences between marketers' and customers' perspective on market orientation, the significance of customers' perspective of market orientation on business performance, and lastly the relationship between firm innovation and business performance. One of the utile contributions of this research is that it confirms customers' perception of market orientation has positively influenced business performance and the customer's perception on market orientation is more valuable as compared to perception on market orientation of company itself. This research also highlighted that the dissimilarities between the perception of marketers and customers on market orientation may affect customer judgment regarding company' market orientation efforts, thus prompt issue of enhancing business performance. The researchers profoundly urge the organization to consolidate both self-evaluation and customers' perspective to assist performance enhancement.

Market Orientation in Context of Web, Webster, and Krepapa

In 2000, Web, Webster, and Krepapa published an article: "An exploration of the meaning and outcomes of a customer-defined market orientation" which introduced the term customer-defined market orientation. The author's view of market-orientation is constructed on the perspective of Deshpandé et al. (1993). Web et al. (2000) proposed that employees define a view of market orientation is myopic and one-sided as it ignores the crucial role that customer play in term of value recognition. Researchers suggested that an organization can appropriately describe as market-oriented only when the customer recognized and perceive that the firm offers considerable value to them. In this study researchers aim to contribute through several ways: firstly, customer-defined market orientation model is conceptualized which extended the framework of market orientation and organizational outcome. Secondly, market orientation tool of Narver and Slater (1990) was amended to accommodate customer vantage. Thirdly, customer-defined market orientation models are examined to test reliability and validity. And last, investigated the relationship between customer define-market orientation and both service quality and customer satisfaction. This study found a significant effect of market orientation with its sub-dimension i.e. customer orientation, competitor orientation, and inter-functional coordination on both service quality and customer satisfaction. The result reveals that competitor orientation, among three sub-dimension of market orientation, has the strongest relationship with both service quality and customer satisfaction.

CUSTOMER-DEFINED MARKET ORIENTATION

The concept of market orientation has been presented and embraced more than 56 years ago (Levitt, 1960). The advancement in the idea of market orientation has induced numerous researchers to conduct research on a different aspect of business and how it can be connected. According to (Narver & Slater, 1990; Lukas & Ferrell, 2000) market orientation perform a critical function in various areas role in different areas of business activities for example, how an organization quickly learn and react to business challenges, new product development, innovation and how to enhanced business performance (Schulze et al., 2022). Researchers (Narver & Slater, 1990; Kohli & Jaworski, 1990) contend that market orientation covers the whole organization in the form of wide application. The organization who adopts market orientation can effectively and efficiently execute the marketing concept in its line of operations.

Numerous researchers try to give a meaningful explanation about the concept of market orientation. The market orientation has conceptualized by Shapiro (1988) as an organizational strategy creating process starts from gathering information and proceed it to implementation. It would be recognized only if the manager of an organization appreciates interdependent sharing of information and permits workers to contribute to the strategy making process at all levels of management. Kohli and Jaworski (1990) characterized the concept of market orientation as an overall organizational generation of market intelligence with respect to present and future needs, information distribution across departments and responsiveness toward market intelligence. According to Narver and Slater (1990) market orientation is the culture of an organization which primarily create superior customer value through customer orientation, competitor orientation, and inter-functional coordination. Deshpandé et al. (1993) viewed market orientation as an ideology which prioritizes customer interest by creating value, however, considering other significant stakeholders such as managers and employees to run venture profitably. Day (1992) presented its perspective and express that, market orientation can be regarded as a predominant capability to understand and satisfy the customer, emphasize on market scanning as well as customer connecting skills that push market-led organizations to regulate in accordance to the market requirement through information anticipation.

Some other researcher viewed market orientation as a vital part of organizational culture and process as it might be encouraged by the internal aspect of an organization (Harris & Ogbonna, 2001; Li et al., 2023). Market orientation would appear to be an essential part of organizations due to intense international competition and rapid changes in consumer preferences, so organizations need to compose their strategies with a strong focus on their target audience, in order to compete in a market (Kurtinaitiene, 2005). Neneh (2016) proposed that business organizations are profoundly influenced by global competition and facing the constant changing need of customers. Subsequently, market orientation has been viewed as a valuable approach for organizations to deal with market fluctuations effectively and sustain superior business performance (Neneh, 2016). Kotler (2009) propose that observing a fluctuation in the market will encourage determining the effect of customer satisfaction, improve product development and strategy execution in developing superior value among players in the industry.

If critically review the explanation given by different researchers with respect to market orientation, one theme that goes through the meaning is that, organizations need to collect information from people who are related to the business and use that information in the execution of strategies in order to create value for stakeholders. Thus, market orientation can be defined as the exertion of getting what customer wants by means of acquiring some idea after that execute these ideas to create value for customers and sustain a competitive position in the industry. Customer-defined market orientation further elaborated in three dimensions by previous researchers (Deshpandé et al., 1993).

Customer Orientation

Customer orientation should introduce the culture which places the customer at priority and requires a comprehensive insight about the customer needs to provide them updated product and service of superior value (Narver & Slater, 1990; Deshpandé et al., 1993). The market-oriented organization has knowledge about adopting different tools to enhance value and benefit to customers and its use in offering benefits results in attaining sustainable competitive advantage (Narver & Slater, 1990). These organizations consistently examine alternatives to identify how the greatest impact can create sustainable better value for existing and potential customers. Therefore, market orientation is essential for an organization to obtain a higher performance level, maintain the capacity building, and formulate a strong positive relationship with customers. Hence, organizations need to gather precise and accurate information about customers which help firms to address the requirement of target customers.

According to Zhou et al. (2005), customer orientation is observed as a part of an organization's strategy for delivering desire value to customers. Narver and Slater (1990) proposed that the objective of customer orientation is to establish an appropriate framework of gathering information concerning current and potential customers for business strategies, and those strategies are taken considering adequate information given by customers, hence results in creating enhanced superior value to the customer base. Kohli and Jaworski (1990) proposed that customer orientation demonstrate the level of gathering customer intelligence and its implementation in a business setup.

The essential element of customer orientation is particularly defined in the management literature, and studies led in the field of strategic management continuously emphasized the idea that focuses on customer been the crucial reason for business operation (Webster, 1988). One can say that customers are the reason for the existence of business hence information which helps the organization to deliver value to customers must be very crucial for management. Therefore, customer orientation should not be relegated since it provides support in delivering value to customers.

Competitor Orientation

To be a competitive organization it is necessary to understand the competitors completely in respect of strength, weaknesses, capabilities as well as their activities. According to researchers the competitor's information help organization to reposition its offering in order to secure future survival (Narver & Slater, 1990; Deshpande et al., 1993). Competitor orientation as an aspect of market orientation viewed as a business strategy which results in creating a business behavior to improve the product they offer to customers. The organization must know that competitors will not relax and unconcerned for customers, so they strive for the same customer base to gain market share. Therefore, it is required for organizations to keep insight over their competitors in order to enhance their offering and sustain their market share.

sThe key objective of competitor orientation is to offer a strong foundation of intelligence for business strategies concerning current and potential competitor. According to Kotler (2009) competitor who provides a substitute product by serving a similar need of customers are viewed as an enterprise. Those substitute product competitors increase the competitive and decrease the potential profit for the organization. Therefore, the organization required to gain insight into the competitor activities and strategies to shape the organization's operation.

Inter-Functional Orientation

Inter-functional Orientation refers that business must have strong coordination among all departments in all aspect of business operations. According to (Narver & Slater, 1990) the organization who practice inter-functional orientation achieve the higher coordination of the firm's resources that perceive as the high performance by the customer. Shapiro (1988) highlights that "market orientation" is not same as "marketing orientation", hence marketing department is not the only one in the organization who play a crucial role, rather it is the effort of all departments.

Market orientation has identified that the attitude of the workforce is very crucial with respect to internal and external customer and all departments as well as workforce should be aware of it. Narver and Slater (1990) suggested that coordinated integration of resources is highly associated with customer and competitor as they are promoting customers experience among departments. Therefore, inter-coordinated operations are required in regular management practices to recognize the full potential of business in maximizing its performance.

THE NEXT FRONTIER IN MARKET ORIENTATION

The future of market orientation is shaped by a number of key trends and developments, including changes in technology, customer behavior, and the business environment. Here is a more in-depth look at some of the key factors that are likely to shape the future of market orientation:

Increased Focus on Data and Analytics

Companies are collecting more data on their customers than ever before, and this trend is likely to continue. In order to remain competitive, companies will need to leverage this data to gain insights into customer preferences and behaviors, and use this information to inform their market orientation strategies. This requires investment in data analytics and the development of data-driven decision-making processes (Kohli & Jaworski, 1990).

Greater Emphasis on Customer Experience

In today's highly competitive marketplace, companies are seeking to differentiate themselves by delivering exceptional customer experiences. This requires companies to understand the needs and preferences of their customers and design their products and services accordingly. Companies will need to focus on creating seamless, intuitive, and personalized experiences that meet the evolving needs of their customers (Batat, 2022).

Greater Use of Technology

Companies are making greater use of technology to improve their market orientation, and this trend is likely to continue. This includes the use of artificial intelligence and machine learning to gain deeper insights into customer data, as well as the use of digital tools and platforms to improve customer engagement and interaction. Companies that are able to effectively integrate technology into their market orientation strategies will be better positioned to succeed (Narver & Slater, 1990).

Greater Emphasis on Sustainability

Companies are placing greater emphasis on sustainability and environmental responsibility in their market orientation strategies. This involves designing products and services that are more environmentally friendly, reducing their carbon footprint, and addressing the sustainability concerns of their customers (Khan et al., 2022b). Companies that are able to effectively integrate sustainability into their market orientation strategies will be better positioned to win over customers who are looking for environmentally responsible products and services (Du & Wang, 2022; Khan et al., 2022b).

MARKET ORIENTATION AND DIGITAL NATIVES

The market orientation and digital natives are interrelated and have a significant impact on businesses and their strategies (Wong et al., 2022). Market orientation refers to a company's focus on creating value for customers by anticipating and fulfilling their needs. Digital natives, on the other hand, are individuals who have grown up with technology and are familiar with digital products and services. In this section, we will examine the connection between market orientation and digital natives and the implications for businesses.

Omnichannel Engagement

Digital natives expect seamless engagement across all touchpoints, including digital and physical channels. Companies that are able to create an omnichannel strategy that integrates digital and physical touchpoints will be better positioned to meet the expectations of digital natives. According to a study by Accenture, 80% of digital natives expect a consistent experience across all touchpoints (Accenture, 2018).

Personalization

Digital natives expect personalization in their interactions with companies. This includes tailored recommendations, custom experiences, and messaging that is relevant to their interests and preferences. Companies that are able to leverage data and technology to deliver personalized experiences will be better positioned to win over digital natives. A study by Epsilon found that personalized experiences can increase customer loyalty by up to 20% (Epsilon, 2019).

Technology Reliant

Digital natives are heavily reliant on mobile devices and expect a mobile-first experience. Companies that are able to create mobile-first strategies that deliver a seamless experience on mobile devices will be better positioned to meet the expectations of digital natives. According to a study by Gkioulos (2017), digital natives are heavily reliant on their mobile devices as their primary source of information.

Social Influence

Digital natives are highly influenced by social media and the opinions of their peers. Companies that are able to effectively leverage social media to engage with digital natives and influence their purchase decisions will be better positioned to win over this demographic. A study by the Nielsen Company found that 92% of digital natives trust recommendations from friends and family more than any other form of advertising (Nielsen, 2016).

Therefore, market orientation is closely linked to the preferences and behaviors of digital natives (Kopalle et al., 2020). Companies that are able to understand and respond to the needs and expectations of digital natives will be better positioned to remain competitive in the future marketplace. By focusing on omnichannel engagement, personalization, mobile-first strategies, and social influence, companies can create a market orientation that meets the needs of digital natives and drives business success.

DIGITAL NATIVES, MARKET ORIENTATION, AND TRADITIONAL BUSINESS MODELS

The rise of digital natives has disrupted traditional business models and challenged the status quo in many industries (Reis & Melão, 2023). Digital natives, who have grown up with technology and are familiar with digital products and services, are changing the way businesses operate and compete. This section will examine the differences in digital natives and traditional business models, and the implications for companies in terms of competitiveness and success.

Data-Driven Strategy

Digital natives are characterized by their market orientation, which is their focus on understanding and responding to customer needs and behaviors. They use technology to collect and analyze customer data, allowing them to quickly respond to changing customer needs and preferences (Schöni, 2022). This market orientation allows digital natives to create products and services that are tailored to the specific needs of their customers, making them more competitive in capturing market share. For example, in the retail industry, e-commerce platforms such as Amazon and Alibaba have disrupted traditional retail models by offering consumers a more convenient and personalized shopping experience. By understanding customer behaviors and preferences, these digital natives have been able to create products and services that are tailored to the specific needs of their customers, leading to their success in capturing market share. In contrast, traditional business models may not have the necessary systems and processes in place to collect and analyze customer data. This can make it difficult for these businesses to respond quickly to changing customer needs, leading to a decline in competitiveness and market share.

Innovation

Digital natives are also known for their innovative approach to business, experimenting with new business models and technologies to create new value for customers. They embrace new technologies, such as artificial intelligence and blockchain, to create products and services that are more efficient and effective (Mariani & Nambisan, 2021). For example, in the financial services industry, fintech companies such as Ant Financial and Grab Financial have disrupted traditional financial services models by offering consumers new and more efficient ways to access financial services. By embracing new technologies, these digital natives have been able to create new products and services that are more convenient and accessible, leading to their success in capturing market share. In contrast, traditional business models may be less willing to experiment with new technologies and business models, leading to a decline in competitiveness and market share.

Customer Centricity

Digital natives are characterized by their customer-centric approach, putting the needs and preferences of customers at the center of their operations. They use technology to understand customer behaviors and preferences, and to create products and services that are tailored to the specific needs of their customers (Kumar & Venkatesan, 2021). For example, in the hospitality industry, the sharing economy platforms such as Airbnb and Grab have disrupted traditional hospitality and transportation models by offering consumers new and more efficient ways to access these services. By putting the needs and preferences of customers at the center of their operations, these digital natives have been able to create products and services that are more convenient and accessible, leading to their success in capturing market share. In contrast, traditional business models without market orientation may be less focused on the needs and preferences of customers, leading to a decline in competitiveness and market share.

Therefore, digital natives are challenging traditional business models and changing the way businesses operate and compete. By adopting a market orientation, embracing innovation, and being customer-centric, companies can remain competitive in the face of digital disruption.

CONCLUSION

All previous studies examined the market orientation agree with the main elements of market orientation such as customer orientation, competitor orientation and inter-functional coordination. Nevertheless, academics' conceptions of market orientation have changed throughout time. At its most essential, market orientation is a concept that emphasizes consumer interest through adding value, while also taking into account other important stakeholders, such managers and staff, in order to operate a business profitably. Market-oriented companies excel in gathering, disseminating, and using market information (consumers, rivals, collaborators, technology, trends, etc.) to drive coordinated choices that result in the development of novel new goods, higher product and service quality, and superior performance. But some businesses are more proactive than others, both in terms of the kind of knowledge they provide and the steps they take. Businesses that are more proactive seek information on present and possible customers' demands as well as competitive threats, in addition to present customer wants and competitor risks. Businesses that take the initiative are more likely to create customer-driven market strategies, in which they actively work to change the way the market is structured and/or establish novel value propositions that allow them to lessen or even eliminate competition. The rise of digital natives has disrupted traditional business models and has challenged companies to understand and respond to the changing needs of their customers. Companies that are able to effectively integrate data analytics, technology, and sustainability into their market orientation strategies, and focus on omnichannel engagement, personalization, mobile-first strategies, and social influence will be better positioned to succeed in the future marketplace. The market orientation of digital natives allows them to create products and services that are tailored to the specific needs of their customers, making them more competitive in capturing market share.

REFERENCES

Accenture. (2018). The Future of Customer Experience. *Accenture.* https://www.accenture.com/us-en/insights/customer-experience/future-of-customer-experience

Alderson, W., & Green, P. E. (1964). *Planning and problem solving in marketing.* RD Irwin.

Batat, W. (2022). What does phygital really mean? A conceptual introduction to the phygital customer experience (PH-CX) framework. *Journal of Strategic Marketing*, 1–24. doi:10.1080/0965254X.2022.2059775

Bisp, S. (1999). Barriers to increased market-oriented activity: What the literature suggests. *Journal of Market Focused Management, 4*(1), 77–92. doi:10.1023/A:1009808112356

Borazon, E. Q., Huang, Y. C., & Liu, J. M. (2022). Green market orientation and organizational performance in Taiwan's electric and electronic industry: The mediating role of green supply chain management capability. *Journal of Business and Industrial Marketing, 37*(7), 1475–1496. doi:10.1108/JBIM-07-2020-0321

Day, G. S. (1992). Marketing's contribution to the strategy dialogue. *Journal of the Academy of Marketing Science, 20*(4), 323–329. doi:10.1007/BF02725208

Day, G. S. (1994). The capabilities of market-driven organizations. *Journal of Marketing, 58*(4), 37–52. doi:10.1177/002224299405800404

Deshpandé, R., Farley, J. U., & Webster, F. E. Jr. (1993). Corporate culture, customer orientation, and innovativeness in Japanese firms: A quadrad analysis. *Journal of Marketing, 57*(1), 23–37. doi:10.1177/002224299305700102

Du, Y., & Wang, H. (2022). Green innovation sustainability: How green market orientation and absorptive capacity matter? *Sustainability (Basel), 14*(13), 8192. doi:10.3390u14138192

Epsilon. (2019). *The Power of Personalization.* Epsilon. https://www.epsilon.com/insights/the-power-of-personalization/

Felton, A. P. (1959). Making the marketing concept work. *Harvard Business Review, 37,* 55–65.

Gkioulos, V., Wangen, G., Katsikas, S. K., Kavallieratos, G., & Kotzanikolaou, P. (2017). Security awareness of the digital natives. *Information (Basel), 8*(2), 42. doi:10.3390/info8020042

Gudlaugsson, T., & Schalk, A. P. (2009). Effects of market orientation on business performance: Empirical evidence from Iceland. *The European Institute of Retailing and Service Studies,* (6), 1–17.

Gummesson, E. (1991). Marketing-orientation revisited: The crucial role of the part-time marketer. *European Journal of Marketing, 25*(2), 60–75. doi:10.1108/03090569110139166

Harris, L. C. (1998). Cultural domination: The key to market-oriented culture? *European Journal of Marketing, 32*(3/4), 354–373. doi:10.1108/03090569810204643

Harris, L. C., & Ogbonna, E. (2001). Strategic human resource management, market orientation, and organizational performance. *Journal of Business Research, 51*(2), 157–166. doi:10.1016/S0148-2963(99)00057-0

Jaworski, B. J., & Kohli, A. K. (1993). Market orientation: Antecedents and consequences. *Journal of Marketing, 57*(3), 53–70. doi:10.1177/002224299305700304

Kelley, S. W. (1992). Developing customer orientation among service employees. *Journal of the Academy of Marketing Science, 20*(1), 27–36. doi:10.1007/BF02723473

Khan, M. R., Khan, N. R., Kumar, V. R., Bhatt, V. K., & Malik, F. (2022). a. Customer-Defined Market Orientation, Brand Image and Customer Satisfaction: A Mediation Approach. *SAGE Open, 12*(4), 21582440221141860. doi:10.1177/21582440221141860

Khan, R. M., Khan, H. R., & Ghouri, A. M. (2022). b. Corporate social responsibility, sustainability governance and sustainable performance: A preliminary insight. *Asian Academy of Management Journal, 27*(1), 1–28.

Kohli, A. K., & Jaworski, B. J. (1990). Market orientation: The construct, research propositions, and managerial implications. *Journal of Marketing, 54*(2), 1–18. doi:10.1177/002224299005400201

Kohli, A. K., & Jaworski, B. J. (1990). Market orientation: The construct, research propositions, and managerial implications. *Journal of Marketing, 54*(2), 1–18. doi:10.1177/002224299005400201

Kohli, A. K., Jaworski, B. J., & Kumar, A. (1993). MARKOR: A measure of market orientation. *JMR, Journal of Marketing Research, 30*(4), 467–477. doi:10.1177/002224379303000406

Kopalle, P. K., Kumar, V., & Subramaniam, M. (2020). How legacy firms can embrace the digital ecosystem via digital customer orientation. *Journal of the Academy of Marketing Science, 48*(1), 114–131. doi:10.100711747-019-00694-2

Kotler, P. (2009). *Marketing management: a South Asian perspective*. Pearson Education India.

Kotler, P., & Armstrong, G. (2010). *Principles of marketing*. Pearson education.

Kotler, P., Kartajaya, H., & Setiawan, I. (2010). *From products to customers to the human spirit; marketing 3.0*. John Wiley & Sons Inc. doi:10.1002/9781118257883

Kotler, P., & Keller, K. (2012). *Management marketing*. Pearson Education Limited.

Kotler, P., & Keller, K. L. (2016). *Marketing management*. Pearson Education.

Kumar, V., & Venkatesan, R. (2021). Transformation of metrics and analytics in retailing: The way forward. *Journal of Retailing, 97*(4), 496–506. doi:10.1016/j.jretai.2021.11.004

Kurtinaitiene, J. (2005). Marketing orientation in the European Union mobile telecommunication market. *Marketing Intelligence & Planning, 23*(1), 104–113. doi:10.1108/02634500510577500

Lavidge, R. J. (1966). Marketing concept often gets only lip service. *Advertising Age, 37*(October), 52.

Levitt, T. (1960). Marketing myopia. *Harvard Business Review, 38*(4), 24–47. PMID:15252891

Li, S., Shi, Y., Wang, L., & Xia, E. (2023). A Bibliometric Analysis of Brand Orientation Strategy in Digital Marketing: Determinants, Research Perspectives and Evolutions. *Sustainability (Basel), 15*(2), 1486. doi:10.3390u15021486

Lukas, B. A., & Ferrell, O. C. (2000). The effect of market orientation on product innovation. *Journal of the Academy of Marketing Science, 28*(2), 239–247. doi:10.1177/0092070300282005

Mariani, M. M., & Nambisan, S. (2021). Innovation analytics and digital innovation experimentation: The rise of research-driven online review platforms. *Technological Forecasting and Social Change, 172*, 121009. doi:10.1016/j.techfore.2021.121009

Matsuno, K., Mentzer, J. T., & Rentz, J. O. (2005). A conceptual and empirical comparison of three market orientation scales. *Journal of Business Research, 58*(1), 1–8. doi:10.1016/S0148-2963(03)00075-4

Narver, J. C., & Slater, S. F. (1990). The effect of a market orientation on business profitability. *Journal of Marketing*, *54*(4), 20–35. doi:10.1177/002224299005400403

Narver, J. C., Slater, S. F., & Tietje, B. (1998). Creating a market orientation. *Journal of Market Focused Management*, *2*(3), 241–255. doi:10.1023/A:1009703717144

Neneh, B. N. (2016). Market orientation and performance: The contingency role of external environment. *Environment and Ecology*, *7*(2), 1–14.

Nielsen. (2016). *The Power of Like-Minded Peers*. Nielsen. https://www.nielsen.com/us/en/insights/report/2016/the-power-of-like-minded-peers/

Ortega, R. T., & Criado, J. R. (2012). Market Orientation of Born Globals Firms: A Qualitative Examination. *International Journal of Business and Management Studies*, *4*(2), 141–150.

Osuagwu, L. (2006). Market orientation in Nigerian companies. *Marketing Intelligence & Planning*, *24*(6), 608–631. doi:10.1108/02634500610701681

Piercy, N. (1991). *Market-led strategic change: Making marketing happen in your organization*. Harper Thorsons.

Reis, J., & Melão, N. (2023). Digital transformation: A meta-review and guidelines for future research. *Heliyon*, *9*(1), 12834. doi:10.1016/j.heliyon.2023.e12834 PMID:36691547

Schöni, W. (2022). Continuing education as value creation: Towards a new orientation beyond market logic. *European Journal for Research on the Education and Learning of Adults*, *13*(3), 261–283. doi:10.3384/rela.2000-7426.3694

Schulze, A., Townsend, J. D., & Talay, M. B. (2022). Completing the market orientation matrix: The impact of proactive competitor orientation on innovation and firm performance. *Industrial Marketing Management*, *103*, 198–214. doi:10.1016/j.indmarman.2022.03.013

Shapiro, B. P. (1988). *What the hell is market oriented?* HBR Reprints.

Slater, S. F., & Narver, J. C. (1994). Market orientation, customer value, and superior performance. *Business Horizons*, *37*(2), 22–28. doi:10.1016/0007-6813(94)90029-9

Webb, D., Webster, C., & Krepapa, A. (2000). An exploration of the meaning and outcomes of a customer-defined market orientation. *Journal of Business Research*, *48*(2), 101–112. doi:10.1016/S0148-2963(98)00114-3

Webster, F. E. Jr. (1988). The rediscovery of the marketing concept. *Business Horizons*, *31*(3), 29–39. doi:10.1016/0007-6813(88)90006-7

Wong, L. W., Tan, G. W. H., Hew, J. J., Ooi, K. B., & Leong, L. Y. (2022). Mobile social media marketing: A new marketing channel among digital natives in higher education? *Journal of Marketing for Higher Education*, *32*(1), 113–137. doi:10.1080/08841241.2020.1834486

Zhao, Y., Peng, B., Iqbal, K., & Wan, A. (2023). Does market orientation promote enterprise digital innovation? Based on the survey data of China's digital core industries. *Industrial Marketing Management*, *109*, 135–145. doi:10.1016/j.indmarman.2022.12.015

Zhou, K. Z., Yim, C. K., & Tse, D. K. (2005). The effects of strategic orientations on technology-and market-based breakthrough innovations. *Journal of Marketing*, *69*(2), 42–60. doi:10.1509/jmkg.69.2.42.60756

Chapter 11
Industrial Revolution 4.0 and the Environment:
The Asian Perspective

Subhanil Banerjee
ⓘ https://orcid.org/0000-0001-7485-9967
Veni Creator Christian University, USA

Souren Koner
ⓘ https://orcid.org/0000-0002-9118-7143
Royal Global University, Guwahati, India

ABSTRACT

Mother Nature has suffered through many industrial revolutions. Ecology suffered after the first industrial revolution. Industrial revolutions quadrupled CO2. Industrial Revolution 4.0 follows the Stockholm Conference in 1972 and Brundtland's report "Our Common Future" (1983-1987) on sustainable development. The emerging and less developed countries are condemned for their carbon footprint and CO2 emissions from manufacturing and consumption. According to the environmental Kuznets curve hypothesis, developed countries advise developing nations to follow their development path to reduce carbon emissions. Industrial Revolution 4.0 replaced the Fordist style of production with information-based production. In this context, is digitization pro-environment? Regrettably, this has not been empirically studied. This chapter examines the environmental effects of digitalization and Industrial Revolution 4.0. The chapter will examine the link between the environment, digitalization, and Industrial Revolution 4.0 using empirical validation and descriptive analysis.

INTRODUCTION

The Emergence of Digital Eras the Prelude of Industry 4.0

The emergence of the digital world during the last decade of the last millennium has put an end to the Fordist mode of production and opened the sluice gate for an informative mode of production. The spread

DOI: 10.4018/978-1-6684-6782-4.ch011

of the World Wide Web and then the mobile phones following the appearance of smartphones led to the conjugation of the internet and mobile phones over time, turning information from static to dynamic. Information remained no longer a slave of space and time; literally, it could be accessed at the tip of a finger at anytime and anywhere. Obviously, this particular incident created an ambiance of information symmetry that arguably improved social welfare. The surfacing of Industry 4.0, often called the fourth industrial revolution, emphasized a production process that was capital-intensive and, more aptly, information-intensive. Over time, automation of the production process through artificial intelligence has made digitalization even more important. This particular rise of information through digitalization gave rise to the famous or infamous digital divide (Banerjee & Gupta, 2022).

A Critical Consideration of the Pro-Environment Ambiance

During these heydays of pro-environment growth and development following the 1972 Stockholm Convention (Chen & McDonough, 2022), and more precisely the Brundtland Commission report that was the outcome of the Brundtland Commission established in 1983 and dissolved following their report 'Our Common Future' in 1987, a new term, sustainable development, has been coined. The essence of sustainable development rests on the pillar of benefiting the present without sacrificing the future. The report tries to identify and address the anthropocentric maladies that the environment is subject to following the industrial revolution, first in Great Britain and then in the United States of America. It is a well-known fact that the level of carbon dioxide (CO_2) in atmospheric air has increased three times from the pre- to post-industrial revolution, and the report is relevant in this context (Brundtland, 1987). Later on, the report has been criticised by experts as ordinal in nature (Butlin, 1989) and replication of Pigouvian externalities (Pigou, 1920). However, the most important shortcomings of the report remained behind the veil. The concerned report has a major lacuna: it considers sustainable development purely from an anthropocentric perspective and disregards the fact that environmental sustainability is much beyond anthropocentric sustainability and depends on all the living and non-living agents of mother nature. The experts who criticised the report never took into account this major shortcoming of the Brundtland Commission report 'Our Common Future'. The influence of 'Our Common Future' on the academic literature can be easily found in the fact that it popularised the discipline of environmental economics like no other factor (Banerjee et al., 2022).

Industry 4.0: Need for an Empirical Evaluation

However, the present chapter does not delve into such a descriptive debate. It rather investigates the fact of whether the so-called Industry 4.0 and its subset, digitalization, are as environmentally friendly as they are promoted. The green sector is perceived through the proliferation of the service sector. Are they really green? Whether Industry 4.0 and digitalization are essential to improve the quality of the environment and lead toward sustainable development (Javaid et al., 2022). These series of questions need both descriptive and empirical validation, as so far these claims are more theoretical in nature. In research, it has often been found that a strong theory lacks the necessary empirical validation and is thus only useful in papers but not in any particular problem scenario. Considering the extremely sensitive nature of the environmental status and problems, it cannot be left to a mere theory to stand as the vanguard of the problem. Without a doubt, such theories need to be empirically investigated and validated before acceptance (Banerjee et al., 2022).

The Discontent Among Developed, Developing and Less Developed Countries Regarding Environmental Resilience and Sustainability

The developing nations have long been criticised by the international bodies lobbied by the developed nations, considering the carbon footprint left through their labour-intensive production process and the higher emission of CO_2 in the atmosphere. A technological improvement developed over a capital-intensive choice of technique has long been extended as a way out of such a trap (the Environmental Kuznets Curve stands on such a theoretical proposition) (Ahmad et al., 2021). On the one hand, the present chapter investigates the validity of such policy prescriptions and tries to find out the relation between digitalization and the environment. Considering the fact that Asia is not only the largest continent but also the largest cluster of developing and less developed nations, the concerned continent has been chosen for investigation. The analysis resorts to a short panel data analysis of select countries in Asia over a certain number of years.

A Bird's Eye View of the Current Chapter

Per capita emission of CO_2 measured in metric tons has been taken as the dependent variable, and per 100 people, availability of mobile phones along with fixed broadband connections have been taken as independent variables. It can be easily understood that where per capita CO_2 acts as a proxy for environmental quality, the per 100 people availability of mobile phones along with fixed broadband stands as a proxy for digitalization. In case a negative and statistically significant relationship is found between the quality of the environment as mentioned and the level of digitalization as portrayed, we may say that a higher level of digitalization leads to a better quality of the environment. The opposite relationship will refute the conventional attributes that are assigned to the dependent and independent variables as described above.

In brief, the concerned chapter is devoted to analyzing the relationship between environmental quality and digitalization in the background of Industry 4.0 for select countries on the Asian continent over a specific time period. The data under consideration is short panel in nature and will follow the established doctrine of short panel analysis while undertaking the econometric analysis. However, the data analysis and the empirical findings are not all that make the chapter stand alone. Existing theories of sustainable development, their loopholes, and a more holistic consideration of sustainable development inclusive of living and non-living environmental agents will also be considered (Banerjee & Gupta, 2022).

LITERATURE REVIEW

Industry 4.0 and Digitalization a Critical Consideration

As defined by Sirimanne, Industry 4.0 in a nutshell is: "Industry 4.0 refers to the "smart" and connected production systems that are designed to sense, predict, and interact with the physical world, so as to make decisions that support production in real-time. In manufacturing, it can increase productivity, energy efficiency, and sustainability. It increases productivity by reducing downtime and maintenance costs" (Sirimanne, 2022). It is obvious that, considering the dependence of Industry 4.0 on the Internet of Things, cloud computing and analytics, artificial intelligence, and machine learning, its close association with digitalization is not surprising (Raja, 2021).

Industry4.0 and Choice of Technique the Dilemma

No doubt, Industry 4.0 and the following digitalization will change many things, but considering the choice of technique, it will shake the very foundation of economic growth and development. The basic principle of choice of technique states that the labour abundant country will resort to labour intensive technology and the capital abundant country will consider capital intensive technology (Thirlwall, 1989). Putting this entire doctrine aside and suggesting the labour intensive countries shift to automation which is at the core of Industry 4.0 might not be a wise suggestion and welcome involuntary unemployment (Fomunyam, 2019). Even if it is assumed that the labourers would be augmented through training to be at par with the changes brought by Industry 4.0, it is no rocket science to understand that automation would require a lower number of employees than before. This aspect raises the very sensitive issue of whether Industry 4.0 is apt for labour-intensive countries as it will require less labour. It must be kept in mind that the continent under the purview of the present chapter, Asia is the largest conglomerate of developing and labour intensive countries. It is also worth mentioning that the developed nations have always kept the developing and less developed nations under pressure to resort to a capital-intensive technology that, in their version, is pro-environment (Dinda, 2004). As per their proposition, a capital intensive choice of technique would eventually lead to growth beyond a certain threshold and restore the environment to its previous status. Such a claim is farcical and lacks proper empirical backing. There are several criticisms of the EKC approach, but they are not necessary for the present chapter (Cole et al., 1997; Dasgupta et al., 2002).

Industry 4.0 and the Digital Debris

Industry 4.0 comes with another dilemma: what will happen to the existing machineries? Is it possible that they will adapt to the changes that will be paved by Industry 4.0, or will they have to be recycled to meet the requirements? Even recycling will reduce the environmental burden measured in terms of carbon footprints following such augmentation of the existing machines (Mourtzis et al., 2020). However, what happens if they cannot be recycled? Would not that add to the non-biodegradable waste?

Then there is also a question regarding digital debris. The improvement in Internet quality and speed from 2G to 5G has made many prior digital types of equipment, such as mobile phones and televisions, obsolete. The peer pressure along with the bandwagon effect made people change their existing digital equipment that was not compatible with 5G Internet speed. As an example, a new kind of router was needed to adjust for such changes, and all these obsolete digital apparatuses became non-biodegradable digital debris. It is obvious that the way from 5G to 6E will follow a similar waste trajectory. With limited lands and an increasing population, following Industry 4.0, accommodating this digital debris would be a massive problem (Wang & Wang, 2018). The world is already riddling under the pressure of nuclear and plastic waste, two anthropocentric atrocities towards Mother Nature, and with the adoption of Industry 4.0, such pressure will increase in a cumulative way. Apart from the televisions and mobiles, desktops, laptops, and tabs might have to go through significant modifications or have to be scrapped following Industry 4.0. Especially the routers that are apt for 5G Internet speed might have to be changed if there is an improvement from 5G to 6E. Such a statement is not baseless, as similar issues have been faced with the increase in speed of the internet from 2G to 3G, 3G to 4G, and finally 4G to 5G. The pro-environment propaganda in favour of Industry 4.0 fails to convince, at least in a theoretical way. A note should also be taken that here only one aspect of Industry 4.0 has been considered, and a multi-aspect consideration of the same would have highlighted several lacunas that are beyond the scope of this chapter.

The Emergence of Pro-Environment Economic Approach: A Critical Review

As mentioned earlier, following the industrial revolution in Great Britain, followed by the United States of America, the CO_2 content in the atmospheric air has increased by three times. Arguably, the environmental concern regarding economic growth and development came following the 1972 Stockholm Convention. It is easy to understand that more than 200 years of atrocities on the environment by anthropocentric activities just got noticed a little more than 50 years ago. Indeed, it is almost impossible to address 200 years of erosion of the environment through 50 years of environmental intervention unless there is any pathbreaking change in technology, which sounds impossible with more and more plastic and nuclear waste and energy intensive consumption. Practically, we are living in an anthropogenic era from the 1950s that has been marked by three characteristics that are alien to any previous time period, namely plastic and atomic garbage, along with the domestication of chicken (Banerjee & Gupta, 2022). The mentioned convention, realisation that the environment is heading towards a chocking point, and the continuous failures of different existing growth and development models that failed to take the environment into consideration paved the way for the Brundtland Commission, which was established in 1983 and dissolved with their famous report Our Common Future in 1987. The report introduced a new term within the realm of growth and development that was more holistic in nature and took the environment within its purview: sustainable development, which proposed benefiting the present without sacrificing the future (Brundtland, 1987).

However, the concerned report was not without its share of loopholes and over time got criticised from many angles, such as its ordinal nature and repetition of pigouvian externalities (it raised a direct question regarding the novelty of the report). However, if these criticisms are neutrally considered, certain facets become clear. First of all, the ordinal nature of the report—not setting any benchmarks for the quality of the environment is a strength rather than a weakness, as environmental quality is subject to population change, so it is dynamic rather than static. Secondly, Pigou definitely mentioned externalities, but not in an exact manner the report considered externalities in the context of the environment. But by no means is the report holistic or inclusive in nature as far as sustainable development or the pro-environment nature of the report are concerned. Even a quick look at the report reveals that it is too anthropogenic and dishonours the other elements of Mother Nature. It fails to comprehend sustainable development as perceived by the report, which rests on the sustainability of the food chain and food pyramid as well as the points covered in the report. It fails to capture the essence that sustainable development is not socio-economic but a bio-socio-economic paradigm where each component is necessary and needs to be handled carefully considering their fragile nature to achieve sustainable development. This aspect remained hidden until Banerjee and Gupta (2022) in their seminal paper briefly mentioned this particular shortcoming of the report. It is apparent now the past, present, and future of the pro-environment economic approach or sustainable development, but the question remains how. Before we delve into such possibilities, it is better to have a brief look at sustainable development as reflected through sustainable development goals and the bio-socio-economic purview that it may have encompassed.

Sustainable Development Goals a Brief Critical Consideration

The sustainable development goals are divided into 17 headings as follows:

1. No poverty
2. Zero hunger
3. Good Health and Well Being
4. Quality Education
5. Gender Equality
6. Clean water and sanitation
7. Affordable and clean energy
8. Decent Work and Economic Growth
9. Industry, Innovation and Infrastructure
10. Reduced inequalities
11. Sustainable cities and communities
12. Responsible consumption and production
13. Climate action
14. Life below water
15. Life on Land
16. Peace, Justice and Strong Institutions
17. Partnerships for the goals(United Nations, 2015)

It is obvious from the above goals that they are set with some socio-economic aspects where energy and environment have been reflected through affordable and clean energy, climate action, life below water, and life on land; however, environmental sustainability is more complex than what is depicted through these 17 goals. To foster a sustainable environment, the two most important aspects are biological and socio-economic. Unless and until the sustainability of the food pyramid and food chain can be ensured, sustainable development will remain the reverie of 'poor Susan'. It should be noted that we are living in an era of biodiversity slum. This has happened before as well, but that was a natural phenomenon. The present biodiversity slum is anthropocentric, and the mother species plant is at risk, which has never happened in previous biodiversity slums (Banerjee & Gupta, 2022).

Sustainable Development Goals and Industry 4.0 a Critical Evolution

Apparently, to naked eyes, there is no association between Industry 4.0 and sustainable development goals. However, if we consider decent work and economic growth, industry, innovation, and infrastructure, as well as responsible production and consumption, then we may say that Industry 4.0 is pro-sustainable development. But two questions loom large: is innovation always environmentally friendly? And what about the digital debris that is closely associated with innovation? A detailed analysis, which is often historical in nature, will help to understand this issue. Considering the hard disk of the computer over the past year, random access memory (RAM), the hard disk of a computer, and computer processors by Intel have undergone huge upgrades. The same can be said for computer monitors. Desktops turned into laptops and then into palmtops or tablets. The software changed in a way that only higher end digital apparatus would be able to perform. This carefully thought-out digital web is definitely successful in running a market with continuous positive variation, but it costs the environment dearly. Amidst this spree of innovation, innovators remained oblivious to what would happen to the obsolete digital apparatus as mentioned previously. The digital debris that is non-biodegradable and mostly non-recyclable does not reflect the three sustainable development goals as mentioned at the beginning of the chapter. Hence, it might be concluded that Industry 4.0 has nothing to do with Sustainable Development Goals and might even be detrimental to the environment. However, the existing literature weaves a wonderland following Industry 4.0 (Talla & McIlwaine, 2022).

Environment, Sustainable Development Goals, Digitalization, and Industry 4.0: An Interactive Consideration

The root of sustainable development goals is embedded in a pro-environment ambience that is considerate and sensitive to our future generation. However, the famous report of the Brundtland Commission, namely, Our Common Future, is absolutely anthropocentric and oblivious to the other living and non-living agents of nature. It absolutely ignores the importance of the food chain and food pyramid, which hold the key to the sustainability of the environment. In this regard, the anthropocentric nature of the concerned report is one of its major shortcomings. To be precise, it is not holistic and does little to guide the human genre toward a better environment (Banerjee & Gupta, 2022). The way we perceive digitalization is also superficial; by no means will digitalization lead to a better environment, as it comes with digital debris, as mentioned above. Apart from the fact that the chapter will empirically evaluate the impact of digitalization on the environment, it might reveal new facets between the environment and digitalization. Finally, the much celebrated Industry 4.0 goes absolutely against the labour intensive developing countries as it is weaved through automation, artificial intelligence, the Internet of Things, cloud computing, and others. This will definitely lead to a higher level of digitalization and follow the same trajectory that has been discussed between the environment and digitalization. Moreover, Industry 4.0 will produce an extremely high volume of non-biodegradable waste that will impact the environment in a pretty negative way. It is obvious considering the fact that the present machineries and tools have to be replaced at least partially to be at par with the changed industrial ambience that Industry 4.0 proposes. With this background, the chapter is now moving towards an empirical analysis to support the arguments that have been raised throughout the chapter.

METHODOLOGY

The current chapter has selected 39 countries from Asian countries over the time frame of 2015 to 2019. Only countries with available and continuous data have been chosen. Three variables have been considered: the per capita emission of carbon dioxide measured in metric tons has been considered the dependent variable (CO), and the percentage of mobile (ms) and broadband (bs) subscriptions have been considered the independent variables. All the mentioned statistics have been acquired from the World Development Indicators database.

Cameron & Trivedi (2013) has mentioned, "fixed and random effects models for short panels introduce an individual-specific effect"; In this background, opting for one-way panel data analyses with individual specific effects for the data under purview is apt. The regression equation might be written as $CO_{it} = a + b. ms_{it} + c. fb_{it} + U_{it}$ where i = 1, 2, 3...39 and t = 2015...2019. a implies the constant term, and b, along with c, are the coefficients U is the stochastic error term. As the data is short panel, at first, multicollinearity, autocorrelation, heteroskedasticity, and contemporaneous correlation of the data are tested.

Econometric Analysis

As depicted in Table 1, there is no multicollinearity. The Wooldridge test for first-order autocorrelation (Wooldridge, 2002) says there is autocorrelation. The Greene (2000) test shows the presence of heteroskedasticity in the fixed effects (within) regression models.

"The Pesaran test (2004) for cross-sectional dependence... (Cameron & Trivedi, 2005) maintain that ignoring heterogeneity and correlation across units and over time might lead to biased statistical inference. Moreover, Chudik et al. (2011) have said that if the number of cross-sectional units (N) is much larger than the time units (T), then cross-sectional dependence should always be taken into account" (Banerjee, 2017, p. 46). However, the Pesaran test (2004) statistics negate the existence of contemporaneous correlation in both the fixed and random effect models. On the other hand, Bera, Sosa-Escudero, and Yoon modified the Lagrange multiplier test for autocorrelation that works unbiased even under random effects (Sosa-Escudero & Bera, 2008) and the Baltagi and Li joint test for serial correlation and random effects have found autocorrelation in the random effects models. The problems of autocorrelation and/or heteroskedasticity in fixed and random effects regressions have been addressed through clustering around the panel variable, i.e., countries. According to Wooldridge, clustering successfully addresses autocorrelation and/or heteroskedasticity problems in short panels. Again, whether autocorrelation and/or heteroskedasticity are present in the data, clustering always reports an asymptotically valid inference (Wooldridge, 2003, 2006). Contrary to the usual belief (Wooldridge, 2006), clustering might also be

Table 1. Test results

	Independent Variable	
	ms_{it}, fb_{it}	
	Group Effect	
CO_{it} (Dependent variable)	Stat	Prob
Multicollinearity	1.04 < 2	NA
Wooldridge test for autocorrelation	18.615	0.0001
Modified Wald test for Heteroskedasticity	34465	0
Pesaran test for Contemporaneous correlation (FE)	-0.348	0.7275
Pesaran test for Contemporaneous correlation (RE)	-0.496	0.6197
Robust F test	1564.05	0
Bera, Sosa-Escudero and Yoon modified Adjusted Lagrange Multiplier Test for random effects (two tail)	155.77	0
Bera, Sosa-Escudero and Yoon modified Adjusted Lagrange Multiplier Test for random effects (one tail)	12.48	0
Bera, Sosa-Escudero and Yoon modified adjusted Lagrange Multiplier Test for serial correlation	13.55	0.0002
Baltagi-Li joint test for serial correlation and random effects	379.06	0
Sargan-Hansen test Statistics for fixed vs random effect	12.525	0.0019

Source: Computed

used with random effects estimators to address autocorrelation and/or heteroskedasticity problems and safeguard against the often false assumption of equi-correlated errors. No attempts have been made to test heteroskedasticity in the random effects model, as autocorrelation is already present for the random effects regression as per the necessary tests, and as mentioned, clustering around the panel variable countries would eventually address autocorrelation and/or heteroskedasticity problems if present. For the choice between pooled OLS regression models and fixed unit effect models, the presence of heteroskedasticity favours the robust F test for poolability over the Chow test of poolability (Baltagi, 2021), and the concerned test supports the presence of fixed unit effects for the regression equation. For the choice between a pooled OLS regression model and a unit random effects model; the presence of autocorrelation discards the use of the Breusch and Pagan Lagrange multiplier test and Honda's version of the same. However, Bera, Sosa-Escudero, and Yoon modified the Lagrange multiplier test for random effects (two and one tail) that is robust under autocorrelation (Sosa-Escudero & Bera, 2008) to reject the null hypothesis of no random effects for the regression equation. Since fixed and random effects estimators are better than the pooled OLS regression estimators as per the necessary tests, one of them has to be chosen for the regression equation. One shouldn't use the usual Hausman test to decide between random and fixed effects models when there is heteroskedasticity. However, a test between fixed and random effects models might also be seen as a test of over-identifying restrictions. The random effects model uses one more orthogonality condition than the fixed effects model in that the regressors are uncorrelated with the group-specific errors. This might also be considered an over-identifying restriction. The Sargan-Hansen test for over-identifying restrictions easily adjusts for heteroskedasticity (Baum, 2009). Schaffer & Stillman (2016) reject the idea that the over identifying restriction is valid for the regression and hence favours the fixed effects model.

DISCUSSION

It is apparent from the above econometric analysis that the state of digitalization measured in terms of digital penetration reflected through availability of mobile subscription measured in percentage of population is directly proportional to per capita CO_2 emissions, and the relation is statistically significant at the 99% level considering the probability associated with the z statistics. The passion surrounding the 4th Industrial Revolution, widely regarded as Industry 4.0, is founded on automation, cloud computing, the Internet of Things, digitalization, and artificial intelligence. These aspects together are perceived as environmentally friendly, reinforcing the sustainable development goals. However, considering the Asian Continent, the pro-environment digitalization as perceived by Industry 4.0 acts just the opposite. The reason is straightforward even if the brunt of digital debris is uncared for; taking into consideration

Table 2. Regression results

	Independent Variables		Value	z-statistics	probability	R^2	Adjusted R^2	F (2, 38)	Probability
Dependent Variable (CO_{it})		Intercept	0.88	8.8	0	0.18	0.17	9.89	0.0003
	ms_{it}	Coefficient (ms_{it})	0.01	2.46	0.019				
	fb_{it}	Coefficient (fb_{it})	0.04	1.35	0.187				

Source: Computed

the incursion of the digital market and its virtual appeal that attracts the consumers to consume more out of their greed than need will certainly promote more consumption and ignite consumerism. Beyond any doubt, this will result in a higher carbon footprint. Hence, it would not be unjust to mention that such an approach has little or nothing to do with sustainable development and is least pro-environment. This discovery is precisely contrary to the findings of Gaglione & Ayiine-Etigo (2021) and Li et al. (2022). The key dilemma possibly embedded in the naïve consideration of anthropogenic sustainable development as promoted by the Brundtland Commission report is that it ignored the food chain and food pyramid and failed to understand that the environment is like a web where all the species are related to each other. If sustainability is human-centric, ignoring other species, it can never be sustainable, as sustainability is a function, and for any species, the function comprises other species.

CONCLUSION

It is apparent from the above conversation following the econometric analysis that anthropocentric sustainable development has its short comings; it is not inclusive and fails to capture the essence that sustainability of the environment and sustainable development in its true form are only achievable if they follow the principle 'Live and Let Live'. Only this can ensure the peaceful coexistence of all the species. One needs to understand that without understanding the importance of ensuring the sustainability of the food chain and the food pyramid, a pro-environment approach and sustainable development goals will remain a mirage. Regarding the digitalization aspect, it is evident that it is far from pro-environment. The green nature of digitalization as usually perceived is absolutely wrong. The much-glorified Industry 4.0, which has digitalization as one of its core components and is regarded as adding to the sustainability of the environment, might have exactly the opposite impact. It is clearly proved in the econometric analysis section that an increased level of mobile penetration is associated with an increased level of per capita emissions of CO_2 measured in metric tons. These are the original findings of the present chapter and augment the present literature. So, the present chapter unfolds a dilemma: development and technological progress are dynamic, they cannot be stopped, and they are relentless. However, give emphasis to green technology, and follow proper empirical investigation and backup as might be of utmost need. Otherwise, as shown by select Asian countries in this chapter, so called green efforts will end up adding more burdens to Mother Nature, and the sole motive of the Brundtland Commission report of benefiting the present without sacrificing the future will remain a daydream.

REFERENCES

Ahmad, M., Muslija, A., & Satrovic, E. (2021). Does economic prosperity lead to environmental sustainability in developing economies? Environmental Kuznets curve theory. *Environmental Science and Pollution Research International*, *28*(18), 22588–22601. doi:10.100711356-020-12276-9 PMID:33420933

Baltagi, B. H. (2021). *Econometric Analysis of Panel Data*. Springer International Publishing. doi:10.1007/978-3-030-53953-5

Banerjee, S. (2017). Revisiting bank mergers: Does size matter? *Economic and Political Weekly, 52*(8), 41–48. https://scholar.google.com/scholar?hl=en&as_sdt=0,5&cluster=11755901839183430510#d= gs_cit&t=1669143363739&u=%2Fscholar%3Fq%3Dinfo%3AbsPj8m9aJaMJ%3Ascholar.google.com %2F%26output%3Dcite%26scirp%3D0%26scfhb%3D1%26hl%3Den

Banerjee, S., & Gupta, S. (2022). Impact of digital connectivity on ease of doing business. In M. N. Almunawar, M. Z. Islam, & P. O. de Pablos (Eds.), *Digital Transformation Management* (1st ed., pp. 73–88). Routledge. doi:10.4324/9781003224532-5

Banerjee, S., Gupta, S., & Koner, S. (2022). Sustainability and Consumerism: How Green Are the Green Sectors. In P. Ordóñez de Pablos, X. Zhang, & M. N. Almunwar (Eds.), *In Handbook of Research on Green, Circular, and Digital Economies as Tools for Recovery and Sustainability* (pp. 186–206). IGI Global. doi:10.4018/978-1-7998-9664-7.ch010

Baum, K. (2009). *st: Re: STATA heteroscedasticity test*. Statalist: The Stata Listserver. https://www.stata. com/statalist/archive/2009-03/msg00776.html

Brundtland. (1987). *Measuring Sustainable Development | Department of Economic and Social Affairs*. SDGS. https://sdgs.un.org/publications/measuring-sustainable-development-17620

Butlin, J. (1989). *Our common future. By World commission on environment and development*. Oxford University Press. https://www.academia.edu/download/47184423/jid.3380010208201607123227-xebmus.pdf

Cameron, A. C., & Trivedi, P. K. (2005). *Microeconometrics: Methods and Applications*. Cambridge University Press. https://books.google.co.in/books?hl=en&lr=&id=TdlKAgAAQBAJ&oi=fnd&pg=PP1&d q=Microeconometrics:Methods+and+Applications&ots=yKiqJZaAxv&sig=PIxeWYTEiiY8XqVmVk cMM-m0u3k&redir_esc=y#v=onepage&q=Microeconometrics%3AMethods and Applications&f=false

Cameron, A. C., & Trivedi, P. K. (2013). Counting panel data. In B. H. Baltagi (Ed.), *The Oxford handbook of panel data* (pp. 233–256). Oxford University Press.

Chen, Y., & McDonough, P. (2022). Conerference: The 1972 Stockholm Declaration at Fifty: Reflecting on a Half-century of International Environmental Law. *Georgia Journal of International and Comparative Law, 50*(3). https://heinonline.org/hol-cgi-bin/get_pdf.cgi?handle=hein.journals/gjicl50&section=22

Chudik, A., Pesaran, M. H., & Tosetti, E. (2011). Weak and strong cross-section dependence and estimation of large panels. *The Econometrics Journal, 14*(1), C45–C90. doi:10.1111/j.1368-423X.2010.00330.x

Cole, M. A., Rayner, A. J., & Bates, J. M. (1997). The environmental Kuznets curve: An empirical analysis. *Environment and Development Economics, 2*(4), 401–416. doi:10.1017/S1355770X97000211

Dasgupta, S., Laplante, B., Wang, H., & Wheeler, D. (2002). Confronting the Environmental Kuznets Curve. *The Journal of Economic Perspectives, 16*(1), 147–168. doi:10.1257/0895330027157

Dinda, S. (2004). Environmental Kuznets Curve Hypothesis: A Survey. *Ecological Economics, 49*(4), 431–455. doi:10.1016/j.ecolecon.2004.02.011

Fomunyam, K. (2019). Education and the Fourth Industrial Revolution: Challenges and possibilities for engineering education. *International Journal of Mechanical Engineering*, *10*(8), 271–284. https://www.academia.edu/download/60492936/IJMET_10_08_02220190905-84363-5660xl.pdf

Gaglione, F., & Ayiine-Etigo, D. A. (2021). Resilience as an urban strategy: The role of green interventions in recovery plans. *TeMA Journal of Land Use Mobility and Environment*, *14*(2), 279–284.

Greene, W. H. (2000). *Econometric Analysis*. 4th Prentice Hall. https://scholar.google.com/scholar?hl=en&as_sdt=0%2C5&q=Greene%2C+W+%282000%29%3A+Econometric+Analysis+%28Upper+Saddle+River%2C+NJ%3A+Prentice–Hall&btnG=

Javaid, M., Haleem, A., Singh, R. P., Suman, R., & Gonzalez, E. S. (2022). Understanding the adoption of Industry 4.0 technologies in improving environmental sustainability. *Sustainable Operations and Computers*, *3*, 203–217. doi:10.1016/j.susoc.2022.01.008

Li, J., Chen, L., Chen, Y., & He, J. (2022). Digital economy, technological innovation, and green economic efficiency—Empirical evidence from 277 cities in China. *MDE. Managerial and Decision Economics*, *43*(3), 616–629. doi:10.1002/mde.3406

Mourtzis, D., Angelopoulos, J., & Panopoulos, N. (2020). Recycling and retrofitting for industrial equipment based on augmented reality. *Procedia CIRP*, *90*, 606–610. doi:10.1016/j.procir.2020.02.134

Pigou, A. C. (1920). *The Economics of Welfare*. Macmillan and Company. https://archive.org/details/dli.bengal.10689.4260

Raja, G. B. (2021). Impact of Internet of Things, Artificial Intelligence, and Blockchain Technology in Industry 4.0. In R. Kumar, Y. Wang, T. Poongodi, & A. L. Imoize (Eds.), *Internet of Things, Artificial Intelligence and Blockchain Technology* (pp. 157–178). Springer. doi:10.1007/978-3-030-74150-1_8

Schaffer, M. E., & Stillman, S. (2016). XTOVERID: Stata module to calculate tests of overidentifying restrictions after xtreg, xtivreg, xtivreg2, xthtaylor. *Statistical Software Components*. https://ideas.repec.org/c/boc/bocode/s456779.html

Sirimanne, S. N. (2022, May 3). *What is "Industry 4.0" and what will it mean for developing countries? | UNCTAD*. United Nations Conference on Trade and Development (UNCATAD). https://unctad.org/news/blog-what-industry-40-and-what-will-it-mean-developing-countries

Sosa-Escudero, W., & Bera, A. K. (2008). Tests for Unbalanced Error-Components Models under Local Misspecification. *Sage Journals,* *8*(1), 68–78. doi:10.1177/1536867X0800800105

Talla, A., & McIlwaine, S. (2022). Industry 4.0 and the circular economy: using design-stage digital technology to reduce construction waste. *Smart and Sustainable Built Environment*. https://doi.org/doi:10.1108/SASBE-03-2022-0050/FULL/XML

Thirlwall, A. P. (1989). *Growth and Development: With Special Reference to Developing Economies* (Fourth Edition). Macmillan Education Ltd. https://books.google.co.in/books?hl=en&lr=&id=WKuvCwAAQBAJ&oi=fnd&pg=PR13&dq=thirlwall+choice+of+#v=onepage&q=thirlwall choice of&f=false

United Nations. (2015). *THE 17 GOALS | Sustainable Development*. United Nations - Department of Economic and Social Affairs. https://sdgs.un.org/goals

Wang, X. V., & Wang, L. (2018). Digital twin-based WEEE recycling, recovery and remanufacturing in the background of Industry 4.0. *International Journal of Production Research*, *57*(12), 3892–3902. doi:10.1080/00207543.2018.1497819

Wooldridge, J. M. (2002). *Econometric Analysis Of Cross Section And Panel Data*. MIT Press.

Wooldridge, J. M. (2003). Cluster-Sample Methods in Applied Econometrics. *The American Economic Review*, *93*(2), 133–138. doi:10.1257/000282803321946930

Wooldridge, J. M. (2006). Cluster-sample methods in applied econometrics: an extended analysis. In *Economics Department Working Paper Series, Department of Economics*. Michigan State University. https://www.academia.edu/download/31182655/Cluster_Sample_Methods_in_Applied_Econometrics.pdf

Chapter 12
Securing Digital Transformation in Healthcare Systems

Nazhatul Hafizah Kamarudin
🆔 https://orcid.org/0000-0002-6972-7967
Universiti Kebangsaan Malaysia, Malaysia

Mohammad Arif Ilyas
UCSI University, Malaysia

ABSTRACT

The Internet of Things (IoT) has experienced rapid growth, and as a result, the e-health system has established a robust infrastructure that enables the delivery of viable healthcare services over the network. Healthcare organizations recognize the importance of adopting the latest technologies to improve healthcare services and reduce operational costs. Integrating IoT into the healthcare system offers numerous benefits, including secure patient identification and efficient data collection. However, many existing e-health systems primarily focus on patient data acquisition and medical embedded components, paying little attention to crucial aspects like real-time monitoring and, most importantly, the security of the e-health system. This chapter strives to enable the smooth integration and sustained expansion of digital transformation within the e-health system by addressing the urgent need to strengthen security measures and improve accountability. Securing the extensive advancements in digital transformation within e-health is of utmost importance. To safeguard the security and accountability of digital transformation in the healthcare system, it is essential to develop multilevel authentication protocols alongside the implementation of deep learning techniques.

INTRODUCTION

With increasing numbers of people visiting the healthcare center, the need for remote healthcare monitoring system is highly needed to assist the situation. Therefore, advancements in electronics and biomedical applications have become growing attention recently since these areas contribute to e-health monitoring systems. Security challenges in e-health systems will lead to an e-health transformation and

DOI: 10.4018/978-1-6684-6782-4.ch012

with the development of IoT applications, e-health security systems need to be improved and upgraded. Acknowledging the current security problems with the digital transformation in the healthcare system and limited constraints faced by e-health system, this chapter will present a comprehensive security method solution in terms of the security authentication protocol and deep learning features in order to provide seamless and secure e-health while ensuring its practicality and efficiency. The proposed security method solution for e-health authentication is mainly to establish secure communication in the mobile e-health networking environment. Through this chapter, the authors aim to discuss the unique identity-based authentication and focus on the e-health authentication scheme. There has been significant research on the mobile e-health authentication system in order to enhance the efficacy and security of the e-health system. As demand for e-health applications has increased, a secure authentication protocol has become the main concern in e-health networking. Improvement in communication technology as well as sensor networking has assisted the development of e-health applications in order to provide effective healthcare services to people.

Considering the progressively advancing digitalization of healthcare systems and the mounting dependence on electronic health (e-health) applications, it is of utmost significance to prioritize the establishment of resilient security protocols. The reinforcement of the authentication process in e-health applications is fundamentally dependent on the pivotal function of image detection security. The authentication process for users operating within the healthcare industry is of paramount importance, primarily due to its ability to safeguard the confidentiality of patient information, facilitate secure entry to medical records, and restrict unlawful access to e-health systems. The range of visual indicators that can be utilized in the field of biometrics encompasses various physical attributes such as facial characteristics, retinal patterns, fingerprints, and other distinctive biometric markers. E-health authentication applications can achieve a robust and dependable approach for validating the identity of healthcare practitioners, patients, and authorized personnel endeavoring to obtain access to sensitive medical information by capitalizing on image detection methodologies.

The implementation of e-health in healthcare organizations offers various well-defined advantages, such as cost reduction, improvement in quality of care, efficient storage of data, and enhanced healthcare services. However, ensuring the security requirements of the e-health system remains a crucial factor. The process of implementing new technology in e-health is often intricate and time-consuming, yielding uncertain results. Throughout the years, extensive research has primarily focused on the implementation process of e-health, neglecting the analysis of outcomes and security requirements for the system. While e-health technology is mostly perceived as a means to enhance service efficiency and reduce errors, concerns regarding security and safety have diminished people's trust in e-health, thus impeding its utilization within healthcare organizations.

The advancements in mobile technology have revolutionized the use of mobile devices, such as smartphones and tablets, across various applications. The development of sensor networking connection and the Internet of Things (IoT), coupled with the widespread adoption of mobile phones, has made it increasingly viable to leverage mobile technology in medical applications. In recent times, individuals have witnessed the rapid growth of portable technology infrastructure and the emergence of diverse applications for mobile devices. These devices now serve a dual purpose, not only facilitating communication but also integrating with sensor networking, thereby simplifying and enhancing mobile e-health communication. The rapid progress in mobile technologies has paved the way for mobile e-health, also known as m-health, initiatives that have introduced personal health monitoring systems. These advancements have significantly improved the healthcare services provided by healthcare professionals.

With the continuous progress of the Internet of Things (IoT), advancements have been made in the development of mobile e-health network architecture, making it more feasible and reliable for data communication systems. The term "mobile e-health network architecture" encompasses the overall layout and design of a comprehensive framework for the mobile e-health network, encompassing hardware, software, connectivity, and communication protocols. The existing three-tier network architecture is no longer considered reliable, as it involves the involvement of a third-party server or an e-health service provider to analyze mobile e-health data before transmitting it to the e-health server. This setup poses significant security risks, as it becomes vulnerable to perilous security attacks that jeopardize the entire mobile e-health system. Insider attacks and man-in-the-middle attacks can compromise the reliability of the mobile e-health network under such circumstances.

The deployment of image recognition security protocols provides numerous benefits in the realm of electronic health authentication. Furthermore, the integration of image detection security leads to enhanced user convenience whereby the obligation to recall intricate login credentials or carry physical authentication tokens is eliminated. This is possible as users can verify their identities utilizing their distinctive visual characteristics. The current study endeavors to investigate the importance of image detection security in relation to e-health authentication applications. This study endeavors to explore the multifarious methodologies and technological advancements utilized in the domain of image detection. These include intricate approaches such as facial recognition and electroencephalogram (EEG).

Through comprehension of the advantages and impediments associated with image detection security in the context of e-health authentication applications, healthcare entities and interested parties can arrive at judicious determinations concerning the implementation and assimilation of such technologies. The primary objective is to establish an e-health environment that is both secure and trustworthy, thus preserving the confidentiality and privacy of patients while simultaneously guaranteeing seamless and efficient delivery of healthcare information and services.

BACKGROUND

Authentication refers to the process of verifying the authenticity or veracity of an individual, entity, or statement. Authentication technology is commonly employed in the domain of computer science to implement access control measures on secure systems by mandating users to furnish explicit credentials, such as passwords or access devices, for the purposes of verification. The significance of authentication systems in the realm of information security is derived from their efficacy in preserving the confidentiality of sensitive data by limiting accessibility solely to authorized users, through their implementation in various computer networks, databases, and services. Facial recognition technology, which can detect, identify, and authenticate human faces by mapping facial features against a pre-existing database, was originally conceptualized in 1960 by the celebrated mathematician and computer scientist, Wondrow Wilson Bledsoe. The aforementioned technology has been the subject of widespread utilization, particularly in the field of user authentication predicated on biometric characteristics.

Access control is a security measure that verifies the authorization of a user to access and utilize data resources within a networking system. It regulates the connections made to the system's data and server. In the context of mobile e-health systems, the access control structure holds immense importance due to the open nature of data transmission in mobile e-health. By implementing an access control structure, user identification can be carried out through proper authentication. The access control system primarily encompasses critical processes, namely authentication, authorization, and accountability. These fundamental security procedures are essential for ensuring a high level of security within the e-health access control structure. The primary objective of credential and trust management systems is to facilitate secure access control among users. However, the distributed nature of Wireless Sensor Networks (WSN), particularly in mobile e-health, makes the access control structure vulnerable to various security attacks, such as replay attacks and node cloning attacks.

The utilization of facial recognition technology has been implemented by an array of industries thus far. Law enforcement agencies employ facial recognition technology to improve security, assist in preventing criminal activity, generate suspect notifications, monitor offenders, and facilitate inquiries via digital imaging or video surveillance. Moreover, the banking industry utilizes facial recognition technology to enhance the accuracy of customer verification and enhance the security of internet banking facilities. Continual exploration and advancement endeavors, conducted by researchers on a global scale utilizing a variety of methodologies, have resulted in significant enhancements in the precision of facial recognition technology.

In the realm of cybersecurity, the authentication process can be rendered relatively straightforward when employing a solitary method of authentication to validate the identity of a user seeking entry to a network or website. The verification mechanism commonly known as single-factor authentication (SFA) involves users satisfying only one credential during the authentication process, as documented by Ometov et al. (2018) One of the prevalent instances of SFA pertains to the utilization of a combination of a username and password for logging into a password-secured network. In order to access the system, individuals are required to authenticate their identity through a distinctive digital profile tailored to their specific persona. The deployment of username and password as an authentication mechanism offers a comparatively simplistic approach in comparison to other methods such as biometric authentication, while still granting a satisfactory degree of protection at a cost that is economically feasible. The reliability of password-based authentication hinges on the ability of the system to compare the furnished credentials with the corresponding information stored in the database (Wiefling et al., 2020)

As technology continues to advance and cyber threats become increasingly sophisticated, password-based authentication is gradually losing its effectiveness and proving inadequate in verifying users' identity. This is particularly evident in situations where users are physically present in front of a screen and may potentially be malicious actors, as highlighted by Ometov et al. (2018) Individuals have a propensity to select uncomplicated passwords due to their inherent convenience. This particular behavior leads to a trade-off between the level of security and expediency. Although uncomplicated passwords may be convenient to memorize, they also present an unambiguous vulnerability for adversaries to surreptitiously manipulate or conjecture. In absence of an added authentication factor, the acquisition of a user's password alone is sufficient for malicious actors to gain access, which poses a significant security challenge (Wiefling et al., 2020)

Over time, the employment of single-factor authentication (SFA) has become less advocated for applications that necessitate elevated levels of cybersecurity. The implementation of multi-factor authentication (MFA) has gained significant traction and is widely endorsed by organizations as a mechanism to augment security management practices in the face of mounting apprehension surrounding cyber threats (Al-Assam et al., 2011; FFIEC, 2011). The implementation of MFA confers an added stratum of safeguarding measures that surpasses that of SFA. This is achieved through the mandatory utilization of multiple verification factors to authenticate the identity of a user.

An inclusion into a security system that frequently appears is the implementation of a biometric system that verifies an individual's identity via analyzing their distinctive biological traits. Facial recognition technology has garnered extensive usage as a biometric identification modality that enables authentication of a user's identity through the analysis of facial architecture and composition (Solanki & Pittalia, 2016). Facial recognition methodologies are commonly employed in the commercial sector as part of access control systems. Specifically, a camera captures and authenticates a user's facial features prior to authorizing network or computer access. Facial recognition systems have been implemented at high-security areas, such as airports, to authenticate the identities of passengers (Huang et al., 2011)

The susceptibility of facial recognition technology to presentation attacks poses a pressing concern. This vulnerability arises from the potential for offenders to simulate the identity of an authorized individual through the use of a photographic representation of their facial features in order to subvert the precision of aforementioned system. Modern technological advancements have become accessible to cyber intruders, who utilize said advancements to acquire facial photos of individuals that are frequently made public on social media platforms. "To develop a facial recognition system that is impervious to security breaches, it is imperative to incorporate anti-spoofing methodologies that can effectively mitigate any potential cyber intrusions (Zhang et al., 2020)"

FACIAL RECOGNITION

The inception of facial recognition technology can be traced to the 1960s, wherein a team of computer scientists devised a methodology for semi-automatically identifying pre-defined facial features to detect faces. While the initial phase of the project entails the manual marking of facial landmarks such as the eyes and mouth, it served as a crucial primary benchmark that establishes the feasibility of utilizing facial recognition in biometric systems (A. Ometov et al., 2018). Thus far, there has been significant progress in the field of facial recognition technology owing to the continuous growth of artificial intelligence and computer vision over the past three decades. In recent years, there has been significant scholarly endeavor dedicated to the development of facial recognition algorithms through diverse approaches across a global network of researchers.

Facial recognition technology has found broad application in commercial, industrial, education, and law enforcement domains, thanks, in part, to the ready availability of face image datasets, the utilization of artificial intelligence, and the rapid advancement of deep learning techniques (I. adjabi et al., 2020). The introduction of facial recognition technology in society is widely perceived to yield potentially beneficial effects in terms of security. However, it is also recognized that this implementation may give rise to negative outcomes, due to the concomitant increase in concerns regarding privacy infringement. In order to address the difficulties impeding the successful deployment of facial recognition technology, it is imperative that its future development prioritizes a non-invasive design that seamlessly integrates with natural human actions and tendencies (M. I. Zarkasyi et al., 2020). The automated facial recognition system is typically characterized by two major operations, namely face detection and face recognition. The diagram in Figure 1 provides a comprehensive representation of the customary procedure for facial recognition.

The preliminary stage involved in the process of facial recognition is face detection, which involves identifying and isolating the facial region within an image by means of localisation and extraction of the extent of the face from the surrounding background. The process frequently entails identification of

Figure 1. General process of a facial recognition system

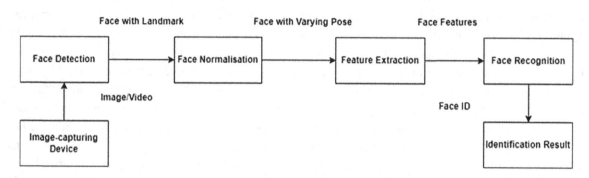

the facial region within the image, which is subsequently demarcated via a bounding box in a typical manner. Facial detection possesses the capability to perform facial landmark localization, encompassing the eyes, nose, and mouth. Subsequently, this feature may potentially improve the efficacy of facial recognition, at a later stage. Subsequent to this, the process of facial normalisation is executed in order to attain geometric and photometric normalisation of the facial features, intended to facilitate feature extraction by rendering the properties of the resulting image similar. The implementation of a suitable face normalisation technique can effectively mitigate detection error propagation and consequently lead to enhanced evaluation accuracy in subsequent recognition stages, as documented in prior research (W. Zhao et al., 2003).

An instance of normalisation techniques encompasses geometrical normalisation, which necessitates the detected facial area to exhibit qualities such as stable eye placement and frontal alignment. The optimal normalization of an image can be achieved through the utilization of scaling or rotation. In the succeeding phase, the facial attributes are derived from the standardised facial representation, encapsulating distinctive information related to an individual's identity. In the field of facial recognition, facial features serve as key identifiers, whereby pertinent information from a given input face is compared against existing data sets within a prepared database for the purpose of verification (R. Johnson et al., 2007). When the facial information corresponds to the enrolled face in the database, the face recognition system generates an output utilizing the prediction type employed during the stage. The output is typically a face identification element that triggers the system to exhibit the label of the input face's possessor, accompanied by a similarity metric.

Facial Recognition Algorithm

The facial recognition algorithm is an established set of directives that instruct a computing system to conduct computation on an input image and construct a mathematical model for the purpose of face detection and recognition. In conformity with established conventions, the fundamental aspect of the facial recognition algorithm pertains to the extraction of facial landmarks or distinctive attributes from the given image of the face. Facial recognition algorithms typically employ an analytical approach to the assessment of facial characteristics, which commonly includes an assessment of the relative spatial relationship and proportional dimensions associated with the ocular features, nose, and oral cavity. The resulting data is subsequently utilized for the purpose of image matching. The field of face recognition encompasses a broad spectrum of algorithms, which can be categorized into two fundamental approaches:

the feature-based method and the holistic models. The former employs techniques for segmenting facial features, such as landmarks and correlating their spatial locations to facial components. In contrast, the latter considers the entire face image as a single unit (Kortli et al., 2020) Each method within its respective category exhibits distinct characteristics and benefits which are uniquely tailored towards specific applications. Moreover, numerous renowned recognition algorithms have integrated machine learning models into their data processing procedures, in addition to conventional image processing techniques. This integration, in turn, enables the accurate generation of predictions, meticulous statistical analysis, and pattern matching (Batta, 2020). The swift progression of device capabilities in recent years, particularly the notable increases in computing power, has led to a widespread adoption of machine learning techniques (Sze et al., 2018) The subsequent discourse features several instances of esteemed facial recognition algorithms.

Haar Cascades Classifier

The Haar Cascades is a machine learning-driven object detection algorithm initially introduced by Paul Viola and Michal Jones in 1960. The Viola-Jones technique for detecting human faces employs Haar features which are derived from the analysis of adjacent rectangular regions that are positioned within a given detection window. These features are calculated through a series of computations that are executed on the sampled regions. In order to comprehend the Haar feature, it is necessary to consider it as the outcome of a scalar product between images and Haar templates utilized in the computation process. The Haar templates are generally comprised of 2 to 4 rectangular partitions. This procedure necessitates the computation of the aggregate pixel intensities within designated regions, followed by the determination of the divergence between said aggregates. Figure 2 exhibits a range of Haar features, encompassing two-rectangular, three-rectangular, and four-rectangular features. These features are characterized by horizontal or vertical adjacency.

The process of evaluating pixel intensities in an image involves the continuous traversal of the entire image by the Haar features. In order to minimize the computational time required for pixel summation in image processing applications, the integral image concept has been introduced. This approach involves the conversion of the original image into an integral image, where each pixel comprises the summation of all the pixels located to the left and above it in the original image. The AdaBoost method employs a boosting algorithm to amalgamate numerous weak classifiers with the aim of producing a powerful classifier that demonstrates resilience in classification. The cascade classifier proceeds to administer features on the image through a successive series of stages. The classifier determines the adequacy of a given window in terms of its facial features to be classified as either a face or not a face. At the speci-

Figure 2. Examples of Haar features

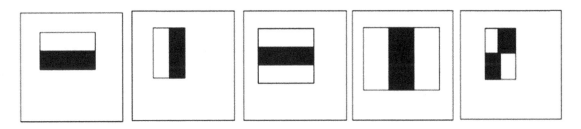

fied stage, the classifier will abruptly eliminate any non-facial entities detected within the sub-window. Once the classifier recognizes a potentially identifiable face, it shall proceed to the subsequent phase within the cascade. The utilization of this particular technique has the potential to diminish the workload and minimize the occurrence of false negative outcomes generated by the algorithm. This, in turn, may result in an improvement in computational efficiency, albeit with a slight compromise in detection accuracy (Chaudhari et al., 2015) The Haar Cascade technique has been found to possess vulnerability under certain circumstances, particularly when an image is characterized by a noisy background featuring changes in brightness or color information (Ahad et al., 2018)

Principle Component Analysis

Principal Component Analysis (PCA), also referred to as eigenface, is a widely recognized holistic-based facial recognition (FR) algorithm that was originally introduced as a statistical methodology in 1990 by Kirby and Sirovich. Its approach involves converting a 2D facial image into a simplified 1D pixel vector representation, which is intended to effectively decrease data dimensionality and enable the creation of a more refined machine learning model. The principal component analysis (PCA) methodology involves implementing an orthogonal transformation to facilitate the process of feature selection, thereby aiding in the identification of distinct patterns and distributions inherent in facial images. According to empirical investigations, the employment of principal component analysis (PCA) methodology has shown to enhance the efficacy of facial recognition systems when identifying facial images that display a range of variations including differences in head orientation (Paul & Sumam, 2012; Sunita, 2014), provided that the criteria for obtaining suitable facial images are met. The present study highlights the sensitivity of the Principal Component Analysis (PCA) technique to expression variation, which poses a critical concern in its application for Facial Authentication (FA). This observation has been supported by earlier research conducted by Jollife and Cadima (2016) and Liu et al. (2003), claiming that FA may require the detection of facial changes for the purpose of user access authentication. The principal component analysis (PCA) method is commonly recognized as a comprehensive approach that entails the use of sophisticated mathematical tools for data dimension reduction and visualization.

Histogram Of Oriented Gradients (HOG)

HOG is one type of feature descriptors used commonly for computer vision tasks, such as object detection, because of its simple and powerful computation algorithm (Dadi & Mohan Pillutla, 2016; Zhu et al., 2006). One distinct capability of HOG feature descriptor is that it provides useful information about features which is generally not given from other feature descriptors. In 2005, Dalal & Triggs, (2005) introduces an effective object detection algorithm that can extract feature vectors of an image by accumulating localized histogram of gradients within a single detection window that scans across the image. The oriented or the direction of gradients of an image can be obtained by filtering the image with kernel and finding out the magnitude and direction using the formula:

$$Magnitude, g = \sqrt{\left(g_x^2 + g_y^2 \right)} \tag{1}$$

$$Direction, \theta = arctan \frac{g_y}{g_x} \qquad (2)$$

At each individual pixel located within an image, the determination of gradient magnitude and direction is derived through the utilization of Equation 1 and Equation 2, respectively. The gradient vectors can be utilized to determine the gradient histogram of each cell within an n x n grid that has been subdivided into block units by the feature descriptor, in order to facilitate the calculation of the Histograms of Oriented Gradients (HOG) for computational purposes. During the computation of Histograms of Oriented Gradients (HOG), it is typical to normalize the image vectors as a means of mitigating the impact of lighting variations on the image data. The final HOG feature vectors of the image are obtained by concatenating the histograms of each block that have been concatenated into a one-dimensional vector, along with the histograms of the remaining blocks. Histogram of Oriented Gradients (HOG)-based features have gained extensive usage and incorporation in numerous object detection applications, ranging from attendance systems to pedestrian monitoring and notably, face recognition systems. This can be primarily attributed to their exceptional detection accuracy and accelerated computing speed, as affirmed by investigations conducted by Rahim and Mohamad (2018), VKulkarni (2020) and Walk et al. (2010)

Convolutional Neural Network (CNN)

One of the notable milestones in the development of facial recognition technology is its early adoption of machine learning techniques to enable the processing of voluminous data involved in its training process. As a member of a subset within the field of machine learning, deep learning has set itself apart from other techniques by endeavoring to replicate the cognitive processes of the human brain. This is achieved through the training of extensive quantities of data that have been duly labeled (Bhatt et al., 2021) Rather than relying on the conventional technique of facial recognition, such as Eigenfaces, that measures statistics of variance among facial images, the deep learning approach utilizes a deep neural network. This network comprises several interconnected layers of nodes, with each node being connected to the preceding layer's node. The deep neural network is designed to execute optimized prediction and classification tasks on various forms of data, including images, textual information, and audio signals (Saez Trigueros et al., 2018)

The Convolution Neural Network (CNN) stands out as one of the most widely recognized algorithms used in deep learning. The original convolutional neural network (CNN) model has its origins dating back to 1989, wherein it was introduced as a basic neural network capable of identifying small hand-written digits. This model, widely recognized as LeNet, was the first to incorporate the backpropagation algorithm to facilitate object recognition tasks (LeCun et al., 1989) The convolutional neural network (CNN) is a formidable tool in the realm of object detection and computer vision owing to its ability to autonomously discern features and patterns within an image. Unlike traditional methods that necessitate manual feature extraction, the CNN can directly identify objects and detect their attributes. The utilization of a highly efficient network architecture enables the attainment of exceptional recognition accuracy, making it particularly suitable for the processing of image data. This assertion is corroborated by the findings of Bharati and Pramanik (2020) as well as Gu et al. (2018b) The depiction of a convolutional neural network (CNN) operation is demonstrated in Figure 2. 3 There exist three primary categories of layers within the CNN network, including the convolutional layer, pooling layer, and the fully-connected layer. In order to derive features from an input image, the convolutional layer convolves the image data through a series of filters, thereby identifying and activating image features. Each convolutional filter that traverses the image is assigned a unique weight value. In accordance with the research conducted by Albelwi and Mahmood (2017), if a filter yields a result that surpasses the designated threshold value, activation of the node containing the corresponding image data will occur. Subsequently, the activated node will be transmitted to the succeeding layer of the network. During the pooling stage, the data contained within images will undergo a process of simplification. This process is executed in order to reduce the number of parameters in the image data, ultimately enhancing computational efficiency and reducing network complexity (Gu et al., 2018a)

Once the feature extraction process has been completed via the convolutional and pooling layers, the CNN network transitions to the classification stage. In the fully connected (FC) layer, every individual node within the layer possesses a direct connection with each of the corresponding nodes located in the preceding layer. This stratum executes the categorization process founded on the distinctive characteristics that have been previously derived via the filters. The fully connected (FC) layer generates the classification outcome as a vector of probabilities for each image class that has been classified, which the convolutional neural network (CNN) can utilize for predictive purposes. In the ultimate layer of the computational model, the output vector transmitted from the fully connected layer will undergo a normalization process by means of the softmax function, giving rise to a probability distribution that encapsulates the likelihoods of each discerned image class. This ultimately results in the classification output, as posited by Alzubaidi et al. (2021)

CHALLENGES IN E-HEALTH SECURITY SYSTEM

The implementation of a three-tier network topology in the mobile e-health system introduces vulnerabilities to security attacks, thereby reducing its overall reliability in network communication. The network architecture is primarily designed to enhance the efficiency of the mobile e-health system by incorporating essential elements throughout the entire system. An insider attack occurs when someone with legitimate system access perpetrates an attack on the mobile e-health network. Insiders may possess authorized ac-

Figure 3. CNN network architecture

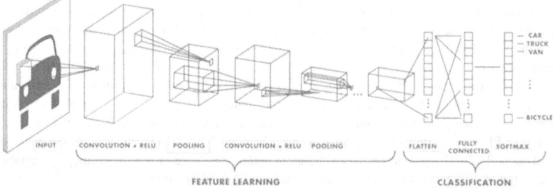

cess to the system and can have specific objectives within the network architecture. Examples of insiders can include third-party servers, e-health service providers, or cloud service providers. According to the NIST Computer Security Resource Center, detecting insider attacks is exceptionally challenging, and protecting the system against such attacks proves to be difficult. Security issues related to third-party servers, cloud services, and e-health service providers, such as insider attacks and spoofing attacks, have been extensively discussed (Khorshed et al, 2012). To address these concerns, the implementation of a trusted authentication scheme is proposed as a security solution within the system. Various issues arise from the implementation of third-party services in cloud service providers, leading to an unknown risk profile and a lack of transparency.

Mobile e-health is increasingly recognized as a valuable approach to improving healthcare system management, primarily driven by the advancements in IoT technology. The structured and efficient nature of IoT technology allows for the transformation of the mobile e-health sector, leveraging its ubiquitous computing capabilities. Recent developments in IoT have facilitated the development of mobile e-health systems with enhanced efficiency and intelligence, aiming to improve their overall capabilities. However, many existing mobile e-health authentication schemes suffer from vulnerabilities, inefficiencies, and a lack of user-friendliness, particularly for elderly users. To address this, low-computation algorithms should be implemented to accommodate the limited computational power of mobile devices.

Given that mobile e-health communication occurs over open access networks, a robust access control structure is crucial to ensuring secure transmission channels. Access control involves employing security techniques that selectively restrict access to mobile e-health data, aligning with the system's requirements. Security and privacy are major obstacles that must be addressed when developing mobile e-health applications, especially considering the insecure transmission of data over open access channels like the Internet. Secure authentication plays a pivotal role in the access control structure, ensuring that only authorized users can communicate with the e-health server and decrypt transmitted data. Access authorization for data resources in mobile e-health applications relies on efficient user access control mechanisms, allowing only authorized users with specific access privileges to access the mobile e-health data system.

While implementing SSL protocol authentication in the mobile e-health network was once reliable, it now poses limitations. SSL establishes encryption between a server and a user, but the communication process becomes slower due to the additional handshakes, encryption, and decryption involved. This increases network traffic and reduces response runtime in the e-health server. Similarly, password-based authentication has become unreliable, as many improved schemes have proven vulnerable to security attacks like parallel session attacks.

Complex and intricate security algorithms are not suitable for implementation in mobile e-health systems due to the constraints of e-health devices. The main objective of developing an authentication framework for mobile e-health is to provide a secure and reliable method for validating e-health sensor nodes to join the network. Additionally, the framework aims to eliminate barriers and enable seamless and efficient communication in mobile e-health by removing the need for an e-health service provider. Cryptographic protocol enhancements are incorporated to mitigate security attacks within the mobile e-health network. While achieving absolute security in e-health systems is challenging, healthcare organizations must adhere to security policies and design measures that make it difficult for intruders to gain access to the network and prolong the time required to breach system security.

Designing a framework that incorporates passwordless authentication using unique identity-based encryption for mobile e-health poses significant challenges. It requires a deep understanding of e-health network architecture concepts and a detailed exploration of unique user identities. Ensuring secure communication between e-health sensor nodes and mobile devices with the e-health server remains a significant challenge in establishing a secure and feasible infrastructure for mobile e-health applications. Passwordless authentication for mobile e-health monitoring systems can replace existing technologies, offering benefits such as low power consumption and ease-of-use, reducing discomfort for elderly users. Healthcare providers can also reduce expenses by eliminating the need for a third-party server, which can introduce unforeseen vulnerabilities. Consequently, mobile e-health applications enhance health communication, making it easier and more practical.

In the context of mobile e-health applications, security attacks on e-health sensor nodes pose emerging security issues in network systems. The deployment of unattended e-health sensor nodes exposes the network to potential vulnerabilities. Therefore, it is imperative to implement additional security features on the e-health sensor network platform to meet the security requirements before its integration into the mobile e-health system.

FUTURE RESEARCH DIRECTIONS

One of the major challenges in creating a secure and viable infrastructure for mobile e-health applications is ensuring secure communication between the e-health sensor node, mobile device, and the e-health server. This thesis introduces innovative methods to secure the e-health sensor network within a two-tier mobile e-health architecture. However, there are still fascinating research problems in this field that require further investigation and have not yet been fully addressed.

The findings presented in the development of the proposed unique identity for the e-health sensor node can be considered groundbreaking in establishing a distinct identity for each sensor node. Future work should focus on conducting a comprehensive analysis of the feasibility and seamless integration of this approach into the mobile e-health system. Additionally, the authentication protocol was developed within a controlled laboratory environment, involving e-health sensor nodes, a mobile device, and a server acting as the e-health server. Further research can be conducted in real medical applications to refine the assumptions made during the protocol design.

For further improvement of the facial recognition system, it is recommended to implement image processing classifier to filter out the reflection color produced by the spectacles. The proposed facial authentication system can be integrated or cascaded with other machine learning algorithm such as Haar cascade, multilater perceptron, or PCA for better system robustness and recognition accuracy. For CNN models, since the recognition accuracy is critical in the application of security system to prevent cyber-threat, it is suggested to provide the CNN model with a greater number of training set with an additional variation of surrounding brightness. As a real-time user login system may not wait for illuminance change happens in user's location. It is recommended to be achieved by using data augmentation technique to modify and transform the captured face image to the required condition.

CONCLUSION

The proposed system exhibits potential as a robust preventative measure against spoofing attacks, thereby potentially enhancing the overall resilience of contemporary facial recognition technologies. The enhanced prosperity of society can be achieved through the heightened level of safety and security facilitated by the deployment of facial recognition technology. Incorporation of an authentication factor and unique feature detection into a facial recognition system can significantly enhance its security capacity and mitigate potential risks associated with cyberthreats. Moreover, the elimination of superfluous human interaction between the system and the user could yield noteworthy modifications to individuals' lifestyle. This may include the preservation of valuable time through the provision of a prompt and unobtrusive authentication procedure. As previously deliberated, the proposed facial authentication system possesses the potential to provide numerous valuable advantages to the larger community especially in e-health authentication application.

REFERENCES

Adjabi, I., Ouahabi, A., Benzaoui, A., & Taleb-Ahmed, A. (2020). Past, present, and future of face recognition: A review. In Electronics (Switzerland), 9(8). doi:10.3390/electronics9081188

Ahad, Md. A. R., Paul, T., Shammi, U., & Kobashi, S. (2018). A Study on Face Detection Using Viola-Jones Algorithm for Various Backgrounds, Angels and Distances. *Applied Soft Computing*.

Al-Assam, H., Sellahewa, H., & Jassim, S. (2011). Accuracy and Security Evaluation of Multi-Factor Biometric Authentication. *International Journal for Information Security Research*, 1(1), 11–19. doi:10.20533/ijisr.2042.4639.2011.0002

Albelwi, S., & Mahmood, A. (2017). A framework for designing the architectures of deep Convolutional Neural Networks. *Entropy (Basel, Switzerland)*, 19(6), 242. doi:10.3390/e19060242

Alzubaidi, L., Zhang, J., Humaidi, A. J., Al-Dujaili, A., Duan, Y., Al-Shamma, O., Santamaría, J., Fadhel, M. A., Al-Amidie, M., & Farhan, L. (2021). Review of deep learning: Concepts, CNN architectures, challenges, applications, future directions. *Journal of Big Data*, 8(1), 53. doi:10.118640537-021-00444-8 PMID:33816053

Batta, M. (2020). Machine Learning Algorithms - A Review. *International Journal of Science and Research*, 9(1), 381.

Bharati, P., & Pramanik, A. (2020). Deep Learning Techniques—R-CNN to Mask R-CNN: A Survey. *Advances in Intelligent Systems and Computing*, 999, 657–668. doi:10.1007/978-981-13-9042-5_56

Bhatt, D., Patel, C., Talsania, H., Patel, J., Vaghela, R., Pandya, S., Modi, K., & Ghayvat, H. (2021). Cnn variants for computer vision: History, architecture, application, challenges and future scope. In Electronics (Switzerland), 10(20). doi:10.3390/electronics10202470

Bledsoe, W. W. (1964). The Model Method In Facial Recognition. *Panoramic Research Inc., Palo Alto, CA, Rep. PR1, 15*(47).

Chaudhari, M., sondur, S., & Vanjare, G. (2015). A review on Face Detection and study of Viola Jones method. *International Journal of Computer Trends and Technology*, 25(1), 54–61. doi:10.14445/22312803/IJCTT-V25P110

Dadi, H. S., & Mohan Pillutla, G. K. (2016). Improved Face Recognition Rate Using HOG Features and SVM Classifier. *IOSR Journal of Electronics and Communication Engineering, 11*(04), 34–44. doi:10.9790/2834-1104013444

Dalal, N., & Triggs, B. (2005). Histograms of oriented gradients for human detection. *Proceedings - 2005 IEEE Computer Society Conference on Computer Vision and Pattern Recognition, CVPR 2005, I.* IEEE. 10.1109/CVPR.2005.177

FFIEC. (2011). Authentication in an Internet Banking Environment. *Federal Financial Institutions Examination Council, 1,* 1–14.

Gu, J., Wang, Z., Kuen, J., Ma, L., Shahroudy, A., Shuai, B., Liu, T., Wang, X., Wang, G., Cai, J., & Chen, T. (2018a). Recent advances in convolutional neural networks. *Pattern Recognition, 77,* 354–377. doi:10.1016/j.patcog.2017.10.013

Gu, J., Wang, Z., Kuen, J., Ma, L., Shahroudy, A., Shuai, B., Liu, T., Wang, X., Wang, G., Cai, J., & Chen, T. (2018b). Recent advances in convolutional neural networks. *Pattern Recognition, 77,* 354–377. doi:10.1016/j.patcog.2017.10.013

Huang, T., Xiong, Z., & Zhang, Z. (2011). Face Recognition Applications. In Handbook of Face Recognition (pp. 617–638). Springer London. doi:10.1007/978-0-85729-932-1_24

Johnson, R., & Bonsor, K. (2007). How facial recognition systems work. *How Stuff Works,* 1–6. https://electronics.howstuffworks.com/gadgets/high-tech-gadgets/facial-recognition.htm

Jollife, I. T., & Cadima, J. (2016). Principal component analysis: A review and recent developments. In Philosophical Transactions of the Royal Society A: Mathematical, Physical and Engineering Sciences, 374(2065). doi:10.1098/rsta.2015.0202

Khorshed, M. T., Ali, A. B. M. S., & Wasimi, S. A. (2012). A survey on gaps, threat remediation challenges and some thoughts for proactive attack detection in cloud computing. *Future Generation Computer Systems, 28*(6), 833–851. doi:10.1016/j.future.2012.01.006

Kirby, M., & Sirovich, L. (1990). Application of the Karhunen-Loéve Procedure for the Characterization of Human Faces. *IEEE Transactions on Pattern Analysis and Machine Intelligence, 12*(1), 103–108. doi:10.1109/34.41390

Kortli, Y., Jridi, M., al Falou, A., & Atri, M. (2020). Face recognition systems: A survey. In Sensors (Switzerland), 20(2). doi:10.339020020342

LeCun, Y., Boser, B., Denker, J. S., Henderson, D., Howard, R. E., Hubbard, W., & Jackel, L. D. (1989). Backpropagation Applied to Handwritten Zip Code Recognition. *Neural Computation, 1*(4), 541–551. doi:10.1162/neco.1989.1.4.541

Liu, X., Chen, T., & Kumar, B. V. K. V. (2003). Face authentication for multiple subjects using eigenflow. *Pattern Recognition, 36*(2), 313–328. doi:10.1016/S0031-3203(02)00033-X

Ometov, A., Bezzateev, S., Mäkitalo, N., Andreev, S., Mikkonen, T., & Koucheryavy, Y. (2018). Multi-factor authentication: A survey. *Cryptography, 2*(1), 1. doi:10.3390/cryptography2010001

Paul, L. C., & al Sumam, A. (2012). Face recognition using principal component analysis method. In Journal of Advanced Research in Computer.

Rahim, A. S., & Mohamad, M. (2018). Biometric Authentication using Face Recognition Algorithms for A Class Attendance System. In Jurnal Mekanikal, 41.

Saez Trigueros, D., Meng, L., & Hartnett, M. (2018). *Face Recognition: From Traditional to Deep Learning Methods*. Research Gate.

Solanki, K., & Pittalia, P. (2016). Review of Face Recognition Techniques. *International Journal of Computer Applications*, *133*(12), 20–24. doi:10.5120/ijca2016907994

Sunita, N. (2014). Face Recognition Using Principal Component Analysis. *International Journal of Computer Science and Information Technologies*, *5*, 6491–6496.

Sze, V., Chen, Y. H., Emer, J., Suleiman, A., & Zhang, Z. (2018). Hardware for machine learning: Challenges and opportunities. *2018 IEEE Custom Integrated Circuits Conference, CICC 2018*. IEEE. 10.1109/CICC.2018.8357072

VKulkarni, S.VKulkarni. (2020). Attendance Marking System using Facial Recognition. *International Journal of Advanced Trends in Computer Science and Engineering*, *9*(3), 3588–3594. doi:10.30534/ijatcse/2020/166932020

Walk, S., Majer, N., Schindler, K., & Schiele, B. (2010). New features and insights for pedestrian detection. *Proceedings of the IEEE Computer Society Conference on Computer Vision and Pattern Recognition*, 1030–1037. 10.1109/CVPR.2010.5540102

Wang, D., Yu, H., Wang, D., & Li, G. (2020). Face recognition system based on CNN. *Proceedings - 2020 International Conference on Computer Information and Big Data Applications, CIBDA 2020*. IEEE. 10.1109/CIBDA50819.2020.00111

Wiefling, S., Dürmuth, M., & lo Iacono, L. (2020). More Than Just Good Passwords? A Study on Usability and Security Perceptions of Risk-based Authentication. *ACM International Conference Proceeding Series*, (pp. 203–218). ACM. 10.1145/3427228.3427243

Zarkasyi, M. I., Hidayatullah, M. R., & Zamzami, E. M. (2020). Literature Review: Implementation of Facial Recognition in Society. *Journal of Physics: Conference Series*, *1566*(1), 012069. doi:10.1088/1742-6596/1566/1/012069

Zhang, M., Zeng, K., & Wang, J. (2020). A Survey on Face Anti-Spoofing Algorithms. *Journal of Information Hiding and Privacy Protection*, *2*(1), 21–34. doi:10.32604/jihpp.2020.010467

Zhao, W., Chellappa, R., Phillips, P. J., & Rosenfeld, A. (2003). Face Recognition: A Literature Survey. *ACM Computing Surveys*, *35*(4), 399–458. doi:10.1145/954339.954342

Zhu, Q., Avidan, S., Yeh, M. C., & Cheng, K. T. (2006). Fast human detection using a cascade of histograms of oriented gradients. *Proceedings of the IEEE Computer Society Conference on Computer Vision and Pattern Recognition*, 2. IEEE. 10.1109/CVPR.2006.119

Chapter 13
Online Learning Satisfaction:
A Comparative Study on Malaysian and Indonesian Students

Soliha Binti Sanusi
Universiti Kebangsaan Malaysia, Malaysia

Istyakara Muslichah
Universitas Islam Indonesia, Indonesia

Nik Herda Nik Abdullah
Taylor's University, Malaysia

Nabilah Rozzani
Teach for Malaysia, Malaysia

ABSTRACT

Far from being optional, teaching and learning for education providers at various levels have made online learning the primary medium of delivery, due to Covid 19. As such, this study investigates how students' preparedness, motivation, internet availability, technical support, and psychological support influence students' online learning satisfaction in Malaysian and Indonesian higher learning institutions. An online survey was administered across Malaysia and Indonesia, with three hundred thirty-six (336) responses from Malaysia and two hundred ninety-two (292) from Indonesia. Structural equation model with smart PLS 3.2.4 was used for data analysis, with five hypotheses being tested. The present study found that motivation, psychological support, and technical support significantly affected student satisfaction in Malaysia, whereas an additional factor, students' preparedness, affected Indonesian students. Future research may investigate other aspects that may have contributed to students' satisfaction and which medium is the best for students to satisfy their learning curve.

INTRODUCTION

To fulfil the need for education, the rapid transfer of knowledge within society has been necessitated by the immense technological development of the present day. This is a result of the rise of online learning

DOI: 10.4018/978-1-6684-6782-4.ch013

as an adjunct teaching and learning tool for educators around the world. As teaching and learning are increasingly distributed over many internet-based platforms, online platforms have become a significant impetus for people to become more adaptable to the rapid shift in global education (Koksal, 2020). With global investments in education technology exceeding $18.66 billion in 2019, the adoption of education technology has increased dramatically. The niche market for language apps, virtual tutoring, video conferencing tools, and online learning software is anticipated to produce US$350 billion by 2025 (Li & Lalani, 2020).

As the Covid-19 pandemic forced schools worldwide to close for physical interactions, the rapid advancement of online learning became even more significant (Zhao et al., 2022). As a result, over 1.2 billion students in 186 countries were forced to leave their regular classrooms (Li & Lalani, 2020). Since then, all education providers have been compelled to integrate online learning as an alternative to blackboard-style learning. Online learning has evolved from a complementary medium to the primary mode of delivery for teaching and learning for education providers at all levels, including universities. Tertiary education educators and students were compelled to participate in synchronous and asynchronous activities on online platforms.

Committed to preserving its high quality for students while simultaneously learning from the challenges of adapting to new methods of teaching and learning, the current study aims to investigate the higher education students' preparedness, motivation, internet availability, technical support, and psychological support that influence their satisfaction with online learning in Malaysia and Indonesia. The subsequent section is a discussion of the literature review, followed by the research methodology, findings and discussion and conclusion of the study.

LITERATURE REVIEW

Student Satisfaction

Student satisfaction is the most significant aspect of encouraging students to continue learning. Astin(1993) defined student satisfaction as a student's perception of their educational experiences at a higher education institution. According to Muilenburg and Berge (2005), students' perceptions of their online learning experiences continue to vary substantially. Therefore, students' satisfaction with their educational experiences can influence their commitment to the course and their levels of happiness with their online learning experiences (Carr, 2000). Student satisfaction is one of the most important factors to consider when determining the success of implementing online learning (Harsasi & Sutawijaya, 2018).

According to Elliott and Healy (2001), student satisfaction is a short-term attitude because evaluation is based entirely on students' educational experiences at the time of evaluation. Consequently, this element influences student retention and is a consequence of the educational system (Navarro et al., 2005). Student satisfaction is defined by Elliott and Shin (2002) as students' subjective judgements of their academic performance and experiences. Consequently, student satisfaction can be described in terms of relative interaction and actual performance regarding educational services supplied during the study (Mukhtar et al., 2015). Multiple criteria are considered when defining student satisfaction as a short-term behaviour based on evaluating the students' personal experience, assistance, and educational facilities (Li et al., 2016).

Satisfaction among online students can be attributed to several different things. In particular, the teacher or educator, the technological tools, and the interaction were identified by Bolliger and Wasilik (2009) as the three most important factors contributing to student satisfaction with online learning. This involved discussions of course and lesson components, management system issues, and website feedback. Essential concepts like students' perspectives on assessment tasks and self-belief, social skills, system quality, and interactive media instruction have been identified by Liaw (2008). On the other hand, students faced challenges related to administration, technical issues, time limits, social connection, academic skills, and limited access to materials when engaging in virtual learning.

Although Mukhtar et al. (2015) and Li et al. (2016) have conducted numerous studies on online learning at the university level, there has been surprisingly little research on determining factors of students' satisfaction towards online teaching and learning during the Covid-19 pandemic. Due to the severity of the pandemic, it is crucial to study the factors that affect university students' satisfaction. It is essential for administrators to hear from students about their experiences in universities so they can better shape institutional policies to enhance instruction and learning.

Students' Preparedness

This investigation was initiated as a response to a series of questions posed by Arif (2001) about the degree to which students were prepared for online learning. As an illustration, the level of preparedness of students will take into consideration questions such as whether or not the student is adequately prepared to make use of computer technology and whether or not the student acquires the required skills for attempting to access and explore through the content of the course. When it comes to educational concepts, the question will be whether or not the student is prepared for self-evaluation and self-belief to adjust to new learning routes. The final question is whether or not the student is willing to forego conventional methods of academic pursuit in favour of more modern approaches.

In a university environment where online learning has become the preferred method for the delivery of lessons, it may appear realistic to assume that students who have been exposed to technology and have digital instincts will do well in an environment characterised by such learning conditions. Students will become more comfortable with the educational technology being utilised for their lectures and classes, at which point they will frequently strive to excel in the online learning environment. In addition, participation rates for online learning classes are typically significantly higher than those for traditional in-person classes (Waugh & Su-Searle, 2014). Students' preparedness for online learning environments at the university level is called into question as a result of these factors.

In spite of the rapid expansion and increasing recognition of online learning at higher education, not a great deal of research has been conducted on the level of preparation or readiness of students for the conditions of online learning. Using participants from the Australian Vocational Education and Training (VET) industry, Warner et al. (1998) conducted one of the earliest studies on student readiness for online learning. This study was one of the first of its kind. According to the findings, students were neither adequately prepared for online learning nor receptive to the idea of doing so. According to Parkes et al. (2015)'s research, the majority of students needed both a sense of being prepared and the competencies necessary for online learning. Students may be adequately prepared to manage the technology involved in online learning; however, they are not sufficiently willing to complete activities such as reading and writing, be concise and clear in feedback, generating new ideas, long term planning, presenting reasoning, and working collaboratively with others.

Abdous's (2019) study shows how important it is to make online learning more enjoyable for students by reducing their worries about finishing online lessons. So, letting students go through an online learning orientation should make them feel more ready to learn. Based on past research and other relevant literature, students' readiness may be a factor that affects how happy they are with their teaching and learning. Because of this, the following hypothesis is made:

H1: Students' preparedness improves students' online learning satisfaction.

Student's Motivation

Johnson et al. (2017) assert that understanding complex behaviours starts with understanding what motivates them. Bekele (2020) suggests that motivation is important for constructive learning because it affects how and when higher-order thinking skills are learned and developed. Motivation is a student's willingness to start learning activities, which can affect how well they learn (Tomy & Pardede, 2019). Based on self-determination theory, the intrinsic and extrinsic motivational orientations are a good way to study motivation in educational settings. Intrinsic and extrinsic motivation are not at opposite ends of a continuum. Instead, they are two things that can exist together and have different effects on learning (Stutz et al., 2017).

Extrinsic motivation is shown by focusing on reaching practical goals beyond the learning process itself. Students motivated by things beyond themselves may pay more attention during an activity to meet their teachers' expectations, get praise from their parents, get a good grade, or be noticed by their peers (Stutz et al., 2017). On the other hand, intrinsically motivated students do something because they enjoy it or because it makes them feel good. Intrinsically motivated students listen since they find it rewarding to do so on its own or because they enjoy doing tasks that require them to attend.

Students might have a better time if they could figure out what drives them (Johnson et al., 2017). Motivation is essential for figuring out what tasks need to be done, making it more likely that good things will happen, making people happier, and making them more likely to stay with a company (Strigas & Jackson, 2003). Johnson et al. (2017) looked into student motivation and satisfaction. They found that students were motivated to learn when they had the chance to share their knowledge, skills, and abilities simultaneously. As such, it makes sense that students will be delighted with teaching and learning as their motivation grows. The next hypothesis is structured as follows:

H2: Students' motivation improves online learning satisfaction.

Internet Availability

Shitta (2002) stated that the internet has been referred to as an interactive high-speed line that connects, webbing, and translates the entire world. This description is supported by the fact that the internet is frequently used. It is a component of a global village in which a large number of people can easily connect, find, and communicate with each other, while simultaneously being able to share information instantly from one point on the globe to another. The development of this technology has made it possible to act as a catalyst in transforming the way academic learning is practised in higher education. It is anticipated that this transformation will continue to be viable in the years to come (Apuke & Iyendo, 2018). In addition, Hussain (2012) argued that the internet's utilisation in tertiary education can improve academic growth and research. Additionally, it has encouraged virtual conversations between researchers to share their findings.

Apuke and Iyendo (2018) give insight on the accessibility of the internet, the limitations of financial resources, and the implementation of online learning. Students anticipate that their instructors will use resources such as messaging applications that are a part of the online learning system because they are aware that students are financially constrained. This finding is in line with the discovery made by Allo (2020), which found that many respondents believe it is more expensive to offer courses through online learning than it is to provide courses that are entirely face-to-face. If the decision between traditional classroom learning and online learning were to be made solely based on cost considerations, then most respondents would choose traditional classroom learning. The current study demonstrates that even though activities are desirable for keeping physical distance during a pandemic, they demand group work to assist friends who do not have access to the internet. This is the case even though widespread access to the internet is available.

It has been discovered, as mentioned in the discussion above, that students would enthusiastically support the online learning system to extend their learning beyond the conventional model of learning that takes place in a face-to-face classroom. The students in this system are instructed to become accustomed to working online without using paper. Therefore, the network's availability and the students' financial capabilities are the issues at hand. Even though the vast majority of students have sufficient funds to purchase an Internet data package and connect to a reliable network, some still need to do so. Therefore, the purpose of this study is to investigate the relationship between access to the internet and the level of satisfaction experienced by students. This leads to the development of the third hypothesis, which is as follows:

H3: Internet availability improves students' online learning satisfaction.

Technical Support

According to Lee et al. (2011), providing students with "technical support" means assisting them with any technical issues that may crop up while participating in online or blended learning. The use of technology in education, whether it be online or blended, has become more prevalent. According to Song et al. (2004), the technical problem is the most important factor determining the level of difficulty in online learning environments and the degree to which students are satisfied with those environments. According to the findings of Muilenburg and Berge (2005), students who are already familiar with the technologies that are utilised in online learning have a significantly easier time navigating their way around the online learning environment compared to students who are less familiar with the technologies. As a consequence, educators and teachers are responsible for ensuring that students have a positive experience when interacting with technologies that are based online. They also need to ensure that they can resolve any technical issues that may arise among the students as they occur (Muilenburg & Berge, 2005; Song et al., 2004).

Students in tertiary education now have easier access to laptops, mobile phones, and other forms of technology (Sanusi et.al, 2018), which has helped alleviate many of the problems that online-based technologies have caused. Consequently, students develop greater confidence in the system, which ultimately increases their level of contentment with educational programs (Itasanmi & Oni, 2021). Providing adequate technical support is indispensable to any open and distance learning infrastructure. It entails activities that are responsive to the needs of students and makes online learning and services extremely accessible to learners by providing a diverse range of support options. This is done to make the activities more student centred.

In this context, "technical support" refers to support for information, support for institutions, support for academics, and support for providing timely feedback to students (Aftab et al., 2019). Recent research, such as that conducted by Aftab et al. (2019) and Itasanmi and Oni (2021), has shown that the provision of technical support services is the factor that contributes the most to the level of satisfaction experienced by learners participating in open distance learning programs. As a result, the conclusion was that providing students with adequate technical support led to an increase in overall satisfaction. The following is the formulation of the fourth hypothesis, which is based on the discussion that was presented earlier:

H4: Technical support improves students' online learning satisfaction.

Psychological Support-Enjoyment

According to Kangas et al. (2017), the joy of having a caring learning ecosystem for student satisfaction can be defined as the satisfaction commonly linked with learning activities and the experience of those activities. This concept places a more considerable emphasis on optimistic attitudes and feelings regarding the learning process, which are generally prompted by a desire to further one's education (Chang & Chang, 2012; Topala & Tomozii, 2014). For instance, Chang and Chang (2012) discovered a stronger association between student satisfaction and enjoyment. As a result, it is reasonable to assume that student satisfaction with their learning environment is directly correlated to the degree to which students engage in learning activities that they find enjoyable.

Teachers could make any lesson more exciting and fun for them and their students. But this skill requires teachers to be playful and develop creative teaching methods (Pongpaew et al., 2017; Hyvonen, 2011). The results show how important it is for teachers to be motivated and involved in pedagogical methods that go along with creative learning settings to ensure students are pleased with them. This finding supports what Frenzel et al. (2009) said about how a teacher's enthusiasm can lead to student enjoyment in a caring environment. Also, research shows that teachers' pedagogical and emotional engagement is linked to student satisfaction and schools' ability to change sustainably (Kangas et al., 2017). Gil-Ariase et al. (2020) found that students will be thrilled with the universities if they have more fun in class. Based on the preceding discussion, psychological support-enjoyment is anticipated to be one of the factors influencing student satisfaction. Thus, the final hypothesis is elaborated as follows:

H5: Psychological support improves online learning satisfaction.

This section covered study variables. It defines, and describes previous studies, methodology, and variable relationships. The hypotheses of this study are based on the gaps and limitations of each variable. The structure and hypotheses for this investigation were derived from this literature. This study evaluates the preparedness, motivation, internet availability, technical support, and psychological support of Malaysian and Indonesian higher education students that influence their satisfaction with online learning. These factors can influence student satisfaction through learning readiness, motivational orientations, network availability, technical support services, and enjoyment of the learning environment, which is essential for influencing students' perceptions of educational institutions and achieving expected learning outcomes.

RESEARCH METHODOLOGY

Researchers used a cross-sectional quantitative approach based on survey data to examine students' satisfaction levels. The seven-part questionnaire, adapted from Bolliger & Wasilik (2009), was designed to assess students' reactions to online instruction in Malaysian and Indonesian settings. It included six items measuring students' satisfaction with online teaching and learning, five items measuring students' preparedness, four items measuring their motivation, four items measuring their access to the internet, four items measuring their technical support, and five items measuring their psychological support. An individual's age, gender, race/ethnicity, level of schooling attained, and current educational status are the five selected demographics for this survey. This questionnaire included 33 questions organised into 7 distinct categories. Students' satisfaction levels with their existing online learning environment, internet use, course tool utilisation, enjoyment, and mental health are a few questions investigated in the survey questionnaire. All questions in this questionnaire included a seven-point Likert-type scale with response options ranging from "strongly disagree" (1) to "strongly agree" (7). Each item required one answer to be responded by the student.

More than 700,000 students were enrolled in higher education institutions in Malaysia in 2019 (Hirschmann, 2020), compared to more than 3,129 million in Indonesia. Considering this population of Malaysian and Indonesian tertiary education students, a total sample of 384 respondents was deemed acceptable for the current study (Krejcie & Morgan, 1970). To attain a medium effect size of 0.15, the current study required complete replies from 117 respondents (Green, 1991).

Respondents received a link to an online survey administered by researchers at the university, which was selected using a purposeful sample method. It is a non-probability sampling approach in which respondents are chosen from the community based on predetermined criteria. The goal of using purposive sampling is to obtain a representative sample of the population for their research. As a result, the current study sampled students from institutes of higher education. The distribution and collection of survey data occurred over five months, commencing in November 2020 and concluding in March 2021. Respondents' participation in completing this survey was entirely voluntary and anonymous. The current study got comprehensive responses from 336 respondents from various academic fields who were selected from both public and private higher education institutions in Malaysia and 292 in Indonesia.

The current study examined the model using Structural Equation Model with Smart Partial Least Squares (PLS) technique (Ringle et al., 2015). This method begins with descriptive analysis using SPSS. It then employs the two-state analytical procedure proposed by Hair et al (2019). It would then move forward through assessing the measurement model's validity and reliability. Following that, the process continued with structural model evaluation to identify the existence of relationships between variables to provide evidence to support or reject the developed hypotheses.

FINDINGS AND DISCUSSION

The total number of acceptable completed questionnaires from Malaysian tertiary students was 336, and 292 from Indonesian students. Respondents were asked to provide background information such as gender, age, ethnicity, current education level, and study background. Table 1 summarises the demographics of the respondents. In summary, approximately three-quarters of Malaysian respondents are female, have a non-science background, and are between the ages of 20 and 24 because this is the age range of Malaysian tertiary students. However, almost equal numbers of respondents were received from Indonesia, with 53.1 percent being female with the same range of age and many of them coming from a non-science background as well.

Analysis of the Measurement Model

Convergent validity is a range in which multiple estimating devices determine whether a linked concept is inconsistent. Multiple measurements, including composite reliability (CR) and average variance extracted (AVE), were employed to explain convergent validity (Hair et al., 2010).

Table 2 highlighted the composite reliability values for the present research, which exceeded the indicated value of 0.70 for the degree to which construct indicators could predict the latent construct (Hair, Sarstedt & Ringle, 2019). The extracted average variance, which surpassed the required value of 0.5, represented the total differences between indicators resulting from the latent construct (Hair et al., 2010). The results for convergent validity are shown in Table 2. It is proposed for the study with five student preparedness items in the Research Methodology section. However, from Table 2, only three constructs were utilised for the final assessment. Two constructs need to be withdrawn for students' preparedness (SS) due to the low loading during the initial analysis.

Discriminant validity indicates the extent to which the measurements failed to interpret other variables, as demonstrated by poor correlations between the construct of interest and the indicators of other constructs (Cheung & Lee, 2010). Establishing discriminant validity by comparing squared correlations

Table 1. Demographic characteristics of respondents

| | | Malaysia | | Indonesia | |
Items	Particular	Frequency	(%)	Frequency	(%)
Gender	Male	93	27.7	137	46.90
	Female	243	72.3	155	53.10
Age	15-19	82	24.4	142	48.60
	20-24	250	74.4	149	51.00
	25-29	2	0.6	1	0.30
	Above 34	2	0.6		
Education level	Certificate	7	2.1		
	Diploma	187	55.7		
	Degree	141	42		
	Master	1	0.3		
	SMA			256	87.70
	S1			36	12.30
Education Background	Science	39	11.6	124	42.5
	Non-Science	297	88.4	168	57.5

Table 2. Convergent validity

Construct	Item	Loading	Cronbach Alpha	Composite Reliability	AVE
Psychological support (PS)	PS1	0.839	0.823	0.876	0.588
	PS2	0.849			
	PS3	0.782			
	PS4	0.663			
	PS5	0.681			
Internet availability (SIA)	SIA1	0.921	0.836	0.893	0.68
	SIA2	0.854			
	SIA3	0.863			
	SIA4	0.633			
Students' motivation	SM1	0.844	0.794	0.866	0.622
	SM2	0.841			
	SM3	0.835			
	SM4	0.61			
Students' satisfaction	SS1	0.811	0.871	0.903	0.608
	SS2	0.794			
	SS3	0.773			
	SS4	0.797			
	SS5	0.753			
	SS6	0.747			
Students' preparedness	SW2	0.772	0.735	0.85	0.654
	SW3	0.798			
	SW4	0.854			
Technical support	TS1	0.741	0.705	0.812	0.522
	TS2	0.634			
	TS3	0.701			
	TS4	0.803			

between constructs and variance for a single concept has become achievable (Fornell & Larcker, 1981). This study investigated discriminant validity using heterotrait-monotrait ratio (HTMT). Even though discriminant validity will be affected when the HTMT value exceeds 0.90 (Gold, Malhotra, & Segars, 2001), all values given in Table 3A for the Malaysian study and Table 3B for the Indonesian study were lower than the proposed value of 0.90. These results demonstrate that discriminant validity has been established.

Analysis of Structural Model

The proposed structural model revealed causal links between all model constructs (Sang, Lee & Lee, 2010). Initially, the variance inflation factor (VIF), R-squared, F-squared, Q-squared, and path coefficients were evaluated (Hair et al., 2014). Collinearity issues should have been addressed in the earliest phases of the structural model development. This was assessed by checking the VIF value. Before hypothesis testing,

Table 3A. HTMT criterion (Malaysia) for discriminant validity analysis

Factors	SIA	PS	SM	SW	SS	TS
Internet availability (SIA)						
Psychological support (PS)	0.527					
Students' motivation (SM)	0.659	0.82				
Students' preparedness (SW)	0.385	0.746	0.867			
Students' satisfaction (SS)	0.557	0.847	0.862	0.682		
Technical support (TS)	0.537	0.556	0.587	0.572	0.564	

Table 3B. HTMT criterion (Indonesia) for discriminant validity analysis

Factors	SIA	PS	SM	SW	SS	TS
Internet availability (SIA)						
Psychological support (PS)	0.673					
Students' motivation (SM)	0.794	0.876				
Students' preparedness (SW)	0.483	0.799	0.828			
Students' satisfaction (SS)	0.505	0.885	0.721	0.65		
Technical support (TS)	0.852	0.689	0.805	0.467	0.485	

the developed model should have a VIF value of less than 5 to ensure no multicollinearity issues. Tables 4A and 4B indicated that there was no potential for multicollinearity problems within the model, as the VIF value was less than 5, i.e., internet accessibility (1.614), psychological support (2.027), students' motivation (2.594), student preparedness (1.901), and technical support (1.463) for Malaysia. Internet availability (1.74), psychological support (2.209), students' motivation (1.828), student preparedness (1.739), and technical support (1.739) all contribute to a VIF value for Indonesian study that was less than 5, together with students' motivation (1.828) and student preparedness (1.739). The analysis will then evaluate the effect size using the F square.

Table 4A. Preliminary Malaysia's structural model analysis

Item	Path Coefficient	VIF	F Square	R square	Q square
Internet availability (SIA)	0.034	1.614	0.002		
Psychological support (PS)	0.409	2.027	0.242		
Students' motivation (SM)	0.387	2.594	0.169	0.658	0.388
Students' preparedness (SW)	0.021	1.903	0.001		
Technical support (TS)	0.093	1.463	0.017		

Table 4B. Initial structural model analysis (Indonesia)

Item	Path Coefficient	VIF	F Square	R square	Q square
Internet availability (SIA)	-0.008	1.740	0.000		
Psychological support (PS)	0.625	2.209	0.438		
Students' motivation (SM)	0.109	1.828	0.016	0.597	0.341
Students' preparedness (SW)	0.109	1.739	0.017		
Technical support (TS)	0.012	1.748	0.000		

In addition, 500 resamples were used in a bootstrapping process to determine t-values. The measuring model presented in Table 4A revealed an R-squared value of 65.8 percent and p-values for the correlations between the constructs. The findings of the tested hypotheses are presented in Table 5A. The effect size of the predictor was determined using Cohen's f2, which assesses the relative influence of an independent variable on a dependent variable. The effect size of the predictor from Table 4A construct suggested f2 values of 0.24 and 0.169 for psychological support and student motivation, respectively, which were medium effect sizes (Cohen, 1992). The effect size of f2 values for all other factors was small (0.002 for SIA, 0.001 for SW, and 0.017 for TS). The Indonesian study from Table 4B's impact size predictor showed that psychological support's f^2 value of 0.438 had a substantial effect size (Cohen,1992). The other factors' f^2 had little or no effect sizes (0.016, 0.017, and 0.000, respectively).

Table 5A displays the structural model's path coefficients, t-values, p-values, and standard error for the Malaysian sample, which were generated from the PLS output. Thus, psychological support (b = 0.409, p<0.05), students' motivation (b = 0.387, p<0.05), and technical support (b = 0.093, p<0.05) were found to be positively linked with students' satisfaction with online learning. Moreover, the developed model could account for 65.8% of the variances. These data supported Hypotheses 2, 3, and 5 of this study. In addition, the study found that the availability of the Internet and students' preparedness had no significant effect on student satisfaction.

The result for the Indonesian study from Table 5B indicated that psychological support (b = 0.625, p<0.05), students' motivation (b = 0.109, p<0.05), and students' preparedness (b = 0.109, p<0.05) were noticed to be associated to students' online learning satisfaction and managed to justify 59.7% of the variances. These results confirmed the current study's **H2, H3, and H4.** The survey also revealed that accessibility to the internet and technical assistance had no obvious influence on students' satisfaction in Indonesia. A significant difference between both countries results in factors influencing students on online learning.

In Malaysia and Indonesia, the three supported hypotheses are consistent with previous research by Jiang et al. (2022), Gil-Ariase et al. (2020), Sanusi et al. (2022), Johnson et al. (2017), Aftab et al. (2019), and Itasanmi and Oni (2019). Their research discovered that psychological support, motivation, and technical support could enhance student satisfaction. In the context of an online platform, the psychological support is consistent with the findings of a study by Pongpaew et al (2017). The importance of user psychology on their engagement with an online platform attitude and behaviour was discovered in this study. However, in the learning activity, this condition depends on the platform, the educator, and the institution's capacity (Hyvonen, 2011; Kangas et al., 2017). Moreover, this analysis revealed that this factor has the most influence compared to others.

Table 5A. Structural model for Malaysia

H	Variable	Beta Coeff.	Std. Error	T Values	P Values	Decision
H1	Internet availability (SIA) -> Students' satisfaction (SS)	0.034	0.046	0.751	0.453	Not supported
H2	Psychological support (PS) -> Students' satisfaction (SS)	0.409	0.047	8.730	0.000	**Supported**
H3	Students' motivation (SM) -> Students' satisfaction (SS)	0.387	0.056	6.917	0.000	**Supported**
H4	Students' preparedness (SW) -> Students' satisfaction (SS)	0.021	0.049	0.434	0.665	Not supported
H5	Technical support (TS) -> Students' satisfaction (SS)	0.093	0.042	2.199	0.028	**Supported**

Table 5B. Structural model for Indonesia

H	Variable	Beta Coeff.	Std. Error	T Values	P Values	Decision
H1	Internet availability (SIA) -> Students' satisfaction (SS)	-0.008	0.051	0.153	0.879	Not supported
H2	Psychological support (PS) -> Students' satisfaction (SS)	0.625	0.051	12.227	0.000	**Supported**
H3	Students' motivation (SM) -> Students' satisfaction (SS)	0.109	0.057	1.921	0.055	**Supported**
H4	Students' preparedness (SP) -> Students' satisfaction (SS)	0.109	0.047	2.33	0.02	**Supported**
H5	Technical support (TS) -> Students' satisfaction (SS)	0.012	0.056	0.218	0.828	Not supported

According to the study's findings, motivation is the second element influencing students' pleasure. As Johnson et al. (2017) previously discovered, students' motivation, such as experiencing joy from imparting their knowledge, skills, and abilities, dramatically impacts their pleasure. Additionally, some research has separated intrinsic and extrinsic motivational types (Stutz et al., 2017). Students' satisfaction may be increased through intrinsic categories like interest and enjoyment. Extrinsic categories, like reward and compliance, can also boost learning motivation and result in satisfaction. And last, technical support, which was found to be the factor that most significantly influenced students' satisfaction in studies by Aftab et al. (2019) and Itasanmi and Oni (2021), continues to have an impact on students' satisfaction with their learning in this study.

On the other hand, Internet accessibility and student readiness have little effect on satisfaction in Malaysia. It contradicts the findings by Apuke and Iyendo (2018) and Allo (2020), which claimed that one of the reasons why online learning is expensive is the expense of an internet connection. This divergent outcome may be attributable to The Malaysian Communications and Multimedia Commission's sponsorship of free internet data for home-based teaching and learning (PdPR) during this epidemic (NST, 2021). Students may no longer need to enrol in the premium internet plan for their online learning activity.

In Malaysia, students' preparedness only significantly affects their pleasure, unlike Indonesian students, for whom it has a considerable effect. This study has shown that learning orientation has little impact on students' satisfaction, even though it may increase their readiness for learning and reduce their anxiety about online courses (Abdous, 2019). This paradox may be resolved by Trembach & Deng's (2018) study, which found that millennial kids can do better academically when technology plays a significant role in their classroom environment. Hence, the more satisfied students are with online classes, the better grade they will get and the more knowledge they can absorb from their lecturers and teachers.

CONCLUSION

This study compared Malaysian and Indonesian students' satisfaction with online learning across two countries. Overall, the current research results for both countries supported three of the five proposed hypotheses. According to the findings, psychological support, motivation, and technical help significantly impact Malaysian students' happiness. In contrast, psychological support, motivation, and students' readiness significantly impact Indonesian students' satisfaction.

Given that the study was conducted during the two years of the Covid-19 pandemic, the results provide new information about the literature on online learning, particularly in pandemic situations. Even after the end of the endemic era, it can still be used in various circumstances. It concludes that psychologically related characteristics, such as psychological support and motivation, were the most significant determinants of students' satisfaction.

Findings from this study contributed to the literature review of teaching and learning, which identified a unique focus on online learning. Due to the paucity of prior research on this topic, particularly within the Malaysian and Indonesian contexts, the current study was conceived. However, there were some restrictions as the survey was conducted online without in-person interaction. Everyone is encouraged to work from home due to government-issued orders to regulate movement and stop the spread of Covid 19. Additionally, the data was only collected for five months, but enough information was collected to generalise the results.

Future studies could concentrate more on the causes of students' satisfaction with online learning. It is feasible that student happiness will increase as online education becomes more established. Therefore, it is crucial to think about how the school and its instructors contribute to this condition in terms of psychological support. According to earlier research by Itasanmi and Oni (2021); Aftab et al. (2019); Stutz et al. (2017), the motivation variable can be further studied by being divided into intrinsic and extrinsic aspects. Furthermore, future research may investigate other aspects that may have contributed to students' satisfaction with online learning at higher education institutions and which medium is the best for students to satisfy their learning curve.

ACKNOWLEDGEMENT

The authors would like to thank Universiti Kebangsaan Malaysia for granting a Teaching and Learning Innovation Grant No. EP-2022-015.

REFERENCES

Abdous, M. H. (2019). Influence of satisfaction and preparedness on online students' feelings of anxiety. *The Internet and Higher Education*, *41*, 34–44. doi:10.1016/j.iheduc.2019.01.001

Aftab, J., Sarwar, H., Khan, A. H., & Kiran, A. (2019). Critical factors which impact on students' satisfaction: A study of e-learning institutes of Pakistan. *Asian Journal of Distance Education*, *14*(2), 32–46.

Allo, M. D. G. (2020). Is the online learning good in the midst of Covid-19 Pandemic? The case of EFL learners. *Jurnal Sinestesia*, *10*(1), 1–10.

Apuke, O. D., & Iyendo, T. O. (2018). University students' usage of the internet resources for research and learning: Forms of access and perceptions of utility. *Heliyon*, *4*(12), 01052. doi:10.1016/j.heliyon.2018. e01052 PMID:30582057

Arif, A. A. (2001). Learning from the Web: Are students ready or not? *Journal of Educational Technology & Society*, *4*(4), 32–38.

Astin, A. W. (1993). *What matters in college? Four critical years visited*. Jossey-Bass.

Bekele, T. A. (2010). Motivation and Satisfaction in Internet-Supported Learning Environments: A Review. *Journal of Educational Technology & Society*, *13*(2), 116–127.

Bolliger, D. U., & Wasilik, O. (2009). Factors influencing faculty satisfaction with online teaching and learning in higher education. *Distance Education*, *30*(1), 103–116. doi:10.1080/01587910902845949

Bozkurt, A., & Sharma, R. C. (2020). Emergency remote teaching in a time of global crisis due to CoronaVirus pandemic. *Asian Journal of Distance Education*, *15*(1), 1–4.

Carr, S. (2000). As distance education comes of age, the challenge is keeping the students. *The Chronicle of Higher Education*, *46*(23), A39–A41.

Chang, I. Y., & Chang, W. Y. (2012). The effect of student learning motivation on learning satisfaction. *International Journal of Organizational Innovation*, *4*, 281–305.

Cheung, C. M. K., & Lee, M. K. O. (2010). A theoretical model of intentional social action in online social network. *Decision Support Systems, 49*(1), 24–30. doi:10.1016/j.dss.2009.12.006

Cohen, J. (1992). A power primer. *Psychological Bulletin, 112*(1), 155–159. doi:10.1037/0033-2909.112.1.155 PMID:19565683

Elliott, K., & Healy, M. (2001). Key factors influencing student satisfaction related to recruitment and retention. *Journal of Marketing for Higher Education, 10*(4), 1–11. doi:10.1300/J050v10n04_01

Elliott, K., & Shin, D. (2002). Student satisfaction: An alternative approach to assessing this Important Concept. *Journal of Higher Education Policy and Management, 24*(2), 197–209. doi:10.1080/1360080022000013518

Fasae, J. K., & Adegbilero-Iwari, I. (2015). Mobile devices for academic practices by students of college of science in selected Nigerian private universities. *The Electronic Library, 33*(4), 749–759. doi:10.1108/EL-03-2014-0045

Fornell, C., & Lacker, D. F. (1981). Evaluation structural equation models with unobserved variables and measurement error. *JMR, Journal of Marketing Research, 18*(1), 39–50. doi:10.1177/002224378101800104

Frenzel, A. C., Goetz, T., Lüdtke, O., Pekrun, R., & Sutton, R. (2009). Emotional transmission in the classroom: Exploring the relationship between teacher and student enjoyment. *Journal of Educational Psychology, 101*(3), 705–716. doi:10.1037/a0014695

Gil-Arias, A., Claver, F., Práxedes, A., Villar, F. D., & Harvey, S. (2020). Autonomy support, motivational climate, enjoyment and perceived competence in physical education: Impact of a hybrid teaching games for understanding/sport education unit. *European Physical Education Review, 26*(1), 36–53. doi:10.1177/1356336X18816997

Gold, A. H., Malhotra, A., & Segars, A. H. (2001). Knowledge management: An organizational capabilities perspective. *Journal of Management Information Systems, 18*(1), 185–214. doi:10.1080/07421222.2001.11045669

Green, S. B. (1991). How many subjects does it take to do a regression analysis. *Multivariate Behavioral Research, 26*(3), 499–510. doi:10.120715327906mbr2603_7 PMID:26776715

Hair, J. F., Anderson, R. E., Babin, B. J., & Black, W. C. (2010). *Multivariate data analysis: A global perspective*. Pearson Education.

Hair, J. F., Sarstedt, M., & Ringle, C. M. (2019). Rethinking some of the rethinking of partial least squares. *European Journal of Marketing, 53*(4), 566–584. doi:10.1108/EJM-10-2018-0665

Harsasi, M., & Sutawijaya, A. (2018). Determinants of student satisfaction in online tutorial: A study of a distance education institution. *Turkish Online Journal of Distance Education, 19*(1), 89–99. doi:10.17718/tojde.382732

Hirschmann, R. (2020). *Students in public higher education institutions in Malaysia 2012-2019, by gender*. Statista. https://www.statista.com/statistics/794845/students-in-public-higher-education-insitutions-by-gender-Malaysia/

Hodges, C. B., Moore, S., Lockee, B., Trust, T., & Bond, A. (2020, March 27). *The difference between emergency remote teaching and online learning. Why IT Matters to Higher Education Educause Review.* Educause. https://er.educause.edu/articles/2020/3/the-difference-between-emergency-remote-teaching-and-online-learning

Hussain, I. (2012). A study to evaluate the social media trends among university students. *Procedia: Social and Behavioral Sciences, 64,* 639–645. doi:10.1016/j.sbspro.2012.11.075

Hyvonen, P. (2011). Play in the school context? The perspectives of Finnish teachers. *The Australian Journal of Teacher Education, 36*(8), 65–83. doi:10.14221/ajte.2011v36n8.5

Itasanmi, S.A. and Oni, M.T. (2021). Determinants of Learners' Satisfaction in Open Distance Learning Programmes in Nigeria. *Pakistan Journal of Distance and Online Learning, 6*(2).

Jiang, H., Islam, A. A., Gu, X., & Spector, J. M. (2021). Online learning satisfaction in higher education during the COVID-19 pandemic: A regional comparison between Eastern and Western Chinese universities. *Education and Information Technologies, 26*(6), 1–23. doi:10.100710639-021-10519-x PMID:33814959

Johnson, J. E., Giannoulakis, C., Felver, N., Judge, L. W., David, P. A., & Scott, B. F. (2017). Motivation, Satisfaction, and Retention of Sport Management Student Volunteers. *Journal of Applied Sport Management, 9*(1), 1–26. doi:10.18666/JASM-2017-V9-I1-7450

Kangas, M., Siklander, P., Randolph, J., & Ruokamo, H. (2017). Teachers' engagement and students' satisfaction with a playful learning environment. *Teaching and Teacher Education, 63,* 274–284. doi:10.1016/j.tate.2016.12.018

Koksal, I. (2020, May 2). The rise of online learning. *Forbes.* https://www.forbes.com/sites/ilkerkoksal/2020/05/02/the-rise-of-online-learning/?sh=5829897772f3

Krejcie, R. V., & Morgan, D. W. (1970). Determining sample size for research activities. *Educational and Psychological Measurement, 30*(3), 607–610. doi:10.1177/001316447003000308

Lee, S. J., Srinivasan, S., Trail, T., Lewis, D., & Lopez, S. (2011). Examining the relationship among student perception of support, course satisfaction, and learning outcomes in online learning. *The Internet and Higher Education, 14*(3), 158–163. doi:10.1016/j.iheduc.2011.04.001

Li, C., & Lalani, F. (2020, Apr 29). The COVID-19 pandemic has changed education forever. This is how. *We Forum.* https://www.weforum.org/agenda/2020/04/coronavirus-education-global-covid19-online-digital-learning/

Li, N., Marsh, V., Rienties, B., & Whitelock, D. (2017). Online learning experiences of new versus continuing learners: A large-scale replication study. *Assessment & Evaluation in Higher Education, 42*(4), 657–672. doi:10.1080/02602938.2016.1176989

Liaw, S. S. (2008). Investigating students' perceived satisfaction, behavioral intention, and effectiveness of e-learning: A case study of the Black board system. *Computers & Education, 51*(2), 864–873. doi:10.1016/j.compedu.2007.09.005

Muilenburg, L. Y., & Berge, Z. L. (2005). Student barriers to online learning: A factor analytic study. *Distance Education*, *26*(1), 29–48. doi:10.1080/01587910500081269

Mukhtar, U., Anwar, S., Ahmed, U., & Baloch, M. A. (2015). Factors effecting the service quality of public and private sector universities comparatively: An empirical investigation. *Research World*, *6*(3), 132–142.

NST. (2021). *Take advantage of free internet data for PdPR purposes*. MCMC. https://www.nst.com.my/news/nation/2021/02/662364/take-advantage-free-internet-data-pdpr-purposes-mcmc

Pongpaew, W., Speece, M., & Tiangsoongnern, L. (2017). Social presence and customer brand engagement on facebook brand pages. *Journal of Product and Brand Management*, *26*(3), 262–281. doi:10.1108/JPBM-08-2015-0956

Ringle, C. M., Wende, S., & Becker, J. M. (2015). *SmartPLS 3*. Bonningstedt: SmartPLS. http://www.smartpls.com

Sahu, P. (2020). Closure of universities due to coronavirus disease 2019 (COVID-19): Impact on education and mental health of students and academic staff. *Cureus*, *12*(4), 1–5. doi:10.7759/cureus.7541 PMID:32377489

Sanusi, S., Firdaus, A., Noor, R., Omar, N., & Sanusi, M. (2018). Technology on Goods and Services Tax compliance among small-medium enterprises in developing countries. *Advanced Science Letters*, *24*(7), 5461–5465. doi:10.1166/asl.2018.11757

Sanusi, S., Nik Abdullah, N. H., Rozzani, N., & Muslichah, I. (2022). Factors influencing the level of satisfaction on online learning among tertiary students during Covid-19 pandemic era – A Malaysian study. *Geografia*, *18*(2), 248–263.

Shitta, M. B. K. (2002). The impact of information technology on vocational and technology education for self reliance. *Journal of VOC & Tech. Education*, *1*(1), 75–82.

Trembach, S., & Deng, L. (2018). Understanding millennial learning in academic libraries: Learning styles, emerging technologies, and the efficacy of information literacy instruction. *College & Undergraduate Libraries*, *25*(3), 1–19. doi:10.1080/10691316.2018.1484835

Turan, Z., & Gurol, A. (2020). Emergency transformation in education: Stress perceptions and views of university students taking online course during the COVID-19 Pandemic. *Hayef: Journal of Education*, *17*(2), 222–242. doi:10.5152/hayef.2020.20018

Vlachopoulos, D. (2011). COVID-19: Threat or opportunity for online education? *Higher Learning Research Communications*, *10*(1), 16–19. doi:10.18870/hlrc.v10i1.1179

Zhao, X., Shao, M., & Su, Y. S. (2022). Effects of Online Learning Support Services on University Students' Learning Satisfaction under the Impact of COVID-19. *Sustainability (Basel)*, *14*(17), 10699. doi:10.3390u141710699

Chapter 14
Automation in Digital Marketing

Hafizah Omar Zaki
Universiti Kebangsaan Malaysia, Malaysia

Dahlia Fernandez
Universiti Kebangsaan Malaysia, Malaysia

ABSTRACT

Marketing automation is becoming an increasingly important topic for marketing managers and practitioners. Despite the well-known use of automation in marketing activities, academic study into marketing automation is minimal compared to, possibly, the recent surge. This chapter addresses this important omission. Findings suggest that to get the most out of automation in digital marketing, organizations need to integrate automation into every part of their operations. Digitalization is an unavoidable prerequisite for the successful adoption of marketing automation. Marketing firms can make better judgments by opting for the excellent use of automation platforms in digital marketing. The creation of effective marketing teams is made more accessible by using marketing automation, although the process is not without its challenges. Automation will allow them to maximize the benefits that marketing automation provides.

INTRODUCTION

Technology and innovation breakthroughs are the two most important pillars on which any industry can rely to thrive in today's highly competitive environment. Simple marketing efforts are insufficient for success in today's market. In today's globalised marketplace, marketing is crucial for the success of any business. Keeping up with the latest trends is likely the most critical responsibility of a marketing professional. The term "digital marketing" describes any marketing that employs digital tools and methodologies instead of conventional methods (Digital Marketing Overview: Types, Challenges, and Required Skills, 2022). Banner advertisements on websites are a common practice in digital marketing. Online communication platforms play a crucial role in this type of marketing. In a global poll of marketing decision-makers conducted in February 2023, 63 percent stated they used automation in their email marketing activities. Half of those polled indicated they used it for social media management, and 40% said they used it to automate their paid advertising efforts (*Most Often Automated Marketing Channels,* 2023). Figure 1 illustrates marketing channels using automation worldwide as of February 2023.

DOI: 10.4018/978-1-6684-6782-4.ch014

Figure 1. Marketing channels using automation in 2023
adopted from Statista.com

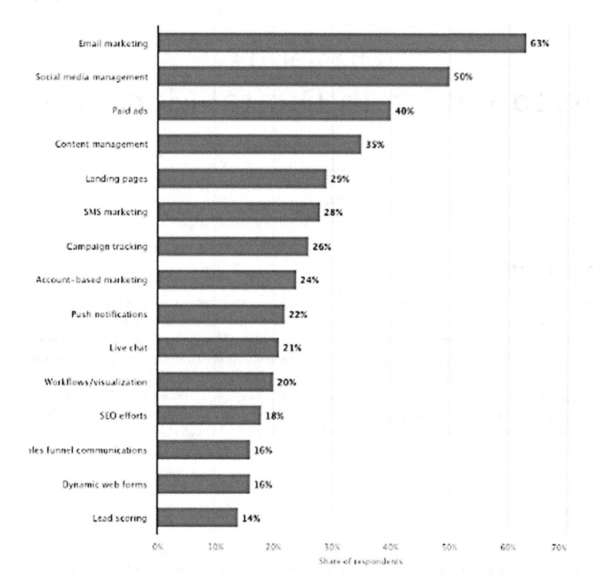

The rise of digital marketing has made inbound marketing a far more efficient strategy. Businesses can narrow their audience and entice prospective buyers through email marketing, social media marketing, monitoring activity, personalised content via Optimisation for Search Engines (SEO), and Content Marketing. These distinct strategies included the term "digital marketing." They provide a comprehensive marketing strategy and a larger audience for a relatively small investment. Following digital marketing, tools, and processes support marketing automation, among the most recent developments in digital marketing (Scully, 2022). Recently, it has become one of the essential tools a business can possess. Numerous thriving companies attribute their market success to the utilisation of such tools. In general, this chapter will discuss the insights, advantages as well as challenges of using automation in digital marketing.

Changing the Marketing Landscape Through Automation

The Oxford Dictionary defines automation as "the substitution of machines for human labour" (Automation Noun - Definition, Pictures, Pronunciation and Usage | Oxford Advanced Learner's Dictionary at OxfordLearnersDictionaries.com, 2022). Therefore, technology reduces the amount of manual or repetitive labour required of an individual. It can streamline processes, decrease turnaround time, and lower costs. Industrial, manufacturing, and factory units have utilised automation technology extensively for many years. As a result, machines now perform the most tedious tasks. This technology is currently being rapidly implemented in many other fields and industries worldwide to accelerate work and increase productivity.

Automation in digital marketing is not limited to performing repetitive tasks and relieving the pressure on humans. As a result of advancements in AI and machine learning, it now has a considerable amount of cognitive depth. AI is no longer a theoretical concept; rather, it permeates our daily lives through the proliferation of AI-powered web advertisements and other services we use without giving it much thought. They are used daily in various contexts, ranging from chatbots and intelligent home speakers, such as Alexa, to internet streaming sites, such as Netflix, to better comprehend consumer behaviour. Artificial intelligence embeds many products, including smartphones, automobiles, banks, and homes. Automation, such as AI, has been embedded in various conventional marketing activities and processes (Figure. 2).

The use of automation in conventional offline marketing operations is subject to a distinct set of limitations. Using customer relationship management software, marketers could automate the flow of its tasks and manage the database. Still, automation is the only viable option for intensive or impulse online marketing activities such as emailing, social networking, advertising, and online purchasing (Scully, 2022; Zaki & Hamid, 2021).

The execution of digital marketing is not as simple as it may initially appear. AI-based online advertisements can help a company manage a new variety of data touchpoints, which is advantageous given many data organisations already possess. However, these businesses remain uncertain about interpreting and forecasting these trends and making sound decisions. It can comprehend all customer interactions and draw accurate conclusions about how to approach them.

Numerous businesses rely heavily on digital marketing to generate a higher ROI at a lower cost. Nonetheless, this will not be a simple exertion. Marketers will need to coordinate their marketing and sales objectives with automation to get the most out of the data and achieve a high return on investment. The foundation of marketing automation is the integration of data and processes, which simplifies and automates these operations (Bagshaw, 2015). They intend to devote more time and effort to strategic planning to achieve their corporate objectives. Automation increases efficiency and decreases the time required to complete a task, thus forming its usage benefits.

ADVANTAGES OF DIGITAL MARKETING AUTOMATION

Effectiveness

First and foremost, marketing automation increases the efficiency of the entire organisation. A business may be able to reduce staffing expenses while freeing up its team's time to focus on more critical,

Figure 2. AI integration in conventional marketing activities

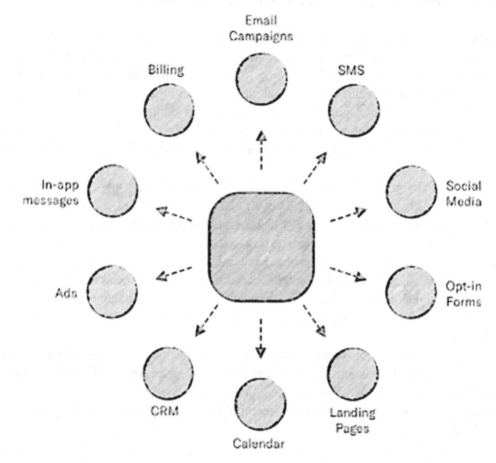

strategic projects. Marketing automation software can automate daily social media posting instead of requiring manual intervention. The automation process allows the business team to devote more time to creative tasks, such as planning and brainstorming for upcoming campaigns and projects (Scully, 2022; Bagshaw, 2015). In addition, working in an automation platform will simplify a team's tasks. Using the same software, a team can create social media posts, email nurturing campaigns, blog posts, and landing pages. The automation software will ultimately save business time when creating campaigns.

Sales-Marketing Alignment

Businesses can align their company's objectives and actions by combining their sales and marketing automation efforts with the same software. It will facilitate the transition from marketing-qualified leads to sales-qualified leads. Marketing automation can increase sales productivity by 14.5% and reduce marketing expenses by 12.2% (Turner-Wilson, 2021). It can also help the company generate more leads and boost sales. The company's marketing team will spend more time strategising ways to increase the conversion rate, whereas the sales team will increase its output. It's a win-win situation.

Increase Conversions

In addition to increasing conversion rates, marketing automation can improve a company's department processes and team efficiency. Marketing automation software can assist businesses in improving their conversion rate and lead management. The company's marketing automation software will track its leads and can even use for retargeting non-converting website visitors, thereby increasing its CRO (Turner-Wilson, 2021). Again, marketing automation should give a company's departments and teams additional time to evaluate their marketing strategy and determine how to convert visitors.

Accuracy

Reporting a company's analytics can be daunting, but marketing automation platforms make it unnecessary. Companies should be able to generate automated reports with their automated marketing software. In addition, marketing automation platforms can provide an overview of the entire process, making a difficult task more accessible. With automation, a precise streamlined marketing reporting, it is possible to remember where things go wrong. Accurate analytics using marketing automation software will help companies promptly identify and address issues (Scully, 2022).

Personalised Marketing

As a marketing team spends less on manual data entry and more time creating, marketing automation software will enable them to make more personalised content through its segmentation and reporting capabilities (Lies, 2021). With marketing automation, marketers can utilise multiple channels to target their persona. They can reach them through social media, search ads, and email campaigns (Tinkler, 2023). How does marketing automation make this possible? Once marketers know who their leads are, they can segment them based on their behaviours or characteristics. The entire information nurturing process should be personalised. A marketer's email nurturing leads includes invitations to a sales conference their team is hosting. This process allows them to send personalised messages to their information and track their engagement. A personalised message in ads can influence the cognition and emotions of consumers (Zaki et al. 2021). Additionally, this will aid in lead scoring.

Frontrunner

When a marketing-qualified lead becomes a sales-qualified lead, marketing automation software can notify the sales team and update the lead's score, which in turn will demonstrate the improved alignment between its marketing and sales departments (Lies, 2021; Tinkler, 2023). In addition, the process is automated, making it easier and more real-time. With automation, the time to sell products and services will be optimised, and the sales team can immediately contact prospects.

Managing Data and Scalability

Fascinatingly, marketing automation platforms will monitor the engagement of a marketing team leads with its website. Marketing automation makes data management more accessible than ever before. Additionally, it updates marketers' data automatically. In terms of the ability to scale, when establishing marketing systems and procedures, it is essential to consider Scalability (Lies, 2021; Scully, 2022; Tinkler, 2023). Can this process expand with the marketer's organisation? It will be difficult for a company to grow if it is not scalable. Marketing automation will help marketing companies create scalable processes. The more manual and dependent on a single individual a process is, the more difficult it will be to scale as the team grows.

Managing Change

In addition, marketing automation facilitates lead nurturing. The software for marketing automation is where marketers can create drip email campaigns and track their success. Without lead nurturing, converting leads into sales prospects will be more difficult. Now, we are not the only ones advocating for marketing automation (Lies, 2021; Tinkler, 2023). Optimus Prime believes that marketing automation is one of the best ways to develop a marketing programme that can scale with the business. Additionally, it can align additional departments, such as sales and customer service, in companies.

SUCCESS OF DIGITAL MARKETING AUTOMATION BASED ON RESEARCH

An academic study into digital marketing is minimal compared to, possibly, the recent surge. Digital marketing research is still in its early stages, but you can learn more by looking at related fields of study and software, such as CRM, promotional tools, email marketing, SMS marketing, web-based and process optimisation, digital advertising, and web personalisation. Unlike consensus publications, there is no shortage of marketing automation use cases, testimonials, surveys, and available research from and sponsored by vendors and agencies.

Doyle's (2000) article on emerging marketing automation systems is one of the earliest examples of this optimism. He predicted a 100-fold rise in the volume of communications sent to clients, citing the merits of both email and SMS as marketing communication tools while cautioning about the organisational consequences. Similarly, Redding (2015) sees marketing automation as the glue to unify sales and marketing and develop a customer-focused firm, with the caveat that success relies on exemplary implementation.

To date, research has primarily focused on improving sales and marketing functions. Benefits identified include generating higher-quality sales prospects (Järvinen & Taiminen, 2016; Sandell, 2016) in more significant numbers (Järvinen & Taiminen, 2016; Murphy, 2018), with more information about and stronger relationships with leads (Sandell, 2016), and through sales and marketing efficiencies, transparency, and strategy (Järvinen & Taiminen, 2016).

Publicly available research from private firms on technology has been less glowing but is still generally optimistic about the automation of the technology and its implementation. Interestingly, while many firms utilise marketing automation for efficiency, transparency, and analytics, mainly return on investment, NCBI (2022) indicates that 18.5% of survey respondents never use dashboards for reporting. Nearly one-fifth of enterprises fail to measure their activities, self-and porting of success may be untrustworthy (Marquis, Marquis, & Polich, 1986), making academic case studies more valuable (Järvinen & Taiminen, 2016).

According to Econsultancy's annual Email Marketing Industry Census, while email marketing is seen as the most effective marketing channel in terms of ROI (Gilliland, 2020), 33% of respondents deemed their automated email marketing programme unsuccessful (Moth, 2017). Similarly, Zhang and Xiao (2020) found in their State of B2B Marketing Automation study that 15% of respondents assessed their marketing automation initiatives as unsuccessful, while 85% ranked them as effective. LeadMD also found that half of the 2061 organisations surveyed in its 2016 research saw no increase in qualified leads after deploying marketing automation.

Despite the well-known use of automation in marketing activities, academic study into marketing automation is minimal compared to, possibly, the recent surge. While marketing automation research is still in its infancy, it is possible to broaden knowledge by learning from complementary digital marketing disciplines and associated software such as CRM, sales automation tools, email marketing, SMS marketing, online testing and optimisation, content marketing, as well as web personalisation. Marketing automation has problems, but it helps develop effective marketing teams. It is undoubtedly the future of digital marketing, combining sophisticated technologies such as email with a touch of automation.

CHALLENGES AND THE FUTURE OF DIGITAL MARKETING AUTOMATION

There are dozens of marketing automation tools and hundreds of marketing software categories. As a result, it is getting more popular. Selecting the best marketing automation tools for a marketing business operation can be challenging (Silva et al. 2023). It takes time for employees to become accustomed to new devices. Expensive and slow to combine several instruments and have a comprehensive perspective costly to have marketing automation due to membership payments for numerous tools. Increased automation and well-designed tools are diverting attention away from marketers' primary focus: creating great content that resonates with their audience and compels them to act. While the impact of automation on marketers' workload may be easily assessed, the effect on revenue, which is dependent on the company's messaging, is more difficult to quantify. Some challenges include a lack of app integration, usage restrictions, international policies, customisation restrictions, and reporting problems.

Data Silos and a Lack of App Integration

These two distressing issues frequently appear together. Because in an era when customer data is currency, any absence of data integration in the stack would cause broad problems (Silva et al. 2023). Root causes in a marketing automation platform include:

- Limited data capabilities or a predefined data structure (marketers will not be able to preserve and use vital data from their leads or contacts).
- API usage and API features are restricted.

Solution: Use a marketing automation platform that runs campaigns and streamlines data warehouse architecture to capture data streams from multiple sources, including third-party apps, via APIs and connections.

Usage Restrictions or Pay-to-Play Features

If a 'free' or very low-cost marketing automation programme seems too good to be true, it probably is. High-end automation, the kind that combines actionable data with AI-powered magic to make everything sing, is not cheap (Silva et al. 2023). Otherwise, marketers will encounter obstacles such as:

- Sends per channel are limited (price highly variable)
- Web traffic allowance is limited.
- SMS service providers are scarce.

Solution: Read the fine print before deciding on a platform or app. And, in the long run, predict the marketing team's needs and marketing volume: If they outgrow the free plan, why not begin with a professional tool to protect their data in the long run?

International Policies and Little Language Support

If a marketing organisation operates globally, its marketing automation platform should also (Silva et al. 2023). Otherwise, regional teams may have to combine improvised solutions for local markets, increasing the likelihood of anticipated data and integration issues. Marketers should keep an eye out for the following:

- There is no or minimal multilingual support.
- There will be no geotagging or localised website versions.
- Consent and opt-in forms under the CCPA and GDPR are missing.

Solution: Involve stakeholders from the marketing firm in the decision-making process of the marketing automation platform. Marketing organisations can also consider platform extensibility to suit future legislation or data privacy requirements.

Restrictions on Customisation and Content Possibilities

Even if marketers automate their interaction marketing, today's customers expect to be treated as people. Once marketers have gathered all the required data to impress customers with intelligent content (Kapoor, 2023), it is a significant let-down when the marketing automation platform slows their roll with:

- Email design options are limited.
- Simple journeys, such as single shots or A/B tests, require complexity to build.
- No one-to-many relationship data, only simple, inclusive filters, no nesting, and so on.
- One-to-one customisation is limited, and dynamic content is fixed (designs cannot be changed).

Solution: To transform automation into intelligent automation, insist on some must-haves in marketing automation platforms, such as A/B testing, audience segmentation, dynamic content, and marketing-specific AI.

Problems With Reporting

Returning to a marketer's first point of contention, a lack of data integration will eventually taint the quality of their overall customer intelligence (Silva et al. 2023). The customer profiles owned by marketers should be able to capture data from all channels, including online, mobile, social, e-commerce, email, and customer service, on a micro level (Kapoor, 2023). Capturing website behaviour and email subscribers for all visitors provides a big-picture perspective. Otherwise, you'll have to settle for the following:

- Journey reporting is limited (no bounces, no device type, no domain differentiation)
- Inability to detect churn
- There is no visibility into abandoned cart journeys, customer complaints, or malfunctioning products and services.

Solution: Choose a marketing automation platform with an integrated data warehouse architecture as the key to relevant messages and properly segmented campaigns, as well as real-time reporting and optimisation to keep automated marketing less focused.

CONCLUSION

Marketing automation is becoming an increasingly important topic for marketing managers and practitioners, with expenditure expected to double to $25 billion by 2023 (Adams, 2019). Two hundred ninety-two platforms currently serve over 2.5 million websites globally (Adams, 2019). This market has grown from only ten media in 2011 (Turner-Wilson, 2021), with software such as Oracle, Adobe, Salesforce, and IBM recently joining the marketing automation specialists Marketo and Infusionsoft via the acquisition of existing platforms or development of their marketing automation products. Despite the well-known use of automation in marketing activities, academic study into marketing automation is minimal compared to, possibly, the recent surge. While marketing automation research is still in its infancy, it is possible to broaden knowledge by learning from complementary digital marketing disciplines and associated software such as CRM, sales automation tools, email marketing, SMS marketing, online testing and optimisation, content marketing, as well as web personalisation. Marketing automation has problems, but it helps develop effective marketing teams. It is undoubtedly the future of digital marketing, combining sophisticated technologies such as email with a touch of automation.

REFERENCES

Adams, J. (2019, April 10). *Global Marketing Automation Spending Will Reach $25 Billion By 2023*. Forrester. https://www.forrester.com/blogs/global-marketing-automation-spending-will-reach-25-billion-by-2023/

Bagshaw, A. (2015). What is marketing automation? *Journal of Direct, Data and Digital Marketing Practice, 17*(2), 84–85. doi:10.1057/dddmp.2015.46

Digital Marketing Overview: Types, Challenges, and Required Skills. (2022, June 23). Investopedia. https://www.investopedia.com/terms/d/digital-marketing.asp

Doyle, P. (2000). Value-based marketing. *Journal of Strategic Marketing*, 8(4), 299–311. doi:10.1080/096525400446203

Gilliland, M. (2020). The value added by machine learning approaches in forecasting. *International Journal of Forecasting*, 36(1), 161–166. doi:10.1016/j.ijforecast.2019.04.016

Järvinen, J., & Taiminen, H. (2016). Harnessing marketing automation for B2B content marketing. *Industrial Marketing Management*, 54, 164–175. doi:10.1016/j.indmarman.2015.07.002

Kapoor, S. (2023). Prospects and challenges of digital marketing. *Digital Marketing Outreach*, 93-107.

Lies, J. (2021). Digital marketing: Incompatibilities between performance marketing and marketing creativity. *Journal of Digital & Social Media Marketing*, 8(4), 376–386.

Marquis, K. H., Marquis, M. S., & Polich, J. M. (1986). Response bias and reliability in sensitive topic surveys. *Journal of the American Statistical Association*, 81(394), 381–389. doi:10.1080/01621459.1986.10478282

Most often automated marketing channels. (2023). Statista. https://www.statista.com/statistics/1269813/marketing-channels-automation/#:~:text=Marketing%20channels%20using%20automation%20world-wide%202023&text=During%20a%20February%202023%20global,automated%20their%20paid%20ads%20efforts

Moth, R., & Lavalette, M. (2017). *Social protection and labour market policies for vulnerable groups from a social investment perspective: The case of welfare recipients with mental health needs in England*. RE-InVEST working paper series D5. 1.

Murphy, D. (2018). Silver bullet or millstone? A review of success factors for implementation of marketing automation. *Cogent Business & Management*, 5(1), 1546416. doi:10.1080/23311975.2018.1546416

NCBI. (2022). *Assessing and Addressing COVID-19 information needs via a weather application*. NCBI. Retrieve on 22 November 2022 https://www.ncbi.nlm.nih.gov/pmc/articles/PMC9037469/

Redding, S. (2015). Can marketing automation be the glue that helps align sales and marketing? *Journal of Direct, Data and Digital Marketing Practice*, 16(4), 260–265. doi:10.1057/dddmp.2015.27

Sandell, N. (2016). Marketing automation supporting sales.

Scully, D. (2022). Marketing Automation: A Design Perspective. The SAGE Handbook of Digital Marketing, 54.

Silva, S. C., Corbo, L., Vlačić, B., & Fernandes, M. (2023). Marketing accountability and marketing automation: Evidence from Portugal. *EuroMed Journal of Business*, 18(1), 145 164. doi:10.1108/EMJB-11-2020-0117

Tinkler, A. (2023). AI, marketing technology and personalisation at scale. *Journal of AI. Robotics & Workplace Automation*, 2(2), 138–144.

Turner-Wilson, L. (2021, April 26). *Using Marketing Automation to Increase Sales Efficiency, Quality Lead Generation and Revenue.* Linkedin. https://www.linkedin.com/pulse/using-marketing-automation-increase-sales-efficiency-turner-wilson

Zaki, H. O., & Ab Hamid, S. N. (2021). The Influence of Time Availability, Happiness, and Weariness on Consumers' Impulse Buying Tendency amidst Covid-19 Partial Lockdown in Malaysia. *Jurnal Pengurusan, 62.*

Zaki, H. O., Kamarulzaman, Y., & Mohtar, M. (2021). Cognition and Emotion: Exploration on Consumers Response to Advertisement and Brand. *Jurnal Pengurusan, 63.*

Zhang, H., & Xiao, Y. (2020). Customer involvement in big data analytics and its impact on B2B innovation. *Industrial Marketing Management, 86,* 99–108. doi:10.1016/j.indmarman.2019.02.020

Chapter 15
Study on Sentence and Question Formation Using Deep Learning Techniques

N. Venkateswaran
Department of Management Studies, Panimalar Engineering College, India

R. Vidhya
Department of Computer Science and Engineering, Sri Krishna College of Technology, India

Darshana A. Naik
Ramaiah Institute of Technology, India

T. F. Michael Raj
Department of Computer Applications, SCLAS, SIMATS University (Deemed), India

Neha Munjal
Department of Physics, Lovely Professional University, India

Sampath Boopathi
ⓘ https://orcid.org/0000-0002-2065-6539
Mechanical Engineering, Muthayammal Engineering College, India

ABSTRACT

Natural language techniques require less personal information to communicate between computers and people. Generative models can create text for machine translation, summarization, and captioning without the need for dataset labelling. Markov chains and hidden Markov models can also be employed. A language model that can produce sentences word by word was created using RNNs (recurrent neural networks), LSTMs (long short-term memory model), and GRUs (gated recurrent unit). The suggested method compares RNN, LSTM, and GRU networks to see which produces the most realistic text and how training loss varies with iterations. Cloze questions feature alternative responses with distractors, whereas open-cloze questions include instructive phrases with one or more gaps. This chapter provides two novel ways to generate distractors for computer-aided exams that are simple and dependable.

DOI: 10.4018/978-1-6684-6782-4.ch015

1. INTRODUCTION

Software for text prediction was developed to help persons who write slowly and to improve communication. It merely uses a few early text fragments to predict the previous phrase that is likely to continue. Currently used methods use a text prediction algorithm to choose the optimal word depending on the current phrase. Artificial Neural Networks, which are machine learning algorithms, are a subset of deep learning. They are constrained, nonetheless, in terms of creating appropriate sentence structures for lengthy sequences. Recently, it has been discovered that deep learning approaches are frequently employed and produce successful outcomes. One of the main factors contributing to their success is their flexibility in choosing the architecture. Machine learning models make judgments based on what they have learnt from the data, whereas neural networks put up algorithms to make decisions on their own that are dependable. Deep learning models can manage more data and anticipate more accurately than machine learning algorithms, producing outcomes that are more precise than those produced by current system technologies(Abujar et al., 2019; Raza et al., 2019).

With categories for voice tagging, word meaning disambiguation, and named entity identification, NLP is a hot issue in academia. An Indo-Aryan language that is descended from Sanskrit, Language is an Indo-Aryan language. For example, Language, the world's 23rd most common language, is processed and pre-processed using methods from Hindi, Sanskrit, Arabic, and English. Many sentences are built using a subject, object, and verb in that sequence. There are two Vachans: single and plural(Ahmad et al., 2020; Sharif et al., 2020). The Objective Nominative Case is expressed by a series of words, phrases, and sentences, with various words standing in for one term, separate terms for one sentence, and different letters for one word. It's derived from a set of letters known as "kakko."

"Sentences are composed of many letters and words."

Language text processing problems can be difficult due to ambiguity, phrase complexity, language grammatical construction, text translation errors, and the difficulty of finding reliable data for text processing algorithms. A language model is a set of estimates made by a self-supervised learning system. Labels are ingested in the data, and by comprehending the specifics of the predicted corpora, researchers may apply transfer learning to enhance the performance of text classifiers. The Indic NLP library offers a general answer to the problems that Indian languages encounter due to their many similarities in terms of writing, phonetics, grammar, and other areas(Al-Aswadi et al., 2020).

Complexities in the Reginal Language: Each noun in the gender-classified Reginal Language designates one of three gender kinds. The past, future, and present tenses are the three that are employed in language processing. There are two varieties of vachans: singular and plural. If a word is only represented in the singular, it cannot be processed or stated in the plural. Language is a regional tongue with five main dialects, each of which conveys a unique meaning based on the environment, society, and community. Due to their numerous quasi-words, these words are known as multiquasi words and can lead to ambiguity in utterances. Different Language Resources: WordNet is a connected lexical positioning system that incorporates social lexical memory ideas from psycholinguistics. Adjectives, verbs, and nouns are all equivalent in English and each expresses a fundamental lexical idea. A group of synonyms are connected by several connections. It is one of the 22 recognised languages of India, and the linguistic WordNet was produced using a Hindi language extension approach. Wikipedia is a web resource having nouns, verbs, lemmas, and other categories represented. Architecture of WordNet is shown in Figure 1.

Figure 1. Architecture of WordNet

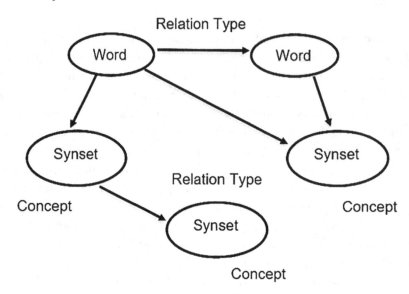

Major challenges in Text Processing: To establish a clear, logical framework for text that provides exact and accurate content descriptions, Language sentence creation is a laborious process. The deep learning series model's sentence building function aids readers in swiftly ascertaining both the specifics of a statement and the topic of the overall statement. The goal of this study was to provide a Long Short-Term Memory (LSTM) model using a Gated Recurrent Unit (GRU), a unique kind of Recurrent Neural Network employed in text based on word arrangements from the past. Language presents a number of difficulties for text processing jobs, such as the ambiguity it introduces between words and phrases, sentence complexity, difficulty with grammatical organisation, and Language text processing methods. With functions including word and script normalisation, tokenization, word segmentation, romanization, indication, script conversion, and translation, the Indic NLP library iNLTK offers a generic solution for these problems. For illiterate persons who struggle to write paragraphs, sentence preaching is helpful, and a special online input technique opens study subjects to all Indic languages. Based on the most accurate review of the literature, three computational models were selected(Prabha & Srikanth, 2019; Zhang & El-Gohary, 2021).

Text Generation: Three steps are involved in building text sentences from of keywords: acquisition, creation, and assessment. With the help of candidate-text phrases that have been formed and generation rules learned, keywords are employed to construct text sentences. Candidate-text phrases are ranked based on assessment scores using a likelihood estimate and language model. For applications like translation, summarization, and human-computer interaction, text production is a crucial strategy. For language model estimation, natural surface sentences and phrases have been generated using datasets and corpora. Natural Language: A subset of machine learning called natural language processing (NLP) uses language models created by machine learning to evaluate and produce natural language data. It serves as an example of how RNN construction works. NLP refers to a computer's capacity to comprehend spoken and written language in a manner similar to that of a person. To interpret human language and comprehend its intent and sentiment, natural language processing integrates statistical, machine learning, and deep learning models with rule-based human language modelling(Zou et al., 2015). The text generation process is shown in Figure 2.

Figure 2. Text generation process

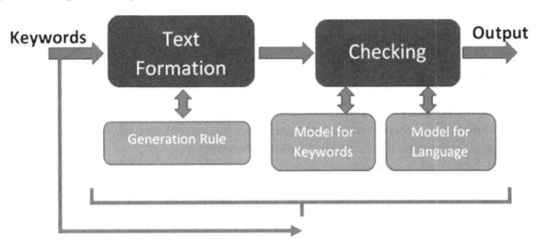

Computer programmes that interpret text, reply to spoken requests, and summarise information in real-time are all powered by NLP. Additionally, it is utilised in corporate solutions to simplify mission-critical business procedures, increase staff productivity, and streamline operations. If natural language-driven systems are to be helpful, programmers must educate them to identify and comprehend ambiguities in human language, such as holonomies, homophones, sarcasm, idioms, metaphors, exceptions to syntax and use, and variances in sentence structure. By converting human text and voice into computer-friendly forms, such as speech recognition, tagging, disambiguation, named entity identification, and co-reference resolution, NLP operations help computers comprehend what they are consuming. Natural Language Processing is carried out using NLTK, Statistical NLP, Machine Learning, and Deep Learning. Individual functions of phrase structure and machine tools are the two main divisions of the computer engineering field known as natural language processing. Learnability, computational capacity, ambiguity, and diversity are the four guiding principles for any language's syntax and semantics. It has been reviewed how Language linguists may utilise NLP to leverage structural ideas(Khan et al., 2021).

While syntactic analysis focuses on understanding phrase grammatical rules, lexical analysis focuses on identifying and categorising each sentence's structure. While syntactic analysis is used to understand phrase grammatical rules, lexical analysis is used to identify and categorise sentences. While Disclosure Integration derives the meaning of each representation of sentence formation from the prior sentence, Semantic Analysis gives meaning to the entire statement representation. It keeps track of how the joined and united phrases' meanings relate to one another. Natural language processing and pragmatic analysis are two crucial elements of the performance of real-world information. Sentence observations and pragmatic analysis both track correctness, which is crucial for the performance of information in the actual world. Word and phrase errors are caused by natural language processing. Language text patterns have been studied in order to understand how pre-processing is used. A language model's objective is to lessen the amount of uncertainty it experiences after viewing a series of texts. Repeating the generator can speed up training as only one language model per domain needs to be created. It frequently takes up the most time during training(Safder et al., 2020).

With the same word embedding for each supplied word, NLP represents words in a sequence using a hidden Markov matrix. It can be used to denote exclamation points or phrases. Automatic text translation techniques include Machine Words, Sentiment Analysis, Text Classification, Question Answering, Sequence Text Generation, and Music Generation. Tokenization is the act of dividing big data or complex ideas into smaller, more understandable chunks. Tokenization breaks down the original text into chunks that aid in context comprehension or model construction. Each text is transformed into an integer sequence using the #texts-to-sequences function. The Stemming Process standardises the presentation of text as a root or fundamental word. The method, which aims to enhance NLP systems, uses Mixed Access Lightweight Stemmer and Language Linguistic Stemmer.

To get the right stems, predictive outputs must be free of prefixes and mid-outputs must remove suffixes. The length of the suffixes was listed from longest to shortest. Depending on the suffix list, a word is stripped when it is input. The bigger ones are removed first, then, if required, the shorter ones, and so on. The book illustrates the lemmatization process using general terms that require diverse interpretations. While stemming employs established rules to change a word into a stem, lemmatization uses context and a lexical vocabulary to construct a lemma. The Language rule set is used by the suffix stripping module to detect where the suffix begins and to separate the stem from the suffix. The Speech Tagging Process clarifies the meaning of the text in a phrase as well as how the language relates to its structure. Depending on the term used in the phrase or the text context, the sentence representation may be broken into many parts. Natural languages detect named items in text and categorise them into predefined groups. Examples include names of businesses, people, and companies as well as places, dates, options, and percentages.

DEEP LEARNING

A three-layer neural network called deep learning makes an effort to imitate how the human brain functions by learning from vast amounts of data. AI apps and services rely on deep learning to increase automation, and hidden layers can assist to optimise and boost accuracy. DNN models, which are capable of retaining text for extended periods of time like CNN and RNN designs, can be utilised to handle text sequence issues. With no unique selection on the DNN model for all NLP challenges, RNN adopts a sequential framework for text processing. CNN is a multitask learning method that combines Deep learning and prediction of event outcomes. Using a lookup table structure, it turns each word in a phrase into a high-dimensional vector(Liu et al., 2016; Xu et al., 2014). For NLP applications including text translation, speech-to-text generation, and conversation building, RNN has grown in popularity. Each semantic input value is provided by the pre-processing method, whilst the representation style makes use of strategies like regulation, pedagogy, and reinforcement learning. The DNN is a trustworthy way for automatic text translation in any language that does not require manual effort. NLP tasks are carried out using deep neural network models as GRU, LSTM, CNN, and RNN. While LSTM classifiers are trained to examine a string of text words and their semantic meaning, two DNN models are used as encoders and decoders. The Deep Neural Network Model has become increasingly popular for NLP-related activities as a result of this. For DNN models to collect complete and helpful data for each word in a sentence, high-dimensional split vectors are necessary.

Deep Neural Network (DNN)

Input and output layers, together with nodes and arcs linking them, are features of artificial neural networks. Each neuron has a weight, and functions like Tangent, Hyperbolic, Step, and Sigmoid are used to activate them. In contrast to non-deep networks, which have just one hidden layer between the input and output layers, deep neural networks have several. Three distinct sorts of artificial neural networks have been considered by scientists as ways to increase their accuracy. While Convolutional Neural Networks enable the insertion of neurons in three dimensions, Artificial Neural Networks are collections of neurons that process inputs forward. While RNNs employ loops to glean information from data to predict the future, CNNs process a tiny section of the visual field using convolutional layers. They are frequently used with images and moving pictures(Zhang & El-Gohary, 2021).

Deep Neural Networks (DNNs) have been used extensively in the field of natural language processing (NLP) for various tasks such as language translation, sentiment analysis, and text generation. In recent years, DNNs have shown promising results in generating high-quality text that is coherent and contextually relevant. A DNN-based text generation model that uses a combination of convolutional and recurrent neural networks to generate high-quality and diverse sentences. The proposed model was trained on a large corpus of text data and was able to generate coherent and semantically meaningful sentences. A language model based on a DNN architecture called the AWD-LSTM, which stands for "ASGD Weight-Dropped LSTM". The proposed model achieved state-of-the-art performance on several benchmark datasets for text generation, including the Penn Treebank dataset and the WikiText-103 dataset.

In addition to these studies, DNNs have also been used in combination with other techniques such as reinforcement learning and adversarial training to improve the quality and diversity of generated text. For example, a text generation model based on a DNN architecture that was trained using a combination of maximum likelihood estimation and reinforcement learning. The proposed model was able to generate high-quality and diverse text by optimizing a trade-off between the quality and diversity of generated text.

Overall, DNNs have shown great potential for text generation tasks and continue to be an active area of research in NLP.

Activation Functions

In neural networks, activation functions are used to create non-linearity and choose whether or not to communicate a value from a particular neuron. They convert the single neuron's summarily weighted input into an output value, which is then passed on to another deep layer. This keeps happening all through the training until the intended result is reached. Three different activation function types—Step Function in Binary, Linear Form, and Not Linear—are used in neural networks in this thesis study. In order to introduce non-linearity to a network and address multi-class problems, SoftMax is a non-linear activation function. NLP techniques for text classification and sentiment the best results come from RNN-GRU, whereas CNN beats LSTM when it comes to question-answering and segmenting speech. In text sequence to-sequence learning, RNN-GRU and RNN-LSTM models perform better than the competition. Improved execution is achieved by using a bidirectional DNN model(Prabha & Srikanth, 2019).

RESEARCH PROBLEM

For text processing tasks, the Language poses a variety of difficulties, including ambiguity resolution, phrase complexity, language grammar development, text translation hiccups, and finding reliable data. The major issue is automatic text production from supplied text information. A language model is utilised to predict the next word from a given sequence of words. The goal of this study is to create a language model that can generate whole phrases automatically, word by word, utilising RNNs (Recurrent Neural Networks) and their variants, LSTM (Long Short-Term Memory model) and GRU (Gated Recurrent Unit). Generative models may be used to create text, and natural language approaches are excellent for conveying data between computers and people. It is possible to produce text using Markov Chains and Hidden Markov Models, although it can be difficult to do so in the form of whole sentences.

Text generation, including speech-to-text, conversational systems, text creation, and text summarization, is an issue in language modelling. Although it learns a word's likelihood of appearing based on the words that came before it in the text, trained models have difficulty anticipating what will come next. Although recurrent neural networks (RNNs) have shown promise in addressing this issue, they still have a significant flaw: they are unable to comprehend the full chain of interactions between the present state and its previous states. To grasp the semantic content of each word location, one must follow the sequential sequence of data, such as time series.

Reviewing by Research Questions

The primary research topic is whether the decreasing gradient causes basic Recurrent Neural Network (RNN) architecture to face the biggest challenge in language modelling. This makes it challenging to analyse the textual structure and compare the relationships between the present and previous texts. Techniques like LSTM and GRU can be utilised to get around constraints.

LSTM and GRU Model

With the use of three gates—the input, output, and forget gates—the LSTM is able to resolve the lengthy dependence and vanishing gradient problems. Backpropagation with an infinite number of time-driven steps is possible. By employing frequent gate updates and direct access to forgotten gate activations, LSTMs leverage an additive gradient structure to induce desirable behaviour from the error gradient. A gated recurrent unit, or GRU, manages data similarly to an LSTM structure without a memory unit using two gates. In RNN, LSTM is a more effective representation since it may expose classified information while dispensing with control strategies.

Research Objective

- One paragraph and a phrase are deep learned using RNNs and LSTMs.
- RNN creation tools are incorporated into TensorFlow.
- We trained RNN, LSTM, and GRU to build a language model.
- comparing models to evaluate the output of text creation.
- A language model that can automatically assemble sentences word-by-word while matching the final word with the series of preceding words was developed using RNNs, LSTMs, and GRUs.

- The goal of the project is to generate sentences using various RNNs and a language model. The method consists of two steps: sampling to produce output text and training RNNs, LSTMs, and GRUs on diverse datasets. To identify which network generates the most realistic text, output texts will be contrasted. Investigated will be the variation in training loss over iterations.
- This research focuses on the pre-processing methods used in Language, which are affected by a number of languages including Hindi, Sanskrit, Arabic, and English.

Methodology Framework

Text generation and development techniques are used in machine translation, abstraction, summarization, and human-computer interaction. Sentences are structured as a model of estimating language in statistical machine translation, and natural surfaces have been employed for a generation.

The suggested study recognises the importance of the Transformation approach, which uses target language corpora to distribute certain root words or exact terms to produce a full sentence representation. The language can be expressed in the following fashion if a statement designates a group of root words in a particular form of the target language as D.

Two feature extraction techniques for sequence prediction are TF-IDF and Vectorization. The Bhagwad Gomandal, a collection of 2.81 lac Language terms with their semantics, was proposed after the study examined numerous categories of sequences based on sentence structure. The second dataset was constructed using 2570 Language news headlines, each of which was given a distinct number to aid with categorization. Every 300–1000 epochs, the outcomes of deep learning models are calculated using pre-processed data.

Every 500 epochs, deep learning models like RNN, LSTM, and GRU determine the average accuracy of computations using pre-processed data. Three phrases are given to the suggested model at random and forecasted in order to test it. Every 300 to 1000 epochs, the findings are computed.

DATA COLLECTION AND PROCESSING

Data Collection

More than 50 million people in Gujarat, India, speak Language as a first language. It has four general terms borrowed from Sanskrit and belongs to the Indo-Aryan language family. Adjectives match the noun's gender and number, and there are three genders and two different sorts of numerals. A Language verb's structure is [root + infinitive].

Variable for Text Sequence Model

On the basis of the suggested methodology, a solution is developed using Google Colab. The initial phase involves adding Python libraries for calculation, which is followed by text cleaning to get rid of punctuation and lowercase every word. The subsequent line's data is subsequently deleted. Tokenization is the act of dividing up big data or big concepts into smaller, more digestible chunks, such words and phrases. By looking at the word order, it is possible to comprehend context and model building for

Natural Language Processing. The function #texts to sequences turns text into a 100-line token sequence that is shown as an integer sequence(Liu et al., 2016; Rao et al., 2018).

Recurrent Neural Networks (RNNs)

A model's training accuracy is plotted by combining its output layer with Hidden Layer 1 (LSTM Layer). RNNs are deep convolutional neural networks with looped versions of the layers that repeatedly combine, multiply matrices, and perform non-linear operations. In order for a network to be recurrent, a loop must be present. For each iteration, it receives the entry of a continuous variable and returns the activations from the previous iteration(Figure 3)f. A description of the subsequent word in a phrase is the result of the final iteration and is supplied via the final tier activation function(Khan et al., 2021; Safder et al., 2020; Xu et al., 2014).

RNNs are excellent in text-related tasks like time series forecasting, text classification, text production, and sequence labelling. For these activities, NLP is employed. With an internal memory that enables more precise word prediction inside phrases, OpenAI's GPT-2 algorithm has changed text output. Due to its recurrent nature, RNN architecture is a strong option for sequential information processing. A fixed vector value that is formed by feeding token values to the recurrent model represents each text sequence. For natural language processing tasks, recent RNN models have gained popularity.

Recurrent neural networks (RNNs) are employed in a number of fields, including the creation of dialogue, music, and text sequences. RNNs are limited in that they can't keep data in memory for very long, which leads to instability. However, if the network is used on a few of the most recent inputs, it may use prior predictions and learn from its failures. The RNN model has been trained by some researchers to look for long-term dependencies. Sequential modelling is used by RNN models to identify the structure of letters, words, or phrases. A phrase's individual words each provide semantic or meaningful information that is impacted by the words that came before it. For instance, adjective-starting nouns have a distinct meaning than those that come before them(Tai et al., 2015).

Since RNN creates a more effective semantic representation and includes a summary function that enhances machine translation efficiency, it is better suited for NLP jobs that call for any length of text,

Figure 3. Recurrent neural networks

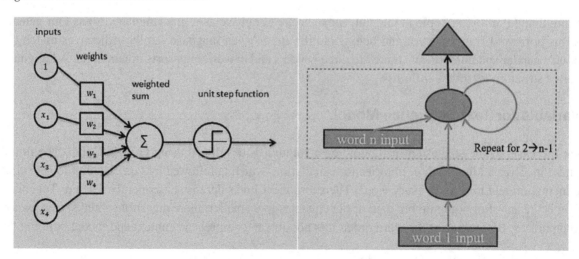

phrases, or paragraphs. Recent studies have favoured CNN architecture over RNN design. By analysing text patterns and examining the connections between current and previous text, GRU and LSTM were able to get over the limitations of basic RNN design.

Long Short-Term Memory (LSTM) Model

LSTMs are a sort of recurrent neural network that can handle long-term dependencies and store network knowledge over time. LSTMs were invented in 1997, and many researchers have worked to enhance them since then. Although the chain architecture of LSTM and RNN is similar, the gated units differ. The LSTM gate unit's three gates are used to store and remove previous information based on model inputs. The gates described above contain sigmoid functions, which are similar to tanh activation in that they set values to a range of 0 to 1, enabling the model to reject or recall input. If the output is less than one and more than zero, the model will keep it(Palangi et al., 2016; Rao et al., 2018; Zhu et al., 2018).

Forget Gate: The sigmoid function filters data in the 0 to 1 range, with values closer to 1 being eliminated and values closer to 0 being preserved by the model.

Input Gate: The tanh function returns values ranging from -1 to 1, which are then sent to the sigmoid function, which decides whether to keep or discard the information from the tanh output.

Output Gate: The last gate of the LSTM cell determines the next hidden state by applying the sigmoid and tanh functions to pass the cell state and get the next hidden layer data.

Cell Status: The forget vector will be multiplied by the cell state of the forget gate, and the data from the input gate will be added point-by-point to update and make the network relevant.

In RNN architecture, LSTM overcomes the lengthy dependence and vanishing gradient problem with an additional gate dubbed the "Forget Gate," which is beneficial for backpropagation with any number of time-driven steps. It consists of three gates: input, output, and forget. All three gates are handled by the Sigmoid function, with the input value Xt representing the concealed value, Pt representing each prior value, and the tanh function storing intermediate-level replies in Qt.

Gated Recurrent Unit (GRU) Model

GRU (Gated Recurrent Units) are a newer RNN generation that is comparable to LSTMs but does not have a cell state or the three gates that LSTMs have. Data is processed by two gates: Reset and Update(Das & Majumder, 2017; Jia et al., 2015; Matsumori et al., 2023).

Reset Gate: The Reset Gate governs how old and new data should be combined and contains a sigmoid function that transforms numbers between 0 and 1. It multiplies hidden state weights by the current input and preceding hidden state, then sums the results and passes them to the sigmoid function.

Update Gate: The gate, like the LSTM's input and forget gate combination, regulates the network's term memory. GRU is a gated recurrent unit composed of two gates: a reset gate and an update gate that manage the full data flow in the same way that an LSTM structure without a memory unit does. Unlike the LSTM structure, it is a more sophisticated RNN representation.

Dataset

The Experiments presented a set of over 2 lac Language words corpus and 2570 Language news headlines using a single organized database. All punctuation signals and special characters from other languages were eliminated, leaving just 853 Language stop words. The suggested model considered 853 Language stop words in total. Here is a selection of Language news headlines.

When it comes to learning grammar and semantic representations and creating more effective sentences, LSTMs outperform other RNN units. Two networks outperform unidirectional RNN networks in terms of fundamental overall scores. For describing the bidirectional flow of hidden vectors and constructing coherent sentence word groupings, the latent position is critical. To create a more advanced model, researchers created a new reference vector after every ten counts. The inference model is used to calculate the network formation weight matrix. Experiment Dataset Characteristics are essential for comprehending a dataset's properties.

RESULTS AND DISCUSSION

Perplexity

Perplexity is a significant component in confusion selection since it assists us in selecting the finest models from a wide number of options. It can also be effective in cases when resources are few, as additional assessment indicators would be costly and time-consuming. This might cause other programs to lag, which is undesirable.

Hyper-parameter Tuning: To enhance predictions, neural networks must be trained with new parameters.

Model Development: Python is a free and open-source programming language that excels in machine learning and deep learning by providing libraries for implementing various algorithms.

Master Model: The LSTM and GRU models were trained with various parameters, using training durations of 6 and 4 hours for 10 epochs, respectively, and a learning rate of 0.01. With prediction periods of 14 and 10 ms, respectively, both models had an accuracy of 0.8762 and 0.7504.

Machine Learning Models: The efficacy of a machine learning system may be measured using a variety of measures and criteria. True positives (tp) are outcomes in which the model predicts the positive class correctly, true negatives (tn) are outcomes in which the model predicts the negative class correctly, false positives (fp) are outcomes in which the model incorrectly predicts the positive class, and false negatives (fn) are outcomes in which the model incorrectly predicts the negative class.

Accuracy: Accuracy is defined as the fraction of right classifications produced out of all classifications made, although it does not work with stable datasets due to a huge class discrepancy. Because of the impact of highly populated classes, the Equilibrium accuracy metric is utilized to achieve extraordinary precision.

Precision: Precision is calculated by dividing the proportion of relevant criteria supplied in the positive class by the number of correctly categorized items, making it a useful indication in instances where false positives are a concern.

Recall: The capacity of the estimator to recognize things that should be categorized favourably is critical for finding the positive class.

AUC-ROC Curve: The Receiver Operator Characteristic (ROC) curve is a binary classification issue evaluation metric that presents True Positive against False Positive at various threshold levels. The AUC is a summary of the ROC curve that indicates a classifier's ability to differentiate across classes. AUC greater than one implies superior performance.

Deep Learning models are trained using datasets, and the evaluation metrics produced by each model are reviewed. The Receiver Operator Characteristic (ROC) curve is a binary classification issue evaluation metric that presents True Positive against False Positive at various threshold levels. The AUC is a summary of the ROC curve that indicates a classifier's ability to differentiate across classes. GRU (Gated Recurrent Units) are a newer RNN generation that is comparable to LSTMs but does not have a cell state or the three gates that LSTMs have. For 50 epochs, the accuracy and loss of the LSTM and GRU models are compared. Because the accuracy of LSTM is higher than that of GRU for all epochs compared, it is preferable to adopt the LSTM model. Because the loss of LSTM is smaller than that of GRU for all comparison epochs, it is preferable to employ the LSTM model.

Based on text creation and a trained deep learning model, deep learning models are used to anticipate the following words in Language Kavitas and Gazals. To evaluate the cost, we trained LSTM and GRU deep learning models for 500 epochs and employed an optimization strategy such as Gradient Descent, RMSprop, or the Adam optimizer to translate projected labels to actual labels. The Adam optimizer produces better results than any other optimization methods, has shorter calculation times, and requires less tuning parameters.

The text synthesis process has been reduced to a prediction issue. To make predictions, a model must be given an initial phrase or sentence to analyze and utilize to generate computational predictions based on the corpus of text on which it was trained. The system predicts the token for the next word, transforms it back to the original word, and displays the entire anticipated string. Deep learning models can generate unique phrases and informed words, but Natural Language Processing has progressed significantly. It can aid deep learning models in comprehending emotion and predicting unknown sentences for a given sequence.

When taking epochs 500 times, the accuracy increases by one. When the LSTM model reaches 300 epochs, it gradually gains accuracy and lowers loss, with accuracy approaching 1 and loss approaching 0. When epochs exceed 100, the GRU model improves its accuracy, outperforming the LSTM when compared to 500 epochs. When reaching 100 epochs, the GRU model improves its accuracy, which is deemed a superior outcome than the LSTM when reaching 300 epochs. This is because epochs are calculated 500 times. When reaching 100 epochs, the GRU model reduces its loss, which is deemed a superior outcome than the LSTM when reaching 300 epochs.

Sentence completion models are built with LSTM and GRU networks, while the output sequence is built with the record detection technique. The following are examples of summaries built with the base model. After 500 epochs, we discovered that GRU outperforms LSTM for text production and prediction tasks. This is due to the increasing number of running epochs.

OPEN-CLOZE QUESTION GENERATION

Open-ended questions test more productive knowledge than other types of objective questions, but multiple-choice questions test less productive information. This chapter provides a hint-based method for making open-ended questions easier to answer, as well as a scoring mechanism for assessing and ranking learners (Figure 4). To assess a learner's grammar, vocabulary, and subject understanding, questions are developed. Factual queries arise from informative content and necessitate a factual response. Factual questions are those that can be answered by referring to a text passage. They enable e-learning specialists to assess a learner's familiarity with the text passage and what they need to know to close the learning gap(Campbell, 2022; Das & Majumder, 2017; Matsumori et al., 2023; Pino et al., 2008).

Factual Open-Cloze Question Generation

Fill-in-the-blank questions with one or more blanks are known as open-cloze questions. They are created from sentences containing the information required to assess the learner's content-based understanding. The procedure is divided into two main steps: phrase selection, answer-key identification, and stem production(Das et al., 2021; Felice, Taslimipoor, & Buttery, 2022).

Sentence Selection

Due to the difficulties of producing complicated or compound phrases, we concentrated on generating questions from basic sentences. Sentence selection entails recognizing basic statements and choosing informative sentences to create inquiries. To detect simple sentences, sentences in the input corpus are classified into three types(Felice & Buttery, 2019; Pino & Eskenazi, 2009).

Simple Sentence: There is only one independent clause in a simple sentence and no dependent clauses.
Compound Sentence: A compound sentence has two independent clauses, but a complex sentence comprises one or more dependent clauses, which are joined together by a subordinate conjunction.
Identify Simple Sentences: Stanford Parser 1 and Core-NLP 2 use the Stanford Typed Dependency Manual and Stanford Deterministic Co-reference Resolution System to recognize simple phrases

Figure 4. Conversion of questions for making answers based on deep learning

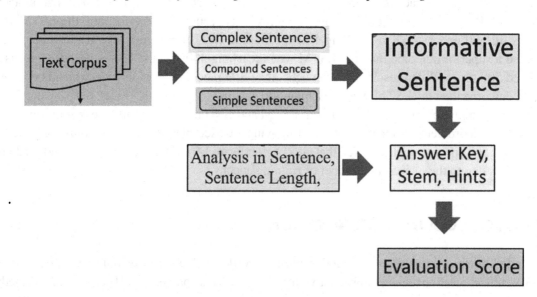

in incoming text. This chapter describes a dependency parsing approach for identifying basic statements and analyzing their dependence patterns. According to the Stanford Typed Dependency Manual, simple phrases have only one nsubj or nsubjpass (subject) and are classified as subject. Three examples of sentences were explored. A simple sentence consists of one independent clause, whereas a complex sentence consists of at least two clauses, as determined by Stanford typed dependency notations. Simple phrases contain one clause (nsubj), but complex sentences have two clauses (Bachchan joined and became) and three clauses (Bachchan joined and became) (Bachchan born and actor)(Malafeev, 2014).

Selection of Informative Sentences: By examining the Part-of-Speech tags, a novel strategy for selecting informative phrases from simple sentences is suggested (POS tags). The sentences must be no more than 25 words long and have at least two disjoint NNP/NNPS tags.

Answer-Key Identification and Stem Generation

The task of identifying a word or combination of words (multi-word) that has the potential to produce the correct response is known as answer-key identification. With a word constraint of three, a novel approach is given for identifying the multi-word answer-key from the informative phrase. There are two parts to the task: multi-word extraction and pattern search.

Multi-word Extraction: Preprocessing of the source text is performed to determine the frequency and co-occurrence of NNP/NNPS (Proper noun). The Dice-coefficient association approach is used to extract a set of multi-word keys G1 from the co-occurrence frequency, whereas set G2 includes the uni-word frequency.

Pattern Search: The main notion is that if no match is detected, the answer-key is chosen from the uni-word key with the highest frequency from G2.

Assessment and Scoring

Open-ended questions are difficult to answer, yet they assess active knowledge. Hints are offered to all examinees in order to decrease the number of potential answers. The first hint reveals the amount of words in the answer-key.

Hints for uni-word answer-key: To determine the correct answer for a uni-word answer-key, learners are provided two hints: the number of words and the first two letters.

Hints for bi-word answer-key: The bi-word answer-key has three hints: the same as the uni-word key, the last word, and comparable to the uni-word key.

Hints for tri-word answer-key: The tri-word answer-key has four hints: the same as the second hint of bi-word answer-keys, the middle word of tri-word answer-keys, and the second clue of uni-word keys. The technique is intended to guarantee that students are informed of the quantity of suggestions and words in an answer-key prior to taking the exam. A learner's score is determined by the correct answer and the number of tips required to answer the question. Uni-word keys are worth two credits, bi-word keys are worth three credits, and tri-word keys are worth four credits. Examiners may give varying or random credit dependent on the amount of difficulty.

Results Analysis

To verify the accuracy of our system, experimental data was taken from 8 Wikipedia pages, including 614 basic phrases. The algorithm classifies 131 sentences as informative, but the datasets given are insufficient for verifying it. As a result, five human language experts' average judgements are employed to analyze the validity of the statements. The algorithm picks just 131 potential sentences for open-cloze question production out of 2275 input sentences, implying that a large input corpus is required to produce enough open-cloze questions. A better pre-processing strategy can increase sentence selection accuracy. A new way for generating open-ended questions based on POS tags and patterns that does not require response keys(Felice, Taslimipoor, Andersen, et al., 2022).

FUTURE WORK

- Overall, multi-criteria optimization techniques are powerful tools for solving complex problems that involve multiple objectives and constraints. By using these techniques, decision-makers can make more informed decisions and find the best possible solution among the available alternatives(Babu et al., 2023; Boopathi, Arigela, et al., 2023; Boopathi, Jeyakumar, et al., 2022; Boopathi, Lewise, et al., 2021; Kavitha et al., 2023; Myilsamy et al., 2021; Sahal et al., n.d.).
- One of the advantages of using ANNs for text generation is their ability to capture complex patterns in the text data, which can lead to more realistic and coherent text outputs. However, training ANNs for text generation can be computationally expensive and requires large amounts of training data to achieve good results. Overall, text generation using ANNs is a promising area of research that has numerous potential applications in areas such as natural language processing, content creation, and chatbots(Boopathi, Venkatesan, et al., 2023; Domakonda et al., 2023; Kumara et al., 2023; Mohanty et al., 2023; S. et al., 2022; Selvakumar et al., 2023).
- Taguchi and response surface method can be a powerful tool for optimizing text generation systems, helping researchers and developers to create more effective and efficient natural language generation models(Boopathi, 2019; Boopathi, Balasubramani, et al., 2021; Boopathi, 2021; Boopathi, Thillaivanan, et al., 2022; Boopathi, 2022b, 2022f, 2022d, 2022e, 2022c, 2022a; Boopathi, Haribalaji, et al., 2022; Boopathi, Balasubramani, et al., 2023; Gunasekaran et al., 2022; Janardhana, Anushkannan, et al., 2023; Kannan et al., 2022; Myilsamy & Sampath, 2021; Sampath & Myilsamy, 2021; Trojovský et al., 2023; Yupapin et al., 2023).
- The combination of IoT and cloud technology offers a powerful platform for generating text content that is both scalable and highly personalized, and has the potential to transform a wide range of industries, from content marketing to customer service and beyond(Arunprasad RV, 2019; Boopathi, 2023; Boopathi, Khare, et al., 2023; Boopathi, Siva Kumar, et al., 2023; Harikaran et al., 2023; Janardhana, Singh, et al., 2023; Palaniappan et al., 2023; Reddy et al., 2023; Samikannu et al., 2023; Sampath et al., 2022; Senthil et al., 2023; Vanitha et al., 2023; Vennila et al., 2023). In recent years, evolutionary algorithms such as Genetic Algorithms (GA), Particle Swarm Optimization (PSO), and Differential Evolution (DE) have gained popularity as effective multi-criteria optimization techniques. These algorithms use the concept of natural selection to iteratively search for the optimal solution in a large search space.

SUMMARY

This work gives a set of more sophisticated processes for implementing Language Linguistics structural and sequential rules using NLP. It analyses text processing challenges such as ambiguity reduction, foreign language detection, stop words, and un annotation task finding, and finds that the LSTM model outperforms the GRU model based on obtained results. Word prediction is critical for speeding up typing and decreasing mistakes, and Language requires a customized, predictive input text system. For this research, three algorithms were chosen: LSTM, GRU, and hybrid. The final result was picked because of its capacity to create not just the next word, but also a few words, a whole phrase, or numerous sentences in Language. Cloze questions involve distractors and alternative replies, whereas open-cloze questions include instructional sentences with one or more gaps. This thesis presents two unique methods for producing simple and reliable distractors for computer-aided tests.

Limitation: Data-driven decision-making procedures are not always required, and other statistical methodologies outperform the hybrid approach since it is responsible for data collection and cleansing. The model's performance may vary based on the data's quality or kind. Improvements should be made to graphing and word form prepositional phrases, as well as a tool to personalize the system and obtain more accurate assessments of noted data.

REFERENCES

Abujar, S., Hasan, M., & Hossain, S. A. (2019). Sentence similarity estimation for text summarization using deep learning. *Proceedings of the 2nd International Conference on Data Engineering and Communication Technology: ICDECT 2017*, (pp. 155–164). Springer. 10.1007/978-981-13-1610-4_16

Ahmad, S., Asghar, M. Z., Alotaibi, F. M., & Khan, S. (2020). Classification of poetry text into the emotional states using deep learning technique. *IEEE Access : Practical Innovations, Open Solutions*, 8, 73865–73878. doi:10.1109/ACCESS.2020.2987842

Al-Aswadi, F. N., Chan, H. Y., & Gan, K. H. (2020). Automatic ontology construction from text: A review from shallow to deep learning trend. *Artificial Intelligence Review*, 53(6), 3901–3928. doi:10.100710462-019-09782-9

Arunprasad, R. V. B. S. (2019). Alternate Refrigerants for Minimization Environmental Impacts: A Review. In *Advances in Engineering Technology,* p. 69. AkiNik Publications New Delhi. https://www.researchgate.net/publication/340939609

Babu, B. S., Kamalakannan, J., Meenatchi, N., M, S. K. S., S, K., & Boopathi, S. (2023). Economic impacts and reliability evaluation of battery by adopting Electric Vehicle. *IEEE Explore*, 1–6. doi:10.1109/ICPECTS56089.2022.10046786

Boopathi, S. (2019). Experimental investigation and parameter analysis of LPG refrigeration system using Taguchi method. *SN Applied Sciences*, 1(8), 892. doi:10.100742452-019-0925-2

Boopathi, S. (2021). Improving of Green Sand-Mould Quality using Taguchi Technique. *Journal of Engineering Research*. doi:10.36909/jer.14079

Boopathi, S. (2022a). An experimental investigation of Quench Polish Quench (QPQ) coating on AISI 4150 steel. *Engineering Research Express*, *4*(4), 45009. doi:10.1088/2631-8695/ac9ddd

Boopathi, S. (2022b). An Extensive Review on Sustainable Developments of Dry and Near-Dry Electrical Discharge Machining Processes. *Journal of Manufacturing Science and Engineering*, *144*(5), 50801. doi:10.1115/1.4052527

Boopathi, S. (2022c). An investigation on gas emission concentration and relative emission rate of the near-dry wire-cut electrical discharge machining process. *Environmental Science and Pollution Research International*, *29*(57), 86237–86246. doi:10.100711356-021-17658-1 PMID:34837614

Boopathi, S. (2022d). Cryogenically treated and untreated stainless steel grade 317 in sustainable wire electrical discharge machining process: A comparative study. *Environmental Science and Pollution Research International*, 1–10. doi:10.100711356-022-22843-x PMID:36057706

Boopathi, S. (2022e). Experimental investigation and multi-objective optimization of cryogenic Friction-stir-welding of AA2014 and AZ31B alloys using MOORA technique. *Materials Today. Communications*, *33*, 104937. doi:10.1016/j.mtcomm.2022.104937

Boopathi, S. (2022f). Performance Improvement of Eco-Friendly Near-Dry Wire-Cut Electrical Discharge Machining Process Using Coconut Oil-Mist Dielectric Fluid. *Journal of Advanced Manufacturing Systems*, 1–20. doi:10.1142/S0219686723500178

Boopathi, S. (2023). An Investigation on Friction Stir Processing of Aluminum Alloy-Boron Carbide Surface Composite. In *Materials Horizons: From Nature to Nanomaterials* (pp. 249–257). Springer. doi:10.1007/978-981-19-7146-4_14

Boopathi, S., Arigela, S. H., Raman, R., Indhumathi, C., Kavitha, V., & Bhatt, B. C. (2023). Prominent Rule Control-based Internet of Things: Poultry Farm Management System. *IEEE Explore*, 1–6. doi:10.1109/ICPECTS56089.2022.10047039

Boopathi, S., Balasubramani, V., Kumar, R. S., & Singh, G. R. (2021). The influence of human hair on kenaf and Grewia fiber-based hybrid natural composite material: An experimental study. *Functional Composites and Structures*, *3*(4), 45011. doi:10.1088/2631-6331/ac3afc

Boopathi, S., Balasubramani, V., & Sanjeev Kumar, R. (2023). Influences of various natural fibers on the mechanical and drilling characteristics of coir-fiber-based hybrid epoxy composites. *Engineering Research Express*, *5*(1), 15002. doi:10.1088/2631-8695/acb132

Boopathi, S., Haribalaji, V., Mageswari, M., & Asif, M. M. (2022). Influences of Boron Carbide Particles on the Wear Rate and Tensile Strength of Aa2014 Surface Composite Fabricated By Friction-Stir Processing. *Materiali in Tehnologije*, *56*(3), 263–270. doi:10.17222/mit.2022.409

Boopathi, S., Jeyakumar, M., Singh, G. R., King, F. L., Pandian, M., Subbiah, R., & Haribalaji, V. (2022). An experimental study on friction stir processing of aluminium alloy (AA-2024) and boron nitride (BNp) surface composite. *Materials Today: Proceedings*, *59*(1), 1094–1099. doi:10.1016/j.matpr.2022.02.435

Boopathi, S., Khare, R., Jaya Christiyan, K. G., Muni, T. V., & Khare, S. (2023). Additive manufacturing developments in the medical engineering field. In Development, Properties, and Industrial Applications of 3D Printed Polymer Composites (pp. 86–106). IGI Global. doi:10.4018/978-1-6684-6009-2.ch006

Boopathi, S., Lewise, K. A. S., Subbiah, R., & Sivaraman, G. (2021). Near-dry wire-cut electrical discharge machining process using water-air-mist dielectric fluid: An experimental study. *Materials Today: Proceedings*, *49*(5), 1885–1890. doi:10.1016/j.matpr.2021.08.077

Boopathi, S., Siva Kumar, P. K., & Meena, R. S. J., S. I., P., S. K., & Sudhakar, M. (2023). Sustainable Developments of Modern Soil-Less Agro-Cultivation Systems. In Human Agro-Energy Optimization for Business and Industry (pp. 69–87). IGI Global. doi:10.4018/978-1-6684-4118-3.ch004

Boopathi, S., Thillaivanan, A., Azeem, M. A., Shanmugam, P., & Pramod, V. R. (2022). Experimental investigation on abrasive water jet machining of neem wood plastic composite. *Functional Composites and Structures*, *4*(2), 25001. doi:10.1088/2631-6331/ac6152

Boopathi, S., Venkatesan, G., & Anton Savio Lewise, K. (2023). Mechanical Properties Analysis of Kenaf–Grewia–Hair Fiber-Reinforced Composite. In *Lecture Notes in Mechanical Engineering* (pp. 101–110). Springer. doi:10.1007/978-981-16-9057-0_11

Campbell, C. (2022). Human-centered artificial intelligence in education: Factual open cloze question generation for assessment of learner's knowledge. *Computers and Education: Artificial Intelligence*, *2*, 10000908.

Das, B., & Majumder, M. (2017). Factual open cloze question generation for assessment of learner's knowledge. *International Journal of Educational Technology in Higher Education*, *14*(1), 1–12. doi:10.118641239-017-0060-3

Das, B., Majumder, M., Phadikar, S., & Sekh, A. A. (2021). Automatic question generation and answer assessment: A survey. *Research and Practice in Technology Enhanced Learning*, *16*(1), 1–15. doi:10.118641039-021-00151-1

Domakonda, V. K., Farooq, S., Chinthamreddy, S., Puviarasi, R., Sudhakar, M., & Boopathi, S. (2023). Sustainable Developments of Hybrid Floating Solar Power Plants. In *Human Agro-Energy Optimization for Business and Industry* (pp. 148–167). IGI Global. doi:10.4018/978-1-6684-4118-3.ch008

Felice, M., & Buttery, P. (2019). Entropy as a proxy for gap complexity in open cloze tests. *Proceedings of the International Conference on Recent Advances in Natural Language Processing (RANLP 2019)*, (pp. 323–327). Cambridge. 10.26615/978-954-452-056-4_037

Felice, M., Taslimipoor, S., Andersen, Ø. E., & Buttery, P. (2022). CEPOC: The Cambridge Exams Publishing Open Cloze dataset. *Proceedings of the Thirteenth Language Resources and Evaluation Conference*, (pp. 4285–4290). ACL.

Felice, M., Taslimipoor, S., & Buttery, P. (2022). Constructing open cloze tests using generation and discrimination capabilities of transformers. *ArXiv Preprint ArXiv:2204.07237*. doi:10.18653/v1/2022. findings-acl.100

Gunasekaran, K., Boopathi, S., & Sureshkumar, M. (2022). Analysis of a Cryogenically Cooled Near-Dry Wedm Process Using Different Dielectrics. *Materiali in Tehnologije, 56*(2), 179–186. doi:10.17222/mit.2022.397

Harikaran, M., Boopathi, S., Gokulakannan, S., & Poonguzhali, M. (2023). Study on the Source of E-Waste Management and Disposal Methods. In *Sustainable Approaches and Strategies for E-Waste Management and Utilization* (pp. 39–60). IGI Global. doi:10.4018/978-1-6684-7573-7.ch003

Janardhana, K., Anushkannan, N. K., Dinakaran, K. P., Puse, R. K., & Boopathi, S. (2023). *Experimental Investigation on Microhardness, Surface Roughness, and White Layer Thickness of Dry EDM*. Engineering Research Express. doi:10.1088/2631-8695/acce8f

Janardhana, K., Singh, V., Singh, S. N., Babu, T. S. R., Bano, S., & Boopathi, S. (2023). Utilization Process for Electronic Waste in Eco-Friendly Concrete: Experimental Study. In Sustainable Approaches and Strategies for E-Waste Management and Utilization (pp. 204–223). IGI Global.

Jia, X., Gavves, E., Fernando, B., & Tuytelaars, T. (2015). Guiding the long-short term memory model for image caption generation. *Proceedings of the IEEE International Conference on Computer Vision*, (pp. 2407–2415). IEEE. 10.1109/ICCV.2015.277

Kannan, E., Trabelsi, Y., Boopathi, S., & Alagesan, S. (2022). Influences of cryogenically treated work material on near-dry wire-cut electrical discharge machining process. *Surface Topography : Metrology and Properties, 10*(1), 15027. doi:10.1088/2051-672X/ac53e1

Kavitha, C., Geetha Malini, P. S., Charan Kantumuchu, V., Manoj Kumar, N., Verma, A., & Boopathi, S. (2023). An experimental study on the hardness and wear rate of carbonitride coated stainless steel. *Materials Today: Proceedings, 74*, 595–601. doi:10.1016/j.matpr.2022.09.524

Khan, L., Amjad, A., Ashraf, N., Chang, H.-T., & Gelbukh, A. (2021). Urdu sentiment analysis with deep learning methods. *IEEE Access : Practical Innovations, Open Solutions, 9*, 97803–97812. doi:10.1109/ACCESS.2021.3093078

Kumara, V., Mohanaprakash, T. A., Fairooz, S., Jamal, K., Babu, T., & B., S. (2023). Experimental Study on a Reliable Smart Hydroponics System. In *Human Agro-Energy Optimization for Business and Industry* (pp. 27–45). IGI Global. doi:10.4018/978-1-6684-4118-3.ch002

Liu, P., Qiu, X., & Huang, X. (2016). Recurrent neural network for text classification with multi-task learning. *ArXiv Preprint ArXiv:1605.05101*.

Malafeev, A. (2014). *Automatic generation of text-based open cloze exercises*. Analysis of Images, Social Networks and Texts: Third International Conference, AIST 2014, Yekaterinburg, Russia.

Matsumori, S., Okuoka, K., Shibata, R., Inoue, M., Fukuchi, Y., & Imai, M. (2023). Mask and Cloze: Automatic Open Cloze Question Generation using a Masked Language Model. *IEEE Access : Practical Innovations, Open Solutions, 11*, 9835–9850. doi:10.1109/ACCESS.2023.3239005

Mohanty, A., Venkateswaran, N., Ranjit, P. S., Tripathi, M. A., & Boopathi, S. (2023). Innovative Strategy for Profitable Automobile Industries: Working Capital Management. In Handbook of Research on Designing Sustainable Supply Chains to Achieve a Circular Economy (pp. 412–428). IGI Global.

Myilsamy, S., Boopathi, S., & Yuvaraj, D. (2021). A study on cryogenically treated molybdenum wire electrode. *Materials Today: Proceedings*, *45*(9), 8130–8135. doi:10.1016/j.matpr.2021.02.049

Myilsamy, S., & Sampath, B. (2021). Experimental comparison of near-dry and cryogenically cooled near-dry machining in wire-cut electrical discharge machining processes. *Surface Topography : Metrology and Properties*, *9*(3), 35015. doi:10.1088/2051-672X/ac15e0

Palangi, H., Deng, L., Shen, Y., Gao, J., He, X., Chen, J., Song, X., & Ward, R. (2016). Deep sentence embedding using long short-term memory networks: Analysis and application to information retrieval. *IEEE/ACM Transactions on Audio, Speech, and Language Processing*, *24*(4), 694–707. doi:10.1109/TASLP.2016.2520371

Palaniappan, M., Tirlangi, S., Mohamed, M. J. S., Moorthy, R. M. S., Valeti, S. V., & Boopathi, S. (2023). Fused deposition modelling of polylactic acid (PLA)-based polymer composites: A case study. In Development, Properties, and Industrial Applications of 3D Printed Polymer Composites (pp. 66–85). IGI Global. doi:10.4018/978-1-6684-6009-2.ch005

Pino, J., & Eskenazi, M. (2009). Measuring Hint Level in Open Cloze Questions. *FLAIRS Conference*.

Pino, J., Heilman, M., & Eskenazi, M. (2008). A selection strategy to improve cloze question quality. *Proceedings of the Workshop on Intelligent Tutoring Systems for Ill-Defined Domains. 9th International Conference on Intelligent Tutoring Systems, Montreal, Canada*, (pp. 22–32). Research Gate.

Prabha, M. I., & Srikanth, G. U. (2019). Survey of sentiment analysis using deep learning techniques. *2019 1st International Conference on Innovations in Information and Communication Technology (ICIICT)*, 1–9.

Rao, G., Huang, W., Feng, Z., & Cong, Q. (2018). LSTM with sentence representations for document-level sentiment classification. *Neurocomputing*, *308*, 49–57. doi:10.1016/j.neucom.2018.04.045

Raza, H., Faizan, M., Hamza, A., Ahmed, M., & Akhtar, N. (2019). Scientific text sentiment analysis using machine learning techniques. *International Journal of Advanced Computer Science and Applications*, *10*(12). doi:10.14569/IJACSA.2019.0101222

Reddy, M. A., Reddy, B. M., Mukund, C. S., Venneti, K., Preethi, D. M. D., & Boopathi, S. (2023). Social Health Protection During the COVID-Pandemic Using IoT. In *The COVID-19 Pandemic and the Digitalization of Diplomacy* (pp. 204–235). IGI Global. doi:10.4018/978-1-7998-8394-4.ch009

S., P. K., Sampath, B., R., S. K., Babu, B. H., & N., A. (2022). Hydroponics, Aeroponics, and Aquaponics Technologies in Modern Agricultural Cultivation. In *Trends, Paradigms, and Advances in Mechatronics Engineering* (pp. 223–241). IGI Global. doi:10.4018/978-1-6684-5887-7.ch012

Safder, I., Hassan, S.-U., Visvizi, A., Noraset, T., Nawaz, R., & Tuarob, S. (2020). Deep learning-based extraction of algorithmic metadata in full-text scholarly documents. *Information Processing \& Management, 57*(6), 102269.

Saha1, B. C., R, D., A, A., Thrinath, B. V. S., Boopathi, S., J. R., & Sudhakar, M. (n.d.). *IOT BASED SMART ENERGY METER FOR SMART GRID*. Research Gate.

Samikannu, R., Koshariya, A. K., Poornima, E., Ramesh, S., Kumar, A., & Boopathi, S. (2023). Sustainable Development in Modern Aquaponics Cultivation Systems Using IoT Technologies. In *Human Agro-Energy Optimization for Business and Industry* (pp. 105–127). IGI Global. doi:10.4018/978-1-6684-4118-3.ch006

Sampath, B., & Myilsamy, S. (2021). Experimental investigation of a cryogenically cooled oxygen-mist near-dry wire-cut electrical discharge machining process. *Strojniski Vestnik. Jixie Gongcheng Xuebao*, *67*(6), 322–330. doi:10.5545v-jme.2021.7161

Sampath, B. C. S., & Myilsamy, S. (2022). Application of TOPSIS Optimization Technique in the Micro-Machining Process. In Trends, Paradigms, and Advances in Mechatronics Engineering (pp. 162–187). IGI Global. doi:10.4018/978-1-6684-5887-7.ch009

Selvakumar, S., Adithe, S., Isaac, J. S., Pradhan, R., Venkatesh, V., & Sampath, B. (2023). A Study of the Printed Circuit Board (PCB) E-Waste Recycling Process. In Sustainable Approaches and Strategies for E-Waste Management and Utilization (pp. 159–184). IGI Global.

Senthil, T. S. R. Ohmsakthi vel, Puviyarasan, M., Babu, S. R., Surakasi, R., & Sampath, B. (2023). Industrial Robot-Integrated Fused Deposition Modelling for the 3D Printing Process. In Development, Properties, and Industrial Applications of 3D Printed Polymer Composites (pp. 188–210). IGI Global. doi:10.4018/978-1-6684-6009-2.ch011

Sharif, O., Hoque, M. M., Kayes, A. S. M., Nowrozy, R., & Sarker, I. H. (2020). Detecting suspicious texts using machine learning techniques. *Applied Sciences (Basel, Switzerland)*, *10*(18), 6527. doi:10.3390/app10186527

Tai, K. S., Socher, R., & Manning, C. D. (2015). Improved semantic representations from tree-structured long short-term memory networks. *ArXiv Preprint ArXiv:1503.00075*. doi:10.3115/v1/P15-1150

Trojovský, P., Dhasarathan, V., & Boopathi, S. (2023). Experimental investigations on cryogenic friction-stir welding of similar ZE42 magnesium alloys. *Alexandria Engineering Journal*, *66*(1), 1–14. doi:10.1016/j.aej.2022.12.007

Vanitha, S. K. R., & Boopathi, S. (2023). Artificial Intelligence Techniques in Water Purification and Utilization. In *Human Agro-Energy Optimization for Business and Industry* (pp. 202–218). IGI Global. doi:10.4018/978-1-6684-4118-3.ch010

Vennila, T., Karuna, M. S., Srivastava, B. K., Venugopal, J., Surakasi, R., & B., S. (2023). New Strategies in Treatment and Enzymatic Processes. In *Human Agro-Energy Optimization for Business and Industry* (pp. 219–240). IGI Global. doi:10.4018/978-1-6684-4118-3.ch011

Xu, C., Xie, L., Huang, G., Xiao, X., Chng, E. S., & Li, H. (2014). A deep neural network approach for sentence boundary detection in broadcast news. *Fifteenth Annual Conference of the International Speech Communication Association*. ISCA. 10.21437/Interspeech.2014-599

Yupapin, P., Trabelsi, Y., Nattappan, A., & Boopathi, S. (2023). Performance Improvement of Wire-Cut Electrical Discharge Machining Process Using Cryogenically Treated Super-Conductive State of Monel-K500 Alloy. *Iranian Journal of Science and Technology. Transaction of Mechanical Engineering*, *47*(1), 267–283. doi:10.100740997-022-00513-0

Zhang, R., & El-Gohary, N. (2021). A deep neural network-based method for deep information extraction using transfer learning strategies to support automated compliance checking. *Automation in Construction*, *132*, 103834. doi:10.1016/j.autcon.2021.103834

Zhu, W., Yao, T., Ni, J., Wei, B., & Lu, Z. (2018). Dependency-based Siamese long short-term memory network for learning sentence representations. *PLoS One*, *13*(3), e0193919. doi:10.1371/journal.pone.0193919 PMID:29513748

Zou, H., Tang, X., Xie, B., & Liu, B. (2015). Sentiment classification using machine learning techniques with syntax features. *2015 International Conference on Computational Science and Computational Intelligence (CSCI)*, (pp. 175–179). IEEE. 10.1109/CSCI.2015.44

Compilation of References

Abd Hamid, M. A. A. C., Khairuddin, M. F., Noor, N. A. M., & Mohamad, N. A. (2023). *The study on factors affecting intention to continuously use financial technology (Fintech) among Universiti Malaysia Kelantan (UMK) students post Covid-19* [Doctoral dissertation, Universiti Malaysia Kelantan].

Abdelhakim, A. S., Abou-Shouk, M., Ab Rahman, N. A. F. W., & Farooq, A. (2023). The fast-food employees' usage intention of robots: A cross-cultural study. *Tourism Management Perspectives*, *45*, 101049. doi:10.1016/j.tmp.2022.101049

Abdous, M. H. (2019). Influence of satisfaction and preparedness on online students' feelings of anxiety. *The Internet and Higher Education*, *41*, 34–44. doi:10.1016/j.iheduc.2019.01.001

Abdul-Rahim, R., Bohari, S. A., Aman, A., & Awang, Z. (2022). Benefit–Risk Perceptions of FinTech Adoption for Sustainability from Bank Consumers' Perspective: The Moderating Role of Fear of COVID-19. *Sustainability (Basel)*, *14*(14), 8357. doi:10.3390u14148357

Abrahamson, E., & Rosenkopf, L. (1993). Institutional and Competitive Bandwagons: Using Mathematical Modeling as a Tool to Explore Innovation Diffusion. *Academy of Management Review*, *18*(3), 487–517. doi:10.2307/258906

Abujar, S., Hasan, M., & Hossain, S. A. (2019). Sentence similarity estimation for text summarization using deep learning. *Proceedings of the 2nd International Conference on Data Engineering and Communication Technology: ICDECT 2017*, (pp. 155–164). Springer. 10.1007/978-981-13-1610-4_16

Accenture. (2018). The Future of Customer Experience. *Accenture*. https://www.accenture.com/us-en/insights/customer-experience/future-of-customer-experience

Adams, J. (2019, April 10). *Global Marketing Automation Spending Will Reach $25 Billion By 2023*. Forrester. https://www.forrester.com/blogs/global-marketing-automation-spending-will-reach-25-billion-by-2023/

Adeiza, A., Malek, M. A., & Ismail, N. A. (2017). An Empirical Analysis of the Influence of Entrepreneurial Orientation on Franchisees' Outlet Performance and Intention to Stay. *The Korean Journal of Franchise Management*, *8*(1), 5–18. doi:10.21871/KJFM.2017.03.8.1.5.

Adjabi, I., Ouahabi, A., Benzaoui, A., & Taleb-Ahmed, A. (2020). Past, present, and future of face recognition: A review. In Electronics (Switzerland), 9(8). doi:10.3390/electronics9081188

Aftab, J., Sarwar, H., Khan, A. H., & Kiran, A. (2019). Critical factors which impact on students' satisfaction: A study of c-learning institutes of Pakistan. *Asian Journal of Distance Education*, *14*(2), 32–46.

Ahad, Md. A. R., Paul, T., Shammi, U., & Kobashi, S. (2018). A Study on Face Detection Using Viola-Jones Algorithm for Various Backgrounds, Angels and Distances. *Applied Soft Computing*.

Ahmad, M., Muslija, A., & Satrovic, E. (2021). Does economic prosperity lead to environmental sustainability in developing economies? Environmental Kuznets curve theory. *Environmental Science and Pollution Research International*, *28*(18), 22588–22601. doi:10.100711356-020-12276-9 PMID:33420933

Ahmad, S., Asghar, M. Z., Alotaibi, F. M., & Khan, S. (2020). Classification of poetry text into the emotional states using deep learning technique. *IEEE Access : Practical Innovations, Open Solutions*, *8*, 73865–73878. doi:10.1109/ACCESS.2020.2987842

Ailawadi, K. L., Neslin, S. A., & Gedenk, K. (2001). Pursuing the value-conscious consumer: store brands versus national brand promotions. *American Marketing Association, 65*(1), 71 – 89. doi:10.1509/jmkg.65.1.71.18132

Aji, H. M., Berakon, I., & Md Husin, M. (2020). COVID-19 and e-wallet usage intention: A multigroup analysis between Indonesia and Malaysia. *Cogent Business and Management*, *7*(1), 1804181. doi:10.1080/23311975.2020.1804181

Ajzen, I. (1985). *From intentions to actions: A theory of planned behaviour*. Springer Berlin Heidelberg.

Ajzen, I., & Fishbein, M. (1975). A Bayesian analysis of attribution processes. *Psychological Bulletin*, *82*(2), 261–277. doi:10.1037/h0076477

Ajzen, I., & Fishbein, M. (1977). Attitude-behavior relations: A theoretical analysis and review of empirical research. *Psychological Bulletin*, *84*(5), 888–918. doi:10.1037/0033-2909.84.5.888

Aksami, N. M. D., & Jember, I. M. (2019). Analisis minat penggunaan layanan e-money pada masyarakat kota Denpasar. *E-Jurnal EP Unud*, *8*(9), 2439–2470.

Al-Assam, H., Sellahewa, H., & Jassim, S. (2011). Accuracy and Security Evaluation of Multi-Factor Biometric Authentication. *International Journal for Information Security Research*, *1*(1), 11–19. doi:10.20533/ijisr.2042.4639.2011.0002

Al-Aswadi, F. N., Chan, H. Y., & Gan, K. H. (2020). Automatic ontology construction from text: A review from shallow to deep learning trend. *Artificial Intelligence Review*, *53*(6), 3901–3928. doi:10.100710462-019-09782-9

Alba, J., Lynch, J., Weitz, B., Janiszewski, C., Lutz, R., Sawyer, A., & Wood, S. (1997). Interactive Home Shopping: Consumer, Retailer, and Manufacturer Incentives to Participate in Electronic Marketplaces. *Journal of Marketing*, *61*(July), 38–53. doi:10.1177/002224299706100303

Albelwi, S., & Mahmood, A. (2017). A framework for designing the architectures of deep Convolutional Neural Networks. *Entropy (Basel, Switzerland)*, *19*(6), 242. doi:10.3390/e19060242

Alderson, W., & Green, P. E. (1964). *Planning and problem solving in marketing*. RD Irwin.

Ali, M., Raza, S. A., Khamis, B., Puah, C. H., & Amin, H. (2021). How perceived risk, benefit and trust determine user Fintech adoption: A new dimension for Islamic finance. *Foresight*, *23*(4), 403–420. doi:10.1108/FS-09-2020-0095

Allen, J. (2018). The logistics of parcel delivery: Current operations and challenges facing the UK market. In M. Browne & S. Behrends (Eds.), Urban logistics: Management, policy and innovation in a economy rapidly changing environment (pp. 144–166).

Allo, M. D. G. (2020). Is the online learning good in the midst of Covid-19 Pandemic? The case of EFL learners. *Jurnal Sinestesia*, *10*(1), 1–10.

Al-Maroof, R. S., Alnazzawi, N., Akour, I. A., Ayoubi, K., Alhumaid, K., AlAhbabi, N. M., Alnnaimi, M., Thabit, S., Alfaisal, R., Aburayya, A., & Salloum, S. (2021). The Effectiveness of Online Platforms after the Pandemic: Will Face-to-Face Classes Affect Students' Perception of Their Behavioural Intention (BIU) to Use Online Platforms? *Informatics (MDPI)*, *8*(4), 83–103. doi:10.3390/informatics8040083

Al-Nawayseh, M. K. (2020). Fintech in COVID-19 and beyond: What factors are affecting customers' choice of FinTech applications? *Journal of Open Innovation*, *6*(4), 1–15. doi:10.3390/joitmc6040153

Alsmadi, A., Alfityani, A., & Alhwamdeh, L., Al_hazimeh, A., & Al-Gasawneh, J. (2022). Intentions to use FinTech in the Jordanian banking industry. *International Journal of Data and Network Science*, *6*(4), 1351–1358. doi:10.5267/j. ijdns.2022.5.016

Altinay, L., & Taheri, B. (2019). Emerging themes and theories in the sharing economy: A critical note for hospitality and tourism. *International Journal of Contemporary Hospitality Management*, *31*(2), 180–193. https://doi.org/10.1108/IJCHM-02-2018-0171. doi:10.1108/IJCHM-02-2018-0171

Alt, R., & Puschmann, T. (2012). The rise of customer-oriented banking-electronic markets are paving the way for change in the financial industry. *Electronic Markets*, *22*(4), 203–215. doi:10.100712525-012-0106-2

Alzubaidi, L., Zhang, J., Humaidi, A. J., Al-Dujaili, A., Duan, Y., Al-Shamma, O., Santamaría, J., Fadhel, M. A., Al-Amidie, M., & Farhan, L. (2021). Review of deep learning: Concepts, CNN architectures, challenges, applications, future directions. *Journal of Big Data*, *8*(1), 53. doi:10.118640537-021-00444-8 PMID:33816053

Amaghouss, J., & Zouine, M. (2022). A Critical Analysis of the Moroccan Education System's Governance in the Online Education Era. In M. Garcia (Ed.), *Socioeconomic Inclusion During an Era of Online Education* (pp. 156–176). IGI Global. doi:10.4018/978-1-6684-4364-4.ch008

Anderson, J. C., & Narus, J. A. (1990). A model of distributor firm and manufacturer firm working partnerships. *Journal of Marketing*, *54*(1), 42–58. doi:10.1177/002224299005400103

Anil, K. (2019a). *Internet and Wold Wide Web (Paper Code: MM-409/IB-419).* DDEG. https://www.ddegjust.ac.in/studymaterial/mcom/mc-201.pdf

Annie E. Casey Foundation. (2022). *What Are the Core Characteristics of Generation Z?* AECF. https://www.aecf.org/blog/what-are-the-core-characteristics-of-generation-z

Ansu-Kyeremeh, E. K., & Goosen, L. (2022). Exploring the Socioeconomic Facet of Online Inclusive Education in Ghana: The Effects of Technological Advancements in Academia. In M. Garcia (Ed.), *Socioeconomic Inclusion During an Era of Online Education* (pp. 47–66). IGI Global. doi:10.4018/978-1-6684-4364-4.ch003

Apuke, O. D., & Iyendo, T. O. (2018). University students' usage of the internet resources for research and learning: Forms of access and perceptions of utility. *Heliyon*, *4*(12), 01052. doi:10.1016/j.heliyon.2018.e01052 PMID:30582057

Arendt, L. (2008). Barriers to ICT adoption in SMEs: How to bridge the digital divide? *Journal of Systems and Information Technology*, *10*(2), 93–108. doi:10.1108/13287260810897738

Arif, A. A. (2001). Learning from the Web: Are students ready or not? *Journal of Educational Technology & Society*, *4*(4), 32–38.

Arifi, N. E. (2022, July 7). The purchasing power of Millennials and Generation Z. *Insight*. https://www.wunderman-thompson.com/insight/the-purchasing-power-of-millennials-and-generation-z#:~:text=According%20to%20two%20US%20studies,on%20their%20Generation%20X%20parents

Arunprasad, R. V. B. S. (2019). Alternate Refrigerants for Minimization Environmental Impacts: A Review. In *Advances in Engineering Technology*, p. 69. AkiNik Publications New Delhi. https://www.researchgate.net/publication/340939609

Ashraf, S., Ilyas, R., Imtiaz, M., & Ahmad, S. (2018). Impact of service quality, corporate image and perceived value on brand loyalty with presence and absence of customer satisfaction: A study of four service sectors of Pakistan. *International Journal of Academic Research in Business & Social Sciences*, *8*(2), 452–474. doi:10.6007/IJARBSS/v8-i2/3885

Astin, A. W. (1993). *What matters in college? Four critical years visited.* Jossey-Bass.

Azizan, M., Kee, Y. S., & Mohammad Idris, B. (2021). Trade Union and Job Changes in Volatile Times: A Systematic Literature Review & Future Research Agenda. *International Journal of Academic Research in Business & Social Sciences, 11*(2), 923–937. doi:10.6007/IJARBSS/v11-i2/9189

Babu, B. S., Kamalakannan, J., Meenatchi, N., M, S. K. S., S, K., & Boopathi, S. (2023). Economic impacts and reliability evaluation of battery by adopting Electric Vehicle. *IEEE Explore*, 1–6. doi:10.1109/ICPECTS56089.2022.10046786

Bagshaw, A. (2015). What is marketing automation? *Journal of Direct, Data and Digital Marketing Practice, 17*(2), 84–85. doi:10.1057/dddmp.2015.46

Bahagian Perkhidmatan Akademik, U. M. S. (2019) Course Structure Faculty of Social Science and Humanities. *Prospectus 2019.* UMS. http://bpa.ums.edu.my/images/dokumen/Prospektus/2019/3YEARS_PROGRAMME_COURSE_STRUCTURE_FKSW_BI.pdf

Balanskat, A., & Engelhardt, K. (2015). *Computing our future: Computer programming and coding.* European Schoolnet.

Baltagi, B. H. (2021). *Econometric Analysis of Panel Data.* Springer International Publishing. doi:10.1007/978-3-030-53953-5

Banerjee, S. (2017). Revisiting bank mergers: Does size matter? *Economic and Political Weekly, 52*(8), 41–48. https://scholar.google.com/scholar?hl=en&as_sdt=0,5&cluster=1175590183918343050510#d=gs_cit&t=1669143363739&u=%2Fscholar%3Fq%3Dinfo%3AbsPj8m9aJaMJ%3Ascholar.google.com%2F%26output%3Dcite%26scirp%3D0%26scfhb%3D1%26hl%3Den

Banerjee, S., & Gupta, S. (2022). Impact of digital connectivity on ease of doing business. In M. N. Almunawar, M. Z. Islam, & P. O. de Pablos (Eds.), *Digital Transformation Management* (1st ed., pp. 73–88). Routledge. doi:10.4324/9781003224532-5

Banerjee, S., Gupta, S., & Koner, S. (2022). Sustainability and Consumerism: How Green Are the Green Sectors. In P. Ordóñez de Pablos, X. Zhang, & M. N. Almunwar (Eds.), *In Handbook of Research on Green, Circular, and Digital Economies as Tools for Recovery and Sustainability* (pp. 186–206). IGI Global. doi:10.4018/978-1-7998-9664-7.ch010

Barratt, T., Goods, C., & Veen, A. (2020) ' I'm my Own Boss…': Active intermediation and 'entrepreneurial' worker agency in the Australian gig-economy. *Environment and Planning A: Economy and Space, 52*(8), 1643–1661. https://doi.org/10.1177/0308518X20914346

Barrett-Maitland, N., Barclay, C., & Osei-Bryson, K. M. (2016). Security in social networking services: A value-focused thinking exploration in understanding users' privacy and security concerns. *Information Technology for Development, 22*(3), 464–486. doi:10.1080/02681102.2016.1173002

Batat, W. (2022). What does phygital really mean? A conceptual introduction to the phygital customer experience (PHCX) framework. *Journal of Strategic Marketing*, 1–24. doi:10.1080/0965254X.2022.2059775

Bates, O., & Friday, A. (2018). Intangible commodities with free delivery [Paper presentation]. Finding the limit in digitally mediated ecommerce and workforce injustice. *Proceedings of the 2018 Workshop on Computing within Limits.* ACM. https://doi.org/10.1145/3232617.3232622

Bates, T. (2015). *Teaching in a Digital Age (Open Textbook).* Open Textbook. https://opentextbc.ca/teachinginadigitalage/

Batta, M. (2020). Machine Learning Algorithms - A Review. *International Journal of Science and Research, 9*(1), 381.

Bauer, R. A. (1960). Consumer behavior as risk taking. In *Proceedings of the 43rd National Conference of the American Marketing Association.* American Marketing Association.

Baum, K. (2009). *st: Re: STATA heteroscedasticity test*. Statalist: The Stata Listserver. https://www.stata.com/statalist/archive/2009-03/msg00776.html

Behera, M. P. C., & Dash, M. C. (2019). Digital Ecosystems: Challenges and Prospects. *International Journal of Research and Analytical Reviews*, 176-183. https://www.ijrar.org/papers/IJRAR19VP026.pdf

Behl, A., Jayawardena, N., Ishizaka, A., Gupta, M., & Shankar, A. (2022). Gamification and gigification: A multidimensional theoretical approach. *Journal of Business Research*, *139*, 1378–1393. doi:10.1016/j.jbusres.2021.09.023

Bekele, T. A. (2010). Motivation and Satisfaction in Internet-Supported Learning Environments: A Review. *Journal of Educational Technology & Society*, *13*(2), 116–127.

Beliaeva, T., Ferasso, M., Kraus, S., & Damke, E. J. (2020). Dynamics of Digital Entrepreneurship and the Innovation Ecosystem: A Multilevel Perspective. *International Journal of Entrepreneurial Behaviour & Research*, *26*(2), 266–284. doi:10.1108/IJEBR-06-2019-0397

Belk, R. (2010). Sharing. *The Journal of Consumer Research*, *36*(February), 715–734. doi:10.1086/612649

Bennett, S. (2012). Digital natives. In *Encyclopedia of cyber behavior* (pp. 212–219). IGI Global. doi:10.4018/978-1-4666-0315-8.ch018

Bennett, S., & Maton, K. (2010). Beyond the 'digital natives' debate: Towards a more nuanced understanding of students' technology experiences. *Journal of Computer Assisted Learning*, *26*(5), 321–331. doi:10.1111/j.1365-2729.2010.00360.x

Bennett, S., Maton, K., & Kervin, L. (2008). The 'digital natives' debate: A critical review of the evidence. *British Journal of Educational Technology*, *39*(5), 775–786. doi:10.1111/j.1467-8535.2007.00793.x

Bhakti, B. N., Nurfaizal, Y., & Anwar, T. (2022). Analisis Komparasi Teknik Rendering Blender Render Dan Cycles Render Pada Video Animasi 3d Tentang Alat Pencernaan Manusia. Technomedia Journal, 6(2), 188–196, 2022

Bhalla, R., Tiwari, P., & Chowdhary, N. (2021). Digital natives leading the world: paragons and values of Generation Z. In *Generation Z Marketing and Management in Tourism and Hospitality: The Future of the Industry* (pp. 3–23). Springer International Publishing. doi:10.1007/978-3-030-70695-1_1

Bharati, P., & Pramanik, A. (2020). Deep Learning Techniques—R-CNN to Mask R-CNN: A Survey. *Advances in Intelligent Systems and Computing*, *999*, 657–668. doi:10.1007/978-981-13-9042-5_56

Bhatt, D., Patel, C., Talsania, H., Patel, J., Vaghela, R., Pandya, S., Modi, K., & Ghayvat, H. (2021). Cnn variants for computer vision: History, architecture, application, challenges and future scope. In Electronics (Switzerland), 10(20). doi:10.3390/electronics10202470

BigBlueButton virtual classroom. (n.d.). https://bigbluebutton.org/

Biggs, J., & Tang, C. (2011). *Teaching for Quality Learning at University What the Student Does* (4th ed) McGraw Hill. https://cetl.ppu.edu/sites/default/files/publications/-John_Biggs_and_Catherine_Tang-_Teaching_for_Quali-BookFiorg-.pd

Bihu, R. (2022). Implications of the COVID-19 Pandemic on Higher Education in Tanzania: A Roadmap for Developing an EPRRM Contingency Plan. In M. Garcia (Ed.), *Socioeconomic Inclusion During an Era of Online Education* (pp. 68–91). IGI Global. doi:10.4018/978-1-6684-4364-4.ch004

Bisp, S. (1999). Barriers to increased market-oriented activity: What the literature suggests. *Journal of Market Focused Management*, *4*(1), 77–92. doi:10.1023/A:1009808112356

Bledsoe, W. W. (1964). The Model Method In Facial Recognition. *Panoramic Research Inc., Palo Alto, CA, Rep. PRI, 15*(47).

BNM. (2019). *List of Regulatees*. BNM.

Böcker, L., & Meelen, T. (2016). 'Sharing for People, Planet or Profit? Analysing Motivations for Intended Sharing Economy Participation.'. *Environmental Innovation and Societal Transitions, 23*, 28–39. doi:10.1016/j.eist.2016.09.004

Bolliger, D. U., & Wasilik, O. (2009). Factors influencing faculty satisfaction with online teaching and learning in higher education. *Distance Education, 30*(1), 103–116. doi:10.1080/01587910902845949

Boopathi, S. (2021). Improving of Green Sand-Mould Quality using Taguchi Technique. *Journal of Engineering Research*. doi:10.36909/jer.14079

Boopathi, S., Arigela, S. H., Raman, R., Indhumathi, C., Kavitha, V., & Bhatt, B. C. (2023). Prominent Rule Control-based Internet of Things: Poultry Farm Management System. *IEEE Explore*, 1–6. doi:10.1109/ICPECTS56089.2022.10047039

Boopathi, S., Khare, R., Jaya Christiyan, K. G., Muni, T. V., & Khare, S. (2023). Additive manufacturing developments in the medical engineering field. In Development, Properties, and Industrial Applications of 3D Printed Polymer Composites (pp. 86–106). IGI Global. doi:10.4018/978-1-6684-6009-2.ch006

Boopathi, S., Siva Kumar, P. K., & Meena, R. S. J., S. I., P., S. K., & Sudhakar, M. (2023). Sustainable Developments of Modern Soil-Less Agro-Cultivation Systems. In Human Agro-Energy Optimization for Business and Industry (pp. 69–87). IGI Global. doi:10.4018/978-1-6684-4118-3.ch004

Boopathi, S. (2019). Experimental investigation and parameter analysis of LPG refrigeration system using Taguchi method. *SN Applied Sciences, 1*(8), 892. doi:10.100742452-019-0925-2

Boopathi, S. (2022a). An experimental investigation of Quench Polish Quench (QPQ) coating on AISI 4150 steel. *Engineering Research Express, 4*(4), 45009. doi:10.1088/2631-8695/ac9ddd

Boopathi, S. (2022b). An Extensive Review on Sustainable Developments of Dry and Near-Dry Electrical Discharge Machining Processes. *Journal of Manufacturing Science and Engineering, 144*(5), 50801. doi:10.1115/1.4052527

Boopathi, S. (2022c). An investigation on gas emission concentration and relative emission rate of the near-dry wire-cut electrical discharge machining process. *Environmental Science and Pollution Research International, 29*(57), 86237–86246. doi:10.100711356-021-17658-1 PMID:34837614

Boopathi, S. (2022d). Cryogenically treated and untreated stainless steel grade 317 in sustainable wire electrical discharge machining process: A comparative study. *Environmental Science and Pollution Research International*, 1–10. doi:10.100711356-022-22843-x PMID:36057706

Boopathi, S. (2022e). Experimental investigation and multi-objective optimization of cryogenic Friction-stir-welding of AA2014 and AZ31B alloys using MOORA technique. *Materials Today. Communications, 33*, 104937. doi:10.1016/j.mtcomm.2022.104937

Boopathi, S. (2022f). Performance Improvement of Eco-Friendly Near-Dry Wire-Cut Electrical Discharge Machining Process Using Coconut Oil-Mist Dielectric Fluid. *Journal of Advanced Manufacturing Systems*, 1–20. doi:10.1142/S0219686723500178

Boopathi, S. (2023). An Investigation on Friction Stir Processing of Aluminum Alloy-Boron Carbide Surface Composite. In *Materials Horizons: From Nature to Nanomaterials* (pp. 249–257). Springer. doi:10.1007/978-981-19-7146-4_14

Boopathi, S., Balasubramani, V., Kumar, R. S., & Singh, G. R. (2021). The influence of human hair on kenaf and Grewia fiber-based hybrid natural composite material: An experimental study. *Functional Composites and Structures*, *3*(4), 45011. doi:10.1088/2631-6331/ac3afc

Boopathi, S., Balasubramani, V., & Sanjeev Kumar, R. (2023). Influences of various natural fibers on the mechanical and drilling characteristics of coir-fiber-based hybrid epoxy composites. *Engineering Research Express*, *5*(1), 15002. doi:10.1088/2631-8695/acb132

Boopathi, S., Haribalaji, V., Mageswari, M., & Asif, M. M. (2022). Influences of Boron Carbide Particles on the Wear Rate and Tensile Strength of Aa2014 Surface Composite Fabricated By Friction-Stir Processing. *Materiali in Tehnologije*, *56*(3), 263–270. doi:10.17222/mit.2022.409

Boopathi, S., Jeyakumar, M., Singh, G. R., King, F. L., Pandian, M., Subbiah, R., & Haribalaji, V. (2022). An experimental study on friction stir processing of aluminium alloy (AA-2024) and boron nitride (BNp) surface composite. *Materials Today: Proceedings*, *59*(1), 1094–1099. doi:10.1016/j.matpr.2022.02.435

Boopathi, S., Lewise, K. A. S., Subbiah, R., & Sivaraman, G. (2021). Near-dry wire-cut electrical discharge machining process using water-air-mist dielectric fluid: An experimental study. *Materials Today: Proceedings*, *49*(5), 1885–1890. doi:10.1016/j.matpr.2021.08.077

Boopathi, S., Thillaivanan, A., Azeem, M. A., Shanmugam, P., & Pramod, V. R. (2022). Experimental investigation on abrasive water jet machining of neem wood plastic composite. *Functional Composites and Structures*, *4*(2), 25001. doi:10.1088/2631-6331/ac6152

Boopathi, S., Venkatesan, G., & Anton Savio Lewise, K. (2023). Mechanical Properties Analysis of Kenaf–Grewia–Hair Fiber-Reinforced Composite. In *Lecture Notes in Mechanical Engineering* (pp. 101–110). Springer. doi:10.1007/978-981-16-9057-0_11

Borazon, E. Q., Huang, Y. C., & Liu, J. M. (2022). Green market orientation and organizational performance in Taiwan's electric and electronic industry: The mediating role of green supply chain management capability. *Journal of Business and Industrial Marketing*, *37*(7), 1475–1496. doi:10.1108/JBIM-07-2020-0321

Botsman, R. (2015). *Where does loyalty lie in the Collaborative Economy?* Collaborative.

Bozkurt, A., & Sharma, R. C. (2020). Emergency remote teaching in a time of global crisis due to CoronaVirus pandemic. *Asian Journal of Distance Education*, *15*(1), 1–4.

Brancheau, J. C., & Wetherbe, J. C. (1987). Key Issues in Information Systems Management. *Management Information Systems Quarterly*, *11*(1), 23–45. doi:10.2307/248822

Brodzik, C., Cuthill, S., Young, N., & Drake, N. (2021, October 19). Authentically inclusive marketing - Winning future customers with diversity, equity, and inclusion. *Deloitte*. https://www2.deloitte.com/us/en/insights/topics/marketing-and-sales-operations/global-marketing-trends/2022/diversity-and-inclusion-in-marketing.html

Brundtland. (1987). *Measuring Sustainable Development | Department of Economic and Social Affairs*. SDGS. https://sdgs.un.org/publications/measuring-sustainable-development-17620

Bryman, A., & Bell, E. (2007). *Business research methods. 2*. Oxford University Press.

Bulian, L. (2021). THE GIG IS UP: WHO DOES GIG ECONOMY ACTUALLY BENEFIT? *Interdisciplinary Description of Complex Systems*, *19*(1), 106–119. doi:10.7906/indecs.19.1.9

Burton, S., Lichtenstein, D. R., Netemeyer, R. G., & Garretson, J. A. (1998). A scale for measuring attitude toward private label products and an examination of its psychological and behavioral correlates. *Journal of the Academy of Marketing Science*, *26*(1), 293–306. doi:10.1177/0092070398264003

Buschow, C. (2020). Why do digital native news media fail? An investigation of failure in the early start-up phase. *Media and Communication*, *8*(2), 51–61. doi:10.17645/mac.v8i2.2677

Butler, J. E., Ko, S., & Chamornmarn, W. (2004). Asian Entrepreneurship Research. In K. Leung & S. White (Eds.), *Handbook of Asian Management*. Springer., doi:10.1007/1-4020-7932-X_7

Butlin, J. (1989). *Our common future. By World commission on environment and development.* Oxford University Press. https://www.academia.edu/download/47184423/jid.338001020820160712-3227-xebmus.pdf

Butt, S., & Khan, Z. A. (2019). Fintech in Pakistan: A qualitative study of bank's strategic planning for an investment in fintech company and its challenges. *Independent Journal of Management & Production*, *10*(6), 2092–2101. doi:10.14807/ijmp.v10i6.947

C.C., S. & Prathap, S.K. (2020). Continuance adoption of mobile-based payments in Covid-19 context: An integrated framework of health belief model and expectation confirmation model. *International Journal of Pervasive Computing and Communications*, *16*(4), 351–369. doi:10.1108/IJPCC-06-2020-0069

Cameron, A. C., & Trivedi, P. K. (2005). *Microeconometrics: Methods and Applications.* Cambridge University Press. https://books.google.co.in/books?hl=en&lr=&id=TdlKAgAAQBAJ&oi=fnd&pg=PP1&dq=Microeconometrics:Meth ods+and+Applications&ots=yKiqJZaAxv&sig=PIxeWYTEiiY8XqVmVkcMM-m0u3k&redir_esc=y#v=onepage&q =Microeconometrics%3AMethods and Applications&f=false

Cameron, A. C., & Trivedi, P. K. (2013). Counting panel data. In B. H. Baltagi (Ed.), *The Oxford handbook of panel data* (pp. 233–256). Oxford University Press.

Camilleri, J., & Neuhofer, B. (2017). Value co-creation and co-destruction in the airbnb sharing economy. *International Journal of Contemporary Hospitality Management*, *29*(9), 2322–2340. doi:10.1108/IJCHM-09-2016-0492

Campbell, C. (2022). Human-centered artificial intelligence in education: Factual open cloze question generation for assessment of learner's knowledge. *Computers and Education: Artificial Intelligence*, *2*, 10000908.

Carr, S. (2000). As distance education comes of age, the challenge is keeping the students. *The Chronicle of Higher Education*, *46*(23), A39–A41.

Castro, F. A. O. (2022). The Asian Entrepreneurship Core in COVID-19 Period: Value Chains, Specialized Education, Massive Participation of Women and Strategic Accompaniment. *Socioeconomic Challenges*, *6*(3), 132–147. doi:10.21 272ec.6(3).132-147.2022

Cham, T. H., Ng, C. K. Y., Lim, Y. M., & Cheng, B. L. (2018). Factors influencing clothing interest and purchase intention: A study of generation Y consumers in Malaysia. *International Review of Retail, Distribution and Consumer Research*, *28*(1), 174–189. doi:10.1080/09593969.2017.1397045

Chang, I. Y., & Chang, W. Y. (2012). The effect of student learning motivation on learning satisfaction. *International Journal of Organizational Innovation*, *4*, 281–305.

Chang, Y., Wong, S. F., Lee, H., & Jeong, S. P. (2016, August). What motivates chinese consumers to adopt FinTech services: a regulatory focus theory. In *Proceedings of the 18th annual international conference on electronic commerce: e-commerce in smart connected world* (pp. 1-3). ACM. 10.1145/2971603.2971643

Chan, R., Troshani, I., Hill, S. R., & Hoffmann, A. (2022). Towards an understanding of consumers' FinTech adoption: The case of Open Banking. *International Journal of Bank Marketing*, *40*(4), 886–917. doi:10.1108/IJBM-08-2021-0397

Charlton, E. (2021). What is the gig economy and what's the deal for gig workers? World Economic Forum.

Chaudhari, M., sondur, S., & Vanjare, G. (2015). A review on Face Detection and study of Viola Jones method. *International Journal of Computer Trends and Technology*, *25*(1), 54–61. doi:10.14445/22312803/IJCTT-V25P110

Chenavaz, R. (2017). Better product quality may lead to lower product price. *The B.E. Journal of Theoretical Economics*, *17*(1), 20150062. doi:10.1515/bejte-2015-0062

Cheng, M., & Foley, C. (2018). The sharing economy and digital discrimination: The case of airbnb. *International Journal of Hospitality Management*, *70*, 95–98. doi:10.1016/j.ijhm.2017.11.002

Chen, M., Sinha, A., Hu, K., & Shah, M. I. (2021). Impact of technological innovation on energy efficiency in industry 4.0 era: Moderation of shadow economy in sustainable development. *Technological Forecasting and Social Change*, *164*, 120521. doi:10.1016/j.techfore.2020.120521

Chen, R. (2013). *Member use of social networking sites - An empirical examination.* Decision Consumption. doi:10.1016/j.dss.2012.10.028

Chen, Y., & McDonough, P. (2022). Conerference: The 1972 Stockholm Declaration at Fifty: Reflecting on a Half-century of International Environmental Law. *Georgia Journal of International and Comparative Law*, *50*(3). https://heinonline.org/hol-cgi-bin/get_pdf.cgi?handle=hein.journals/gjicl50&section=22

Chetioui, Y., Lebdaoui, H., & Chetioui, H. (2021). Factors influencing consumer attitudes toward online shopping: The mediating effect of trust. *EuroMed Journal of Business*, *16*(4), 544–563. doi:10.1108/EMJB-05-2020-0046

Cheung, C. M. K., & Lee, M. K. O. (2010). A theoretical model of intentional social action in online social network. *Decision Support Systems*, *49*(1), 24–30. doi:10.1016/j.dss.2009.12.006

Chitra, A. (2020). Impact of socio-economic status of parents' on the emotional intelligence of generation alpha kids. *International Journal of Latest Technology in Engineering, Management &. Applied Sciences (Basel, Switzerland)*, *9*(5), 46–49.

Christensen, G., & Alcorn, B. (2014). Are Free Online University Courses an Educational Panacea? *New Scientist*, *221*(2959), 24–25. doi:10.1016/S0262-4079(14)60484-X

Christie, N., & Ward, H. (2019). The health and safety risks for people who drive for work in the gig economy. *Journal of Transport & Health*, *13*, 115–127. https://doi.org/10.1016/j.jth.2019.02.007. doi:10.1016/j.jth.2019.02.007

Chuang, L. M., Liu, C. C., & Kao, H. K. (2016). The adoption of fintech service: TAM perspective. *International Journal of Management and Administrative Sciences*, *3*(7), 1–15.

Chudik, A., Pesaran, M. H., & Tosetti, E. (2011). Weak and strong cross-section dependence and estimation of large panels. *The Econometrics Journal*, *14*(1), C45–C90. doi:10.1111/j.1368-423X.2010.00330.x

Clark-Murphy, M., & Soutar, G. N. (2004). What individual investors value: Some Australian evidence. *Journal of Economic Psychology*, *25*(4), 539–555. doi:10.1016/S0167-4870(03)00056-4

Cohen, J. (1992). A power primer. *Psychological Bulletin*, *112*(1), 155–159. doi:10.1037/0033-2909.112.1.155 PMID:19565683

Cohen, J. (2013). *Statistical power analysis for the behavioral sciences*. Routledge. doi:10.4324/9780203771587

Cojoianu, T. F., Clark, G. L., Hoepner, A. G., Pažitka, V., & Wójcik, D. (2021). Fin vs. tech: Are trust and knowledge creation key ingredients in fintech start-up emergence and financing? *Small Business Economics*, *57*(4), 1715–1731. doi:10.100711187-020-00367-3

Cole, M. A., Rayner, A. J., & Bates, J. M. (1997). The environmental Kuznets curve: An empirical analysis. *Environment and Development Economics*, *2*(4), 401–416. doi:10.1017/S1355770X97000211

Commission Factory. (2022). *Marketing to Generation Alpha in Malaysia*. Commission Factory. https://blog.commissionfactory.com/ecommerce-marketing/generation-alpha-malaysia

Conceição, P. (Director and lead author) (2022). *Human development report 2021/2022. Uncertain times, unsettled lives. Shaping our future in a transforming world*. UNDP. https://hdr.undp.org/system/files/documents/global-report-document/hdr2021-22pdf_1.pdf

Cornell, J. (2019, January 14). Cultivating behavioral loyalty and attitudinal loyalty among consumers. *Zinrelo*. https://www.zinrelo.com/cultivating-behavioral-loyalty-attitudinal-loyalty.html

Crawford, I. (1997). Marketing Research and Information Systems. Food and Agriculture organization of the UN. FAO. https://www.fao.org/docrep/W3241E/W3241E00.htm [2012-04-02]

Creswell, J. W. (2003). *Research Design: Qualitative, Quantitative, and Mixed Method Approaches*. Sage Publications.

Dablanc, L. (2017). The rise of on-demand 'instant deliveries' in European cities. *Supply Chain Forum: An International Journal*, *18*(4), 203–217. https://doi.org/10.1080/16258312.2017.1375375

Dablanc, L. (2019). E-commerce trends and implications for urban logistics. In M. Browne, S. Behrends, J. Woxenius, G. Giuliano, & J. Holguin-Veras (Eds.), *Urban logistics. Management, policy, and innovation in a rapidly changing environment* (pp. 167–195).

Dadi, H. S., & Mohan Pillutla, G. K. (2016). Improved Face Recognition Rate Using HOG Features and SVM Classifier. *IOSR Journal of Electronics and Communication Engineering*, *11*(04), 34–44. doi:10.9790/2834-1104013444

Daft, R. L. (1982). Bureaucratic Versus Nonbureaucratic Structure and the Process of Innovation and Change. In S. B. Bacharach (Ed.), *Research in the Sociology of Organizations, V.(1)* (pp. 129–166). JAI Press.

Dalal, N., & Triggs, B. (2005). Histograms of oriented gradients for human detection. *Proceedings - 2005 IEEE Computer Society Conference on Computer Vision and Pattern Recognition, CVPR 2005, I*. IEEE. 10.1109/CVPR.2005.177

Damanpour, F. (1991). Organizational Innovation: A Meta-Analysis of Effects of Determinants and Moderators. *Academy of Management Journal*, *34*(3), 555–590. doi:10.2307/256406

Das, B., & Majumder, M. (2017). Factual open cloze question generation for assessment of learner's knowledge. *International Journal of Educational Technology in Higher Education*, *14*(1), 1–12. doi:10.118641239-017-0060-3

Das, B., Majumder, M., Phadikar, S., & Sekh, A. A. (2021). Automatic question generation and answer assessment: A survey. *Research and Practice in Technology Enhanced Learning*, *16*(1), 1–15. doi:10.118641039-021-00151-1

Dasgupta, S., Laplante, B., Wang, H., & Wheeler, D. (2002). Confronting the Environmental Kuznets Curve. *The Journal of Economic Perspectives*, *16*(1), 147–168. doi:10.1257/0895330027157

Dash, B., Sharma, P., Ansari, M. F., & Swayamsiddha, S. (2022). *A review of ONDC's digital warfare in India taking on the e-commerce giants*. Available at SSRN 4323963.

Dastane, O., & Haba, H. F. (2023). The landscape of digital natives research: a bibliometric and science mapping analysis. *FIIB Business Review*, 23197145221137960.

Dastane, O., Fandos-Roig, J. C., & Sánchez-García, J. (2023). It's free! Still, would I learn? Unearthing perceived value of education apps for better entrepreneurial decisions. Management Decision. doi:10.1108/MD-09-2022-1292

Dastane, O., Goi, C. L., & Rabbanee, F. (2023). The development and validation of a scale to measure perceived value of mobile commerce (MVAL-SCALE). *Journal of Retailing and Consumer Services*, *71*, 103222. doi:10.1016/j.jret-conser.2022.103222

Dastane, O., & Haba, H. F. (2023). What drives mobile MOOC's continuous intention? A theory of perceived value perspective. *International Journal of Information and Learning Technology*, *40*(2), 148–163. doi:10.1108/IJILT-04-2022-0087

Davis, F. D. (1989). Perceived usefulness, perceived ease of use, and user acceptance of information technology. *Management Information Systems Quarterly*, *13*(3), 319–340. doi:10.2307/249008

Day, G. S. (1992). Marketing's contribution to the strategy dialogue. *Journal of the Academy of Marketing Science*, *20*(4), 323–329. doi:10.1007/BF02725208

Day, G. S. (1994). The capabilities of market-driven organizations. *Journal of Marketing*, *58*(4), 37–52. doi:10.1177/002224299405800404

De Stefano, V. (2015). The rise of the 'just-in-time workforce': On-demand work, crowdwork and labour protection in the 'gig economy. *International Labour Office*, *13*(01).

Decouz, H. (n.d). Loyalty programs are failing to engage consumers. *Sogeti*. https://www.sogeti.com/explore/reports/reinventing-loyalty-programs-for-the-digital-age/

Decree of the President of the Republic of Uzbekistan (2019). *Concept of development of the system of higher education of the Republic of Uzbekistan till 2030*. DP-5847 08.10.2019.

Decree of the President of the Republic of Uzbekistan (2020a). *Digital Development Strategy of Uzbekistan until 2030*. DP-6079, 05. doi:10.2020.https://lex.uz/en/docs/5031048

Decree of the President of the Republic of Uzbekistan. (2020b). *On the State Program for the Implementation of the Strategy of Actions in five priority areas for the development of the Republic of Uzbekistan in 2017 - 2021 in the "Year of the Development of Science, Education, and the Digital Economy."* DP-5953 02.03.2020. https://lex.uz/ru/docs/-4751561

Delgado-Ballester, E., Munuera-Alemán, J. L., & Yagüe-Guillén, M. J. (2003). Development and validation of a brand trust scale. *International Journal of Market Research*, *45*(1), 35–53. doi:10.1177/147078530304500103

Deloitte. (2021, October 19). *Authentically inclusive marketing*. https://www2.deloitte.com/xe/en/insights/topics/marketing-and-sales-operations/global-marketing-trends/2022/diversity-and-inclusion-in-marketing.html

Deshpandé, R., Farley, J. U., & Webster, F. E. Jr. (1993). Corporate culture, customer orientation, and innovativeness in Japanese firms: A quadrad analysis. *Journal of Marketing*, *57*(1), 23–37. doi:10.1177/002224299305700102

Dess, G. G., & Origer, N. (1987). Environment, Structure, and Consensus in Strategy Formulation: A Conceptual Integration. *Academy of Management Review*, *12*(2), 313–330. doi:10.2307/258538

Digital Marketing Overview: Types, Challenges, and Required Skills. (2022, June 23). Investopedia. https://www.investopedia.com/terms/d/digital-marketing.asp

DiMaggio, P., & Powell, W. W. (1983). The Iron Cage Revisited: Institutional Isomorphism and Collective Rationality in Organizational Fields. *American Sociological Review*, *48*(2), 147–160. doi:10.2307/2095101

Dinda, S. (2004). Environmental Kuznets Curve Hypothesis: A Survey. *Ecological Economics*, *49*(4), 431–455. doi:10.1016/j.ecolecon.2004.02.011

Dingli, A., & Seychell, D. (2015). *The new digital natives*. JB Metzler. doi:10.1007/978-3-662-46590-5

Diversityintech. (2018, October 1). *Top 20 survey questions for measuring inclusion at work*. https://www.diversityintech.co.uk/top-20-survey-questions-for-measuring-inclusion-at-work

Domakonda, V. K., Farooq, S., Chinthamreddy, S., Puviarasi, R., Sudhakar, M., & Boopathi, S. (2023). Sustainable Developments of Hybrid Floating Solar Power Plants. In *Human Agro-Energy Optimization for Business and Industry* (pp. 148–167). IGI Global. doi:10.4018/978-1-6684-4118-3.ch008

DOSM. (2021). Current population estimates, Malaysia. *Department of Statistics Malaysia*. https://www.dosm.gov.my/v1/index.php?r=column/pdfPrev&id=ZjJOSnpJR21sQWVUcUp6ODRudm5JZz09#:~:text=Malaysia's%20population%20in%202021%20is,to%202.7%20million%20(2021)%20

Doyle, P. (2000). Value-based marketing. *Journal of Strategic Marketing*, *8*(4), 299–311. doi:10.1080/096525400446203

Durr, M. (2020). *World Health Organization says cash may contribute to spread of coronavirus, promotes paperless spending* [WWW Document]. M Live. https://www.mlive.com/coronavirus/2020/03/world-health-organizationsays-cash-may-contribute-to-spread-of-coronavirus-promotes-paperlessspending.html (accessed 12.1.22).

Du, Y., & Wang, H. (2022). Green innovation sustainability: How green market orientation and absorptive capacity matter? *Sustainability (Basel)*, *14*(13), 8192. doi:10.3390u14138192

Elad, N. (2022). TikTok, Facebook & Generation Alpha Will Shape The Future Of.... *Forbes*. https://www.forbes.com/sites/eladnatanson/2022/06/28/tiktok-facebook--generation-alpha-will-shape-the-future-of-social-shopping/

Elliott, K., & Healy, M. (2001). Key factors influencing student satisfaction related to recruitment and retention. *Journal of Marketing for Higher Education*, *10*(4), 1–11. doi:10.1300/J050v10n04_01

Elliott, K., & Shin, D. (2002). Student satisfaction: An alternative approach to assessing this Important Concept. *Journal of Higher Education Policy and Management*, *24*(2), 197–209. doi:10.1080/1360080022000013518

Epsilon. (2019). *The Power of Personalization*. Epsilon. https://www.epsilon.com/insights/the-power-of-personalization/

Erdumlu, N., Saricam, C., Tufekyapan, M., Cetinkaya, M., & Donmez, A. C. (2017). Analysing the consumer behaviour and the influence of brand loyalty in purchasing sportswear products. *Proceedings of IOP Conference Series: Materials Science and Engineering*, *254*(17), 172010. 10.1088/1757-899X/254/17/172010

Evans, C., & Robertson, W. (2020). The four phases of the digital natives debate. *Human Behavior and Emerging Technologies*, *2*(3), 269–277. doi:10.1002/hbe2.196

Evans, D. S., & Schmalensee, R. (2016). *Matchmakers: The New Economics of Multisided Platforms*. Harvard Business Review Press.

Fan, X., Ning, N., & Deng, N. (2020). The impact of the quality of intelligent experience on smart retail engagement. *Marketing Intelligence & Planning*, *38*(7), 877–891. doi:10.1108/MIP-09-2019-0439

Fasae, J. K., & Adegbilero-Iwari, I. (2015). Mobile devices for academic practices by students of college of science in selected Nigerian private universities. *The Electronic Library*, *33*(4), 749–759. doi:10.1108/EL-03-2014-0045

Fauziah, Z., Latifah, H., Omar, X., Khoirunisa, A., & Millah, S. (2020). Application of Blockchain Technology in Smart Contracts: A Systematic Literature Review [ATT]. *Aptisi Transactions on Technopreneurship*, *2*(2), 160–166. doi:10.34306/att.v2i2.97

Felice, M., Taslimipoor, S., & Buttery, P. (2022). Constructing open cloze tests using generation and discrimination capabilities of transformers. *ArXiv Preprint ArXiv:2204.07237*. doi:10.18653/v1/2022.findings-acl.100

Felice, M., & Buttery, P. (2019). Entropy as a proxy for gap complexity in open cloze tests. *Proceedings of the International Conference on Recent Advances in Natural Language Processing (RANLP 2019)*, (pp. 323–327). Cambridge. 10.26615/978-954-452-056-4_037

Felice, M., Taslimipoor, S., Andersen, Ø. E., & Buttery, P. (2022). CEPOC: The Cambridge Exams Publishing Open Cloze dataset. *Proceedings of the Thirteenth Language Resources and Evaluation Conference*, (pp. 4285–4290). ACL.

Felton, A. P. (1959). Making the marketing concept work. *Harvard Business Review, 37*, 55–65.

Fetters, M. D., Curry, L. A., & Creswell, J. W. (2013). Achieving integration in mixed methods designs – principles and practices. *Health Services Research, 48*(6pt2), 2134–2156. doi:10.1111/1475-6773.12117 PMID:24279835

FFIEC. (2011). Authentication in an Internet Banking Environment. *Federal Financial Institutions Examination Council, 1*, 1–14.

Fincham, J. E. (2008). Response rates and responsiveness for surveys, standards, and the journal. *American Journal of Pharmaceutical Education, 72*(2), 1–3. doi:10.5688/aj720243 PMID:18483608

Fishbein, M., & Ajzen, I. (1975). *Belief, Attitude, Intention, and Behavior: An Introduction to Theory and Research.* Addison-Wesley.

Fomunyam, K. (2019). Education and the Fourth Industrial Revolution: Challenges and possibilities for engineering education. *International Journal of Mechanical Engineering, 10*(8), 271–284. https://www.academia.edu/download/60492936/IJMET_10_08_02220190905-84363-5660xl.pdf

Fornell, C., & Lacker, D. F. (1981). Evaluation structural equation models with unobserved variables and measurement error. *JMR, Journal of Marketing Research, 18*(1), 39–50. doi:10.1177/002224378101800104

Frenken, K., & Schor, J. (2017). 'Putting the Sharing Economy into Perspective.'. *Environmental Innovation and Societal Transitions, 23*, 3–10. doi:10.1016/j.eist.2017.01.003

Frenzel, A. C., Goetz, T., Lüdtke, O., Pekrun, R., & Sutton, R. (2009). Emotional transmission in the classroom: Exploring the relationship between teacher and student enjoyment. *Journal of Educational Psychology, 101*(3), 705–716. doi:10.1037/a0014695

Fu, J., & Mishra, M. (2020). The global impact of COVID-19 on FinTech adoption. *Swiss Finance Institute Research Paper*, (20-38).

Fung, A., Meadows, M., & Xu, Z. (2022a). Online Learning in Higher Education during COVID-19: A Review of Evidence. *International Journal of Educational Research, 109*, 101865. doi:10.1016/j.ijer.2021.101865

Fung, C. Y., Su, S. I., Perry, E. J., & Garcia, M. B. (2022b). Development of a Socioeconomic Inclusive Assessment Framework for Online Learning in Higher Education. In M. Garcia (Ed.), *Socioeconomic Inclusion During an Era of Online Education* (pp. 23–46). IGI Global. doi:10.4018/978-1-6684-4364-4.ch002

Gaglione, F., & Ayiine-Etigo, D. A. (2021). Resilience as an urban strategy: The role of green interventions in recovery plans. *TeMA Journal of Land Use Mobility and Environment, 14*(2), 279–284.

Ganis, M. R., & Waszkiewicz, M. (2018). Digital Communication Tools as a Success Factor of Interdisciplinary Projects. *Problemy Zarzadzania, 16*, 4(77), 85-96. doi:10.7172/1644-9584.77.5

Gerrard, P., & Cunningham, J. B. (2003). The diffusion of internet banking among Singapore consumers. *International Journal of Bank Marketing, 21*(1), 16–28. doi:10.1108/02652320310457776

Gibson, R. (2023). *International Trade Fairs and Inter-Firm Knowledge Flows: Understanding Patterns of Convergence-Divergence in the Technological Specializations of Firms.* Springer Nature. doi:10.1007/978-3-031-20557-6

Gikas, J., & Grant, M. M. (2013). Mobile computing devices in higher education: Student perspectives on learning with cellphones, smartphones & social media. *The Internet and Higher Education, 19,* 18–26. doi:10.1016/j.iheduc.2013.06.002

Gil-Arias, A., Claver, F., Práxedes, A., Villar, F. D., & Harvey, S. (2020). Autonomy support, motivational climate, enjoyment and perceived competence in physical education: Impact of a hybrid teaching games for understanding/sport education unit. *European Physical Education Review, 26*(1), 36–53. doi:10.1177/1356336X18816997

Gilliland, M. (2020). The value added by machine learning approaches in forecasting. *International Journal of Forecasting, 36*(1), 161–166. doi:10.1016/j.ijforecast.2019.04.016

Gkioulos, V., Wangen, G., Katsikas, S. K., Kavallieratos, G., & Kotzanikolaou, P. (2017). Security awareness of the digital natives. *Information (Basel), 8*(2), 42. doi:10.3390/info8020042

Glazer, R. (1991). Marketing in an Information-Intensive Environment: Strategic Implications of Knowledge as an Asset. *Journal of Marketing, 55*(October), 1–19. doi:10.1177/002224299105500401

Godoe, P., and Johansen, T. (2012). Understanding adoption of new technologies: Technology readiness and technology acceptance as an integrated concept. *Journal of European psychology students, 3*(1).

Goel, P., Kulsrestha, S., & Maurya, S. K. (2022). Fintech Unfolding: Financial Revolution in India. *Thailand and The World Economy, 40*(2), 41–51.

Gogul, K. (2021). A STUDY ON CONSUMER SATISFACTION ON UBER EATS -AN ONLINE FOOD DELIVERY SYSTEM WITH SPECIAL REFERENCE TO KALAPATTI, COIMBATORE. [IJCRT]. *International Journal of Creative Research Thoughts, 9*(4), 4890–4897.

Gold, A. H., Malhotra, A., & Segars, A. H. (2001). Knowledge management: An organizational capabilities perspective. *Journal of Management Information Systems, 18*(1), 185–214. doi:10.1080/07421222.2001.11045669

Goods, C., Veen, A., & Barratt, T. (2019). "Is your gig any good?" Analysing job quality in the Australian platform-based food-delivery sector. *The Journal of Industrial Relations, 61*(4), 502–527. doi:10.1177/0022185618817069

Government of Brazil. (2022). *The Wi-Fi Brazil program: high-speed internet to places with little or no connection.* Government of Brazil. https://www.gov.br/en/government-of-brazil/latest-news/2022/the-wi-fi-brasil-program

Granstrand, O., & Holgersson, M. (2020). Innovation Ecosystems: A Conceptual Review and a New Definition. *Technovation, 90,* 102098. doi:10.1016/j.technovation.2019.102098

Green, D., Walker, C., Alabulththim, A., Smith, D., & Phillips, M. (2018). Fueling the Gig Economy: A Case Study Evaluation of Upwork.com. *Management and Economics Research Journal, 4,* 104–112. doi:10.18639/MERJ.2018.04.523634

Greene, W. H. (2000). *Econometric Analysis.* 4th Prentice Hall. https://scholar.google.com/scholar?hl=en&as_sdt=0%2C5&q=Greene%2C+W+%282000%29%3A+Econometric+Analysis+%28Upper+Saddle+River%2C+NJ%3A+Prentice–Hall&btnG=

Green, S. B. (1991). How many subjects does it take to do a regression analysis. *Multivariate Behavioral Research, 26*(3), 499–510. doi:10.120715327906mbr2603_7 PMID:26776715

Grewal, R., Corner, J. M., & Mehta, R. (2001). An Investigation Into the Antecedents of Organizational Participation in Business-to-Business Electronic Markets. *Journal of Marketing, 65*(July), 17–33. doi:10.1509/jmkg.65.3.17.18331

Gudlaugsson, T., & Schalk, A. P. (2009). Effects of market orientation on business performance: Empirical evidence from Iceland. *The European Institute of Retailing and Service Studies*, (6), 1–17.

Gu, J., Wang, Z., Kuen, J., Ma, L., Shahroudy, A., Shuai, B., Liu, T., Wang, X., Wang, G., Cai, J., & Chen, T. (2018a). Recent advances in convolutional neural networks. *Pattern Recognition*, 77, 354–377. doi:10.1016/j.patcog.2017.10.013

Gummesson, E. (1991). Marketing-orientation revisited: The crucial role of the part-time marketer. *European Journal of Marketing*, 25(2), 60–75. doi:10.1108/03090569110139166

Gunasekaran, K., Boopathi, S., & Sureshkumar, M. (2022). Analysis of a Cryogenically Cooled Near-Dry Wedm Process Using Different Dielectrics. *Materiali in Tehnologije*, 56(2), 179–186. doi:10.17222/mit.2022.397

Haba, H. F., Bredillet, C., & Dastane, O. (2023). Green consumer research: Trends and way forward based on bibliometric analysis. *Cleaner and Responsible Consumption*, 100089.

Haba, H. F., & Dastane, D. O. (2019). Massive open online courses (MOOCs)–understanding online learners' preferences and experiences. *International Journal of Learning. Teaching and Educational Research*, 18(8), 227–242.

Haghjooye Javanmard, N., Keymasi, M., & Shah Hosseini, M. (2022). Developing a Model for Measuring the Quality of Fintech Customer Service Using a Systematic Review Approach. *New Marketing Research Journal*, 12(2), 189–216.

Hair, J. F., Anderson, R. E., Babin, B. J., & Black, W. C. (2010). *Multivariate data analysis: A global perspective*. Pearson Education.

Hair, J. F. Jr, Sarstedt, M., Ringle, C. M., & Gudergan, S. P. (2017). *Advanced issues in partial least squares structural equation modeling*. Sage publications.

Hair, J. F., Sarstedt, M., & Ringle, C. M. (2019). Rethinking some of the rethinking of partial least squares. *European Journal of Marketing*, 53(4), 566–584. doi:10.1108/EJM-10-2018-0665

Halim, F., Efendi, E., Butarbutar, M., Malau, A. R., & Sudirman, A. (2020, October). Constituents driving interest in using e-wallets in generation Z. In *Proceeding on International Conference of Science Management Art Research Technology* (Vol. 1, pp. 101-116). Semantic Scholar.

Hallikainen, H., & Laukkanen, T. (2016). How technology readiness explains acceptance and satisfaction of digital services in B2B healthcare sector? *PACIS 2016 Proceedings*. AIS. https://aisel.aisnet.org/pacis2016/294

Hannák, A. (2017). Bias in online freelance marketplaces: Evidence from taskrabbit and fiverr, *In Proceedings of the 2017 ACM conference on computer supported cooperative work and social computing*, (*vol.* 12, pp. 1914–1933). ACM. 10.1145/2998181.2998327

Harikaran, M., Boopathi, S., Gokulakannan, S., & Poonguzhali, M. (2023). Study on the Source of E-Waste Management and Disposal Methods. In *Sustainable Approaches and Strategies for E-Waste Management and Utilization* (pp. 39–60). IGI Global. doi:10.4018/978-1-6684-7573-7.ch003

Harris, L. C. (1998). Cultural domination: The key to market-oriented culture? *European Journal of Marketing*, 32(3/4), 354–373. doi:10.1108/03090569810204643

Harris, L. C., & Ogbonna, E. (2001). Strategic human resource management, market orientation, and organizational performance. *Journal of Business Research*, 51(2), 157–166. doi:10.1016/S0148-2963(99)00057-0

Harsasi, M., & Sutawijaya, A. (2018). Determinants of student satisfaction in online tutorial: A study of a distance education institution. *Turkish Online Journal of Distance Education*, 19(1), 89–99. doi:10.17718/tojde.382732

Hassard, J., & Morris, J. (2018). Contrived competition and manufactured uncertainty: Understanding managerial job insecurity narratives in large corporations. *Work, Employment and Society*, *32*(3), 564–580. doi:10.1177/0950017017751806

Healy, M., & Perry, C. (2000). Comprehensive criteria to judge validity and reliability of qualitative research within the realism paradigm. *Qualitative Market Research*, *3*(3), 118–126. doi:10.1108/13522750010333861

HEMIS OTM. (n.d.). *The information management system for educational processes*. HEMIS. https://hemis.uz/

Hendrikse, R., Van Meeteren, M., & Bassens, D. (2020). Strategic coupling between finance, technology and the state: Cultivating a Fintech ecosystem for incumbent finance. *Environment and Planning A. Environment & Planning A*, *52*(8), 1516–1538. doi:10.1177/0308518X19887967

Henseler, J., Ringle, C. M., & Sarstedt, M. (2015). A new criterion for assessing discriminant validity in variance-based structural equation modeling. *Journal of the Academy of Marketing Science*, *43*(1), 115–135. doi:10.100711747-014-0403-8

Hinkin, T. R. (1995). A review of scale development in the study of behavior in organizations. *Journal of Management*, *21*(1), 967–988. doi:10.1177/014920639502100509

Hirschmann, R. (2020). *Students in public higher education institutions in Malaysia 2012-2019, by gender*. Statista. https://www.statista.com/statistics/794845/students-in-public-higher-education-insitutions-by-gender-Malaysia/

Hodges, C. B., Moore, S., Lockee, B., Trust, T., & Bond, A. (2020, March 27). *The difference between emergency remote teaching and online learning. Why IT Matters to Higher Education Educause Review*. Educause. https://er.educause.edu/articles/2020/3/the-difference-between-emergency-remote-teaching-and-online-learning

Hoffman, D. L., & Novak, T. P. (1996). Marketing in Hypermedia Computer-Mediated Environments: Conceptual Foundations. *Journal of Marketing*, *60*(July), 50–68. doi:10.1177/002224299606000304

Holmes, W. S. A., Schaumburg, H., & Mavrikis, M. (2018). *Technology-Enhanced Personalized Learning: Untangling the Evidence*. http://www.studie-personalisiertes-lernen.de/en

Hoyland, N. (2022) *What Is A Digital Workplace?* Huler Webpage. https://huler.io/blog/what-is-a-digital-workplace

Hoyland, N. (2022). *Who Are Digital Natives And What Do They Want From The Workplace?* Huler Webpage. https://huler.io/blog/who-are-digital-natives

Huang, T., Xiong, Z., & Zhang, Z. (2011). Face Recognition Applications. In Handbook of Face Recognition (pp. 617–638). Springer London. doi:10.1007/978-0-85729-932-1_24

Hull, F., & Hage, J. (1982). Organizing for Innovation: Beyond Burns and Stalker's Organic Type. *Sociology*, *16*(4), 564–577. doi:10.1177/0038038582016004006

Hussain, I. (2012). A study to evaluate the social media trends among university students. *Procedia: Social and Behavioral Sciences*, *64*, 639–645. doi:10.1016/j.sbspro.2012.11.075

Hyvonen, P. (2011). Play in the school context? The perspectives of Finnish teachers. *The Australian Journal of Teacher Education*, *36*(8), 65–83. doi:10.14221/ajte.2011v36n8.5

iED (2020, April 4). *ICT and Entrepreneurship*. IED. https://ied.eu/blog/ict-and-entrepreneurship/

Ilias, S., & Shamsudin, M. F. (2020). Customer satisfaction and business growth. *Journal of Undergraduate Social Science and Technology*, *2*(2). http://abrn.asia/ojs/index.php/JUSST/article/view/60

Immaniar, D., Cholisoh, N., Putra, F. J. E., Pangestu, P. S., & Sunarya, P. O. A. (2022). Sistem Kartu Ujian Online Menggunakan Framework Yii Pada Universitas Raharja. Technomedia Journal, 6(2), 163–175.

Ince, F. (2021c). Creating Synergic Entrepreneurship as Support of Sustainability: Opportunities and Challenges. In R. Perez-Uribe, D. Ocampo-Guzman, N. Moreno-Monsalve, & W. Fajardo-Moreno (Eds.), Handbook of Research on Management Techniques and Sustainability Strategies for Handling Disruptive Situations in Corporate Settings (pp. 464-486). IGI Global. doi:10.4018/978-1-7998-8185-8.ch022

Ince, F. (2018). Entrepreneurship Tendency of Z Generation: A Study on Undergraduates. *Pamukkale University Journal of Social Sciences Institute*, (32), 105–113. doi:10.30794/pausbed.424969

Ince, F. (2020a). Financial Literacy in Generation Z: Healthcare Management Students. *Smart Journal*, 6(36), 1647–1658. doi:10.31576mryj.616

Ince, F. (2020b). The Effects of COVID-19 Pandemic on the Workforce in Turkey. *Smart Journal*, 6(32), 1125–1134. doi:10.31576mryj.546

Ince, F. (2021a). COVID-19 Pandemic Made Me Use It: Attitude of Generation Z Towards E-Learning. *Smart Journal*, 7(54), 3489–3494. doi:10.31576mryj.1215

Ince, F. (2021b). Opportunities and Challenges of E-Learning in Turkey. In B. Khan, S. Affouneh, S. Hussein Salha, & Z. Najee Khlaif (Eds.), *Challenges and Opportunities for the Global Implementation of E-Learning Frameworks* (pp. 202–226). IGI Global., doi:10.4018/978-1-7998-7607-6.ch013

Ince, F. (2021d). A Revolutionary Business Model for Global Purpose-Driven Corporations: Mobility as a Service (MaaS). In R. Perez-Uribe, C. Largacha-Martinez, & D. Ocampo-Guzman (Eds.), *Handbook of Research on International Business and Models for Global Purpose-Driven Companies* (pp. 22–42). IGI Global. doi:10.4018/978-1-7998-4909-4.ch002

Ince, F. (2022a). The Human Resources Perspective on the Multigenerational Workforce. In F. Ince (Ed.), *International Perspectives and Strategies for Managing an Aging Workforce* (pp. 274–297). IGI Global. doi:10.4018/978-1-7998-2395-7.ch013

Ince, F. (2022b). Creative Leadership: A Multidisciplinary Approach to Creativity. In Z. Fields (Ed.), *Achieving Sustainability Using Creativity, Innovation, and Education: A Multidisciplinary Approach* (pp. 30–49). IGI Global. doi:10.4018/978-1-7998-7963-3.ch002

Ince, F. (2022c). Digital Literacy Training: Opportunities and Challenges. In M. Taher (Ed.), *Handbook of Research on the Role of Libraries, Archives, and Museums in Achieving Civic Engagement and Social Justice in Smart Cities* (pp. 185–199). IGI Global. doi:10.4018/978-1-7998-8363-0.ch009

Ince, F. (2023a). Digital Transformation and Well-Being. In M. Anshari, A. Razzaq, M. Fithriyah, & A. Kamal (Eds.), *Digital Psychology's Impact on Business and Society* (pp. 1–27). IGI Global. doi:10.4018/978-1-6684-6108-2.ch001

Ince, F. (2023b). Socio-Ecological Sustainability Within the Scope of Industry 5.0. In M. Sajid, S. Khan, & Z. Yu (Eds.), *Implications of Industry 5.0 on Environmental Sustainability* (pp. 25–50). IGI Global. doi:10.4018/978-1-6684-6113-6.ch002

Ince, F. (2023c). Transformational Leadership in a Diverse and Inclusive Organizational Culture. In R. Perez-Uribe, D. Ocampo-Guzman, & N. Moreno-Monsalve (Eds.), *Handbook of Research on Promoting an Inclusive Organizational Culture for Entrepreneurial Sustainability* (pp. 188–201). IGI Global. doi:10.4018/978-1-6684-5216-5.ch010

Ince, F. (2023d). Sustainable Eco-Innovation: Some Points to Ponder. In F. Ince (Ed.), *Leadership Perspectives on Effective Intergenerational Communication and Management* (pp. 16–35). IGI Global. doi:10.4018/978-1-6684-6140-2.ch002

Inegbedion, H., & Obadiaru, E. (2019). Modelling brand loyalty in the Nigerian telecommunications industry. *Journal of Strategic Marketing*, 27(7), 583–598. doi:10.1080/0965254X.2018.1462842

Ing, A. Y., Wong, T. K., & Lim, P. Y. (2021). Intention To Use E-Wallet Amongst the University Students in Klang Valley. *International Journal of Business and Economy*, *3*(1), 75–84.

Insights, C. B. (2023, April 3). The Complete List of Unicorn Companies. CB Insights. https://www.cbinsights.com/research-unicorn-companies

Itasanmi, S.A. and Oni, M.T. (2021). Determinants of Learners' Satisfaction in Open Distance Learning Programmes in Nigeria. *Pakistan Journal of Distance and Online Learning, 6*(2).

Iyer, L. S., Bharadwaj, S., Shetty, S. H., Verma, V., & Devanathan, M. (2022). Advancing Equity in Digital Classrooms: A Personalized Learning Framework for Higher Education Institutions. In M. Garcia (Ed.), *Socioeconomic Inclusion During an Era of Online Education* (pp. 225–245). IGI Global. doi:10.4018/978-1-6684-4364-4.ch011

Jaafar, S. N., Lalp, P. E., & Naba, M. M. (2012). Consumers' perceptions, attitudes and purchase intention towards private label food products in Malaysia. *Asian Journal of Business and Management Sciences*, *2*(8), 73–90. https://www.researchgate.net/publication/312762017_Consumers'_perception_attitudes_and_purchase_intention_towards_private_label_food_products_in_Malaysia

James, D. (2022, December 7). Gen Z didn't kill brand loyalty, but it looks different. *Retail Dive*. https://www.retaildive.com/news/gen-z-brand-loyalty-retailers-individuality-pricing/636558/

Janardhana, K., Singh, V., Singh, S. N., Babu, T. S. R., Bano, S., & Boopathi, S. (2023). Utilization Process for Electronic Waste in Eco-Friendly Concrete: Experimental Study. In Sustainable Approaches and Strategies for E-Waste Management and Utilization (pp. 204–223). IGI Global.

Janardhana, K., Anushkannan, N. K., Dinakaran, K. P., Puse, R. K., & Boopathi, S. (2023). *Experimental Investigation on Microhardness, Surface Roughness, and White Layer Thickness of Dry EDM*. Engineering Research Express. doi:10.1088/2631-8695/acce8f

Järvinen, J., & Taiminen, H. (2016). Harnessing marketing automation for B2B content marketing. *Industrial Marketing Management*, *54*, 164–175. doi:10.1016/j.indmarman.2015.07.002

Javaid, M., Haleem, A., Singh, R. P., Suman, R., & Gonzalez, E. S. (2022). Understanding the adoption of Industry 4.0 technologies in improving environmental sustainability. *Sustainable Operations and Computers*, *3*, 203–217. doi:10.1016/j.susoc.2022.01.008

Javalgi, R. G., Todd, P. R., Johnston, W. J., & Granot, E. (2012). Entrepreneurship, Muddling Through, and Indian Internet-Enabled SMEs. *Journal of Business Research*, *65*(6), 740744. doi:10.1016/j.jbusres.2010.12.010

Jaworski, B. J., & Kohli, A. K. (1993). Market orientation: Antecedents and consequences. *Journal of Marketing*, *57*(3), 53–70. doi:10.1177/002224299305700304

Jensen, C. S. (2011). Between industrial and employment relations – the practical and academic implications of changing labour markets, *Arbetsmarknad & Arbetsliv*, *17*(3), 53-65. https://www.diva-portal.org/smash/get/diva2:513619/FULLTEXT01.pdf

Jiang, H., Islam, A. A., Gu, X., & Spector, J. M. (2021). Online learning satisfaction in higher education during the COVID-19 pandemic: A regional comparison between Eastern and Western Chinese universities. *Education and Information Technologies*, *26*(6), 1–23. doi:10.100710639-021-10519-x PMID:33814959

Jia, X., Gavves, E., Fernando, B., & Tuytelaars, T. (2015). Guiding the long-short term memory model for image caption generation. *Proceedings of the IEEE International Conference on Computer Vision*, (pp. 2407–2415). IEEE. 10.1109/ICCV.2015.277

Johnson, R., & Bonsor, K. (2007). How facial recognition systems work. *How Stuff Works*, 1–6. https://electronics. howstuffworks.com/gadgets/high-tech-gadgets/facial-recognition.htm

Johnson, J. E., Giannoulakis, C., Felver, N., Judge, L. W., David, P. A., & Scott, B. F. (2017). Motivation, Satisfaction, and Retention of Sport Management Student Volunteers. *Journal of Applied Sport Management*, *9*(1), 1–26. doi:10.18666/ JASM-2017-V9-I1-7450

Johnson, L., Adams Becker, S., Estrada, V., & Freeman, A. (2015). *NMC horizon report: 2015 higher education edition.* The New Media Consortium.

Jollife, I. T., & Cadima, J. (2016). Principal component analysis: A review and recent developments. In Philosophical Transactions of the Royal Society A: Mathematical, Physical and Engineering Sciences, 374(2065). doi:10.1098/ rsta.2015.0202

Jukes, I., McCain, T., & Crockett, L. (2010). *Understanding the digital generation: Teaching and learning in the new digital landscape.* Corwin Press.

Jünger, M., & Mietzner, M. (2020). Banking goes digital: The adoption of FinTech services by German households. *Finance Research Letters*, *34*, 101260. doi:10.1016/j.frl.2019.08.008

Kahawandala, N., & Peter, S. (2020). Factors affecting purchasing behaviour of Generation Z. *Proceedings of the international conference on industrial engineering and operations management.* 1153 – 1161. https://www.researchgate.net/ publication/349915999_Factors_affecting_Purchasing_Behaviour_of_Generation_Z

Kangas, M., Siklander, P., Randolph, J., & Ruokamo, H. (2017). Teachers' engagement and students' satisfaction with a playful learning environment. *Teaching and Teacher Education*, *63*, 274–284. doi:10.1016/j.tate.2016.12.018

Kannan, E., Trabelsi, Y., Boopathi, S., & Alagesan, S. (2022). Influences of cryogenically treated work material on near-dry wire-cut electrical discharge machining process. *Surface Topography : Metrology and Properties*, *10*(1), 15027. doi:10.1088/2051-672X/ac53e1

Kaplan, A., & Haenlein, M. (2020). Rulers of the world, unite! The challenges and opportunities of artificial intelligence. *Business Horizons*, *63*(1), 37–50. doi:10.1016/j.bushor.2019.09.003

Kapoor, S. (2023). Prospects and challenges of digital marketing. *Digital Marketing Outreach*, 93-107.

Karim, M. W., Haque, A., Ulfy, M. A., Hossain, M. A., and Anis, M. Z. (2020). Factors influencing the use of E-wallet as a payment method among Malaysian young adults. *Journal of International Business and Management, 3*(2), 01-12.

Kathan, W., Matzler, K., & Veider, V. (2016). 'The Sharing Economy: Your Business Model's Friend or Foe?'. *Business Horizons*, *59*(6), 663–672. doi:10.1016/j.bushor.2016.06.006

Kaufman, B. E. (2006). *The Global Evolution of Industrial Relations: Events, Ideas and the IIRA.* International Labour Organization and Academic Foundation of India.

Kavitha, C., Geetha Malini, P. S., Charan Kantumuchu, V., Manoj Kumar, N., Verma, A., & Boopathi, S. (2023). An experimental study on the hardness and wear rate of carbonitride coated stainless steel. *Materials Today: Proceedings*, *74*, 595–601. doi:10.1016/j.matpr.2022.09.524

Keeney, R. L. (1999). The Value of Internet Commerce to the Customer. *Management Science*, *45*(4), 533–542. doi:10.1287/mnsc.45.4.533

Kee, Y., Sabariah, K. M. Y., Mahadirin, A., Jalihah, M. S., Jurry, F. M., Ramlah, D., Hafizi, M., & Liew, T. S. (2021). Penggunaan E-Pembelajaran dan kesannya terhadap kesejahteraan kakitangan akademik di Institusi Pengajian Tinggi di Sabah [MJSSH]. *Malaysian Journal of Social Sciences and Humanities*, *6*(4), 108–116. doi:10.47405/mjssh.v6i4.761

Kelley, S. W. (1992). Developing customer orientation among service employees. *Journal of the Academy of Marketing Science*, *20*(1), 27–36. doi:10.1007/BF02723473

Kesharwani, A. (2020). Do (how) digital natives adopt a new technology differently than digital immigrants? A longitudinal study. *Information & Management*, *57*(2), 103170. doi:10.1016/j.im.2019.103170

Khan, A., & Qureshi, M. (2018). A Systematic Literature Review and Case Study On Influencing Factor And Consequences Of Freelancing In Pakistan. *International Journal of Scientific and Engineering Research*, *9*(12).

Khan, L., Amjad, A., Ashraf, N., Chang, H.-T., & Gelbukh, A. (2021). Urdu sentiment analysis with deep learning methods. *IEEE Access : Practical Innovations, Open Solutions*, *9*, 97803–97812. doi:10.1109/ACCESS.2021.3093078

Khan, M. R., Khan, N. R., Kumar, V. R., Bhatt, V. K., & Malik, F. (2022). a. Customer-Defined Market Orientation, Brand Image and Customer Satisfaction: A Mediation Approach. *SAGE Open*, *12*(4), 21582440221141860. doi:10.1177/21582440221141860

Khan, M. T. I., Yee, G. H., & Gan, G. G. G. (2021). Antecedents of Intention to Use Online Peer-to-Peer Platform in Malaysia. *Vision (Basel)*, 09722629211039051.

Khan, N. F., Ikram, N., Murtaza, H., & Asadi, M. A. (2023). Social media users and cybersecurity awareness: Predicting self-disclosure using a hybrid artificial intelligence approach. *Kybernetes*, *52*(1), 401–421. doi:10.1108/K-05-2021-0377

Khan, R. M., Khan, H. R., & Ghouri, A. M. (2022). b. Corporate social responsibility, sustainability governance and sustainable performance: A preliminary insight. *Asian Academy of Management Journal*, *27*(1), 1–28.

Khatri, A., Gupta, N., & Parashar, A. (2020). Application of Technology Acceptance Model (TAM) in Fintech Services. [IJM]. *International Journal of Management*, *11*(12). doi:10.34218/IJM.11.12.2020.328

Khorshed, M. T., Ali, A. B. M. S., & Wasimi, S. A. (2012). A survey on gaps, threat remediation challenges and some thoughts for proactive attack detection in cloud computing. *Future Generation Computer Systems*, *28*(6), 833–851. doi:10.1016/j.future.2012.01.006

Khusanov, K., & Kakharov, R. (2020). Impact of the Covid-19 pandemic on the development of digital training in higher education in Uzbekistan (Rus). In *Collection "Interconf" (36): with the Proceedings of the 7th International Scientific and Practical Conference "Challenges in Science of Nowadays" (November 26-28, 2020) in Washington, USA,* (pp. 513-522). Endeavors Publisher, 10.4018/978-1-6684-4364-4.ch010

Khusanov, K., Khusanova, G., & Khusanova, M. (2022). Compulsory Distance Learning in Uzbekistan During the COVID-19 Era: The Case of Public and Senior Secondary Vocational Education Systems. In M. Garcia (Ed.), *Socioeconomic Inclusion During an Era of Online Education* (pp. 111–133). IGI Global. doi:10.4018/978-1-6684-4364-4.ch006

Kimberly, J. R., & Evanisko, M. J. (1981). Organizational Innovation: The Influence of Individual, Organizational, and Contextual Factors on Hospital Adoption of Technological and Administrative Innovation. *Academy of Management Journal*, *24*(December), 689–713. doi:10.2307/256170 PMID:10253688

Kimura, F., Shrestha, R., & Narjoko, D. (2019). The Digital and Fourth Industrial Revolution and ASEAN Economic Transformation. In F. Kimura, V. Anbumozhi, & H. Nishimura (Eds.), *Transforming and Deepening the ASEAN Community* (pp. 1–23). ERIA. https://www.eria.org/uploads/media/5.AV2040_VOL3_Digital_and_4th_Industrial_Re volution.pdf

Kim, Y., Choi, J., Park, Y. J., & Yeon, J. (2016). The adoption of mobile payment services for "Fintech". *International Journal of Applied Engineering Research: IJAER, 11*(2), 1058–1061.

Kirby, M., & Sirovich, L. (1990). Application of the Karhunen-Loéve Procedure for the Characterization of Human Faces. *IEEE Transactions on Pattern Analysis and Machine Intelligence, 12*(1), 103–108. doi:10.1109/34.41390

Kitchen, P. J., & Proctor, T. (2015). Marketing communications in a post-modern world. *The Journal of Business Strategy, 36*(5), 34–42. doi:10.1108/JBS-06-2014-0070

Kohli, A. K., & Jaworski, B. J. (1990). Market Orientation: The Construct, Research Propositions, and Managerial Implications. *Journal of Marketing, 54*(2), 1–18. doi:10.1177/002224299005400201

Kohli, A. K., Jaworski, B. J., & Kumar, A. (1993). MARKOR: A measure of market orientation. *JMR, Journal of Marketing Research, 30*(4), 467–477. doi:10.1177/002224379303000406

Koksal, I. (2020, May 2). The rise of online learning. *Forbes.* https://www.forbes.com/sites/ilkerkoksal/2020/05/02/the-rise-of-online-learning/?sh=5829897772f3

Kopalle, P. K., Kumar, V., & Subramaniam, M. (2020). How legacy firms can embrace the digital ecosystem via digital customer orientation. *Journal of the Academy of Marketing Science, 48*(1), 114–131. doi:10.100711747-019-00694-2

Kortli, Y., Jridi, M., al Falou, A., & Atri, M. (2020). Face recognition systems: A survey. In Sensors (Switzerland), 20(2). doi:10.339020020342

Kotler, P. (2009). *Marketing management: a South Asian perspective.* Pearson Education India.

Kotler, P., & Armstrong, G. (2010). *Principles of marketing.* Pearson education.

Kotler, P., Kartajaya, H., & Setiawan, I. (2010). *From products to customers to the human spirit; marketing 3.0.* John Wiley & Sons Inc. doi:10.1002/9781118257883

Kotler, P., & Keller, K. (2012). *Management marketing.* Pearson Education Limited.

Kotler, P., & Keller, K. L. (2016). *Marketing management.* Pearson Education.

Koutropoulos, A. (2011). Digital natives: Ten years after. *Journal of Online Learning and Teaching, 7*(4), 525–538.

Kovács, G., & Spens, K. (2005). Abductive reasoning in logistics research. *International Journal of Physical Distribution & Logistics Management, 35*(2), 132–144. doi:10.1108/09600030510590318

Krejcie, R. V., & Morgan, D. W. (1970). Determining sample size for research activities. *Educational and Psychological Measurement, 30*(1), 607–610. https://psycnet.apa.org/record/1971-03263-001. doi:10.1177/001316447003000308

Kressmann, F., Sirgy, M. J., Herrmann, A., Huber, F., Huber, S., & Lee, D. J. (2006). Direct and indirect effects of self-image congruence on brand loyalty. *Journal of Business Research, 59*(9), 955–964. doi:10.1016/j.jbusres.2006.06.001

Kretschmer, T., Leiponen, A., Schilling, M., & Vasudeva, G. (2022). Platform Ecosystems as Metaorganizations: Implications for Platform Strategies. *Strategic Management Journal, 43*(3), 405–424. doi:10.1002mj.3250

Kumar, V., Lahiri, A., & Dogan, O. B. (2018). A strategic framework for a profitable business model in the sharing economy. *Industrial Marketing Management* [Preprint]. doi:10.1016/j.indmarman.2017.08.021

Kumara, V., Mohanaprakash, T. A., Fairooz, S., Jamal, K., Babu, T., & B., S. (2023). Experimental Study on a Reliable Smart Hydroponics System. In *Human Agro-Energy Optimization for Business and Industry* (pp. 27–45). IGI Global. doi:10.4018/978-1-6684-4118-3.ch002

Kumar, S., & Pandey, M. (2017). The impact of psychological pricing strategy on consumers' buying behaviour: A qualitative study. *International Journal of Business and Systems Research*, *11*(1/2), 101–117. https://EconPapers.repec. org/RePEc:ids:ijbsre:v:11:y:2017:i:1/2:p:101-117. doi:10.1504/IJBSR.2017.080843

Kumar, V., & Venkatesan, R. (2021). Transformation of metrics and analytics in retailing: The way forward. *Journal of Retailing*, *97*(4), 496–506. doi:10.1016/j.jretai.2021.11.004

Kurtinaitiene, J. (2005). Marketing orientation in the European Union mobile telecommunication market. *Marketing Intelligence & Planning*, *23*(1), 104–113. doi:10.1108/02634500510577500

Lamsal, B. (2022). Exploring Issues Surrounding a Safe and Conducive Digital Learning Space in Nepal: A Preparation for Online Education in the Post-Pandemic Era. In M. Garcia (Ed.), *Socioeconomic Inclusion During an Era of Online Education* (pp. 246–263). IGI Global. doi:10.4018/978-1-6684-4364-4.ch012

Landis, T. (2022, April 12). Customer retention marketing vs. customer acquisition marketing. *outbound engine*. https://www. outboundengine.com/blog/customer-retention-marketing-vs-customer-acquisition-marketing/#:~:text=Acquiring%20 a%20new%20customer%20can,customer%20is%205%5D20%25

Lau, G. T., & Lee, S. H. (1999). Consumers' trust in a brand and the link to brand loyalty. *Journal of Market Focused Management*, *4*(1), 341–370. doi:10.1023/A:1009886520142

Lavidge, R. J. (1966). Marketing concept often gets only lip service. *Advertising Age*, *37*(October), 52.

Lavuri, R., Jindal, A., & Akram, U. (2022). How perceived utilitarian and hedonic value influence online impulse shopping in India? Moderating role of perceived trust and perceived risk. *International Journal of Quality and Service Sciences*, *14*(4), 615–634. doi:10.1108/IJQSS-11-2021-0169

LeCun, Y., Boser, B., Denker, J. S., Henderson, D., Howard, R. E., Hubbard, W., & Jackel, L. D. (1989). Backpropagation Applied to Handwritten Zip Code Recognition. *Neural Computation*, *1*(4), 541–551. doi:10.1162/neco.1989.1.4.541

Lee, M. K., & Turban, E. (2001). A trust model for consumer internet shopping. *International Journal of Electronic Commerce*, *6*(1), 75–91. doi:10.1080/10864415.2001.11044227

Lee, S. J., Srinivasan, S., Trail, T., Lewis, D., & Lopez, S. (2011). Examining the relationship among student perception of support, course satisfaction, and learning outcomes in online learning. *The Internet and Higher Education*, *14*(3), 158–163. doi:10.1016/j.iheduc.2011.04.001

Lee, S. K., & Dastane, O. (2019). Building a sustainable competitive advantage for Multi-Level Marketing (MLM) firms: An empirical investigation of contributing factors. *Journal of Distribution Science*, *17*(3), 5–19. doi:10.15722/jds.17.3.201903.5

Le, M. T. (2021). Examining factors that boost intention and loyalty to use Fintech post-COVID-19 lockdown as a new normal behavior. *Heliyon*, *7*(8), e07821. doi:10.1016/j.heliyon.2021.e07821 PMID:34458639

Leong, K., & Sung, A. (2018). FinTech (Financial Technology): What is it and how to use technologies to create business value in fintech way? *International Journal of Innovation, Management and Technology*, *9*(2), 74–78. doi:10.18178/ijimt.2018.9.2.791

Lestari, N. P., Durachman, Y., Watini, S., & Millah, S. (2021, July). Manajemen Kontrol Akses Berbasis Blockchain untuk Pendidikan Online Terdesentralisasi. *Technomedia Journal*, *6*(1), 111–123. doi:10.33050/tmj.v6i1.1682

Levitt, T. (1960). Marketing myopia. *Harvard Business Review*, *38*(4), 24–47. PMID:15252891

Li, C., & Lalani, F. (2020, Apr 29). The COVID-19 pandemic has changed education forever. This is how. *We Forum.* https://www.weforum.org/agenda/2020/04/coronavirus-education-global-covid19-online-digital-learning/

Liaw, S. S. (2008). Investigating students' perceived satisfaction, behavioral intention, and effectiveness of e-learning: A case study of the Black board system. *Computers & Education, 51*(2), 864–873. doi:10.1016/j.compedu.2007.09.005

Liébana-Cabanillas, F., García-Maroto, I., Muñoz-Leiva, F., & Ramos-de-Luna, I. (2020). Mobile payment adoption in the age of digital transformation: The case of Apple Pay. *Sustainability (Basel), 12*(13), 5443. doi:10.3390u12135443

Lien, C. H., & Cao, Y. (2014). Examining WeChat users' motivations, trust, attitudes, and positive word-of-mouth: Evidence from China. *Computers in Human Behavior, 41*(1), 104–111. doi:10.1016/j.chb.2014.08.013

Lies, J. (2021). Digital marketing: Incompatibilities between performance marketing and marketing creativity. *Journal of Digital & Social Media Marketing, 8*(4), 376–386.

Liew, T. S., Haifzi, A., Mahadirin, A., & Dris, M. A. (2019). *Quick Start Guide For UMS Learning Management System*. Institute for Biological Tropical and Conservation, Universiti Malaysia Sabah, OER UMS. https://oer.ums.edu.my/handle/oer_source_files/1099

Li, J., Chen, L., Chen, Y., & He, J. (2022). Digital economy, technological innovation, and green economic efficiency—Empirical evidence from 277 cities in China. *MDE. Managerial and Decision Economics, 43*(3), 616–629. doi:10.1002/mde.3406

Lim, W. M., Gupta, S., Aggarwal, A., Paul, J., & Sadhna, P. (2021). How do digital natives perceive and react toward online advertising? Implications for SMEs. *Journal of Strategic Marketing*, 1–35. doi:10.1080/0965254X.2021.1941204

Li, N., Marsh, V., Rienties, B., & Whitelock, D. (2017). Online learning experiences of new versus continuing learners: A large-scale replication study. *Assessment & Evaluation in Higher Education, 42*(4), 657–672. doi:10.1080/0260293 8.2016.1176989

Lin, E. C., & Yeh, A. J. (2022). Fighting Through COVID-19 for Educational Continuity: Challenges to Teachers. In M. Garcia (Ed.), *Socioeconomic Inclusion an Era of Online Education* (pp. 177–203). IGI Global. doi:10.4018/978-1-6684-4364-4.ch009

Ling, C. H., & Mansori, S. (2018). The effects of product quality on customer satisfaction and loyalty: Evidence from Malaysian engineering industry. *International Journal of Industrial Marketing, 3*(1), 20–35. doi:10.5296/ijim.v3i1.13959

Li, S., Shi, Y., Wang, L., & Xia, E. (2023). A Bibliometric Analysis of Brand Orientation Strategy in Digital Marketing: Determinants, Research Perspectives and Evolutions. *Sustainability (Basel), 15*(2), 1486. doi:10.3390u15021486

Liu, P., Qiu, X., & Huang, X. (2016). Recurrent neural network for text classification with multi-task learning. *ArXiv Preprint ArXiv:1605.05101.*

Liu, T., Walley, K., Pugh, G., & Adkins, P. (2020). Entrepreneurship Education in China: Evidence from a Preliminary Scoping Study of Enterprising Tendency in Chinese University Students. *Journal of Entrepreneurship in Emerging Economies, 12*(2), 305–326. doi:10.1108/JEEE-01-2019-0006

Liu, X., Chen, T., & Kumar, B. V. K. V. (2003). Face authentication for multiple subjects using eigenflow. *Pattern Recognition, 36*(2), 313–328. doi:10.1016/S0031-3203(02)00033-X

Li, W., Badr, Y., & Biennier, F. (2012, October). Digital Ecosystems: Challenges and Prospects. In *Proceedings of the International Conference on Management of Emergent Digital EcoSystems* (pp. 117-122). ACM. 10.1145/2457276.2457297

López-Fernández, A. M. (2020). Price sensitivity versus ethical consumption: A study of Millennial utilitarian consumer behavior. *Journal of Marketing Analytics, 8*(2), 57–68. doi:10.105741270-020-00074-8

Lord, C. (2022). The sustainability of the gig economy food delivery system (Deliveroo, UberEATS and Just-Eat): Histories and futures of rebound, lock-in and path dependency. *International Journal of Sustainable Transportation, 15.*

LRU. (2020). *Law of the Republic of Uzbekistan on Education, 23.09.2020, LRU-637.* LRU. https://lex.uz/ru/docs/5700831

Lu, J., Yao, J. E., & Yu, C. S. (2005). Personal innovativeness, social influences and adoption of wireless Internet services via mobile technology. *The Journal of Strategic Information Systems, 14*(3), 245–268. doi:10.1016/j.jsis.2005.07.003

Lukas, B. A., & Ferrell, O. C. (2000). The effect of market orientation on product innovation. *Journal of the Academy of Marketing Science, 28*(2), 239–247. doi:10.1177/0092070300282005

Lundvall, B. Å. (2007). National Innovation Systems—Analytical Concept and Development Tool. *Industry and Innovation, 14*(1), 95–119. doi:10.1080/13662710601130863

Lusch, R., & Nambisan, S. (2015). Service Innovation: A Service-Dominant Logic Perspective. *Management Information Systems Quarterly, 39*(1), 155–175. doi:10.25300/MISQ/2015/39.1.07

M. S., N. & Siddiqui, I. (2022). How Inclusive Is Online Education in India: Lessons from the pandemic. In M. Garcia (Ed.), *Socioeconomic Inclusion During an Era of Online Education,* 135-155. IGI Global. doi:10.4018/978-1-6684-4364-4.ch007

Macchiavello, E., & Siri, M. (2022). Sustainable Finance and Fintech: Can Technology Contribute to Achieving Environmental Goals? A Preliminary Assessment of 'Green Fintech' and 'Sustainable Digital Finance'. *European Company and Financial Law Review, 19*(1), 128–174. doi:10.1515/ecfr-2022-0005

Magoulas, G. D., & Chen, S. Y. (Eds.). (2006). *Advances in Web-Based Education: Personalized Learning Environments.* IGI Global. doi:10.4018/978-1-59140-690-7

Maguire, M. (2017). Doing a thematic analysis: A practical, step-by-step guide for learning and teaching scholars. *All Ireland Journal of Higher Education, 8*(3), 33510 - 33514. https://ojs.aishe.org/index.php/aishe-j/article/view/335

Mahadirin, A. (2020). HA12 Notice Board – Blog, *Open Electronics Resources (OER),* Jabatan Teknologi Maklumat dan Komunikasi (JTMK) Universiti Malaysia Sabah. https://oer.ums.edu.my/handle/oer_source_files/1484

Mahadirin, A. (2022). *Aku Dan Sesuatu Diari.* e-learning Cafe FSSK, UMS. https://indiework.usm.my/index.php?route=product/product&product_id=458

Malafeev, A. (2014). *Automatic generation of text-based open cloze exercises.* Analysis of Images, Social Networks and Texts: Third International Conference, AIST 2014, Yekaterinburg, Russia.

Malaysian Quality Assurance. (2011). *Guidelines to Good Practices: Curriculum Design and Delivery.* Kuala Lumpur: The Public and International Affairs. https://www2.mqa.gov.my/QAD/garispanduan/2014/GGP%20REKA%20BEN-TUK%20N%20KURIKULUM.pdf

Mariani, M. M., & Nambisan, S. (2021). Innovation analytics and digital innovation experimentation: The rise of research-driven online review platforms. *Technological Forecasting and Social Change, 172,* 121009. doi:10.1016/j.techfore.2021.121009

Markey, R. (2020, February 1). Are you undervaluing your customers? *Harvard Business Review.* https://hbr.org/2020/01/are-you-undervaluing-your-customers

Marquis, K. H., Marquis, M. S., & Polich, J. M. (1986). Response bias and reliability in sensitive topic surveys. *Journal of the American Statistical Association*, *81*(394), 381–389. doi:10.1080/01621459.1986.10478282

Martinčević, I., Črnjević, S., & Klopotan, I. (2020). Fintech Revolution in the Financial Industry. In *Proceedings of the ENTRENOVA-ENTerprise REsearch InNOVAtion Conference* (Vol. 6, No. 1, pp. 563-571).

Martono, S. (2021). Analisis Faktor-Faktor Yang Mempengaruhi Minat Menggunakan Fintech Lending. *Jurnal Ekonomi Bisnis Dan Kewirausahaan*, *10*(3), 246. doi:10.26418/jebik.v10i3.45827

Masnita, Y., Rasyawal, M., & Yusran, H. L. (2021). Halal Transaction: Implication For Digital Retail By Using Financial Technology. *Jurnal Ilmiah Ekonomi Islam*, *7*(1), 16–22. doi:10.29040/jiei.v7i1.1492

Mason, R. M., Barzilai, K., & Lou, N. (2008) The Organizational Impact of Digital Natives: How Organizations are Responding to the Next Generation of Knowledge Workers. *Proceedings of the 17th International Conference on Management of Technology Dubai*. RM Mason. http://faculty.washington.edu/rmmason/Publications/IAMOT_DN_2008.pdf

Mastor, H. (2021). Factors that Affect the Usage Of E-Wallet Among Youth: A Study at a Public Institution of Higher Learning in South Sarawak. Advanced International Journal of Business. *Entrepreneurship and SMEs.*, *3*(7), 40–48. doi:10.35631/AIJBES.37004

Matsumori, S., Okuoka, K., Shibata, R., Inoue, M., Fukuchi, Y., & Imai, M. (2023). Mask and Cloze: Automatic Open Cloze Question Generation using a Masked Language Model. *IEEE Access : Practical Innovations, Open Solutions*, *11*, 9835–9850. doi:10.1109/ACCESS.2023.3239005

Matsuno, K., Mentzer, J. T., & Rentz, J. O. (2005). A conceptual and empirical comparison of three market orientation scales. *Journal of Business Research*, *58*(1), 1–8. doi:10.1016/S0148-2963(03)00075-4

Mauri, A. G., Minazzi, R., Nieto-García, M., & Viglia, G. (2018). Humanize your business. the role of personal reputation in the sharing economy. *International Journal of Hospitality Management*, *73*, 36–43. doi:10.1016/j.ijhm.2018.01.017

Meeuwse, K., & Mason, D. (2018). *Personalized Professional Learning for Educators: Emerging Research and Opportunities*. IGI Global. doi:10.4018/978-1-5225-2685-8

Meria, L., Aini, Q., Lestari Santoso, N. P., Raharja, U., & Millah, S. (2021) Management of Access Control for Decentralized Online Educations using Blockchain Technology. *2021 Sixth International Conference on Informatics and Computing (ICIC)*, (pp. 1–6). IEEE. 10.1109/ICIC54025.2021.9632999

Miller, L. J., & Lu, W. (2018, August 20). Gen Z is set to outnumber millennials within a year. *Bloomberg*. https://www.bloomberg.com/news/articles/2018-08-20/gen-z-to-outnumber-millennials-within-a-year-demographic-trends?leadSource=uverify%20wall

Ministry of Electronics & Information Technology. (n.d.). *Digital India*. MEIT. https://www.digitalindia.gov.in/

Mohammad. (2016). *The effects of utilitarian and hedonic online shopping value on consumer perceived value* [Bachelor thesis, Muhammadiyah University Of Surakarta]. https://eprints.ums.ac.id/47992/1/NASKAH%20PUBLIKASI%20PERPUS.pdf

Mohanty, A., Venkateswaran, N., Ranjit, P. S., Tripathi, M. A., & Boopathi, S. (2023). Innovative Strategy for Profitable Automobile Industries: Working Capital Management. In Handbook of Research on Designing Sustainable Supply Chains to Achieve a Circular Economy (pp. 412–428). IGI Global.

Monsalve-Pulido, J., Aguilar, J., & Montoya, E. (2023). Framework for the Adaptation of an Autonomous Academic Recommendation System as a Service-oriented Architecture. *Education and Information Technologies*, *28*(1), 321–341. doi:10.100710639-022-11172-8

Morgan, B. (2019, December 2). Customer of the future: 5 ways to create a customer experience for Gen-Z. *Forbes.* https://www.forbes.com/sites/blakemorgan/2019/12/02/customer-of-the-future-5-ways-to-create-a-customer-experience-for-gen-z/?sh=73c0c3835a40

Morrow, S. L. (2005). Quality and trustworthiness in qualitative research. *Journal of Counseling Psychology, 52*(2), 250–260. doi:10.1037/0022-0167.52.2.250

Most often automated marketing channels. (2023). Statista. https://www.statista.com/statistics/1269813/marketing-channels-automation/#:~:text=Marketing%20channels%20using%20automation%20worldwide%202023&text=During%20a%20February%202023%20global,automated%20their%20paid%20ads%20efforts

Moth, R., & Lavalette, M. (2017). *Social protection and labour market policies for vulnerable groups from a social investment perspective: The case of welfare recipients with mental health needs in England.* RE-InVEST working paper series D5. 1.

Mourtzis, D., Angelopoulos, J., & Panopoulos, N. (2020). Recycling and retrofitting for industrial equipment based on augmented reality. *Procedia CIRP, 90,* 606–610. doi:10.1016/j.procir.2020.02.134

Muilenburg, L. Y., & Berge, Z. L. (2005). Student barriers to online learning: A factor analytic study. *Distance Education, 26*(1), 29–48. doi:10.1080/01587910500081269

Mukhtar, U., Anwar, S., Ahmed, U., & Baloch, M. A. (2015). Factors effecting the service quality of public and private sector universities comparatively: An empirical investigation. *Research World, 6*(3), 132–142.

Munsch, A. (2021). Millennial and generation Z digital marketing communication and advertising effectiveness: A qualitative exploration. *Journal of Global Scholars of Marketing Science, 31*(1), 10–29. doi:10.1080/21639159.2020.1808812

Murphy, D. (2018). Silver bullet or millstone? A review of success factors for implementation of marketing automation. *Cogent Business & Management, 5*(1), 1546416. doi:10.1080/23311975.2018.1546416

Myilsamy, S., Boopathi, S., & Yuvaraj, D. (2021). A study on cryogenically treated molybdenum wire electrode. *Materials Today: Proceedings, 45*(9), 8130–8135. doi:10.1016/j.matpr.2021.02.049

Myilsamy, S., & Sampath, B. (2021). Experimental comparison of near-dry and cryogenically cooled near-dry machining in wire-cut electrical discharge machining processes. *Surface Topography : Metrology and Properties, 9*(3), 35015. doi:10.1088/2051-672X/ac15e0

Nam, K., & Lee, N. H. (2010). Typology of Service Innovation from Service-dominant Logic Perspective. *Journal of Universal Computer Science, 16*(13), 1761–1775.

Nangin, M. A., Barus, I. R. G., & Wahyoedi, S. (2020). The Effects of Perceived Ease of Use, Security, and Promotion on Trust and Its Implications on Fintech Adoption. *Journal of Consumer Sciences, 5*(2), 124–138. doi:10.29244/jcs.5.2.124-138

Narver, J. C., & Slater, S. F. (1990). The effect of a market orientation on business profitability. *Journal of Marketing, 54*(4), 20–35. doi:10.1177/002224299005400403

Narver, J. C., Slater, S. F., & Tietje, B. (1998). Creating a market orientation. *Journal of Market Focused Management, 2*(3), 241–255. doi:10.1023/A:1009703717144

Naudé, W., & Liebregts, W. (2023). Digital Entrepreneurship. In W. Liebregts, W. J. Van-den-Heuvel, & A. Van-den-Born (Eds.), *Data Science for Entrepreneurship. Classroom Companion: Business.* Springer. doi:10.1007/978-3-031-19554-9_12

NCBI . (2022). *Assessing and Addressing COVID-19 information needs via a weather application.* NCBI. Retrieve on 22 November 2022 https://www.ncbi.nlm.nih.gov/pmc/articles/PMC9037469/

Neneh, B. N. (2016). Market orientation and performance: The contingency role of external environment. *Environment and Ecology, 7*(2), 1–14.

Neuhofer, B., & Johnson, A.-G. (2017). Airbnb – an exploration of value co-creation experiences in Jamaica. *International Journal of Contemporary Hospitality Management, 29*(9), 2361–2376. doi:10.1108/IJCHM-08-2016-0482

Ng, I. C. L. (2013). *Value and Worth: Creating New Markets in the Digital Economy.* Innovorsa Press.

Ngoasong, M. Z. (2015). Digital Entrepreneurship in Emerging Economies: The role of ICTs and local context. In: *42nd AIB-UKI Conference.* Metropolitan University, UK.

Nielsen. (2016). *The Power of Like-Minded Peers.* Nielsen. https://www.nielsen.com/us/en/insights/report/2016/the-power-of-like-minded-peers/

Nowell, L. S., Norris, J. M., & Moules, N. J. (2017). Thematic Analysis: Striving to Meet the Trustworthiness Criteria. *International Journal of Qualitative Methods, 2*(1). https://doi.org/10.1177/1609406917733847. doi:10.1177/1609406917733847

NST. (2021). *Take advantage of free internet data for PdPR purposes.* MCMC. https://www.nst.com.my/news/nation/2021/02/662364/take-advantage-free-internet-data-pdpr-purposes-mcmc

Nurlaily, F., Aini, E. K., & Asmoro, P. S. (2021). Understanding the FinTech continuance intention of Indonesian users: The moderating effect of gender. *Business: Theory and Practice, 22*(2), 290–298. doi:10.3846/btp.2021.13880

Nusantoro, H., Supriati, R., Azizah, N., Santoso, N. P. L., & Maulana, S. (2021). Blockchain Based Authentication for Identity Management. *In 2021 9th International Conference on Cyber and IT Service Management (CITSM),* (pp. 1–8). IEEE. 10.1109/CITSM52892.2021.9589001

OECD. (2021). The State of Higher Education: One Year into the COVID-19 Pandemic. OECD Publishing. doi:10.1787/83c41957-

OECD. (2023, April 4). *4th Digital for SMEs Roundtable.* OECD. https://www.oecd.org/digital/sme/

Oganda, F. P., Lutfiani, N., Aini, Q., Rahardja, U., & Faturahman, A. (2020) Blockchain Education Smart Courses of Massive Online Open Course Using Business Model Canvas. *2nd International Conference on Cybernetics and Intelligent System (ICORIS),* (pp. 1–6). IEEE. 10.1109/ICORIS50180.2020.9320789

Ometov, A., Bezzateev, S., Mäkitalo, N., Andreev, S., Mikkonen, T., & Koucheryavy, Y. (2018). Multi-factor authentication: A survey. *Cryptography, 2*(1), 1. doi:10.3390/cryptography2010001

Orendorff, A. (2019). *Global ecommerce statistics and trends to launch your business beyond borders.* Global Ecommerce.

Ortega, R. T., & Criado, J. R. (2012). Market Orientation of Born Globals Firms: A Qualitative Examination. *International Journal of Business and Management Studies, 4*(2), 141–150.

Osuagwu, L. (2006). Market orientation in Nigerian companies. *Marketing Intelligence & Planning, 24*(6), 608–631. doi:10.1108/02634500610701681

Oxford Economics. (2021, March 10). *Gen Z's role in shaping the digital economy.* Oxford Economics. https://www.oxfordeconomics.com/resource/gen-z-role-in-shaping-the-digital-economy/

Oyer, P. (2020). Non-traditional employment is a great opportunity for many, but it won't replace traditional employment. Stanford University Graduate School of Business. doi:10.15185/izawol.471

Palangi, H., Deng, L., Shen, Y., Gao, J., He, X., Chen, J., Song, X., & Ward, R. (2016). Deep sentence embedding using long short-term memory networks: Analysis and application to information retrieval. *IEEE/ACM Transactions on Audio, Speech, and Language Processing*, *24*(4), 694–707. doi:10.1109/TASLP.2016.2520371

Palaniappan, M., Tirlangi, S., Mohamed, M. J. S., Moorthy, R. M. S., Valeti, S. V., & Boopathi, S. (2023). Fused deposition modelling of polylactic acid (PLA)-based polymer composites: A case study. In Development, Properties, and Industrial Applications of 3D Printed Polymer Composites (pp. 66–85). IGI Global. doi:10.4018/978-1-6684-6009-2.ch005

Pamastillero. (2017 August 11). Redefining marketing in the digital economy. *Digital Entrepreneur*. http://www.pamastillero.com/2017/08/11/4-redefining-marketing-in-the-digital-economy/

Parasuraman, A., & Colby, C. L. (2015). An updated and streamlined technology readiness index: TRI 2.0. *Journal of Service Research*, *18*(1), 59–74. doi:10.1177/1094670514539730

Park, C., & Kim, Y. (2003). Identifying key factors affecting consumer purchase behavior in an online shopping context. *International Journal of Retail & Distribution Management*, *31*(1), 16–29. doi:10.1108/09590550310457818

Parker, S. C. (2005). The Economics of Entrepreneurship: What We Know and What We Don't. *Foundations and Trends in Entrepreneurship*, *1*(1), 1–54. doi:10.1561/0300000001

Paul, L. C., & al Sumam, A. (2012). Face recognition using principal component analysis method. In Journal of Advanced Research in Computer.

Petrillo, A., De Felice, F., Cioffi, R., & Federico Zomparelli, F. (2018). Fourth Industrial Revolution: Current Practices, Challenges, and Opportunities. In A. Petrillo, R. Cioffi, & F. De Felice (Eds.), *Digital Transformation in Smart Manufacturing*. IntechOpen. doi:10.5772/intechopen.72304

Piercy, N. (1991). *Market-led strategic change: Making marketing happen in your organization*. Harper Thorsons.

Pigou, A. C. (1920). *The Economics of Welfare*. Macmillan and Company. https://archive.org/details/dli.bengal.10689.4260

Pino, J., Heilman, M., & Eskenazi, M. (2008). A selection strategy to improve cloze question quality. *Proceedings of the Workshop on Intelligent Tutoring Systems for Ill-Defined Domains. 9th International Conference on Intelligent Tutoring Systems, Montreal, Canada*, (pp. 22–32). Research Gate.

Pino, J., & Eskenazi, M. (2009). Measuring Hint Level in Open Cloze Questions. *FLAIRS Conference*.

Pitic, L., Brad, S., & Pitic, D. (2014). Study on perceived quality and perceived fair price. *Procedia Economics and Finance*, *15*(1), 1304–1309. doi:10.1016/S2212-5671(14)00592-9

Pongpaew, W., Speece, M., & Tiangsoongnern, L. (2017). Social presence and customer brand engagement on facebook brand pages. *Journal of Product and Brand Management*, *26*(3), 262–281. doi:10.1108/JPBM-08-2015-0956

Prabha, M. I., & Srikanth, G. U. (2019). Survey of sentiment analysis using deep learning techniques. *2019 1st International Conference on Innovations in Information and Communication Technology (ICIICT)*, 1–9.

Prensky, M. (2001). Digital natives, digital immigrants. *On the Horizon*, *9*(5), 1–6. doi:10.1108/10748120110424816

Prensky, M. R. (2010). *Teaching digital natives: Partnering for real learning*. Corwin press.

Priporas, C.V. (2017). Unraveling the diverse nature of service quality in a sharing economy: a social exchange theory perspective of airbnb accommodation. *Emerald Insight, 29*(9), 2279–2301.

Purnama, S., Aini, Q., Rahardja, U., Santoso, N. P. L., & Millah, S. (2021, November). Design of Educational Learning Management Cloud Process with Blockchain 4.0 based EPortfolio. *Journal of Education Technology*, *5*(4), 628. doi:10.23887/jet.v5i4.40557

Purnomo, A., Susanti, T., Anisah, H. U., Sari, A. K., & Maulana, F. I. (2021, August). Value of M-commerce Research: A Bibliometric Perspective. In *2021 International Conference on Information Management and Technology (ICIMTech)*, (pp. 813-818). IEEE. 10.1109/ICIMTech53080.2021.9534928

Rahim, A. S., & Mohamad, M. (2018). Biometric Authentication using Face Recognition Algorithms for A Class Attendance System. In Jurnal Mekanikal, 41.

Rahi, S., Abd Ghani, M., & Ngah, A. (2020). Factors propelling the adoption of internet banking: The role of e-customer service, website design, brand image and customer satisfaction. *International Journal of Business Information Systems*, *33*(4), 549–569. doi:10.1504/IJBIS.2020.105870

Raj, M., Sundararajan, A., & You, C. (2021). *COVID-19 and Digital Resilience: Evidence from Uber Eats.* The Social Science Research Network. doi:10.2139/ssrn.3625638

Raja, G. B. (2021). Impact of Internet of Things, Artificial Intelligence, and Blockchain Technology in Industry 4.0. In R. Kumar, Y. Wang, T. Poongodi, & A. L. Imoize (Eds.), *Internet of Things, Artificial Intelligence and Blockchain Technology* (pp. 157–178). Springer. doi:10.1007/978-3-030-74150-1_8

Raja, M., Kumar, A. V., Makkar, N., Kumar, S., & Varma, S. B. (2022). The Future of the Gig Professionals: A Study Considering Gen Y, Gen C, and Gen Alpha. In *Sustainability in the Gig Economy* (pp. 305–324). Springer. doi:10.1007/978-981-16-8406-7_23

Raj, L. V., Amilan, S., Aparna, K., & Swaminathan, K. (2023). Factors influencing the adoption of cashless transactions during COVID-19: An extension of enhanced UTAUT with pandemic precautionary measures. *Journal of Financial Services Marketing*, ●●●, 1–20. doi:10.105741264-023-00218-8

Ramachandran, K. (2020). How will millennials and Gen Z use 5G? *Deloitte.* https://www2.deloitte.com/us/en/insights/industry/technology/5g-impacts-millennials-and-gen-z-technology-usage.html

Ramesh, R., Prabhu, S., Sasikumar, B., Devi, B., Prasath, P., & Kamala, S. (2021). An empirical study of online food delivery services from applications perspective. *Materials Today: Proceedings*, *12*. doi:10.1016/j.matpr.2021.05.500

Rana, M. (2022, December 2). *Digital native brands - transforming retail landscape.* RedSeer Strategy Consultants. https://redseer.com/newsletters/digital-native-brands-transforming-retail-landscape/

Ranta, V., Aarikka-Stenroos, L., & Väisänen, J. M. (2021). Digital Technologies Catalyzing Business Model Innovation for Circular Economy—Multiple Case Study. *Resources, Conservation and Recycling*, *164*, 105155. doi:10.1016/j.resconrec.2020.105155

Rao, G., Huang, W., Feng, Z., & Cong, Q. (2018). LSTM with sentence representations for document-level sentiment classification. *Neurocomputing*, *308*, 49–57. doi:10.1016/j.neucom.2018.04.045

Ratnasingam, P., & Pavlou, P. A. (2003). Technology trust in internet-based interorganizational electronic commerce. [JECO]. *Journal of Electronic Commerce in Organizations*, *1*(1), 17–41. doi:10.4018/jeco.2003010102

Raza, H., Faizan, M., Hamza, A., Ahmed, M., & Akhtar, N. (2019). Scientific text sentiment analysis using machine learning techniques. *International Journal of Advanced Computer Science and Applications*, *10*(12). doi:10.14569/IJACSA.2019.0101222

Razan, S. (2022). Gen Alpha: How to win the customer of 2030. *InfoBip.* https://www.infobip.com/blog/how-to-win-the-customer-of-2030

Razavi, A., Moschoyiannis, S., & Krause, P. (2009). An Open Digital Environment to Support Business Ecosystems. *Peer-to-Peer Networking and Applications, 2*(4), 367–397. doi:10.100712083-009-0039-5

Redding, S. (2015). Can marketing automation be the glue that helps align sales and marketing? *Journal of Direct, Data and Digital Marketing Practice, 16*(4), 260–265. doi:10.1057/dddmp.2015.27

Reddy, M. A., Reddy, B. M., Mukund, C. S., Venneti, K., Preethi, D. M. D., & Boopathi, S. (2023). Social Health Protection During the COVID-Pandemic Using IoT. In *The COVID-19 Pandemic and the Digitalization of Diplomacy* (pp. 204–235). IGI Global. doi:10.4018/978-1-7998-8394-4.ch009

Reis, J., & Melão, N. (2023). Digital transformation: A meta-review and guidelines for future research. *Heliyon, 9*(1), 12834. doi:10.1016/j.heliyon.2023.e12834 PMID:36691547

Ringle, C. M., Wende, S., & Becker, J. M. (2015). *SmartPLS 3.* Bonningstedt: SmartPLS. http://www.smartpls.com

Ritala, P., & Jovanovic, M. (2024). Platformizers, Orchestrators, and Guardians: Three Types of B2B Platform Business Models. In A. Aagaard & C. Nielsen (Eds.), *Business Model Innovation: Game Changers and Contemporary Issues.* Palgrave Macmillan.

Robertson, T., & Gatignon, H. (1986). Competitive Effects on Technology Diffusion. *Journal of Marketing, 50*(July), 1–12. doi:10.1177/002224298605000301

Rogers, E. M. (1995). *Diffusion of Innovations* (4th ed.). The Free Press.

Romaniuk, J., & Nenycz-Thiel, M. (2013). Behavioral brand loyalty and consumer brand associations. *Journal of Business Research, 66*(1), 67–72. doi:10.1016/j.jbusres.2011.07.024

Roy, S. K., Balaji, M. S., Sadeque, S., Nguyen, B., & Melewar, T. C. (2017). Constituents and consequences of smart customer experience in retailing. *Technological Forecasting and Social Change, 124*(C), 257–270. doi:10.1016/j.techfore.2016.09.022

Ruff, C. (2019 February, 26). Price and rewards are crucial to Gen Zers and young millennials. *Retail Dive.* https://www.retaildive.com/news/price-and-rewards-are-crucial-to-gen-zers-and-young-millennials/549166/

Ruipérez-Valiente, J. A. (2022). A Macro-Scale MOOC Analysis of the Socioeconomic Status of Learners and Their Learning Outcomes. In M. Garcia (Ed.), *Socioeconomic Inclusion During an Era of Online Education* (pp. 1–22). IGI Global., doi:10.4018/978-1-6684-4364-4.ch001

S., P. K., Sampath, B., R., S. K., Babu, B. H., & N., A. (2022). Hydroponics, Aeroponics, and Aquaponics Technologies in Modern Agricultural Cultivation. In *Trends, Paradigms, and Advances in Mechatronics Engineering* (pp. 223–241). IGI Global. doi:10.4018/978-1-6684-5887-7.ch012

Saad, M. A., Fisol, W. B. M., & Bin, M. (2019). Financial technology (Fintech) services in Islamic financial institutions. In *International postgraduate conference* (pp. 1-10).

Saez Trigueros, D., Meng, L., & Hartnett, M. (2018). *Face Recognition: From Traditional to Deep Learning Methods.* Research Gate.

Safder, I., Hassan, S.-U., Visvizi, A., Noraset, T., Nawaz, R., & Tuarob, S. (2020). Deep learning-based extraction of algorithmic metadata in full-text scholarly documents. *Information Processing \& Management, 57*(6), 102269.

Saha1, B. C., R, D., A, A., Thrinath, B. V. S., Boopathi, S., J. R., & Sudhakar, M. (n.d.). *IOT BASED SMART ENERGY METER FOR SMART GRID*. Research Gate.

Sahni, A. (2022). How Each Generation Shops in 2020. *Sales Floor*. https://salesfloor.net/blog/generations-shopping-habits/

Sahu, P. (2020). Closure of universities due to coronavirus disease 2019 (COVID-19): Impact on education and mental health of students and academic staff. *Cureus*, *12*(4), 1–5. doi:10.7759/cureus.7541 PMID:32377489

Salam, A., & Abdiyanti, S. (2022). Analisis Pengaruh Celebrity Endorser, Brand Image Dan Brand Trust Terhadap Keputusan Pembelian (Studi Kasus Pada Konsumen Wanita Produk Skin Care Merek Ms Glow Di Kecamatan Sumbawa): Manajemen Pemasaran. *Accounting and Management Journal*, *6*(1), 60–68. doi:10.33086/amj.v6i1.2204

Salimyanova, G. (2019). Economy digitalization: Information impact on market entities. *Journal of Environmental Treatment Techniques*, *7*(4), 654–658.

Salleh, N. M., & Ab Rahman, B. (2020). Part 2 Country Chapter Malaysia. In Nankervis, A.R. Connell, J. and John Burgess, J. (editor) *The Future of Work in Asia and Beyond*. London & New York: Routledge. https://www.taylorfrancis.com/books/edit/10.4324/9780429423567/future-work-asia-beyond-alan-nankervis-julia-connell-john-burgess?refId=b41d9dd3-ffec-414f-be8b-ffa7b1a1a687

Samikannu, R., Koshariya, A. K., Poornima, E., Ramesh, S., Kumar, A., & Boopathi, S. (2023). Sustainable Development in Modern Aquaponics Cultivation Systems Using IoT Technologies. In *Human Agro-Energy Optimization for Business and Industry* (pp. 105–127). IGI Global. doi:10.4018/978-1-6684-4118-3.ch006

Sampath, B. C. S., & Myilsamy, S. (2022). Application of TOPSIS Optimization Technique in the Micro-Machining Process. In Trends, Paradigms, and Advances in Mechatronics Engineering (pp. 162–187). IGI Global. doi:10.4018/978-1-6684-5887-7.ch009

Sampath, B., & Myilsamy, S. (2021). Experimental investigation of a cryogenically cooled oxygen-mist near-dry wire-cut electrical discharge machining process. *Strojniski Vestnik. Jixie Gongcheng Xuebao*, *67*(6), 322–330. doi:10.5545v-jme.2021.7161

Sandell, N. (2016). Marketing automation supporting sales.

San, S. S., & Dastane, O. (2021). Key Factors Affecting Intention to Order Online Food Delivery (OFD). *Journal of Industrial Distribution & Business*, *12*(2), 19–27.

Santander. (2020 October, 1). *Malaysia: Reaching the consumer*. Satander. https://santandertrade.com/en/portal/analyse-markets/malaysia/reaching-the-consumers

Sanusi, S., Firdaus, A., Noor, R., Omar, N., & Sanusi, M. (2018). Technology on Goods and Services Tax compliance among small-medium enterprises in developing countries. *Advanced Science Letters*, *24*(7), 5461–5465. doi:10.1166/asl.2018.11757

Sanusi, S., Nik Abdullah, N. H., Rozzani, N., & Muslichah, I. (2022). Factors influencing the level of satisfaction on online learning among tertiary students during Covid-19 pandemic era – A Malaysian study. *Geografia*, *18*(2), 248–263.

Sarwar, F., Aftab, M., & Iqbal, M. T. (2014). The impact of branding on consumer buying behavior. *International Journal of New Technology and Research.*, *2*(2), 54–64. https://www.researchgate.net/publication/309563927_The_Impact_of_Branding_on_Consumer_Buying_Behavior

Satalkina, L., & Steiner, G. (2020a). Digital Entrepreneurship and Its Role in Innovation Systems: A Systematic Literature Review as a Basis for Future Research Avenues for Sustainable Transitions. *Sustainability (Basel)*, *12*(7), 2764. doi:10.3390u12072764

Satalkina, L., & Steiner, G. (2020b). Digital Entrepreneurship: A Theory-Based Systematization of Core Performance Indicators. *Sustainability (Basel)*, *12*(10), 4018. doi:10.3390u12104018

Satar. M., N.S., H., Azizan, M., & Dastane, O. (2020) Success Factors for e-Learning Satisfaction during COVID-19 Pandemic Lockdown, *International Journal of Advanced Trends in Computer Science and Engineering*, *9*(5), 7859-7865. https://www.warse.org/IJATCSE/static/pdf/file/ijatcse136952020.pdf

Sawhney, M., & Zabin, J. (2001). *The Seven Steps to Nirvana*. McGraw-Hill.

Schaffer, M. E., & Stillman, S. (2016). XTOVERID: Stata module to calculate tests of overidentifying restrictions after xtreg, xtivreg, xtivreg2, xthtaylor. *Statistical Software Components*. https://ideas.repec.org/c/boc/bocode/s456779.html

Schlossberg, M. (2016, February, 11). Teen Generation Z is being called 'millennials on steroids' and that could be terrifying for retailers. *Business Insider*. http://uk.businessinsider.com/millennials-vs-gen-z-2016-2

Schmuck, R. (2015). *Online üzleti modellek.* [Doctoral Thesis, University of Pécs, Pécs].

Schöni, W. (2022). Continuing education as value creation: Towards a new orientation beyond market logic. *European Journal for Research on the Education and Learning of Adults*, *13*(3), 261–283. doi:10.3384/rela.2000-7426.3694

Schulze, A., Townsend, J. D., & Talay, M. B. (2022). Completing the market orientation matrix: The impact of proactive competitor orientation on innovation and firm performance. *Industrial Marketing Management*, *103*, 198–214. doi:10.1016/j.indmarman.2022.03.013

Scully, D. (2022). Marketing Automation: A Design Perspective. The SAGE Handbook of Digital Marketing, 54.

Sekaran, U., & Bougie, R. (2016). *Research methods for business: A skill-building approach* (7th ed.). Wiley & Sons.

Selvakumar, S., Adithe, S., Isaac, J. S., Pradhan, R., Venkatesh, V., & Sampath, B. (2023). A Study of the Printed Circuit Board (PCB) E-Waste Recycling Process. In Sustainable Approaches and Strategies for E-Waste Management and Utilization (pp. 159–184). IGI Global.

Semerikov, S., Babenko, V., Kulczyk, Z., Perevosova, I., Syniavska, O., Davydova, O., Soloviev, V., Kibalnyk, L., Chernyak, O., & Danylchuk, H. (2019). Factors of the development of international e-commerce under the conditions of globalization. *SHS Web of Conferences*. SHS. 10.1051hsconf/20196504016

Senthil, T. S. R. Ohmsakthi vel, Puviyarasan, M., Babu, S. R., Surakasi, R., & Sampath, B. (2023). Industrial Robot-Integrated Fused Deposition Modelling for the 3D Printing Process. In Development, Properties, and Industrial Applications of 3D Printed Polymer Composites (pp. 188–210). IGI Global. doi:10.4018/978-1-6684-6009-2.ch011

Setiani, R. (2018). *Faktor- Faktor Yang Mempengaruhi Penggunaan Alat Pembayaran Non Tunai (Studi di Kota Purbalingga).* Unviersitas Islam Indonesia. Skripsi.

Setiawan, B., Nugraha, D. P., Irawan, A., Nathan, R. J., & Zoltan, Z. (2021). User innovativeness and fintech adoption in Indonesia. *Journal of Open Innovation*, *7*(3), 188. doi:10.3390/joitmc7030188

Shankar, A., Charles, J., Preeti, N., Haroon Iqbal, M., Aman, K., & Achchuthan, S. (2022). Online food delivery: A systematic synthesis of literature and a framework development. *International Journal of Hospitality Management*, *104*(103240), 103240. Advance online publication. doi:10.1016/j.ijhm.2022.103240

Shapiro, B. P. (1988). *What the hell is market oriented?* HBR Reprints.

Sharif, O., Hoque, M. M., Kayes, A. S. M., Nowrozy, R., & Sarker, I. H. (2020). Detecting suspicious texts using machine learning techniques. *Applied Sciences (Basel, Switzerland)*, *10*(18), 6527. doi:10.3390/app10186527

Sharma, M. (2020). A study on digital transformation and its impact on education sector. *PJAEE, 17*(7), 16105–16108.

Sharma, S., Mahajan, S., & Rana, V. (2019). A semantic framework for ecommerce search engine optimization. *International Journal of Information Technology : an Official Journal of Bharati Vidyapeeth's Institute of Computer Applications and Management, 11*(1), 31–36. doi:10.100741870-018-0232-y

Shaw, E. H., Pirog, S. F. III, & Hall, J. R. (2020). Household purchasing productivity: Concept and consequences. *Journal of Macromarketing, 40*(2), 156–168. doi:10.1177/0276146720906539

Shiau, W. L., Yuan, Y., Pu, X., Ray, S., & Chen, C. C. (2020). Understanding fintech continuance: Perspectives from self-efficacy and ECT-IS theories. *Industrial Management & Data Systems, 120*(9), 1659–1689. doi:10.1108/IMDS-02-2020-0069

Shin, D. H. (2010). The effects of trust, security and privacy in social networking: A security-based approach to understand the pattern of adoption. *Interacting with Computers, 22*(5), 428–438. doi:10.1016/j.intcom.2010.05.001

Shin, H. (2022). A critical review of robot research and future research opportunities: Adopting a service ecosystem perspective. *International Journal of Contemporary Hospitality Management, 34*(6), 2337–2358. doi:10.1108/IJCHM-09-2021-1171

Shitta, M. B. K. (2002). The impact of information technology on vocational and technology education for self reliance. *Journal of VOC & Tech. Education, 1*(1), 75–82.

Shukla, A., Kushwah, P., Jain, E., & Sharma, S. K. (2021). Role of ICT in Emancipation of Digital Entrepreneurship Among New Generation Women. *Journal of Enterprising Communities: People and Places in the Global Economy,* 1750-6204. doi:10.1108/JEC-04-2020-0071

Siemens, G., Gašević, D., & Dawson, S. (2015). *Preparing for the Digital University: A review of the history and current state of distance, blended, and online learning*. Link Research Lab.

Silva, S. C., Corbo, L., Vlačić, B., & Fernandes, M. (2023). Marketing accountability and marketing automation: Evidence from Portugal. *EuroMed Journal of Business, 18*(1), 145–164. doi:10.1108/EMJB-11-2020-0117

Simplilearn. (2023). *11 of the Most Popular Digital Business Models and Strategies in 2023*. Simplilearn. https://www.simplilearn.com/digital-business-model-article

Singh, I. J. S. S., Dastane, O., & Haba, H. F. (2022). A Fresh Look on Determinants of Online Repurchase Intention. In *Handbook of Research on Digital Transformation Management and Tools* (pp. 87–116). IGI Global. doi:10.4018/978-1-7998-9764-4.ch005

Singh, S., Sahni, M. M., & Kovid, R. K. (2020). What drives FinTech adoption? A multi-method evaluation using an adapted technology acceptance model. *Management Decision, 58*(8), 1675–1697. doi:10.1108/MD-09-2019-1318

Sinha, M., Majra, H., Hutchins, J., & Saxena, R. (2018). Mobile payments in India: The privacy factor. *International Journal of Bank Marketing, 37*(1), 192–209. doi:10.1108/IJBM-05-2017-0099

Sirimanne, S. N. (2022, May 3). *What is "Industry 4.0" and what will it mean for developing countries? | UNCTAD*. United Nations Conference on Trade and Development (UNCATAD). https://unctad.org/news/blog-what-industry-40-and-what-will-it-mean-developing-countries

Skan, J., Dickerson, J., & Masood, S. (2015). *The future of Fintech and banking: digitally disrupted or reimagined?* Accenture.

Slater, S. F., & Narver, J. C. (1994). Market orientation, customer value, and superior performance. *Business Horizons*, *37*(2), 22–28. doi:10.1016/0007-6813(94)90029-9

Smith, K. T. (2019). Mobile advertising to Digital Natives: Preferences on content, style, personalization, and functionality. *Journal of Strategic Marketing*, *27*(1), 67–80. doi:10.1080/0965254X.2017.1384043

Solanki, K., & Pittalia, P. (2016). Review of Face Recognition Techniques. *International Journal of Computer Applications*, *133*(12), 20–24. doi:10.5120/ijca2016907994

Solarz, M., & Swacha-Lech, M. (2021). *Determinants of the adoption of innovative fintech services by millennials*. D Space. https://dspace5.zcu.cz/handle/11025/45451

Song, A. K. (2019). The Digital Entrepreneurial Ecosystem—A Critique and Reconfiguration. *Small Business Economics*, *53*(3), 569–590. doi:10.100711187-019-00232-y

Soni, V. D. (2020). Emerging Roles of Artificial Intelligence in ecommerce. *International Journal of trend in scientific research and development, 4*(5), 223-225.

Sosa-Escudero, W., & Bera, A. K. (2008). Tests for Unbalanced Error-Components Models under Local Misspecification. *Sage Journals, 8*(1), 68–78. doi:10.1177/1536867X0800800105

Spence, M., Stancu, V., Elliott, C. T., & Dean, M. (2018). Exploring consumer purchase intentions towards traceable minced beef and beef steak using the theory of planned behavior. *Food Control*, *91*(1), 138–147. doi:10.1016/j.foodcont.2018.03.035

Srinivasan, R., Lilien, G., & Rangaswamy, A. (2002). Technological Opportunism and Radical Technology Adoption: An Application to E-Business. *Journal of Marketing*, *66*(July), 47–60. doi:10.1509/jmkg.66.3.47.18508

Stam, E. (2015). Entrepreneurial Ecosystems and Regional Policy: A Sympathetic Critique. *European Planning Studies*, *23*(9), 1759–1769. doi:10.1080/09654313.2015.1061484

Statistica. (2023, January 6). Leading factors motivating Gen Z consumers to engage with a new brand on social media in the United States in May 2022. *Statista Research Department*. https://www.statista.com/statistics/1324765/top-factors-driving-gen-z-engagement-new-brands-social-media-us/

Stephany, F. (2019). Online Labour Index 2020: New ways to measure the world's remote freelancing market. *Online labour observatory*. https://doi.org/www.onlinelabourobservatory.org

Student Feedback. (2020). AH10203 and AH32403. In *SmartUMS. Pusat E-Pembelajaran (PEP) dan Jabatan Teknologi Maklumat dan Komunikasi (JTMK)*. Universiti Malaysia Sabah. https://smartv3.ums.edu.my/

Suleimankadieva, A., Petrov, M., & Kuznetsov, A. (2021). Digital Educational Ecosystem as a Tool for the Intellectual Capital Development. In *SHS Web of Conferences. 116: 00060*. EDP Sciences. 10.1051hsconf/202111600060

Sunita, N. (2014). Face Recognition Using Principal Component Analysis. *International Journal of Computer Science and Information Technologies*, *5*, 6491–6496.

Suprapto, Y. (2022). Analisis pengaruh brand image, trust, security, perceived usefulness, perceived ease of use terhadap adoption intention fintech di Kota Batam. *Journal of Applied Business Administration*, *6*(1), 17–26. doi:10.30871/jaba.v6i1.3396

Sussan, F., & Acs, Z. J. (2017). The Digital Entrepreneurial Ecosystem. *Small Business Economics*, *49*(1), 55–73. doi:10.100711187-017-9867-5

Sutherland, W. (2019). Work Precarity and Gig Literacies in Online Freelancing. *SAGE Journals, 34*(3). https://doi.org/10.1177/0950017019886511

Sze, V., Chen, Y. H., Emer, J., Suleiman, A., & Zhang, Z. (2018). Hardware for machine learning: Challenges and opportunities. *2018 IEEE Custom Integrated Circuits Conference, CICC 2018*. IEEE. 10.1109/CICC.2018.8357072

Tai, K. S., Socher, R., & Manning, C. D. (2015). Improved semantic representations from tree-structured long short-term memory networks. *ArXiv Preprint ArXiv:1503.00075*. doi:10.3115/v1/P15-1150

Talin, B. (2022, Nov 28). 11 Digital Business Models You Should Know. *More than Digital*. https://morethandigital.info/en/11-digital-business-models-you-should-know-incl-examples/

Talin, B. (2023, Jan 20). What is a Digital Ecosystem? Understanding the Most Profitable Business Model. *More Than Digital*. https://morethandigital.info/ru/chto-takoyetzifrovaya-ekosistyema-ponimaniye-naibolyeyeviguodnoy-biznyes-modyeli/

Talla, A., & McIlwaine, S. (2022). Industry 4.0 and the circular economy: using design-stage digital technology to reduce construction waste. *Smart and Sustainable Built Environment*. https://doi.org/ doi:10.1108/SASBE-03-2022-0050/FULL/XML

Tapscott, D. (2008). *Grown up digital: How the Net generation is changing the world* (1st ed.). McGraw-Hill.

Temkin, B. (2008, February 19). The state of experience-based differentiation. *Forrester*. https://www.forrester.com/report/The-State-Of-ExperienceBased-Differentiation/RES45114

Teoh Teng Tenk, M., Yew, H. C., & Heang, L. T. (2020). E-wallet Adoption: A case in Malaysia. *International Journal of Research In Commerce and Management Studies (ISSN: 2582-2292), 2*(2), 216-233.

The ASEAN Post Team. (2020, May 11). Gen Z's use of social media has evolved. *The Asean Post*. https://theaseanpost.com/article/gen-zs-use-social-media-has-evolved

The State Committee of the Republic of Uzbekistan on Statistics. (n.d.). *Social Protection*. SCRUS. https://stat.uz/en/official-statistics/social-protection

Theory Hub. (2022). Social Exchange Theory: A review (2nd ed., Ser. 1). In S. Papagiannidis (Ed), *Theory Hub Book*. TheoryHub. http://open.ncl.ac.uk

Thirlwall, A. P. (1989). *Growth and Development: With Special Reference to Developing Economies* (Fourth Edition). Macmillan Education Ltd. https://books.google.co.in/books?hl=en&lr=&id=WKuvCwAAQBAJ&oi=fnd&pg=PR13&dq=thirlwall+choice+of+#v=onepage&q=thirlwall choice of&f=false

Thistle Initiatives. (2022, December 19). *Digital wallet users expected to exceed 5.2 billion globally by 2026*. Thistle Initiatives. https://www.thistleinitiatives.co.uk/blog/digital-wallet-users-expected-to-exceed-5.2-billion-globally-by-2026#:~:text=A%20new%20study%20has%20found,are%20currently%20considered%20cash%2Dheavy

Thomas, M. R., & Shivani, M. P. (2020). Customer Profiling of Alpha: The Next Generation Marketing. *Ushus Journal of Business Management, 19*(1), 75–86. doi:10.12725/ujbm.50.5

Tilson, D., Lyytinen, K., & Sørensen, C. (2010). Research Commentary-Digital Infrastructures: The Missing IS Research Agenda. *Information Systems Research, 21*(4), 748–759. doi:10.1287/isre.1100.0318

Tinkler, A. (2023). AI, marketing technology and personalisation at scale. *Journal of AI. Robotics & Workplace Automation, 2*(2), 138–144.

Tjiptono, F., Khan, G., Yeong, E. S., & Kunchamboo, V. (2020). Generation Z in Malaysia: The Four 'E' Generation. In E. Gentina & E. Parry (Eds.), *The New Generation Z in Asia: Dynamics, Differences, Digitalisation* (pp. 149–163). Emerald Publishing Limited., doi:10.1108/978-1-80043-220-820201015

Tomte, C. E., Fossland, T., Aamodt, P. O., & Degn, L. (2019). Digitalization in higher education: Mapping institutional approaches for teaching and learning. *Quality in Higher Education*, *25*(1), 98–114. doi:10.1080/13538322.2019.1603611

Treceñe, J. K. (2022). COVID-19 and Remote Learning in the Philippine Basic Education System: Experiences of Teachers, Parents, and Students. In M. Garcia (Ed.), *Socioeconomic Inclusion During an Era of Online Education* (pp. 92–110). IGI Global., doi:10.4018/978-1-6684-4364-4.ch005

Trembach, S., & Deng, L. (2018). Understanding millennial learning in academic libraries: Learning styles, emerging technologies, and the efficacy of information literacy instruction. *College & Undergraduate Libraries*, *25*(3), 1–19. doi:10.1080/10691316.2018.1484835

Trojovský, P., Dhasarathan, V., & Boopathi, S. (2023). Experimental investigations on cryogenic friction-stir welding of similar ZE42 magnesium alloys. *Alexandria Engineering Journal*, *66*(1), 1–14. doi:10.1016/j.aej.2022.12.007

Tun-Pin, C., Keng-Soon, W. C., Yen-San, Y., Pui-Yee, C., Hong-Leong, J. T., & Shwu-Shing, N. (2019). An adoption of fintech service in Malaysia. *South East Asia Journal of Contemporary Business*, *18*(5), 134–147.

Tunsakul, K. (2020). Gen Z consumers' online shopping motives, attitude, and shopping intention. *Human Behavior. Development and Society*, *21*(2), 7–16. https://so01.tci-thaijo.org/index.php/hbds/article/view/240046

Turan, Z., & Gurol, A. (2020). Emergency transformation in education: Stress perceptions and views of university students taking online course during the COVID-19 Pandemic. *Hayef: Journal of Education*, *17*(2), 222–242. doi:10.5152/hayef.2020.20018

Turner-Wilson, L. (2021, April 26). *Using Marketing Automation to Increase Sales Efficiency, Quality Lead Generation and Revenue*. Linkedin. https://www.linkedin.com/pulse/using-marketing-automation-increase-sales-efficiency-turner-wilson

Um, S. R., Shin, H. R., & Kim, Y. S. (2020). An Analysis of the Factors Affecting Technology Acceptance: Focusing on Fintech in high-end technology. *Journal of Digital Convergence*, *18*(2), 57–71.

UNESCO. (2020). *Education: from school closure to recovery*. UNESCO. https://www.unesco.org/en/covid-19/education-response

United Nations. (2015). *THE 17 GOALS | Sustainable Development*. United Nations - Department of Economic and Social Affairs. https://sdgs.un.org/goals

Utami, N. (2023). Analysis of the Use of Financial Technology and Financial Literacy Among MSMEs. *MBIA*, *22*(1), 11–21. doi:10.33557/mbia.v22i1.2217

Vaicondam, Y., Jayabalan, N., Tong, C. X., Qureshi, M. I., & Khan, N. (2021). Fintech Adoption Among Millennials in Selangor. *Academy of Entrepreneurship Journal*, *27*, 1–14.

Vaismoradi, M., Jones, J., Turunen, H., & Snelgrove, S. (2016). Theme development in qualitative content analysis and thematic analysis. *Journal of Nursing Education and Practice*, *6*(5), 100–110. doi:10.5430/jnep.v6n5p100

Valaskova, K., Durana, P., & Adamko, P. (2021). Changes in consumers' purchase patterns as a consequence of the COVID-19 Pandemic. *Mathematics*, *9*(15), 1788. doi:10.3390/math9151788

Van der Heijden, H., Verhagen, T., & Creemers, M. (2003). Understanding online purchase intentions: Contributions from technology and trust perspectives. *European Journal of Information Systems*, *12*(1), 41–48. doi:10.1057/palgrave.ejis.3000445

van Wyk, A. (2022). *Gen Alpha: The next economic force.* Alberton Record. https://albertonrecord.co.za/322037/gen-alpha-the-next-economic-force/

Vanitha, S. K. R., & Boopathi, S. (2023). Artificial Intelligence Techniques in Water Purification and Utilization. In *Human Agro-Energy Optimization for Business and Industry* (pp. 202–218). IGI Global. doi:10.4018/978-1-6684-4118-3.ch010

Vasileiou, K., Barnett, J., Thorpe, S., & Young, T. (2018). Characterising and justifying sample size sufficiency in interview-based studies: Systematic analysis of qualitative health research over a 15-year period. *BMC Medical Research Methodology*, *18*(148), 2–18. doi:10.118612874-018-0594-7 PMID:30463515

Venkatesh, V., & Davis, F. D. (2000). A theoretical extension of the technology acceptance model: Four longitudinal field studies. *Management Science*, *46*(2), 186–204. doi:10.1287/mnsc.46.2.186.11926

Venkatesh, V., Morris, M. G., Davis, G. B., & Davis, F. D. (2003). User acceptance of information technology: Toward a unified view. *Management Information Systems Quarterly*, *27*(3), 425–478. doi:10.2307/30036540

Venkatesh, V., Thong, J. Y., & Xu, X. (2012). Consumer acceptance and use of information technology: Extending the unified theory of acceptance and use of technology. *Management Information Systems Quarterly*, *36*(1), 157–178. doi:10.2307/41410412

Vennila, T., Karuna, M. S., Srivastava, B. K., Venugopal, J., Surakasi, R., & B., S. (2023). New Strategies in Treatment and Enzymatic Processes. In *Human Agro-Energy Optimization for Business and Industry* (pp. 219–240). IGI Global. doi:10.4018/978-1-6684-4118-3.ch011

Vize, R., Rooney, T., & Murphy, L. E. (2020). *Digital Technology We Trust: A FinTech B2B Context. In Interdisciplinary Approaches to Digital Transformation and Innovation.* IGI Global. doi:10.4018/978-1-7998-1879-3.ch003

VKulkarni, S.VKulkarni. (2020). Attendance Marking System using Facial Recognition. *International Journal of Advanced Trends in Computer Science and Engineering*, *9*(3), 3588–3594. doi:10.30534/ijatcse/2020/166932020

Vlachopoulos, D. (2011). COVID-19: Threat or opportunity for online education? *Higher Learning Research Communications*, *10*(1), 16–19. doi:10.18870/hlrc.v10i1.1179

Voyado. (2023, January 19). *How is Generation Z shopping?* Apptus. https://www.apptus.com/blog/generation-z-online-shopping-habits/#:~:text=Gen%20Z%20consumers%20are%20more,of%20view%20on%20political%20issues

Walczuch, R., Lemmink, J., & Streukens, S. (2007). The effect of service employees' technology readiness on technology acceptance. *Information & Management*, *44*(2), 206–215. doi:10.1016/j.im.2006.12.005

Walk, S., Majer, N., Schindler, K., & Schiele, B. (2010). New features and insights for pedestrian detection. *Proceedings of the IEEE Computer Society Conference on Computer Vision and Pattern Recognition*, 1030–1037. 10.1109/CVPR.2010.5540102

Wang, D., Yu, H., Wang, D., & Li, G. (2020). Face recognition system based on CNN. *Proceedings - 2020 International Conference on Computer Information and Big Data Applications, CIBDA 2020.* IEEE. 10.1109/CIBDA50819.2020.00111

Wang, J. S. (2021). Exploring biometric identification in FinTech applications based on the modified TAM. *Financial Innovation*, *7*(1), 1–24. doi:10.118640854-021-00260-2

Wang, Q. X., & Wang, Q. (2018). The labor relationship identification and rights protection of my country's 'online hire workers,'. *Law Science*, *4*, 57–72.

Wang, X. V., & Wang, L. (2018). Digital twin-based WEEE recycling, recovery and remanufacturing in the background of Industry 4.0. *International Journal of Production Research*, *57*(12), 3892–3902. doi:10.1080/00207543.2018.1497819

Warshaw, P. R., & Davis, F. D. (1985). Disentangling behavioral intention and behavioral expectation. *Journal of Experimental Social Psychology*, *21*(3), 213–228. doi:10.1016/0022-1031(85)90017-4

Webb, D., Webster, C., & Krepapa, A. (2000). An exploration of the meaning and outcomes of a customer-defined market orientation. *Journal of Business Research*, *48*(2), 101–112. doi:10.1016/S0148-2963(98)00114-3

Webster, F. E. Jr. (1988). The rediscovery of the marketing concept. *Business Horizons*, *31*(3), 29–39. doi:10.1016/0007-6813(88)90006-7

Wei, W., & MacDonald, I. T. (2021). Modeling the job quality of 'work relationships' in China's gig economy. *Asia Pacific Journal of Human Resources*, *5*. https://doi.org/doi:10.1111/1744-7941.12310

Westphal, J. D., Gulati, R., & Shortell, S. M. (1997). Customization or Conformity? An Institutional and Network Perspective on the Content and Consequences of TQM Adoption. *Administrative Science Quarterly*, *42*(2), 366–394. doi:10.2307/2393924

What is Generation Alpha, and why is it the most influential ? (2022). The Drum. https://www.thedrum.com/profile/infobip/news/gen-alpha-the-most-influential-generation-for-cx

Wiefling, S., Dürmuth, M., & lo Iacono, L. (2020). More Than Just Good Passwords? A Study on Usability and Security Perceptions of Risk-based Authentication. *ACM International Conference Proceeding Series,* (pp. 203–218). ACM. 10.1145/3427228.3427243

Wong, L. W., Tan, G. W. H., Hew, J. J., Ooi, K. B., & Leong, L. Y. (2022). Mobile social media marketing: A new marketing channel among digital natives in higher education? *Journal of Marketing for Higher Education*, *32*(1), 113–137. doi:10.1080/08841241.2020.1834486

Wood, A. (2019). The Taylor Review: Understanding the gig economy, dependency and the complexities of control. *New Technology, Work and Employment*, *34*(2), 111–115. doi:10.1111/ntwe.12131

Wooldridge, J. M. (2006). Cluster-sample methods in applied econometrics: an extended analysis. In *Economics Department Working Paper Series, Department of Economics*. Michigan State University. https://www.academia.edu/download/31182655/Cluster_Sample_Methods_in_Applied_Econometrics.pdf

Wooldridge, J. M. (2002). *Econometric Analysis Of Cross Section And Panel Data*. MIT Press.

Wooldridge, J. M. (2003). Cluster-Sample Methods in Applied Econometrics. *The American Economic Review*, *93*(2), 133–138. doi:10.1257/000282803321946930

World Bank. (2020). *Remote Learning During the Global School Lockdown: Multi-Country Lessons*. World Bank. https://www.worldbank.org/en/topic/edutech/brief/how-countries-are-using-edtech-to-support-remote-learning-during-the-covid-19-pandemic

Worldline. (2020, June 15). *How generation affect shopping behavior.* Bambora. https://www.bambora.com/articles/how-do-generation-affect-shopping-behavior/

Wu, J., Si, S., & Liu, Z. (2022). Entrepreneurship in Asia: Entrepreneurship Knowledge When East Meets West. *Asian Business & Management*, *21*(3), 317–342. doi:10.105741291-022-00187-1

Xu, C., Xie, L., Huang, G., Xiao, X., Chng, E. S., & Li, H. (2014). A deep neural network approach for sentence boundary detection in broadcast news. *Fifteenth Annual Conference of the International Speech Communication Association.* ISCA. 10.21437/Interspeech.2014-599

Xu, X., Li, Q., Peng, L., Hsia, T. L., Huang, C. J., & Wu, J. H. (2017). The impact of informational incentives and social influence on consumer behavior during Alibaba's online shopping carnival. *Computers in Human Behavior, 76,* 245–254. doi:10.1016/j.chb.2017.07.018

Yahya, M., Isma, A., Alisyahbana, A. N. Q. A., & Abu, I. (2023). Contributions of Innovation and Entrepreneurship Education to Entrepreneurial Intention with Entrepreneurial Motivation as an Intervening Variable in Vocational High School Students. *Pinisi Entrepreneurship Review, 1*(1), 42-53. https://journal.unm.ac.id/index.php/PEREV/article/view/49

Yin, R. (2004) *Case study methods.* Cosmo Corp. https://www.cosmoscorp.com/Docs/AERAdraft.pdf

Yong, S. M., & Renganathan, T. S. (2019). Malaysian Millennial buying behavior and country-of-origin effect. *Jurnal Pengguna Malaysia, 32*(1), 55 - 67. https://macfea.com.my/wp-content/uploads/2020/03/JPM-32-Jun-2019-article-5.pdf

Yupapin, P., Trabelsi, Y., Nattappan, A., & Boopathi, S. (2023). Performance Improvement of Wire-Cut Electrical Discharge Machining Process Using Cryogenically Treated Super-Conductive State of Monel-K500 Alloy. *Iranian Journal of Science and Technology. Transaction of Mechanical Engineering, 47*(1), 267–283. doi:10.100740997-022-00513-0

Zaharuddin, U. Rahardja, Q. Aini, F. P. Oganda, & Devana, V. (2021) Secure Framework Based on Blockchain for E-Learning During COVID-19. In *2021 9th International Conference on Cyber and IT Service Management (CITSM),* (pp. 1–7). IEEE. 10.1109/CITSM52892.2021.9588854

Zaki, H. O., & Ab Hamid, S. N. (2021). The Influence of Time Availability, Happiness, and Weariness on Consumers' Impulse Buying Tendency amidst Covid-19 Partial Lockdown in Malaysia. *Jurnal Pengurusan, 62.*

Zaki, H. O., Kamarulzaman, Y., & Mohtar, M. (2021). Cognition and Emotion: Exploration on Consumers Response to Advertisement and Brand. *Jurnal Pengurusan, 63.*

Zarkasyi, M. I., Hidayatullah, M. R., & Zamzami, E. M. (2020). Literature Review: Implementation of Facial Recognition in Society. *Journal of Physics: Conference Series, 1566*(1), 012069. doi:10.1088/1742-6596/1566/1/012069

Zhang, H., & Xiao, Y. (2020). Customer involvement in big data analytics and its impact on B2B innovation. *Industrial Marketing Management, 86,* 99–108. doi:10.1016/j.indmarman.2019.02.020

Zhang, M., Zeng, K., & Wang, J. (2020). A Survey on Face Anti-Spoofing Algorithms. *Journal of Information Hiding and Privacy Protection, 2*(1), 21–34. doi:10.32604/jihpp.2020.010467

Zhang, R., & El-Gohary, N. (2021). A deep neural network-based method for deep information extraction using transfer learning strategies to support automated compliance checking. *Automation in Construction, 132,* 103834. doi:10.1016/j.autcon.2021.103834

Zhang, T. C., Jahromi, M. F., & Kizilldag, M. (2018). Value co-creation in a sharing economy: The end of price wars? *International Journal of Hospitality Management, 71,* 51–58. doi:10.1016/j.ijhm.2017.11.010

Zhao, W., Chellappa, R., Phillips, P. J., & Rosenfeld, A. (2003). Face Recognition: A Literature Survey. *ACM Computing Surveys, 35*(4), 399–458. doi:10.1145/954339.954342

Zhao, X., Shao, M., & Su, Y. S. (2022). Effects of Online Learning Support Services on University Students' Learning Satisfaction under the Impact of COVID-19. *Sustainability (Basel), 14*(17), 10699. doi:10.3390u141710699

Zhao, Y., Peng, B., Iqbal, K., & Wan, A. (2023). Does market orientation promote enterprise digital innovation? Based on the survey data of China's digital core industries. *Industrial Marketing Management*, *109*, 135–145. doi:10.1016/j.indmarman.2022.12.015

Zheng, P., Lin, T. J., Chen, C. H., & Xu, X. (2018). A systematic design approach for service innovation of smart product-service systems. *Journal of Cleaner Production*, *201*, 657–667. doi:10.1016/j.jclepro.2018.08.101

Zhou, K. Z., Yim, C. K., & Tse, D. K. (2005). The effects of strategic orientations on technology-and market-based breakthrough innovations. *Journal of Marketing*, *69*(2), 42–60. doi:10.1509/jmkg.69.2.42.60756

Zhu, G., So, K. K. F., & Hudson, S. (2017). Inside the sharing economy: Understanding consumer motivations behind the adoption of mobile applications. *International Journal of Contemporary Hospitality Management*, *29*(9), 2218–2239. doi:10.1108/IJCHM-09-2016-0496

Zhu, Q., Avidan, S., Yeh, M. C., & Cheng, K. T. (2006). Fast human detection using a cascade of histograms of oriented gradients. *Proceedings of the IEEE Computer Society Conference on Computer Vision and Pattern Recognition*, 2. IEEE. 10.1109/CVPR.2006.119

Zhu, W., Yao, T., Ni, J., Wei, B., & Lu, Z. (2018). Dependency-based Siamese long short-term memory network for learning sentence representations. *PLoS One*, *13*(3), e0193919. doi:10.1371/journal.pone.0193919 PMID:29513748

Zou, H., Tang, X., Xie, B., & Liu, B. (2015). Sentiment classification using machine learning techniques with syntax features. *2015 International Conference on Computational Science and Computational Intelligence (CSCI)*, (pp. 175–179). IEEE. 10.1109/CSCI.2015.44

About the Contributors

Omkar Dastane obtained his Ph.D. in Business from Curtin University and is working as an Assistant Professor and Head of Program (MBAs) at the UCSI Graduate Business School, UCSI University, Kuala Lumpur, Malaysia. Dr. Omkar's research mainly emphasizes digital consumer behavior, consumer perception and values, technological impact on businesses, and scale development studies in the marketing domain. His research has been published in several international journals and books including the Journal of Retailing and Consumer Services, Marketing Intelligence & Planning among others. He is also an active reviewer for Web of Science and Scopus Indexed Journals.

Aini Aman is the Dean of Faculty of Economic and Management at the National University of Malaysia or better known as Universiti Kebangsaan Malaysia. She received her first BSc in Accounting from Purdue University, USA in 1991. She joined Moore and Stephen Audit Firm as an Audit Assistant and later joined Apex Securities as Credit Margin Officer before joining UKM in 1993. She completed her Master in Business Administration (MBA) at Manchester Business School, United Kingdom in 1995 and her PhD in Accounting Information System at the University of Manchester, United Kingdom in 2005. She later continued with her Post-doctoral Research at the same university in 2006. She was a visiting Professor at Loughborough in 2016, National Cheng Kung University, Taiwan in 2015 and Tashkent University in 1998. Her main research interest include Accounting Information System, Digital Economy and Global Business Services (GBS).

Nurhizam Safie Satar is the Dean of the Faculty of Information Technology & Science. Prior to holding this administrative position, he was a Research Fellow at the United Nations University, He was awarded a Technologist (.Ts/P.Tech (Information Technology) from the Malaysian Board of Technology (MBoT) in 2018. Doctoral Degree (PhD) in Systems Management Information (MIS) was received from the International Islamic University of Malaysia in 2010. He received a National Science Fellowship (NSF) from the Ministry of Science, Technology and Innovation Malaysia (MoSTI) to continue his studies for a doctoral degree. A Master's Degree in Information Technology was accepted from Universiti Kebangsaan Malaysia (UKM) in 1999 and he was awarded a Masters in Business Administration (MBA) from Anglia Ruskin University, United Kingdom in 2019.

***

Darshana A. Naik is working as Assistant Professor in the Department of Computer Science and Engineering at Ramaiah Institute of Technology, located in Bengaluru, Karnataka, India.

Badariah Ab Rahman started her academic career at Universiti Malaysia Sabah and was attached to the Industrial Relations Programme since 2014. At the same time being was appointed as a Research Fellow at Borneo Institute of Indigenous Studies (BorIIS) and actively involved in research and publication. Her research interest was on democracy and employee participation which include employee voice, employer-employee harmonious working relationship, partnership and organizational culture. Dr Badariah obtained her PhD in 2019 from Universiti Malaysia Sabah and currently as an independent academic writer and researcher.

Kausar Alam works as an Assistant Professor at BRAC Business School, BRAC University. He completed his PhD from Universiti Putra Malaysia (UPM). He graduated on time from UPM. He completed his MBA & BBA from the Department of Accounting and Information Systems, Jagannath University Dhaka. Dr. Kausar is currently working in several qualitative and quantitative research projects. He published numerous articles and book chapters in several international Scopus and Web of Science indexed journals and publishers respectively in the area of accounting, finance, Islamic finance, corporate governance, and qualitative research. His research works have been published in Asian Review of Accounting, Pacific Accounting Review, Journal of Public Affairs, Journal of Islamic Accounting and Business Research, Qualitative Research in Organizations and Management, Asian Journal of Accounting Research, Journal of Asian Finance, Economics and Business, International Journal of Sociology and Social Policy and Asian Economic and Financial Review. He serves as ad-hoc reviewer of different accounting and finance journals. He participated in international seminars, and research workshops. He has expertise in qualitative research and NVivo software analysis. He is a trainer and facilitator in qualitative research and NVivo software. He is involved with social activities and voluntary functions.

Meraj Farheen Ansari works as a cybersecurity engineer for a Fortune 500 financial firm in Chicago, IL. She received her PhD in information technology and Master of Science in Information Security Systems from University of the Cumberlands, and an MBA in management in information systems – human resource management from Concordia University in Mequon, WI. Her research interests include emerging technologies such as cybersecurity, AI, big data, blockchain, Internet of Things, and cloud computing

Subhanil Banerjee is an Economist currently working as resource person in Veni creator christian University, Florida, USA.. Doctor Banerjee has 19 years of experience in Core Social Science Research. His Research interests are International Trade, Foreign Direct Investment, Health Economics, Digital Economy, Sustainable Development, Environmental Economics, Econometrics, History of economics, Gender Studies and others. So far he has 17 publications 9 of them are SCOPUS indexed Journal Articles, 4 of them are International book chapters, 1 Conference proceeding and 3 other peer reviewed publications.

Sampath Boopathi completed his undergraduate in Mechanical Engineering and postgraduate in the field of Computer-Aided Design. He completed his Ph.D. from Anna University and his field of research includes Manufacturing and optimization. He published 60 more research articles in Internationally Peer-reviewed journals, one Patent grant, and three published patents.He has 16 more years of academic and research experiences in the various Engineering Colleges in Tamilnadu, India.() .

Bibhu Dash is a research scholar and Lead Data architect in Wisconsin, USA. He is a tech. guide, author, and research fellow with a special interest in AI, Bigdata, IoT, Cloud computing, Data modeling and governance, and Cybersecurity.

Kazi Ferdaous is at BRAC Business School, BRAC University, Bangladesh.

Dahlia Fernandez is a lecturer at Universiti Kebangsaan Malaysia (UKM), Faculty of Economics and Management in Bangi, Selangor. She earned a doctorate in accounting from Universiti Kebangsaan Malaysia (UKM), a master's degree in accounting from Universiti Islam Antarabangsa Malaysia (UIA), and a bachelor's degree in accounting from Universiti Kebangsaan Malaysia (UKM).

Aziatul Waznah Ghazali holds a Diploma in Accounting and Bachelor in Accounting from Universiti Teknologi MARA and a Masters degree in the same field from University of Strathclyde, Scotland. She obtained another Masters degree in 2014 and pursue her PhD, which is also in the area of accounting from Kingston University London in 2018. Dr Aziatul's academic career began with her appointment as a lecturer at Universiti Teknologi MARA (UiTM) in 2010. She was then appointed as a senior lecturer in 2019 at Universiti Sains Malaysia (USM). As for her research interest, she specialises in quantitative studies involving financial reporting, corporate governance, auditing and financial criminology. She also has a keen interest in social enterprises, as well as in environmental and sustainable reporting.

Herman Fassou Haba is an analyst for BMO financial group and researcher who does research studies in management, marketing, project management and finance. Having BSC in accounting and finance and an MBA from Anglia Ruskin University. I am currently doing MSC in project management research studies at L'université du Québec à Trois-Rivières.

Mahadirin Hj.Ahmad, Phd, currently works as Senior Lecture at the Industrial Relations Programme, Faculty of Social Science and Humanities, Universiti Malaysia Sabah (UMS). Interested in research relating to Trade Union Movement, Industrial Disputes, Industrial Conflict, Labor History, Sociological Of Work and Phenomenological research.

Mohammad Imtiaz Hossain is a PhD Fellow and Graduate research assistant (GRA) at Multimedia University, Malaysia. He pursued MSc in Business Economics from the School of Business and Economics, Universiti Putra Malaysia (UPM), Malaysia [AACSB & EQUIS accredited]. He has completed Bachelor in Business Management from Binary University, Malaysia and Diploma in Business from Mahsa Prima International College, Malaysia. His research interests include sustainability, SME, entrepreneurship, ambidexterity, leadership, technology adoption, tourism, service quality, human resource management, innovation, and many other interdisciplinary areas. Mr. Imtiaz has published numerous scholarly articles in Web of science, ABDC, Scopus, ERA, Google scholar and other indexed journals. Additionally, he is also serving as a reviewer for some prominent journals.

Mohammad Arif Ilyas is a lecturer in the Faculty of Engineering, Technology, and Built Environment at UCSI University. He received his PhD in Electrical Engineering from Universiti Tun Hussein Onn Malaysia in 2020. He also earned his bachelor's degree in electronic engineering at the same university.

C His main areas of research interest are machine learning, artificial intelligence, the Internet of Things, embedded systems, and optical wireless communication, especially visible light communication.

Fatma İnce received her Ph.D. degree in Management and Organization. Currently, she is an Associate Professor of Organization at Mersin University in Türkiye, where she teaches Organizational Behavior, Entrepreneurship, Creative Thinking, Leadership, and Teamwork at the undergraduate and graduate levels. Her research interests include entrepreneurship, leadership, creativity, synergy, generations, sustainability, and learning organizations. And besides, she serves as Assistant Director at the University Career Center to provide strategic oversight and management for the students' careers as they enhance their skills. However, she performs as the chairman of the faculty internship committee within the scope of the national internship program. In addition, the author gives awareness and mindfulness training so that individuals can concentrate on themselves and experience the true beauty and miracles of life.

Nurul Atasha Jamaludin is a Senior Lecturer at the Faculty of Economics & Management, Universiti Kebangsaan Malaysia (UKM). She received her BBA at UKM, her MBA from UKM-GSB, and her PhD from FEP UKM. Her research interests include entrepreneurship issues, particularly on the process of entrepreneurship, immigrant entrepreneurs, and social capital.

Zainudin Johari has been in the Education industry since 1987. That makes almost 34 years of training, teaching, listening, presenting, planning, accessing, collaborating, and managing for the sake of improving the Education Industry. He also involves in research and very active writer in local magazines. He also lectures in diversified topics like Unified Modelling Language (UML), Social Entrepreneurship, Advanced Systems Analysis Designs, and Social Communications. A Senior Lecturer at Alfa University College and a Faculty Member from School of Business, Management & Technology. Apart from lecturing, Zainudin also hold responsibilities as a Head of School. In the past 34 years, he has conducted lots of training programs which emphasizes hands-on experiences, such as the following key training in management, IT, and education domain. Zainudin is the Finalist for National Outstanding Educator Award 2015 and 2017 organize by the Educoop- Koperasi Pendidikan Swasta Malaysia Berhad [Private Education Cooperative of Malaysia].

Ravshanjon Kakharov graduated from Namangan State University with a specialty in mathematics and Information technologies. His research interests are digital technologies in education and computer sciences.

Nazhatul Hafizah Kamarudin currently is a Senior Lecturer in Center for Cyber Security, Faculty of Information Science and Technology Universiti Kebangsaan Malaysia. Received her first Degree in Electrical Engineering at Stevens Institute of Technology, USA. She furthered her master`s study in the area of Wireless Network Security at Stevens Institute of Technology, USA. Later, she continued her Ph.D. study in the area of Cryptography & Security at Faculty of Electrical Engineering, Universiti Teknologi MARA. Her research interests are authentication, network security, wireless sensor network and artificial intelligence.

Kee. Y. Sabariah Kee Mohd Yussof, PhD, senior lecturer in Industrial Relations program, Faculty of Social Sciences and Humanities, University Malaysia Sabah (UMS). Research focus in the field of management and Industrial Relations, specialize in trade unions and collective bargaining. In addition, she is active in research related to contemporary issues in the field of Social Sciences, namely studies related to online learning, the relationship between employment and digital poverty and issues related to the COVID-19 pandemic. Currently she teaches the topics of Collective Bargaining and Arbitration Strategies, Workplace Ethics and Employee Democracy and Participation.

Khamidulla Khabibullaev graduated in 2017 with a bachelor's degree from Turin polytechnic university in Tashkent and got a master's diploma from Politecnico di Torino in 2022. His research interests are Digital Technologies in Education, Information technology, Big data, Machine learning, Algorithms, and programming.

Naveed R. Khan is an Assistant Professor of Management in the Faculty of Business and Management at the UCSI University, Malaysia. He received his Ph.D. in Management Sciences from University Pendidikan Sultan Idris. His research focuses on sustainability in organization.

Sam Yee Kho Sam's life motto, "Be different, be unique," reflects her belief in embracing diversity and individuality. Growing up in an international community and studying in the United States, she developed a global perspective and a passion for women's empowerment. Sam's dedication to overcoming gender biases led her to pursue an impressive academic journey, including an MBA and a Doctorate. With over a decade of corporate management experience in banking and network marketing, Sam excels in operational excellence, cost management, and relationship governance. She is driven by the principle of "life influencing life" and strives to inspire and positively impact those around her. As CEO and co-founder of Return Legacy, Sam oversees a network of over 120,000 distributors across five countries. Additionally, she actively engages in philanthropy through Legacy Care Association Malaysia, working towards a brighter future for underprivileged children through education and improved living conditions.

Kasim Khusanov graduated from S. Petersburg State University with Applied Mathematics. He got P.H.D. there. His research interests are e-learning, digital technologies in education, and computer sciences.

Mukhsina Khusanova received a Master's in Financial Management from the Technical University of Uzbekistan. Her research interests are digital technologies in Education, Human Research, and Employability of persons.

Mushtariybonu Khusanova graduated from YEOJU Technical Insitute in Tashkent with a Business Administration specialty. Her research interests are Digital marketing, Digital Education Technologies.

Souren Koner (B. Sc., MBA, Ph.D.) has been acting as an Associate Professor at the Royal Global University, Guwahati, Assam since March 2013. He has more than 19 years of experience teaching in different management institutions all over India. His area of specialization is Marketing. He has been teaching in the areas of Marketing Management, Advertising, Sales Management, Service Marketing, etc. So far, he has 17 publications. 2 of them are SCOPUS indexed Journal Articles, 2 of them is in UGC care, 3 of them are international book chapters, 2 Conference proceedings, and 8 other peer-reviewed publications.

Siew Keong Lee a Chartered Accountant in Malaysia, a Chartered Management Accountant in England and ASA of CPA in Australia, holds an MBA, Doctorate in Business and Administration and is pursuing a PhD. With unwavering conviction, Lee recognizes people as the paramount value in the direct selling industry, where equal opportunities for learning, growth, and transformation thrive. His dream is to revolutionize the industry by reestablishing and aligning its essence of sharing and seizing opportunities harmoniously with the company's mission and vision. Thus, Return Legacy was born from these deeply rooted beliefs. As the driving force behind Return Legacy, Lee's leadership encompasses strategic guidance and unwavering support, ensuring adherence to the company's vision and growth strategies. He firmly believes that Return Legacy's unparalleled distinction as an industry-leading brand lies in its unwavering commitment to empowering Legacians in the field, fostering their triumph, and ultimately contributing to Return Legacy's success.

Azizan Morshidi currently works at the School of Social Sciences, Universiti Malaysia Sabah (UMS). Interested in Quantitative & Qualitative Social Research Methodologies. His current project is related to trade union membership, Industry 4.0.

Istyakara Muslichah joined as a lecturer and researcher at the Faculty of Business and Economics, Universitas Islam Indonesia in 2015. She obtained her degree in Management at the Faculty of Economics and Business, Universitas Gadjah Mada and finished her MBA at the Graduate School of Business, Universiti Kebangsaan Malaysia, under Khazanah Asia Scholarship Program in 2014. She has an interest in consumer behavior, tourism and hospitality and digital marketing.

Nik Herda Nik Abdullah is a senior lecturer at the School of Accounting and Finance, Taylor's Business School, Taylor's University, Malaysia. She received her PhD in management accounting from Universiti Teknologi MARA and her MBA from the University of Malaya. Throughout her career, she has taught a range of management accounting modules and has published a number of Scopus-indexed journal articles. Prior to pursuing an academic discipline, she worked in the accounting field for over 13 years in businesses such as manufacturing, retailing, services, and non-profit organizations. Her research interests include management accounting, sustainability, value creation, supply chain, and digitalization.

Hafizah Omar Zaki is a Senior Lecturer in Marketing at the Faculty of Economics and Management (FEP), Universiti Kebangsaan Malaysia (UKM). She is currently the Head of the Emerging Technology & Big Data (ETBD) cluster at the Centre of Global Business and Digital Economy (GloBDE), FEP-UKM. She holds a PhD in Marketing - specializing in advertising and branding from the University of Malaya (UM); an MBA - specialising in Human Resource Management from UKM; and a Degree in Multimedia Management from Multimedia University (MMU). Her research and publications involve advertising, branding, digital marketing and digital business amidst the advancement of technology use.

Hafizah Omar Zaki is a Senior Lecturer in Marketing at the Faculty of Economics and Management (FEP), National University of Malaysia. She is currently the Head of the Emerging Technology & Big Data (ETBD) cluster at the Centre of Global Business and Digital Economy (GloBDE), FEP-UKM. She holds a PhD in Marketing - specializing in advertising and branding from the University of Malaya (UM); an MBA - specialising in Human Resource Management from UKM; and a Degree in Multimedia

Management from Multimedia University (MMU). Her research and publications involve advertising, branding, digital marketing and digital business amidst the advancement of technology use.

Tanima Pal is a formal student of Brac Business School of Brac Univeristy.

Nabilah Rozzani is currently contributing in the impact sector with Teach for Malaysia as an Operations Manager. She received her PhD in accounting information systems for Islamic microfinance from Universiti Teknologi MARA. Prior to her current role with a non-profit organisation, she was in the academia for over 8 years teaching a range of accounting and finance modules, as well as publishing a number of Scopus-indexed journal articles. Her research interests include accounting information systems, management accounting, Islamic microfinance, accounting for non-profit institutions, and digitalization.

Murugan S. is involved with the Department of Physics, Lovely Professional University.

Soliha Sanusi is a Senior Lecturer at the Faculty of Economics and Management under the Centre of Global Business and Digital Economy Studies, Universiti Kebangsaan Malaysia (UKM). She is a Chartered Accountant (CA) of the Malaysian Institute of Accountants (MIA) and obtained her PhD from the Universiti Teknologi MARA Malaysia in 2019. She was SLAB/SLAI scholarship recipient for her MBA and PhD studies. Her research interests are in direct tax, indirect tax, financial criminology, small-medium enterprises, mixed-method, and public-sector accounting. She has published and presented her research work in various conferences and journals. She also reviews Management & Accounting Review, Asian Academy of Management Journal of Accounting & Finance, and a few more journals.

Maherin Tasnim is working at BRAC Business School, BRAC University, Bangladesh.

Michael Raj T.F. is a faculty member in the Department of Computer Applications at SCLAS, SIMATS Deemed University, situated in Chennai, Tamil Nadu, India.

Ramya Thatikonda is a researcher and software professional. She received her Ph.D. in IT from the University of Cumberlands, KY. Her research interests are in AI, BigData, Cloud, DevOps, and Cybersecurity.

Srinivas Vaddadi is a PhD Student with 8+ years of experience in the industry.

Narayanaswamy Venkateswaran, working as Professor at Panimalar Engineering College, having 26 years of teaching experience published more papers in International journals and also member of editorial board in more reputed journals. Published books on International Business Management, HR Analytics, Entrepreneurship Development, Professional Ethics and Human Values, Fundamentals of Management. Area of expertise is on Business Analytics, Artificial Intelligence and Supply Chain Management"

R. Vidhya is an Associate Professor in the Department of Computer Science and Engineering at Sri Krishna College of Technology, situated in Coimbatore, Tamil Nadu, India.

Shee Mun Yong is working with UOW Malaysia University College Sdn Bhd

Index

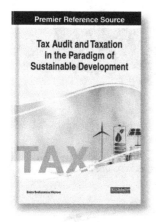

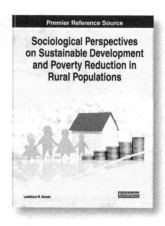

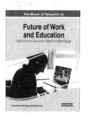

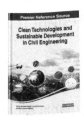